All about making -

FLORAL BUCKS POINT LACE

by Alexandra Stillwell

First published in the UK 2013 by
Salex Publishing
26 Willow Park, Haywards Heath, West Sussex, RH16 3UA, UK
alexandrastillwell1@gmail.com
www.alexstillwell.wordpress.com

Also by the author
The Technique of Teneriffe Lace, Batsford, 1980, reprinted 1987
Laced with Laughs, Lace Guild, 1984, revised edition Salex Publishing 2007
Drafting Torchon Lace Patterns, Dryad, 1986, reprinted Batsford, 1992, revised edition Salex Publishing 2012
Cassell Illustrated Dictionary of Lacemaking, Cassell, 1996
revised and reprinted as Salex Illustrated Dictionary of Lacemaking, Salex Publishing, 2009
All about making—Geometrical Bucks Point Lace, Salex Publishing, 2006
Techniques used in the East Midlands to make the Footside of Point Ground Lace, Salex Publishing 2007
The art of making the Buckingham Bobbin Lace, Georgina Roberts 1926,
completed and edited by Alexandra Stillwell, Salex Publishing 2007

Text, photographs and illustrations by Alexandra Stillwell 2013 ©
The right of Alexandra Stillwell to be identified as
the author of this work has been asserted by her in
accordance with the provisions of the UK Copyright,
Design and Patent Act 1988

All rights reserved
The patterns and grids may be reproduced for personal
use only, but no other part of this book may be reproduced or
transmitted in any form or by any means, electronic or
mechanical, including photocopying, recording or any
information storage or retrieval system,
without prior permission in writing from the author.

ISBN 978-0-9554694-7-3

All about making - FLORAL BUCKS POINT LACE

CONTENTS

Introduction

The Projects are described in order of technical difficulty, thus Projects 20c, 20d and 20e are placed after Project 21 and Projects 25b and Project 27b after Project 28.

Part 1 Standard Floral Bucks		**Chapters 1-9, Projects 1-14**	**1**
Chapter 01	Project 01	Buttercup edging	3
	Project 02	Oval buttercup motif	8
Chapter 02	Project 03	Brooch motif with nook pins	18
	Project 04	Church doll with more nook pins	23
	Project 05	Church doll edging with corners	29
Chapter 03	Project 06	Bookmark with scrolls, hearts and vertical gimps	34
Chapter 04	Project 07	A birthday gift	40
Chapter 05	Project 08	A tablecloth with a reversing corner and a side reverse	52
Chapter 06	Project 09	An anniversary present with the edge worked radially and the centre from top to bottom.	66
	Project 10	An anniversary present worked from top to bottom	72
Chapter 07	Project 11	Insert for a book cover with old mayflower filling	82
	Project 12	Insert for a card with a honeycomb and pin chain filling	84
Chapter 08	Project 13	Shaped jabot	88
Chapter 09	Project 14	Tray insert made in three strips with fine joining	94
Part 2 Kat stitch		**Chapters 10-13, Projects 15-19**	**101**
Chapter 10	Project 15a	Edging	105
	Project 15b	Matching insertion for edging Project 15a	109
Chapter 11	Project 16	Non-reversing corner and pin chain bars	115
Chapter 12	Project 17	A Willow Pattern picture, an exercise in designing	125
Chapter 13	Project 18	Fan leaf worked with a single direction	131
	Project 19	Fan leaf worked with four changes of direction	138
Part 3 Regency Bucks.		**Chapters 14-19, Projects 20-23**	**147**
		Christening set for Emily, a 43cm (17 in) doll	
Chapter 14	Project 20a	Gown bodice insertion	150
	Project 20b	Gown bodice, heading used as an insertion	154
Chapter 15	Project 21	Underdress	159
Chapter 16	Project 20c	Gown, skirt panel upper insertion	162
Chapter 17	Project 20d	Gown, skirt panel lower insertion	166
Chapter 18	Project 20e	Gown, skirt panel central insertion	170
Chapter 19	Project 22	Bonnet with decorated crown	175
	Project 23	Card with decoration	179

Part 4 Very Fine Bucks Chapters 20-27, Projects 24-29   **181**
                         Clothes for Lynette, a 45cm (18in) doll   **182**
    Chapter 20   Project 24   Drawers   183
    Chapter 21   Project 25a   Camisole edging   186
    Chapter 22   Project 26   Petticoat   188
    Chapter 23   Project 27a   Bodice insertion   190
    Chapter 24   Project 28   Skirt edging   193
    Chapter 25   Project 25b   Camisole galloon   196
    Chapter 26   Project 27b   Cuffs   199
    Chapter 27   Project 29   Fichu   201

Part 5 Black holey   **215**
    Chapter 28   Project 30a   Box lid edging   216
    Chapter 29   Project 31   Fingerplate   220
    Chapter 30   Project 30b   Lid insert   227
    Chapter 31   Project 32   Galloon decoration for a lid   235
    Chapter 32   project 33   A Shaped piece made on a Traditional Pricking 240

Part 6 Bobbins and threads   **243**

Bibliography   **248**

Index   **249**

INTRODUCTION

Bucks Point Lace, frequently called the Queen of English laces, is a fine bobbin lace that is traditionally made using white, cream, ecru or black thread. Originally called Point Lace, from the French 'point' meaning stitch, the prefix Buckingham or Bucks was added in the early 20th century. The name is usually abbreviated and Bucks point Lace referred to as Bucks Point or Bucks and Floral Bucks Point Lace to Floral Bucks. However, making

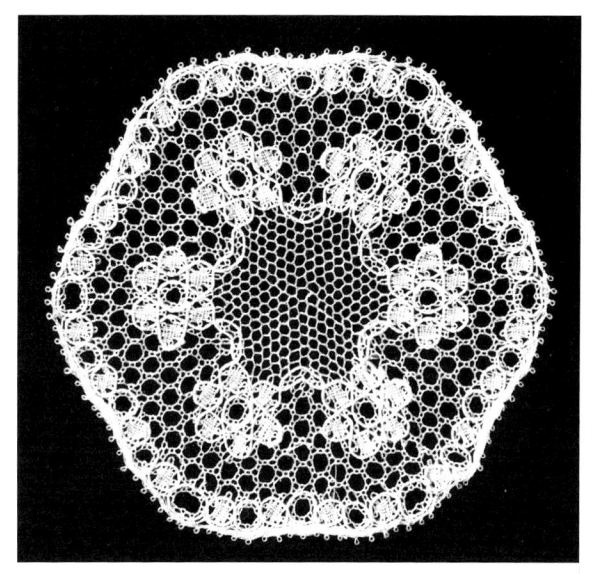

Figure 1 Geometrical Bucks Point

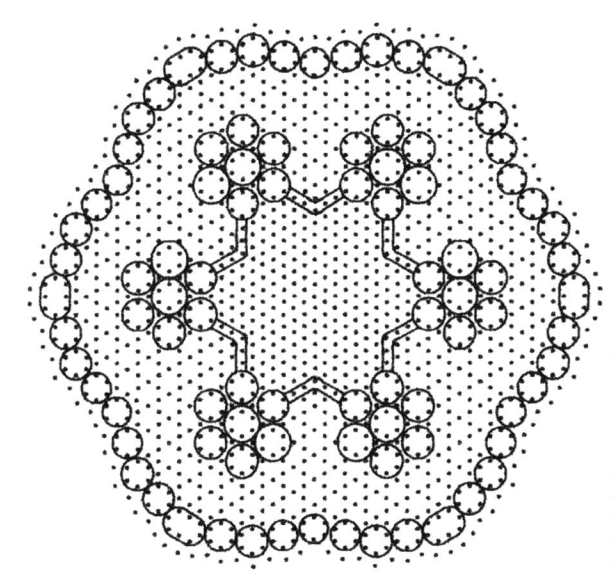

Figure 2 Geometrical Bucks Point

point lace was not restricted to the county of Buckinghamshire; it was also made in the neighbouring counties, particularly Northamptonshire and in other parts of the country including Devon, Suffolk, Wiltshire and Yorkshire. Point Lace made in Devon is known as Trolly Lace and in Wiltshire known as Downton and Malmsbury according to the locality where it is made. Each area has its own characteristics and minor differences in the techniques used; there are even differences between the northern and southern areas of the county of Buckinghamshire, and there were probably differences between adjacent villages as well as the individual lacemakers. These all add to the wealth of techniques that we can use when making our own lace. As with other types of lace the name should be considered generic rather than an indication of the place where the lace was made. When making Bucks Point each technique used should be judged on its own merit, bearing in mind the context in which it is being used.

Although the freestyle version of Bucks Point (figures 3 & 4) is called 'Floral', this does not mean that it is restricted to flowery designs. Nor does it mean that flowery designs are

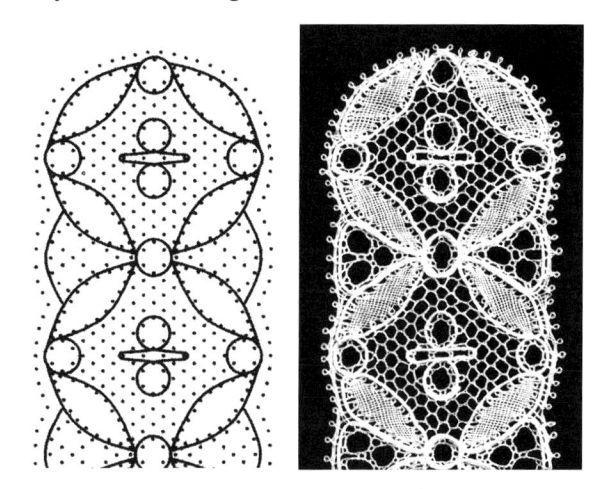

Figure 3 & 4 Floral Bucks Point

All about making—Floral Bucks Point Lace

necessarily Floral Bucks. The distinction between the two depends on the arrangement of the pins. The geometrical form (figures 1 & 2) has all the pinholes, with the exception of the picots, matching the grid for the ground (figures 1& 2). In Floral Bucks the pinholes for the freestyle design elements follow the lines of the design and therefore do not necessarily match the grid (see the long, pointed shapes in figures 3 & 4). To test whether a design is freestyle or geometrical, use a ruler to line up the pins within the design with the lines of pins in the ground. If they line up in both directions the lace is geometrical; if they do not it is Floral.

Figure 5 Regency Bucks Point

Whilst researching my previous book[1], I became aware that there are forms of Floral Bucks other than the ones currently made and my research has included them. (The number in superscript [(1)] is the reference number of the End Note containing further information found at the end of the chapter.) Apart from the standard freestyle version of the Floral Bucks with which we are familiar there is a another style, from the first half of the 19th century which is usually

Figure 6 Very fine Bucks Point

called 'Regency Bucks Point', abbreviated to 'Regency Bucks', in which the gimp is worked within the clothwork, not surrounding it (figure 5).

There is also a very fine version of Bucks Point sometimes referred to as Lille style Bucks Point, in which the design relies mainly on gimp work with a little clothwork and the occasional filling (figure 6). Many of the pieces I have studied are 18th century, but there are some pieces in the 19th century Lace Dealer's book in Luton Museum. This style of Bucks has the majority of the pinholes for the rather sparse clothwork placed outside the gimp. When I first came across the very fine version it answered the question 'How could pins be sufficiently fine that the clothwork of the very fine laces was not entirely choked with them?' The answer is that the pins were placed outside the gimp, as in the Flanders laces. The techniques used for the very fine Bucks are, in many cases the same as or similar to, those used for Beverse, the Flanders member of the Point Lace family.

Samples and prickings of the version of Bucks Point known as black holey are occasionally seen but I have not been able to find any references to it in books. This lace is similar to some black Blonde and the black lace of Pays-d'Enhaut but there are differences in the techniques used, in particular the use of stays across the bases of the ovals which, in my experience, is unique to Black holey. I have found no information concerning the time when the Black Holey was made, but as there are four prickings for making the lace of Pays-d'Enhaut[2] dating from 1823-1866, it is reasonably safe to assume that laces of this style, including Black Holey, were fashionable and made at about the same time.

Figure 7 Black holey

All about making—Floral Bucks Point Lace

Allied to Floral Bucks is the English version of Mechlin sometimes known as Macklin. Unfortunately I have seen so few pieces that I am not confident that I understand the techniques sufficiently well to include them in this book.

From my earliest attempts to make lace, Floral Bucks has been my favourite. When I started, in the mid 1960s, there was no one within reach from whom I could learn and I had to rely on books and very soon found what I liked and disliked about them, what was helpful and what was missing. So many books on Bucks Point contain mainly edgings, but nothing on how to use them. Therefore my previous book[1] was designed so that the reader could learn through a series of finished pieces with all information necessary on how to start and complete the item as illustrated. This book also provides patterns for finished items, sometimes alongside edgings from which they were designed. Extra skills as well as extra knowledge are required when moving from Geometrical to Floral Bucks. In Geometrical Bucks the pinholes, apart from the picots and perhaps the pinholes immediately inside them, follow a geometrical grid and therefore the making of the lace follows a definite set of rules. On the other hand, the pinholes of the design motifs in Floral Bucks follow the line of the design. Thus, there can no longer be a definite set of rules for making the lace. When a known technique fits it can be used; at other times there may be two or more options, none of which will give a perfect result. It is a question of choices. Because these pins are not rigidly spaced they may be adjusted slightly, sometimes by less than the width of the pinhole, to make clothwork more even and avoid adding another pair; sometimes leaning the pin one way or the other will achieve the desired result. Rows may be closed up or given more space and pairs must be spaced evenly across the rows. The tension required becomes much lighter when finer threads are used. For this reason it is necessary to practice by repeating the same pattern several times rather than making several different small items.

Since the revival that started in the 1960s the style of Floral Bucks has changed. We no longer make it for the income, we make it for enjoyment. Our standards are different and we have the time to indulge ourselves. When I learned to make Floral Point in the 1970s I was taught when, where and how to add and remove pairs. My research has found some, but not much, evidence that this was done in the past. However, I have seen very many pieces of antique lace that would have benefited from this technique. Today we tend to use comparatively finer threads than were used in the past, resulting in a more delicate lace and a greater need to adjust the number of threads. When I learnt I was told that the rule was to keep the workers horizontal and the passives vertical. This did not always happen in the past. The tulip pattern is a good example of aligning the pairs in sympathy with the design. We now strive for perfection, but Floral Bucks is not a perfect lace, don't become disheartened if you cannot achieve it.

Before learning to make Floral Bucks, the lacemaker requires a sound understanding of the techniques used for making Geometrical Bucks and references to my previous book *'All about making - Geometrical Bucks Point Lace'* have been inserted at the request of my various friends and helpers who have worked these patterns. At the boundary between a free style motif and the geometrical ground there are times when a geometrical technique will work. When none of the geometrical techniques will produce the desired result, judgment must be used to select, adapt or devise an alternative technique. When making Geometrical Bucks all pairs have exact positions to go to when making a stitch. However, when making Floral Bucks, there are many situations in which the pairs required to make a stitch are not immediately obvious; there may be several methods that could be used to achieve the required result and the lacemaker has to use judgement rather than follow a rule. Often there are options and while all may be appropriate for the situation none will achieve a perfect result. Hence, a sound understanding of Geometrical Bucks is vital. Geometrical perfection may be unobtainable but it is the visual effect that is important, and this can be achieved. In Geometrical Bucks the repeats can and should be made identically, but in Floral Bucks pattern repeats are unlikely to be the same; there is no attempt to remember the choices made so that they can be repeated exactly, and different choices may be made when making subsequent repeats. This does not mean that one repeat will necessarily be better than the others; in fact, they should look much the same. Again, it is the visual effect that matters. This does not detract from the final appearance, it enhances it. Since the techniques are continually being weighed one against another, making this lace remains stimulating and never becomes boring.

To develop the skills required to space rows and pairs, and use new techniques, work an edging first. As you make subsequent repeats remove the appropriate pins from the previous repeat to expose the relevant working. Check the spacing of rows and of the pairs across the rows and also where you have used new techniques and see if anything can be improved. Work several repeats like this until you are happy with the result; each time exposing the previous working so you can see any imperfections that need improving. It is easy to overcompensate by adding extra pairs in a subsequent repeat only to return to the previous number and improve the effect by more careful firming up. This is part of the learning process. Continue making repeats until you are satisfied with the result. Do not expect perfect results first time. Then, with a little extra help, pass on to the adaptation of that edging. The techniques introduced for working the edging will be useful, but not necessarily in exactly the same context; and at times a little creative thinking will be necessary.

Except for the picots, the pinholes for Geometrical Bucks patterns are placed according to a grid with the pinholes for the footside and catch-pin slightly offset. For Floral Bucks, the pinholes within the gimps follow the curves of the design whereas the areas of ground, honeycomb and other fillings follow the grid, although they may be distorted adjacent to it to complement the design. It is easy to design a new pattern for Floral Bucks but, unlike Geometrical Bucks, it is extremely difficult to copy a Floral pattern. Therefore learning to draft Floral Bucks patterns is better left until the techniques for making the lace have been mastered, and then design your own. It is surprisingly easy.

We make lace mainly because we enjoy making it, and most of us also enjoy the added benefit of a finished piece that we can enjoy or give to others for their enjoyment. My advice to someone starting her first Floral Bucks pattern has always been 'When you know the technique that fits the situation use it; if you don't, fudge it'. To be more correct I should say 'choose the best option available' or 'use your initiative' but these phrases imply that you have to be very clever and many lacemakers are not confident that they have these abilities, but the result is the same - trust me.

The original 'Buttercup' pattern, now trued up, came from Mrs Winifred Millar's Collection via Vi Bullard. My thanks to the late Joan Tyler-Smith, Diana Smith and Shirley Burness-Smith, for generously allowing me to include their lace and prickings in this book. I also wish to thank

All about making—Floral Bucks Point Lace

Elaine Woodhams[2] of Becky Dolls for making Emily who wears the christening robe and Maureen Bromley for courageously tackling the traditional pricking that is the last project. It is not for the faint hearted. All the modern lace has been designed and made by myself.

I wish to thank all my friends, including those met through Arachne, who have encouraged, helped me and taken time to send me suggestions. In particular my thanks go to Aurelia Loveman, Maureen Bromley, Ruth Budge, Opal McCleary, Judith Adkins, Corinne Jones, Valerie Sims and Lindsay Norris for proofreading, to Maureen, Ruth and Corinne for checking my prickings and instructions and to Corinne's husband Ed for making the box for project 32. Also to Ann Day for advising me about bobbins, Leonard Bazar for explaining how to use nook pins twice and Judy Aycock for advising me on fine sewing, in particular making up the bonnet. Also to my friends who helped by checking my prickings and working samples and projects including Phyllis Hadden, Diane Kelly, Maureen Philpott, Penelope Piip, Dawn White, Beryl Wilson, Scilla Stephenson, Pat Hamilton, Joy Frusher, Miriam Gidron, Serena Oddie, Janet Norman, Lesley Hilditch and Jacquie Mitchener. All these friends have helped make this book what it is.

Above all ENJOY.

Alex

END NOTES
1 *All about making*—Geometrical Bucks Point Lace, Alexandra Stillwell, Salex Publishing

2 Elaine Woodhams, buttonbearaccessories@yahoo.com

PART 1

STANDARD FLORAL BUCKS

Due to social changes resulting from the First World War, and changes in fashion, the making of bobbin lace for profit declined during the first part of the 20th century, and by the end of the Second World War, it was rarely made. Even as late as the 1940s, to admit that your mother made lace was to admit that your grandmother went to a lace school and was illiterate; it was a social stigma. During that time a few lacemakers, mainly middle class ladies who had been trying to keep the sales of lace going for the lace workers, became concerned that the craft would die out and started writing instruction books.

With the revival of crafts in the mid 20th century, lacemaking became a recreational craft; books describing the craft were sought and the techniques relearned. I have only found three books and an unfinished, unpublished manuscript[1] containing information about Bucks Point techniques written before the revival. While researching my previous book describing how to make Geometrical Bucks, I came across techniques I had not seen before and, over time, realized that the techniques in current use were limited to those recorded in these three books and the manuscript. The techniques for Geometrical Bucks discovered during my researches are detailed in my book[2].

Figure 8 Tulip, 19th century Bucks Point, a traditional design reduced, maximum width approximately 8cm (3.1 in)

Floral Bucks, as it is made today, has the standard point ground and an off-set footside as for Geometrical Bucks Point. In most cases, there are clothwork areas surrounded by gimps and these areas are pinned within the gimps; when lace is made in black these areas are usually made in half stitch. When the gimps at the sides of the clothwork are vertical the worker usually passes out across the gimp into the ground to make an ordinary ground stitch or a catch-pin stitch[3] before returning across the gimp. Honeycomb stems are sometimes present and are worked using the geometrical techniques when they are appropriate and modifying them when necessary.

End Notes

1. Instructions in the art of Making the Buckingham Pillow Lace, G. Roberts 1926, unfinished and unpublished manuscript completed and revised by A Stillwell, Salex Publishing 2007
Practical Lacemaking, C. Channer, Dryad 1928.
A Manual of Hand-made Bobbin Lacework, M. Maidment, Pitman & Sons 1931.
Guide to Lace-making, M. E. W. Milroy, Brown 1934.
2. *All about making–* Geometrical Bucks Point Lace, Alexandra Stillwell, Salex Publishing.
3. Ibid., page 60. (The term Ibid refers to the book previously listed in the End Notes, in this case End Note 2.)

All about making—Floral Bucks Point Lace

CHAPTER 1

PROJECTS 1 & 2: Buttercup

Project 1: Buttercup edging
Project 2: Buttercup design adapted to form an oval motif

PROJECT 1: Buttercup edging

Materials Required for Projects 1 & 2
Egyptian cotton no. 80/2[1]
gimp D.M.C perle no. 12

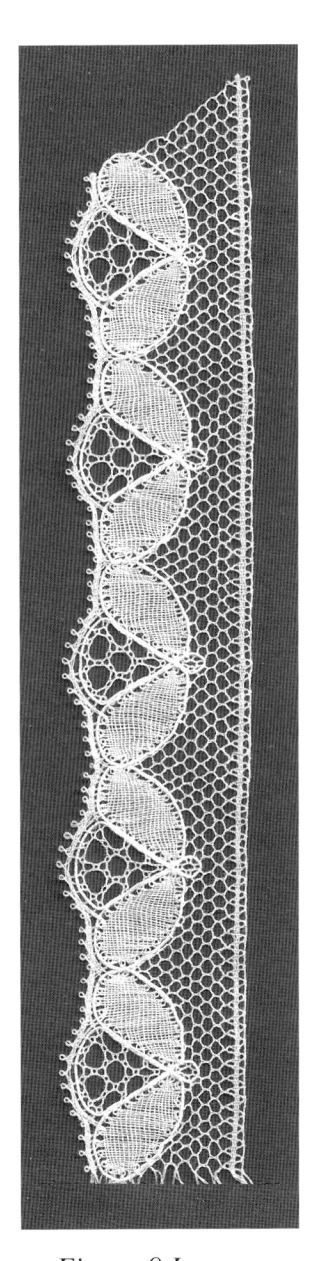

Figure 9 Lace

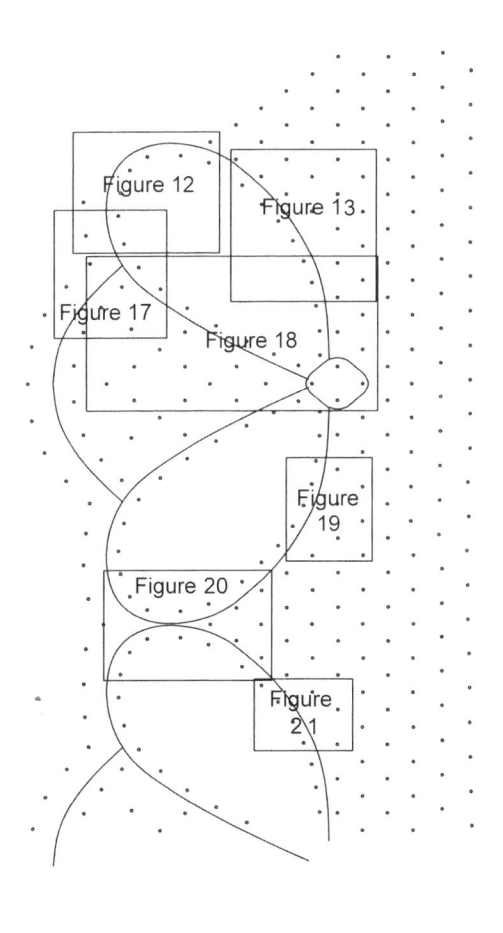

Figure 11 Plan of pricking figure 10, indicating the locations of the techniques described in figures 12-21

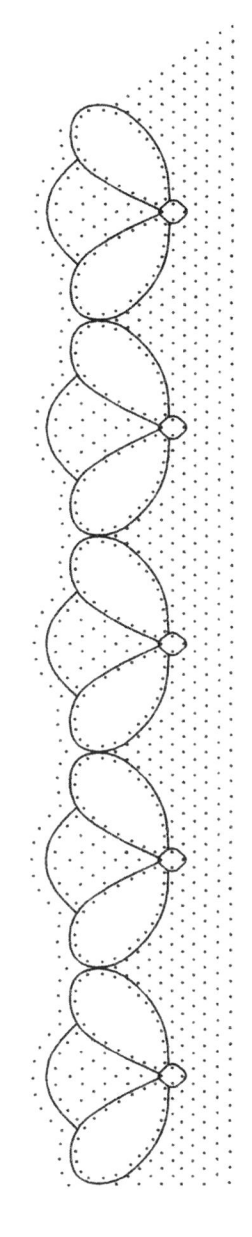

Figure 10 Pricking

3

All about making—Floral Bucks Point Lace

Starting Floral Bucks

If you are new to Floral Bucks it is recommended that the edging (figures 9 & 10) is worked before the motif. Do not expect perfect results first time; making good quality Floral Bucks relies more on skill than does Geometrical Bucks. The answer to each problem is rarely an exact one but is a choice of techniques, none of which can give a perfect result; a different choice may be made when working different repeats. These differences do not show; in fact it is probably this variety that makes the lace so attractive. Of course, the big problem when learning is knowing which techniques are appropriate for a particular situation so that the choice made is appropriate, and this only comes with experience[2]. Therefore work several pattern repeats, each time removing only sufficient pins to expose the previous working of that section. Check the spacing of the pairs etc. and try to improve any imperfections in the next repeat. Although not traditional, today we use long loops[4] to reduce the number of gimps added and removed. Keep working repeats until you are satisfied with the results. Do not expect your first pieces to be perfect, they are learning pieces and it will take some practice before you are making quality Floral Bucks.

Setting in

Start the edging (figures 9 & 10) by working a triangular area of ground[3]. (This is not the best place to start if the lace is to be joined end to start but is the most suitable place when starting a practice piece.) Pass the gimp through some of the ground pairs and add new pairs to the left. Because the top of the cloth stitch area is relatively flat, more than one pair will be added between the top pins (figure 12). The direction of the first row has to be established[5]; in this case the workers start towards the left. An extra pair is included with the headside passives to allow for the wider honeycomb area.

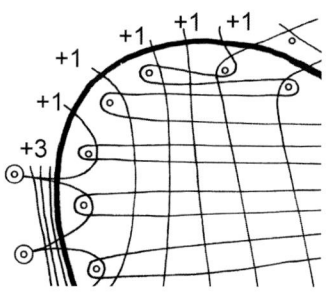

Figure 12 Adding extra pairs to start the clothwork

Avoiding holes by working stitches without pins

Because the edge of the clothwork is curved and bends away from the ground a new row of ground appears, and at the point at which the new row appears a hole may occur in the lace. If an extra pin was placed at the top of this row, its very width would deflect the gimp. However, a stitch may be made without pinning it; thus we have a stitch but there is no pin to affect the line of the gimp (figures 13 & 16).

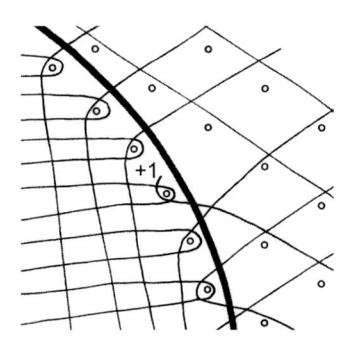

Figure 13 Adding a pair to make a ground stitch without a pin

Adding a new pair to be left out[6]

The clothwork should have as even a texture as possible. The clothwork is not solid; it is usually lighter in Floral Bucks than in Geometrical Bucks, i.e. the background behind the lace shows through. Although lacemakers in the past added pairs into the clothwork, the technique is found in comparatively few pieces, probably because it was time consuming. Today we have more time and it is regular practice to add and throw out pairs from clothwork to maintain the density. A shadow hole may occur when a new row of point ground starts and it may be avoided by working a stitch without a pin. Frequently as in this case (figure 13), there are insufficient pairs in the clothwork to allow for the pair that must be left out to make the ground stitch, therefore a pair is added at the end of the clothwork row

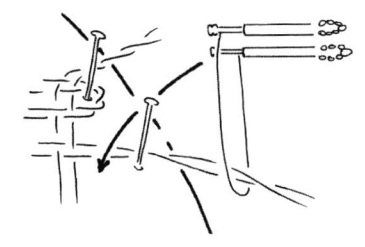

Figure 14 Slipping on a new pair

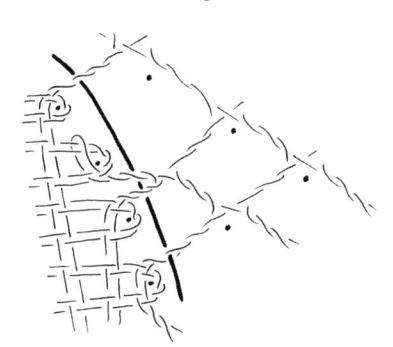

so that it can be left out of it for use in the ground. This is done thus: at the end of the row, pin and twist the workers as usual. Take a new pair and slip them up the workers (figure 14), take them round behind the pin, leave them between the pin and the nearest pair of passives (figure 15) and work the next row. Twist the new pair and pass it out across the gimp to work a ground stitch, which may or may not be pinned (figure 16 unpinned). Continue the clothwork taking pairs in from the ground and leaving them out for the ground as appropriate. Ground stitches adjacent to the vertical gimp may be worked as usual or as catch-pin stitches. It all depends on the space between the pin and the gimp and your personal preference.

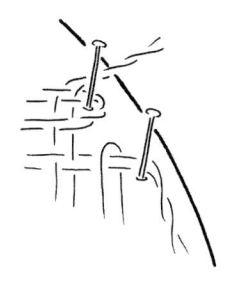

Figure 15 New pair added to be left out

Figure 16 (left) New pair left out to make a ground stitch

The Clothwork

The clothwork is more dense at the start and finish of the petals where the shape curves and rows become shorter. To maintain an even density i.e. to keep it light, a second passive pair may be left out to become another headside passive pair (figure 17).

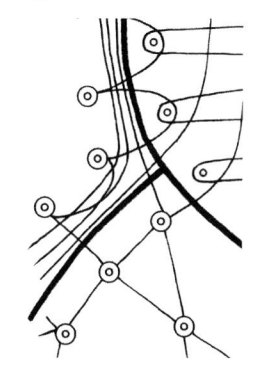

Figure 17 (right) Leaving out pairs from the clothwork

Moving surplus pairs from one area to another

The passive pairs reduce and the gimp will need binding on[7] as the clothwork reaches its lowest point, but there is still one more pair than would be present in Geometrical Bucks Point (figure 18). As there is a gimp adjacent to the unwanted pair, this pair is twisted, passed across the gimp, left lying against the gimp and used together with the gimp as far as necessary. To keep this extra, or spare pair and the gimp together the pair can be twisted a few times around the gimp or the two can be secured loosely together using an elastic band as when joining threads. (Up to three pairs can be carried along a gimp). Cross the gimps below the clothwork, take the gimp from the underside of the petal through the pairs for the four-pin honeycomb ring[8] and work the ring. Then pass the nearest gimp through the pairs from the clothwork and when it reaches the outer gimp double that back through the same pairs[9].

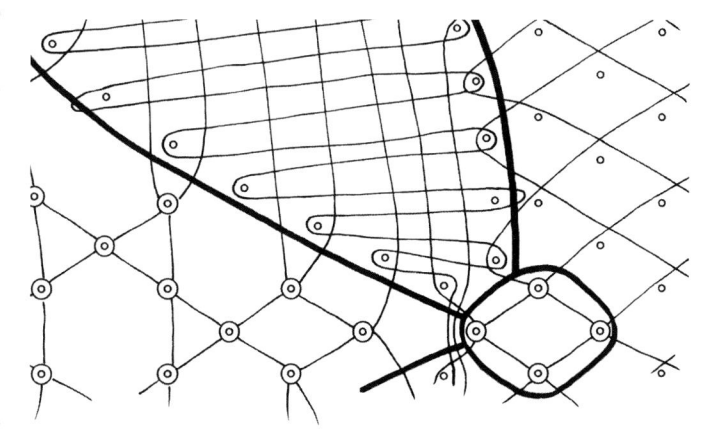

Figure 18 Finishing the clothwork and starting the honeycomb

All about making—Floral Bucks Point Lace

The honeycomb row adjacent to the headside
Start the honeycomb with a gap row using the inner passive pair and a pair from the clothwork. The last honeycomb stitch of the row is worked as a continuous row. This was found necessary because the honeycomb area tapers down towards the four-pin honeycomb ring. If the honeycomb grid were strictly adhered to there would be a single honeycomb stitch and it would not look as good, also the honeycomb stitches inside the headside gimp are distorted to accommodate the shape. Where possible the line of honeycomb immediately inside the headside gimp is worked as a continuous row in Floral Bucks. In many cases, such as this one, this entails working a blind spot[10], in this case one at the centre of each head. After completing the honeycomb, bring the headside gimp through the honeycomb pairs, across the other gimp and, at an appropriate point, move the pair lying along the gimp onto the other gimp.

Carrying spare pairs on a gimp

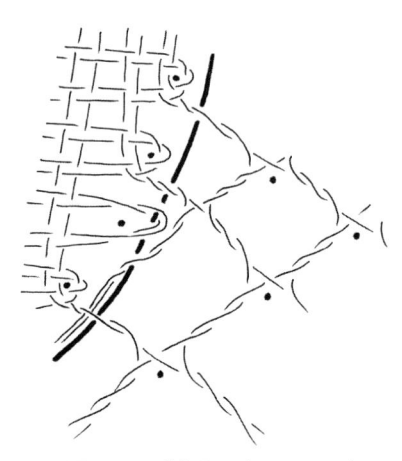

Figure 19 Laying a pair on a gimp

Start the lower petal mirroring the finish of the first petal. This time the stitch without a pin is at the end of a row and there will be an extra pair. This extra pair may be incorporated into the ground and a pair thrown out[11] or left lying on the gimp (figure 19); it depends on the density of the cloth work. To bring the pair to lie on the gimp first pass the gimp through the pair, then twist the pair and lay it along the gimp. Twist the gimp and the pair several times or secure together with an elastic band to prevent the spare pair going astray. Up to three pairs may be carried on a gimp. For this piece, the extra or spare pair can be carried on the gimps until needed in the next repeat (figure 20), moving it from one gimp to the other when the gimps cross. If the spare pair will not be needed again, after three pairs have crossed the gimp with the spare pair lying on it, the spare pair can be laid out over the back of the work and cut off later.

Moving from one area of cloth stitch to the next
The cloth stitch area does not end with two pairs at the last pin; there is an extra passive pair. The extra pair may be left either side of the last pin of the clothwork; choose which looks best (figure 20). The gimps cross as they pass through these pairs. When too many pairs accumulate in the headside lift two threads out and lay them back. If a pair is needed, add it in. The aim is to produce a piece of work that is beautiful, with good tension; this does not mean tight. The tension for Floral Bucks is lighter than for Geometrical Bucks. Tensioning means spacing the passives and rows to get a smooth texture that may shade lighter and darker but does not have stripes either horizontally or vertically. Tension 'by eye' not by feeling the tension with your fingers. It is unnecessary to work all the repeats exactly the same way.

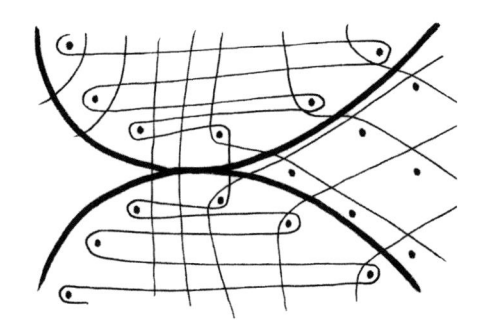

Figure 20 Passives passing from one petal to the next

All about making—Floral Bucks Point Lace

Bringing a pair on a gimp back into the work
When the next point is reached at which a stitch without a pin is to be made, the pair on the gimp is released, twisted if necessary and used to make the stitch without a pin (figure 21).

Although I initially tried to keep the repeats identical when I made this sample I kept making minor changes; this is how Floral Bucks is made. Each time a geometrical rule does not work assess the situation, don't try to remember it for the following repeat. Therefore, although the samples made for this book will usually have the first repeat made as described, following repeats may contain minor differences.

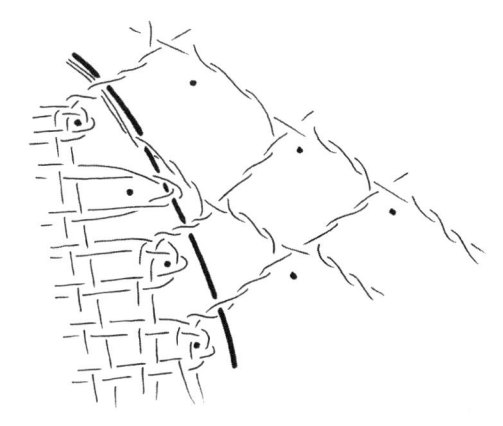

Figure 21 Bringing the pair back into the work

All about making—Floral Bucks Point Lace

PROJECT 2: Oval motif using the buttercup design

Figure 22 Oval motif mounted in a pot

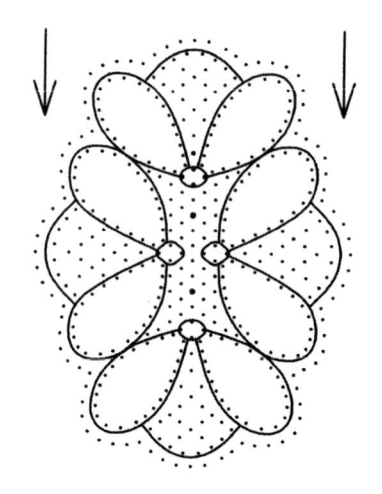

Figure 23 Oval motif, pricking (arrows indicate working direction)

Materials Required for Project 2
Egyptian cotton no. 80/2[1]
gimp D.M.C. perle no. 12
porcelain pot or oval frame kit with
70mm (1¾ in) x 50mm (2 in) approx. aperture

Figure 24 (left) Oval motif

This oval motif has the buttercup repeat from the edging on both sides, and these are made as for the edging. The motif was turned and used at the top and bottom, and since they were adjusted to fit the space available these motifs are not made exactly the same as for the edging. The piece was set in with false picots[12] (+2), pairs added by the traditional method and by slipping them on[13] (+1) and two pairs laid across to travel in two directions[14] (+2B) for the two central honeycomb stitches at the top (figure 25). This may not be the only way to set in this motif, there may be others that will work equally as well. Continue making the petals using clues from making the edging and adding gimps as required.

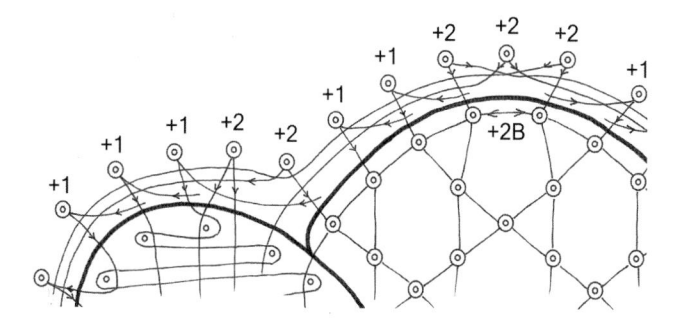

Figure 25 Setting in the motif

All about making—Floral Bucks Point Lace

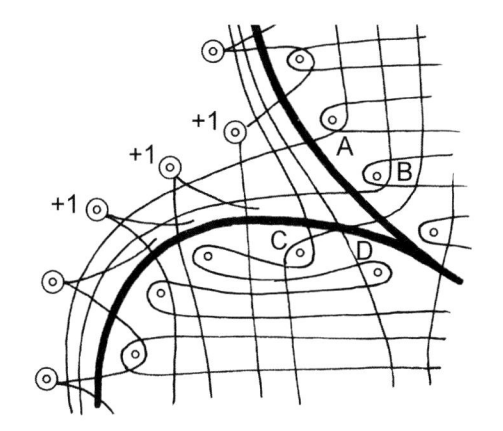

Starting the side flower

When the petal for the side flower is reached, the pairs left out from the top flower at pins A and B work through the current edge passives to become the edge passives for the side flower (figure 26) and the current edge passives pass into the clothwork of the new petal at pins C and D. Extra pairs will be needed for this petal and they may be added by slipping them on or by the traditional method.

Figure 26 (left) Starting the side petals

The central section of point ground starts with the pins in the top two corners using two pairs from the petal above (figure 27) and the large black dots indicate tallies[15]. As the end approaches throw out unwanted pairs that accumulate as headside passives, as in casting off[16], and finish as at a point[17].

Figure 27 (right) Starting the central section of point ground

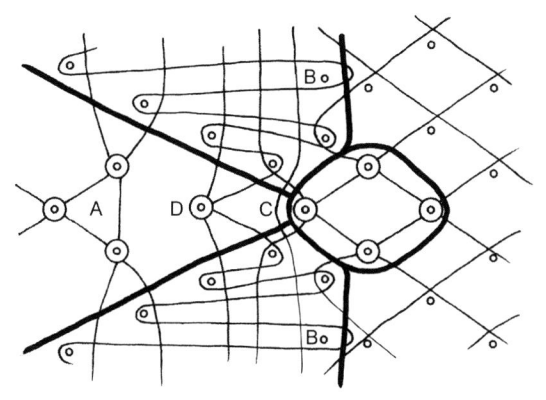

Figure 28 Moving from one petal to the next

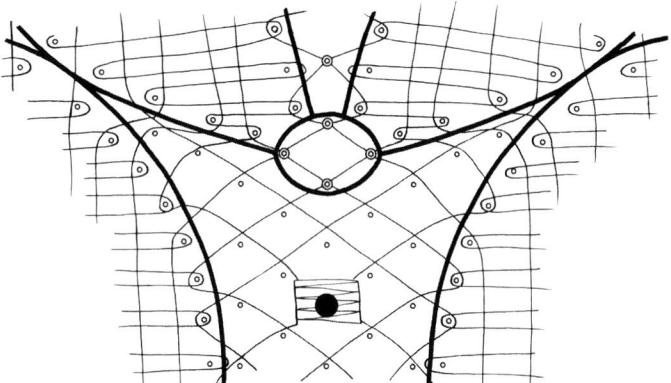

There may not always be a pair coming out from the ground to enter the clothwork, so bind the gimp on (figure 28, B). There may be too many pairs at the bottom of the four-pin honeycomb ring; just lay spare pairs along a gimp as at C and either throw them out or carry them along until needed. You may wish to change the honeycomb triangle A to form a diamond by including the pin on its right, pin D. This will result in the pair from the last pin of the clothwork being laid along the gimp at C, making two on the gimp. This is also acceptable.

It is useful to make a double size photocopy[18] of the pattern and draw the pairs in as in these diagrams. This is not 'making lace by numbers', this is working out your own interpretation. Making Floral Bucks is making lace 'by the seat of your pants', i.e. by choosing the technique you think will work best at the time not by following a rule book. Do not expect your first attempt to be perfect. You will need practice and experience and more practice and more experience. It takes a lot of lacemaking time to master Floral Bucks.

All about making—Floral Bucks Point Lace

END NOTES

1 Substituting threads
See Part 6.

2 Moving from ground to clothwork
Traditionally pairs from the ground become passives when they enter clothwork and the workers of the clothwork do not exchange their roles. Recently techniques have been circulating that involve the pair entering from the ground exchanging roles with the worker (figures 29-32), i.e. the workers make a cloth stitch with the ground pair and become the new ground pair while the former ground pair becomes the workers. The gimp passes through adjacent to the cloth stitch without any twists separating the two. The pin may be set up between the cloth stitch and gimp (figures 29 & 30) or between the cloth stitch and the twists for the ground (figures 31 & 32). Exchanging the roles of the pairs is not typical of Geometrical or standard Floral Bucks and the effect of exchanging roles may be very subtle, but there is a definite change in character. However, Part 4 describes the techniques for making very fine Bucks Point and in this form the ground pairs and workers continually exchange. If you mix techniques you may find that the thread and accompanying design flow along the gimp is interrupted, resulting in an unsatisfactory effect and compromising the character of the lace. I have tried mixing techniques but been dismayed with the results. I am now much more careful to keep like with like. Treat these techniques with caution.

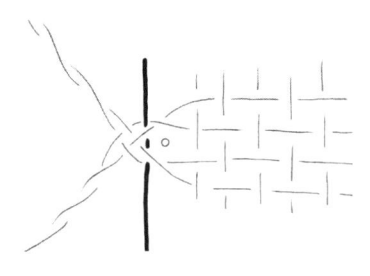

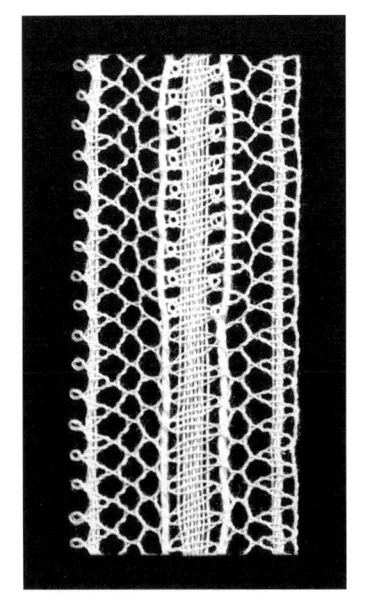

Figure 29 (left) Exchanging ground with workers, gimp inside cloth stitch

Figure 30 (right) Upper half standard catch-pin stitches, lower half, exchanging ground pair with workers, gimp inside cloth stitch

Figure 31 (left) Upper half standard catch-pin stitches, lower half, exchanging ground pair with workers, cloth stitch inside gimp

Figure 32 (lower right) Exchanging ground pair with workers, cloth stitch inside gimp

Lace figures 30 & 32 worked on pricking figure 56 *All about making - Geometrical Bucks Point Lace*, A. Stillwell, Salex Publishing

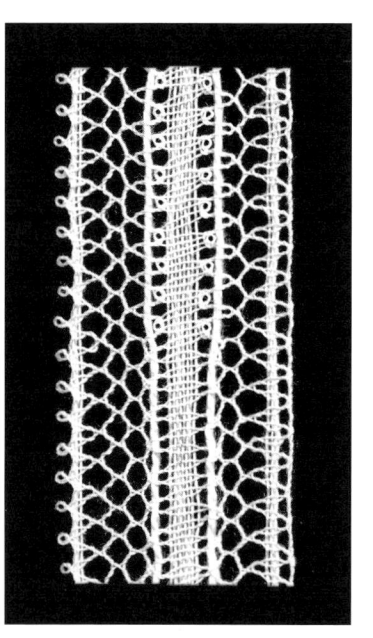

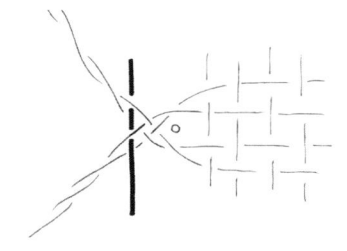

3 Point ground
All about making - Geometrical Bucks Point Lace, A. Stillwell, Salex Publishing, page 19.

4 Long loops
Ibid., pages 188-193

5 Checking the working direction of the first row.
When working clothwork the workers should travel at right angles to the line of work, and the starting direction can either help or hinder. To check for the best direction to start use a pin in each hand. Place the point of the pin held in your right hand in the top hole, place point of the other pin in the hole on the left, move the pin in your right hand to the next hole on the right, then the one on the other side to the next hole on the left. Continue moving the pins alternately down the sides of the clothwork and note how close lines joining them are to a horizontal line across the right (figure 33). Starting this petal towards the right results in the line of work dropping downwards on the right hand side. Therefore this petal is best started with the first row working towards the left. Always check the starting direction of cloth stitch areas before working them; sometimes there is a definite advantage in starting in a particular direction, sometimes there is not.

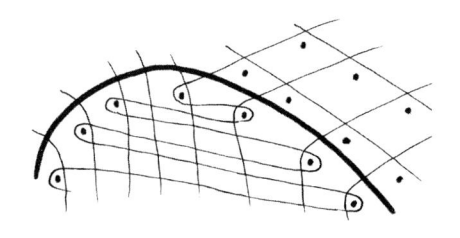

Figure 33 If the first row is started by working towards the right there is a definite 'list to starboard'

6 Adding a new pair to be left out, alternative method
The new pair may be slipped onto the worker as it passes round the pin and the workers returned without making a stitch with the new pair (figure 34). This technique was probably a shortcut used when time was of the essence and in some cases this technique may make it easier to preserve the line of the ground pair. However, this technique has two disadvantages. Firstly, it is much weaker than the standard technique, but this is only relevant when strength is required. Secondly the loop of the workers around the pin and the gimp may be displaced when the ground is worked and the displacement cannot be corrected.

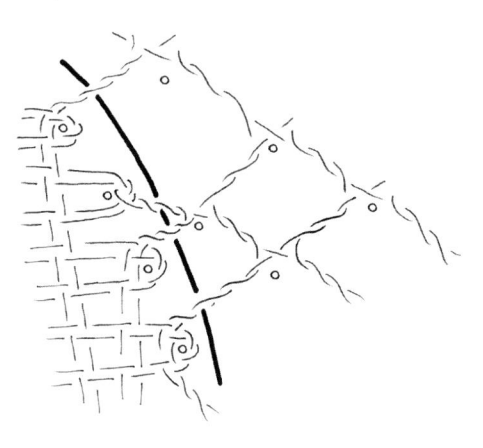

Figure 34 Adding a new pair to be left out, alternative method

7 Binding on a gimp
Ibid. page 154, figure 386, page 174, figure 440.

8 Honeycomb and four-pin honeycomb ring
Honeycomb, Ibid., page 38
Four-pin honeycomb ring, ibid., page 115.

9 Doubling gimps
Ibid., page 57.

10 Blind spot
Ibid., page 47, figure 132.

All about making—Floral Bucks Point Lace

11 Throwing Pairs out
The density of the clothwork can be reduced by lifting pairs out and throwing them back.

12 False picot
Ibid., page 114.

13 Slipping pairs on
Ibid., page 114.

14 Pairs laid across to travel in two directions.
Sometimes, at the very start of a piece the pairs entering honeycomb across the gimp do not start the first two stitches comfortably. When working this piece, I started the top of the area with two pairs travelling between the first two pins. To do this attach two pairs to a pin at the side of the work using clove hitches (lark's head) or a double half hitch (figure 35), loops that attach the pairs must disappear without leaving knots when the pin is removed, or use a thread clamp (figures 36 & 37). Then one bobbin from each of these pairs is used to form new 'pairs' to make a honeycomb stitch, the top one on the left hand side. This new pair will have to work at least three stitches to stabilise the threads before removing the pin around which the two pairs were hitched, or the thread clamp. Then twist the 'pairs' twice and use them to work the next honeycomb stitch on the right.

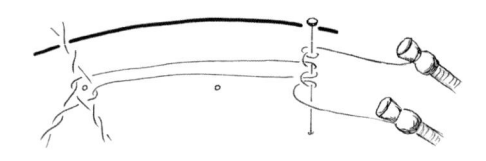

Figure 35 Securing pairs that will travel in two directions with half hitches

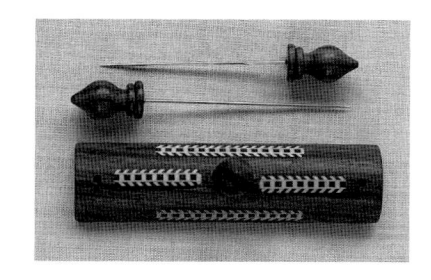

Figure 36 Thread clamp. Place the bar across the threads to be restrained and secure in place by inserting the pins through the holes

15 Tallies
Ibid., pages 97-98, 108-109, 118.

16 Casting off
Ibid., pages 115-116, 125-126.

17 Neatening at a point
Ibid., page 120

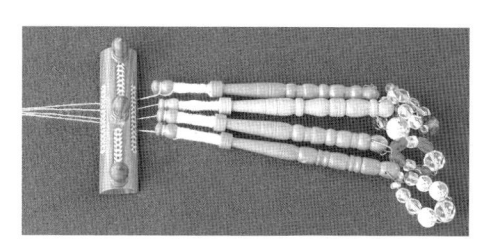

Figure 37 Securing pairs that will travel in two directions with a thread clamp

18 Working with photocopies
Some copying machines are designed to narrow the page to prevent loss of words near the edges. This means that after repeated copying the pattern becomes unacceptably distorted. However, repeated copying is a useful tool when drafting, and the distortion can be avoided by changing the direction of the page being copied. When the second copy is made, place the page at right angles to its direction when it was first copied, the third in the original position and the fourth in the same direction as the second etc. I always add the new number to each subsequent copy so that the odd numbers go in normally and the even numbers at right angles. The final pattern should have the same angle to the footside but may be a slightly different size and this can be adjusted more easily. Making a new photocopy at each stage can be very useful. If you find you do not like changes you have made you can return to a previous situation.

All about making—Floral Bucks Point Lace

19 Drafting the pattern

Computers are excellent for producing accurate patterns, repeating patterns, turning corners, truing up, etc. (see Bibliography). However, I find it easier to design with pencil and paper first then scan the drawing and, using the scan as my 'tracing' continue as for Method 1. It is much harder and more time-consuming to copy a Floral Bucks pattern exactly than it is to design a new one and in this situation, although it is generally easier to learn by copying first and then moving to the next stage of working from your own design, it is probably better to draw a simple design or trace an existing edging and turn that into a pricking. If you use this design do not expect or even aim to have all the pinholes in exactly the same place; it would be too time consuming and frustrating. When making Floral Bucks the pattern repeats usually work up in very slightly different ways. It is the same with drafting the patterns. The process of drafting the pattern is straightforward, but it is not worth the time and frustration trying to get the pinholes in exactly the same place as in the original. In any case the lines of your gimps are unlikely to be exactly the same and the pinholes for the clothwork must relate to your gimps and ground, not the original ones. Providing a draft is made using the same design it will look the same even if pins are in slightly different places.

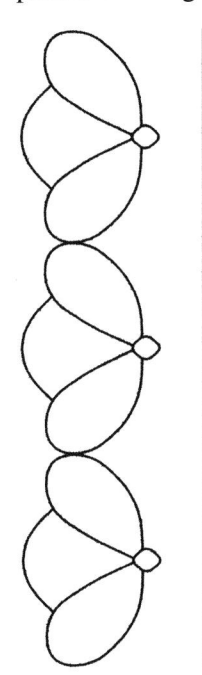

To draft your version of the Buttercup edging trace (or photocopy onto tracing paper) three pattern repeats and draw the line for the footside (figure 38). (When tracing do not forget to fold the paper to get both halves of the design exactly the same, tracing paper has two sides, try using both.) Using three repeats allows you to see the relationship between the centre repeat and the one on either side of it, the effect of which you will not be aware if you only use one repeat. There are various ways of continuing, two are described or you may wish to follow a different route.

Figure 38 (left) Tracing three pattern repeats and the footside line.

19a Method 1a Placing the grid for the ground over the design

Select a suitable grid (see Part 6) and make an accurate pricking using a transparent medium e.g. acetate. Attach a white sheet of paper to the back of the tracing and place the grid over the tracing of the pattern with the footside of the transparent grid parallel to the footside of the traced design and a line of pins at right angles to the footside passing through the centre of the design where the petals meet. Check the positions of the pinholes around the design looking for the places where holes may occur in the lace, especially where rows disappear or new rows appear. Move the grid towards the left and right across the design, keeping the footsides of the tracing and grid parallel, and try to minimize these problems. With so many places requiring attention it is not possible to deal with them all. It is a case of getting as many pinholes as possible in ideal positions coping with those that are not in good positions when making the lace, i.e. making the stitch without a pin near the centre of the outer curve of the petal (figure 39). Transfer the grid to the tracing and white paper by pricking through the grid.

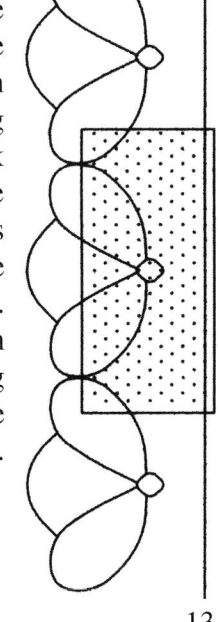

Figure 39 Design with transparent grid in place

All about making—Floral Bucks Point Lace

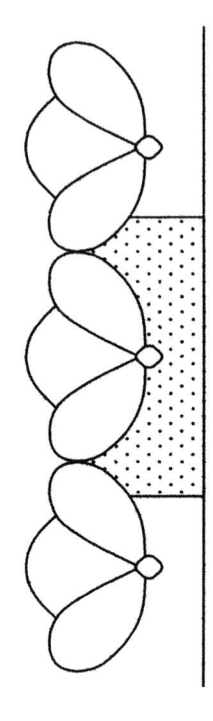

19a Method 2 Placing the grid for the ground under the design

Make a photocopy of the design and cut away the area for the grid, i.e. between the outer line of the petals and the footside line. Place this grid under the design with the footside of the transparent pricking parallel to the footside of the traced design and a line of pins through the centre of the design where the petals meet. Check the positions of the pinholes around the design looking for the places where holes may occur in the lace, especially where rows disappear or new rows appear. Move the grid to the left and right across the design, keeping the footsides of the tracing and grid parallel and try to minimize these problems. With so many places requiring attention it is not possible to deal with them all. It is a case of doing what is possible and dealing with the others when making the lace. Hence the necessity for making the stitch without a pin near the centre of the outer curve of the petal (figure 40). Stick the design to the grid.

Figure 40 (left) Grid placed under the design (Method 2)

19b Method 1 Adding the honeycomb filling with the grid over the design

Prepare a transparent grid of the honeycomb filling. Place over the central part of the buttercup so that a horizontal line of pinholes of the grid passing through the centres of the diamond-shaped spaces lines up with the junction where the petals meet. For this piece the dots of the honeycomb filling and the four-pin bud line up with those of the ground, but they need not. The grid may be moved slightly to the left or right to get the best position for the pins next to the gimp (figure 41).

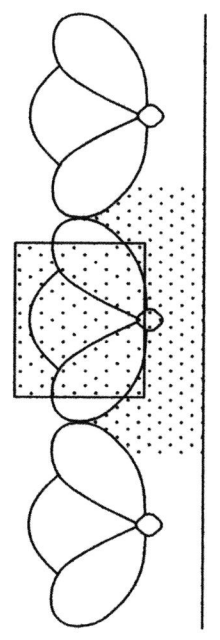

Figure 41 (right) Honeycomb filling placed over the design (Method 1)

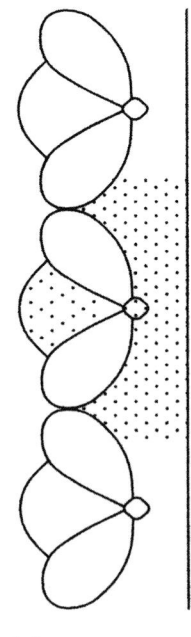

19b Method 2 Adding the honeycomb filling with the grid under the design

Prepare a grid for the honeycomb. Using a copy of the draft with the ground added (figure 30), cut away the space for the honeycomb ground and place the grid under the central part of the buttercup with a line of pins through the centre between the petals; this line must be one through the centres of the diamond-shaped spaces of the grid. For this piece it happens that the dots of the honeycomb filling and the four-pin bud line up with those of the ground, but they need not. The grid may be moved slightly to the left or right to get the best position for the pins next to the gimp (figure 42).

Figure 42 (left) Honeycomb filling added (Method 2)

All about making—Floral Bucks Point Lace

19c Adjusting the honeycomb pinholes adjacent to the gimp (both methods)

The holes around the edges of the honeycomb should be adjusted so that they complement the design without distorting them too far. Another pinhole is added in the corner where the petals meet. (figure 43).

Figure 43 (right) Adjusting the honeycomb pinholes

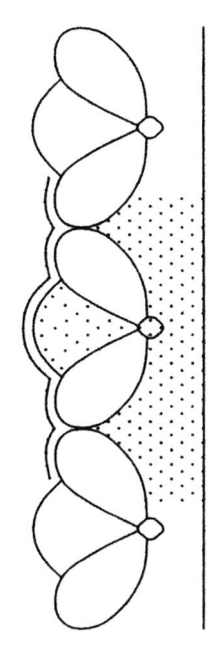

19d Picot line (both methods)
Draw the picot line allowing a little more than the space between two vertical rows of ground, plus a little more in the valleys where pairs are stacked. Continue these lines across part of the adjacent repeats so that you will be aware of how the repeats react towards each other. Then add the picots by eye (figure 44) and remove the picot line.

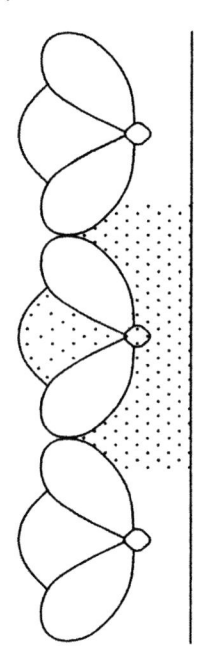

Figure 44 (left) Adding the picot line

19e Clothwork pinholes (both methods)
At this stage the pinholes for the clothwork can be added by eye. There should be one pinhole approximately in line with each horizontal row of ground or honeycomb, but as each must also lie an equal distance from the gimp this can only be a rough guide. The position of the pins is always a compromise between the requirements of the geometrical ground and the freestyle clothwork. (figure 45). I find, even now after years of designing and pattern drafting, that my ability as a lacemaker to position these pinholes is better than my ability as a designer. Therefore I prepare the draft as far as figure 43 and position the pinholes when I make the lace.

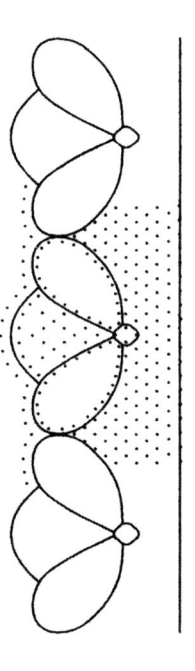

Figure 45 (right) Adding picots.

All about making—Floral Bucks Point Lace

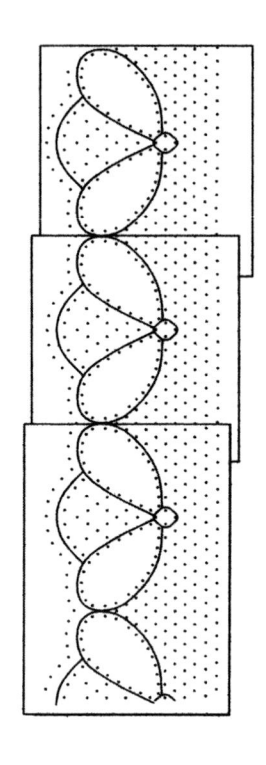

19f Check the junction of the repeats
Make three photocopies and trim to about 1cm (½ in) around the central pattern repeat, then carefully trim the top of each through the row of dots in line with the junction of two repeats. If this row is not in line with the junction take the best one and position each repeat over the one above. By cutting through the dots it is possible to place the cut dots of one repeat across the corresponding dots of another repeat and get a nearly perfect match (figure 46). If necessary the gimps at the junctions and the pinholes within them may need some adjusting so that the repeats meet exactly along a row of ground pins.

Figure 46 (left) Checking the junctions of the repeats

19g Adjust the footside
When you are satisfied with the result adjust the catch-pin and footside pinholes (figure 10), Ibid, page 26, and make a final copy.

20 Drafting the motif
The motif is an adaptation of the 'Buttercup' edging (figure 9).

20a Side motifs
Make a copy of the edging pattern (figure 10) and cut out two repeats. Trim one down the second vertical row of dots from the four-pin honeycomb ring, turn it round and place on the other repeat, lining up the cut dots with the second row of dots from the four-pin honeycomb ring. Attach the pieces together (figure 47).

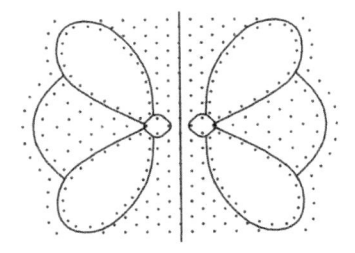

Figure 47 Side motifs

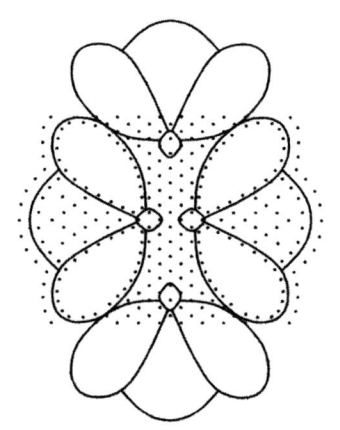

20b Gimps for the upper and lower motifs
Cut out two buttercup flowers along their gimp lines and place them at right angles to the two side motifs, one above and one below the side motifs (figure 48).

Figure 48 Upper and lower motifs in place

20c Honeycomb ground

Remove any unwanted ground pinholes, they can be removed from a paper copy by blocking them out with a white liquid paper pen, add the honeycomb ground as described in End Note 19b and adjust any edge pinholes as described in End Note 19c (figure 49).

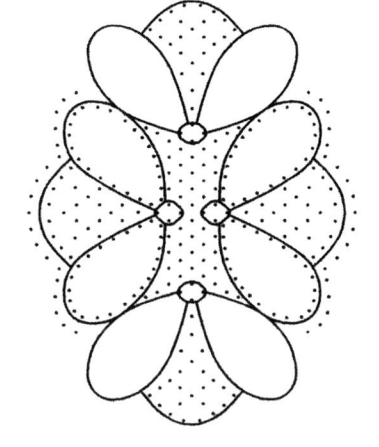

Figure 49 Honeycomb ground

20d Picot pinholes, clothwork pinholes and tallies

Add the clothwork pinholes and picot pinholes as described in End Notes 19d and 19e, and because the point ground looks rather bare add two tallies (figure 23).

All about making—Floral Bucks Point Lace

CHAPTER 2

PROJECTS: 3-5 Nook Pins

Project 3: Brooch motif
Project 4: Church doll
Project 5: Edging with corner

PROJECT 3: Brooch motif

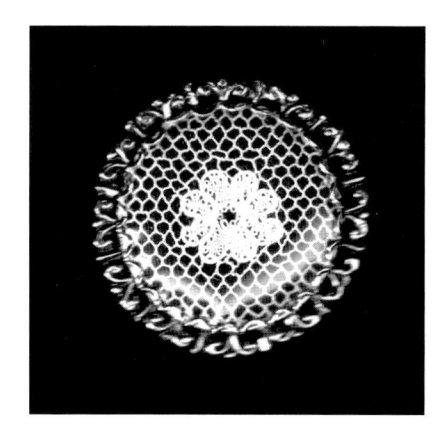

Figure 50 Brooch motif

Adjust the numbers of rows of ground around the central motif according to the size of the frame, allowing for at least four rows to be folded back around the mount.

Materials Required for Projects 3-5
Egyptian cotton no. 100/2[1]
gimp D.M.C. perle no. 12
circular brooch mount with 30mm ($1^3/_8$ in) aperture

Gimp lines where there are nook pins
Frequently gimps are not drawn going around nook pins but by-passing them (pricking, figure 51). The heavy gimp lines of the working diagram (figure 53) indicate the true position of the gimp; the dotted line shows the path of the gimp as indicated on the pricking.

All about making—Floral Bucks Point Lace

Setting in

This motif design has no edging around the ground, therefore start by tying pairs to pins above the pricking and work the ground with the pairs as they lie. At the sides the point ground pairs just pass around the pins to start the next row. When the lace is mounted the edges will be folded back around the mount and will not show. Work the ground as far as the flower motif.

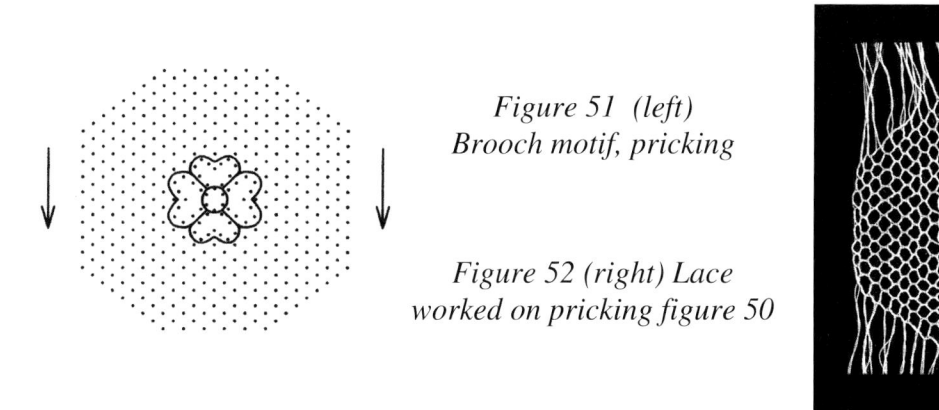

Figure 51 (left) Brooch motif, pricking

Figure 52 (right) Lace worked on pricking figure 50

Working the right lobe of the upper petal (nook pin dipping down into clothwork)

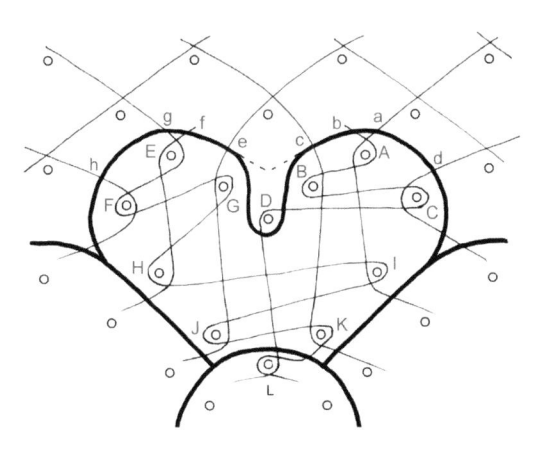

Figure 53 Working the upper petal

Work the ground as far as the gimp line (figure 53). Support a pair of gimps over a pin placed in any pinhole to the right of the right hand lobe, pass pair 'a' across the gimp and twist. Slip a new pair, pair 'b', over the gimp[2] to the left of pair 'a' and twist them. Then start the clothwork at pin A by working cloth stitch, pin, cloth stitch with pairs 'a' and 'b'. Continue by working towards the left taking in pair 'c' at pin B and returning across the row adding pair 'd' at pin C. This has used all the pins of the right lobe above the nook pin[3], pin D. Work back across from pin C but do not twist before passing the gimp through, set up the nook pin, pin D, twist the pair two or three times and pass the gimp through again. Do not twist this pair but allow it to drop down to become a passive pair.

Working the left lobe of the upper petal

Pass the gimp through the next pair on the left, pair 'e', slip a new pair on the gimp, pair 'f', and pass the gimp through the next two pairs on the left, pairs 'g' and 'h'. Twist pairs 'e' to 'h'. It is usual to start working both lobes in the same direction unless the pinholes dictate otherwise, therefore start the clothwork with pairs 'f' and 'g' at pin E and work the first row towards the left, taking in pair 'h' at pin F, then work back to the right taking in pair 'e' and pin at G. This has used the remaining pins on the left above the nook pin, pin D.

Working the lower part of the upper petal

Work back across the pairs of the left hand lobe, leaving out the last pair of the row at pin H. Return leaving out the last pair, pin I. Work two more rows leaving out a pair at pins J and K and cover pin K. Twist the pairs leaving the petal.

All about making—Floral Bucks Point Lace

Gimp path around the upper petal

Having completed the top petal, pass the gimps through the pairs until they cross in the centre (figure 54). Pass the gimp now on the left towards the left through the pairs left out of the top petal and two more pairs. Pass the gimp now on the right towards the right through the pairs left out of the top petal and two more pairs. There are no twists between the gimps[4]. Place a new pair of gimps over a pin in any hole in the pattern, pass the central pair from the top petal and the pair to its right across the new gimp (again there are no twists between the gimps); then twist these pairs. With the same two pairs work the top honeycomb stitch of the centre (figure 53, pin L).

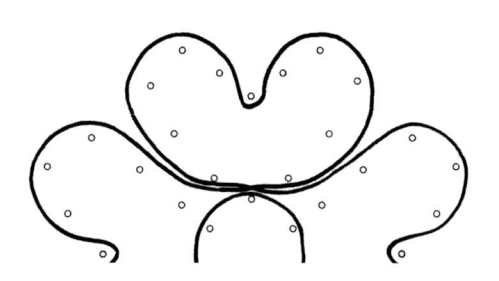

Figure 54 Gimp path around the upper petal

Working the right hand petal (nook pin protruding into the side of clothwork)

Starting with top two pairs, pairs a and b (figure 55), work rows of cloth stitch adding a pair each side as it widens, pairs c, d and e at pins B, C and D. Then leave out pairs as it narrows, pairs f and g at pins C and E. At the end of the next row take the workers across the gimp to make the honeycomb stitch to the right of the one at the top of the honeycomb ring, pin F, and return it across the gimp; there are no twists between the gimp and the clothwork when a worker passes out from clothwork across a gimp or returns back across it. A modified honeycomb stitch[5] may be necessary at pin F. Work back across the row and pass the gimp through the workers (no twists before the gimp), set up the nook pin, pin G, and twist the workers two or three times. Return the workers back across the gimp and through the passives, pass the gimp through the workers and make the next honeycomb stitch, pin H. Work some point ground so that two pairs can be added into the lower lobe on this side while pairs are left out after working each pin on the other side of the clothwork.

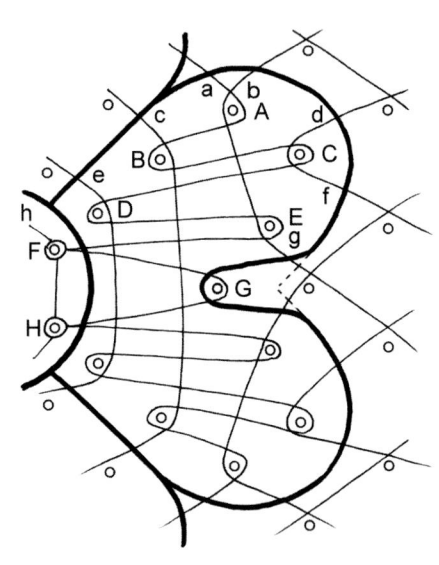

Figure 55 Working the right hand petal

Work the left hand petal as a mirror image of the right hand petal and make the last honeycomb stitch of the centre ring. Cross the gimps that have passed around the honeycomb ring (figure 56), double them up and throw them out.

Gimp path to the lower petal

Bring the gimps from the side petals through until they meet in the centre, cross them and pass each out through the pairs of the other side petal (figure 56).

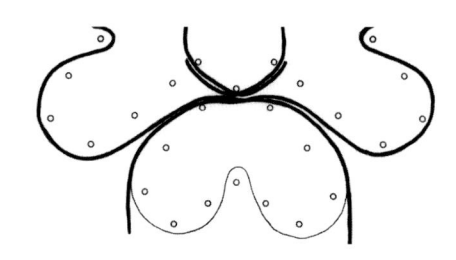

Figure 56 Gimp path to the lower petal

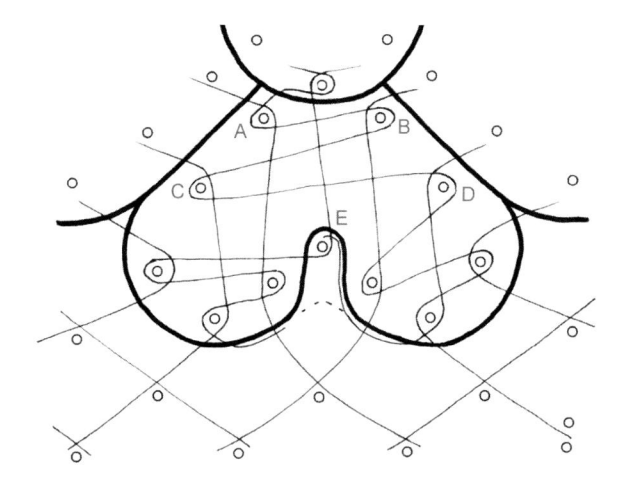

All about making—Floral Bucks Point Lace

Working the upper part of the lower petal
Start the upper section of the petal at pin A using the first pair left out from the left hand petal and a pair from the last honeycomb stitch of the central ring (figure 57). Work across taking in the first pair left out from the right hand petal and set up pin B. Add a pair at the end of each of the next two rows at pins C and D.

Figure 57 (left) Working the upper part of the lower petal

Working the right hand lobe of the lower petal
Divide the passives in half, adding the central pair to the left side (figure 57). (These will become the workers for the left hand lobe.) Complete the right hand lobe using the passives on the right.

Gimp path enclosing the right hand lobe
Bring the right hand gimp through the pairs left out from the right hand lobe (figure 58) and the next pair (the central pair). Set up the nook pin, pin E, to the left of the central pair, twist this pair two or three times and pass the gimp back through.

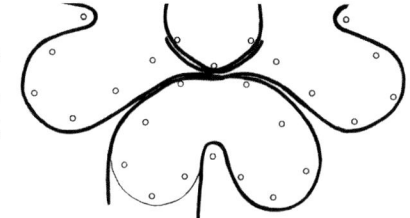

Figure 58 (right) Gimp path around the right hand lobe

Working the left hand lobe of the lower petal
Using the former central pair as workers, continue by working across the row towards the left and complete the lobe (figure 57).

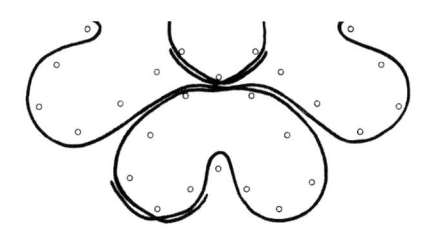

Closing the gimp path around the lower petal
After completing the left hand lobe, bring the gimps through until they meet (figure 59), cross them, double up and throw them back.

Figure 59 (left) Completing the gimp

Throwing out surplus pairs
Line up the pairs that are left out with the ground pins and it is obvious that there is an extra pair each side (figure 57); these correspond to the new pairs that were added, one to each of the lobes of the top petal, that are necessary to fill the petals, but they are not needed for the ground. For each lobe, from the last pinhole used, take the pair nearest the nook pin along the gimp through two pairs, if possible, and throw back. After working several rows these bobbins may be cut off leaving a long thread, ensuring that these bobbins are cut off before the pins surrounding the throw out point are removed. If not, the weight of the bobbins may distort the lace. The long ends should be trimmed off close to the lace, preferably when there are still pins a few rows away that will keep the lace stable during the cutting process.

Twist the remaining pairs and continue the point ground until all pinholes have been used. This piece is not 'finished off', the pairs may be finished in twos with reef knots or just cut off 1cm ($^3/_8$ in) from the end of the point ground.

Mounting the brooch motif
Select a suitable backing and stiffen with interfacing if necessary. Cut the backing to size and pin the lace in position. Fold the surplus lace over at the top, the bottom and the sides and pin at the back. At the back, make a circle of running stitches through the ground one or two meshes from the fold, gather up gently and trim the point ground as necessary. Still at the back, work long stitches across from one side to the other as required. Mount according to the brooch manufacturers instructions.

All about making—Floral Bucks Point Lace

PROJECT 4: Church doll[6]

Figure 58 Church doll

Materials Required for Project 4
Egyptian cotton no. 100/2[1]
gimp D.M.C. perle no. 12
gent's handkerchief approximately
36 cm (14¼ in) square
or fine lawn 40 cm (15¾ in) square
cotton wool ball
fine sewing needle
strong white thread and sewing needle
black stranded embroidery thread
red stranded embroidery thread
embroidery needle
20 cm (8 in) 3mm (⅛ in) ribbon

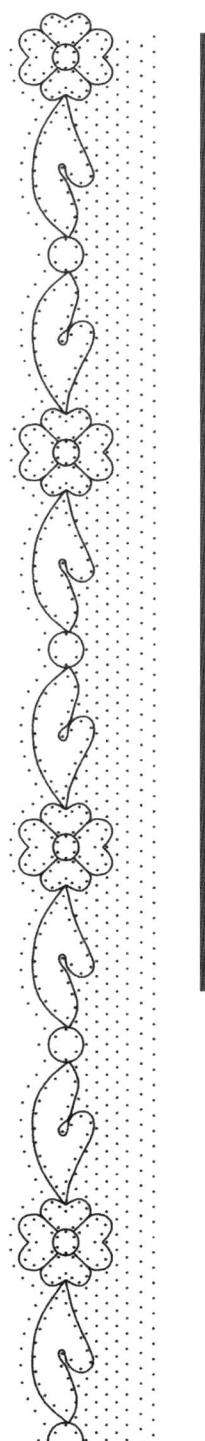

*Figure 60
Bonnet brim,
pricking*

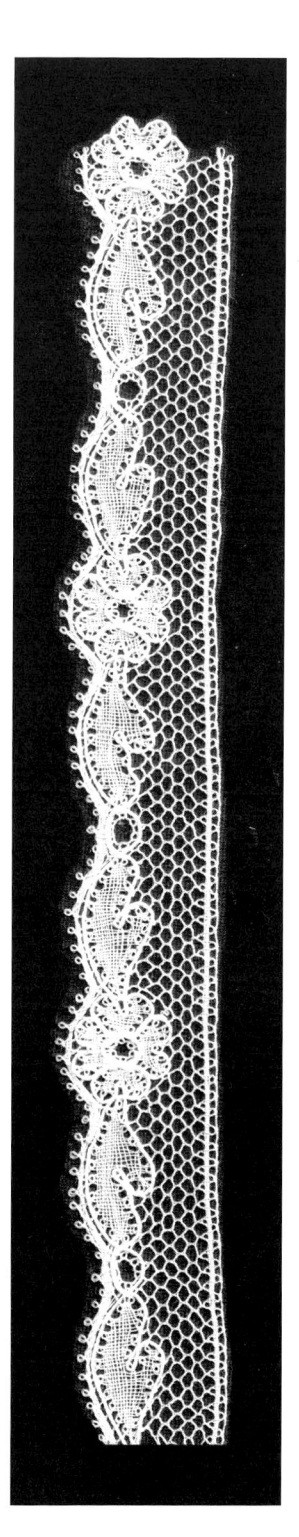

*Figure 62
Bonnet brim made
on pricking figure 60*

23

All about making—Floral Bucks Point Lace

Estimating the length of lace for the bonnet brim
After making the doll, see pages 26 & 27, gather a length of machine lace or fine fabric, the same width as the lace, into a circle. Try it round the head and adjust the length until it looks right. Straighten out the gatherings and measure the length.

Setting in
As this edging will be joined end to start, set in horizontally across the ground at the point where the ground is at its narrowest. Set in a flower, (which is the same as the Brooch Motif Flower, figure 47) by adding pairs in across the gimps at the top of the petal. Place the pairs on support pins behind the starting point and pass the gimp through. Twist the pairs the usual number of times and start working. After covering the first pin let down the workers; the other pairs may remain on the support pins for a few rows before being let down (figure 63). Take care not to firm up too strongly or you may deflect the gimp; firming up the gimp will help to counteract this.

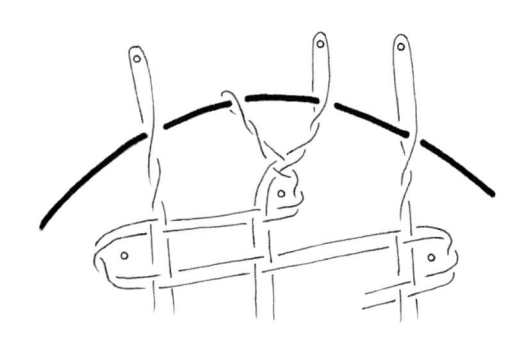

Figure 63 Starting with pairs on support pins

Start the ground[7] and add pairs until it meets the petal and add the headside passives. Work the flower as for the motif (figures 53-58), but do not throw out the final two gimps, instead cross them in preparation for making the first leaf.

The first leaf
Make an enlargement of the pricking and plan the line of the workers and where pairs enter the leaf so that you have the same number of pairs when you reach pin A as shown in figure 64. Then work the leaf until the following row crosses the nook pin, i.e. when you set up pin A and complete the small lobe, pins B-D. Take the gimp round the small lobe and through the next passive pair, set up the nook pin E, twist the pair twice and take across the gimp. Continue working, taking in pairs that bridge the gimp at pins G and J. Complete the leaf, first planning the routes of the pairs on the enlarged pricking and work the six-pin honeycomb ring[8].

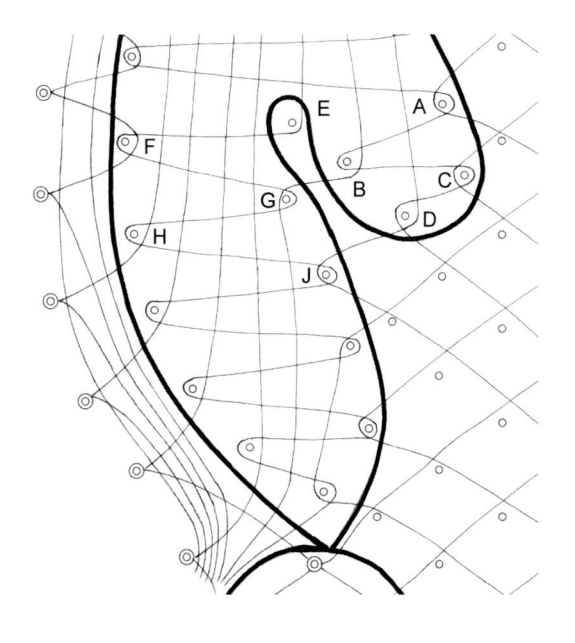

Figure 64 First leaf

All about making—Floral Bucks Point Lace

Second leaf
Work the leaf as far as pin A (figure 65), which is a nook pin; the workers for that section are now left as passives. Take the gimp through ground pairs to the right and work the small lobe, pins B-E, this last pin being the start of the row that works right across the leaf to pin F. Complete the leaf and work the flower.

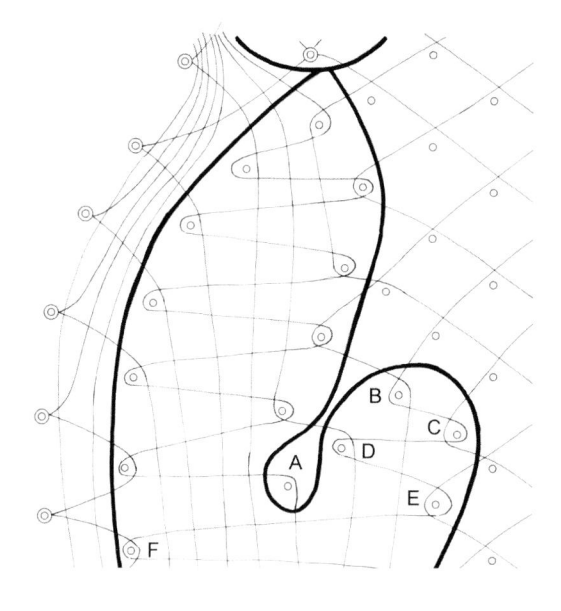

Figure 65 Second leaf with nook pin

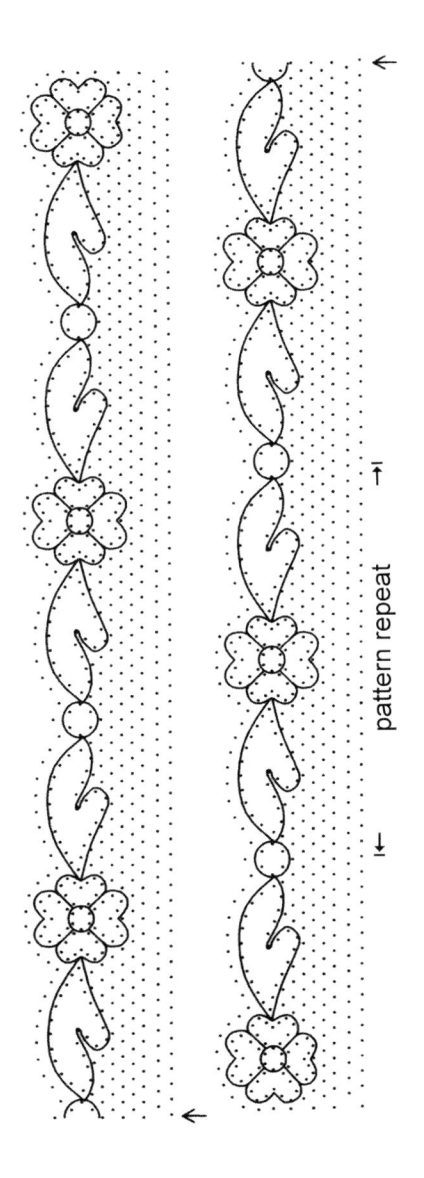

Figures 66a & 66b Prickings for skirt edging

Preparing the pricking for the skirt edging
Estimate the length of lace required for along one side of the square of fabric. Use one pricking figure 66a and two of pricking 66b. Cut across the dots along the arrowed line at the lower end of pricking 66a and place over the arrowed first line of pricking 66b with the cut dots matching. Cut across the top arrowed line of dots of the second pricking 66b and match the appropriate arrowed line of the previous section of the pricking according to the length required. Lace should always be made a little longer than required and eased in when it is mounted.

All about making—Floral Bucks Point Lace

Setting in horizontally along a picot edge

Set in horizontally with a whole stitch round the pin[9] at A and false picots B-F (figures 67 & 68). Work two 'headside passive' pairs across from right to left. Pass appropriate pairs from the false picots[10] pins D-F across a gimp and work ground with appropriate pairs from false picots B-D. Work the ground and add two footside passive pairs supported on a pin. Use the lower headside passive pair to make picot G and slip on a pair[11] to work the next picot. Start working the ground using pairs from pins A and B and add a gimp when starting the flower. Add further pairs as required by slipping them on and make the edging. Adjust pins to keep the footside straight and the clothwork even[12].

Figure 67 (left) Setting in along a picot edge

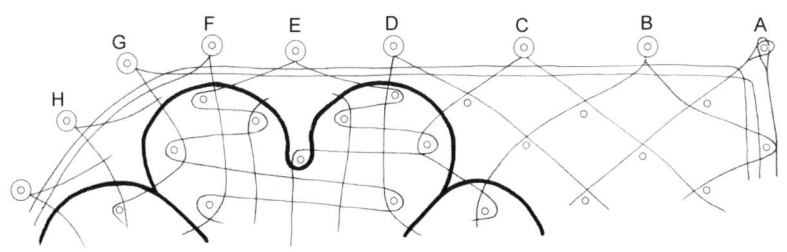

Figure 68 Setting in along a picot edge

Casting off horizontally along a picot edge

As the end is reached cast off pairs[13] after working pins A-E (figures 69 & 70). The next pins F-H each have two pairs approaching them. For each of these work the pair approaching from the right towards the left through all pairs available except for the edge passive pair, then throw them out. Then make the picot with the last pair that is approaching the pin from the left and take through the footside passives. After making up the edge at pin J bring the new workers back through three pairs and leave out. Work the edge pair through two pairs. Finally tie off these pairs using reef knots.

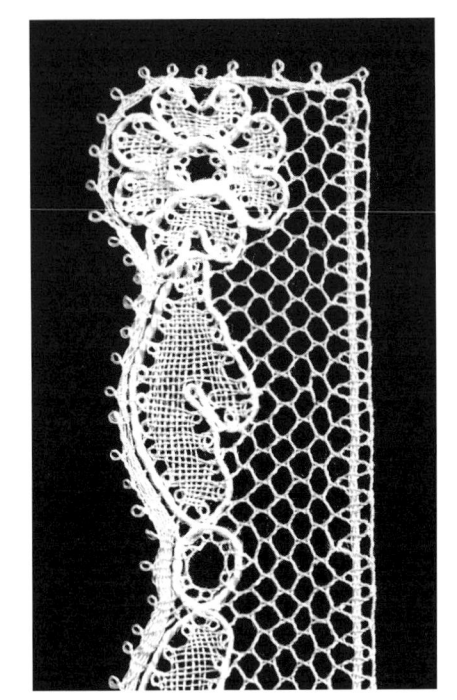

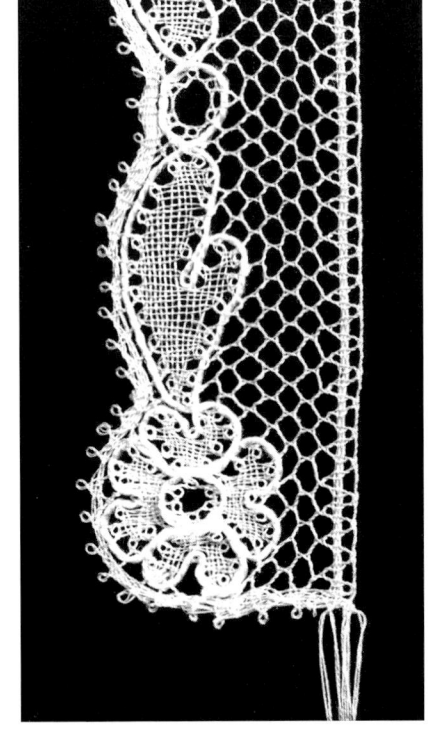

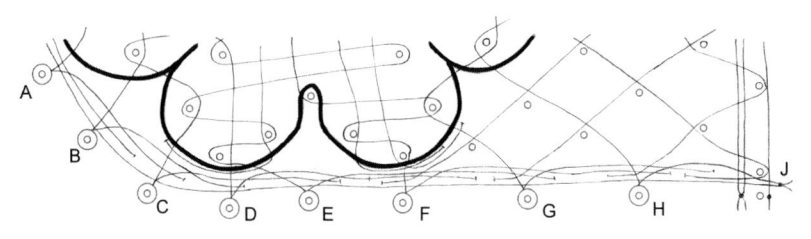

Figure 69 (above) Finishing along a picot edge

Figure 70 (right) Finishing along a picot edge

All about making—Floral Bucks Point Lace

Rolling the hem and attaching the lace along the edge of her skirt
Ensure the edge of the fabric is straight by pulling a thread and cutting along the space it has left and press. Moisten the thumb and forefinger and starting with the edge folded over about 1cm (½ in) roll the fold back towards the edge; this will cause the fabric to curl. (I prefer to start a little away from the edge and work outwards.) When you are a couple of threads from the edge start rolling it up; repeat unrolling and rolling three or four times and a tight roll will form along the edge (figure 71). It takes a little practice to judge how close to the edge you have to go before rolling back. I usually roll the fabric along the length of the edge, then start at one end and repeat the rolling a couple of times as I slip stitch along (figure 72).

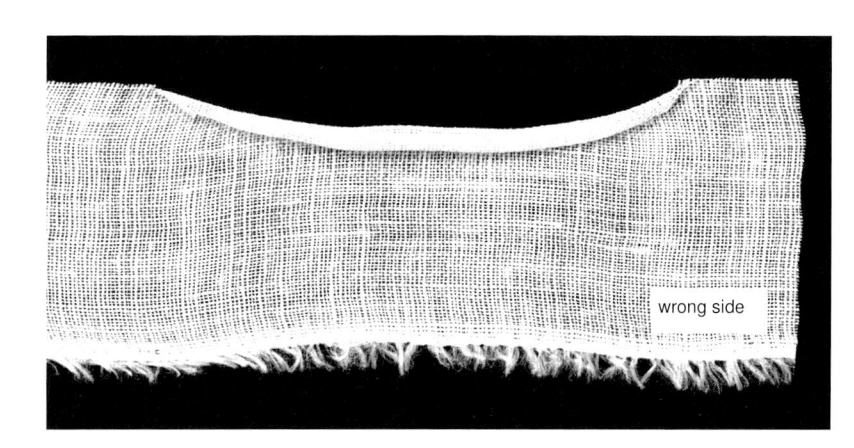

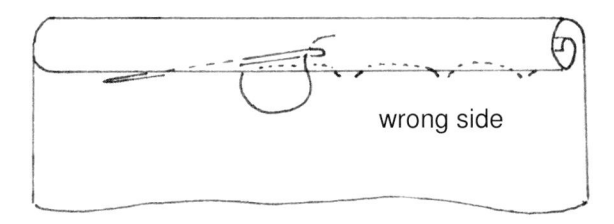

Figure 71 (right) Preparing the roll

Figure 72 (left) Slip stitching a rolled hem

Attaching lace to a hem
To attach the lace, fasten a thread to the edge of the hem, bring the needle up through a pinhole in the footside of the lace and slide the needle inside the hem until it reaches the next pinhole in the lace. Bring the needle up through that hole and repeat as required (figure 73).

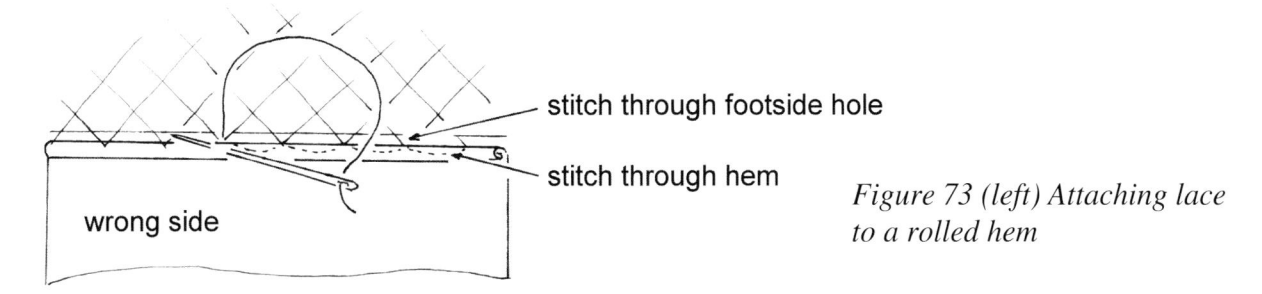

Figure 73 (left) Attaching lace to a rolled hem

All about making—Floral Bucks Point Lace

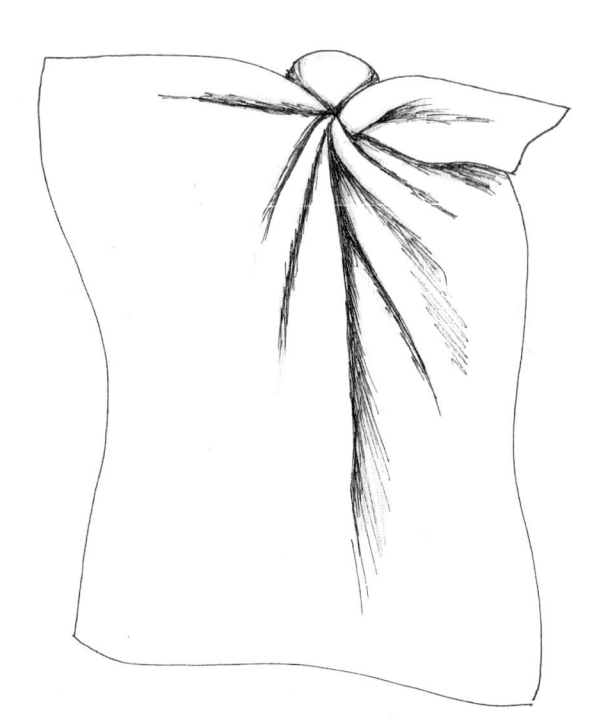

Making the doll
Roll some cotton wool into a ball (mine is 3.3 cms ($1^5/_{16}$ ins) across), place at the centre of the edge opposite the lace edging, fold the fabric round it to make the head, bind a piece of strong thread round to make the neck and knot securely (figure 74).

The arms
Hold one corner of the edge along the side with the head and twist it to make an arm (figure 75).

Figure 74 The doll's head

Take the end of the arm round to make a loop (figure 76) and pass the end through the loop. Push the knot up close to the head as you tighten it, to make her puff sleeve. Repeat for the other arm.

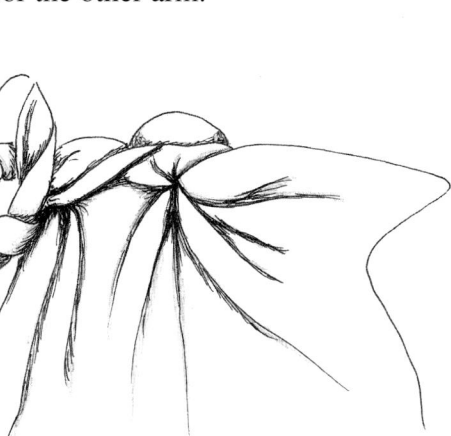

Figure 75 Twisting an arm

Figure 76 (left) Knotting an arm

Bonnet brim
Gather along the footside by passing a thread through the footside pinholes, pull up until it fits around the head (figure 60) and stitch in place.

Eyes and mouth
Embroider her black French knot eyes[14] and her pink back stitch mouth[15]. Finally tie a ribbon around her neck, making a bow under her chin.

All about making—Floral Bucks Point Lace

PROJECT 5: Church doll edging with corners

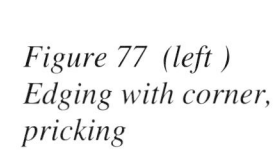

Figure 77 (left) Edging with corner, pricking

Figure 78 (right) Edging with corner worked on pricking figure 77

Materials Required for Project 5
Egyptian cotton no. 100/2[1]
gimp D..M.C. perle no. 12

Figure 79 (right) Setting in at the corner

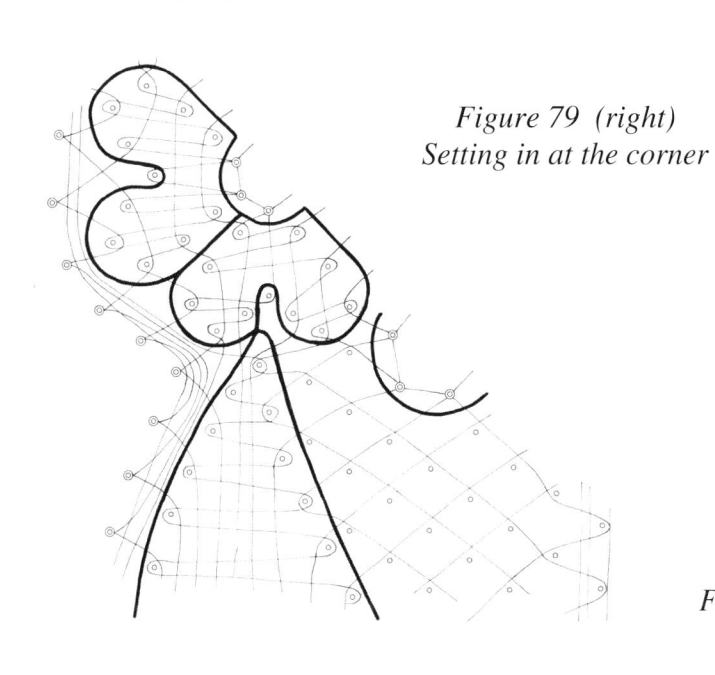

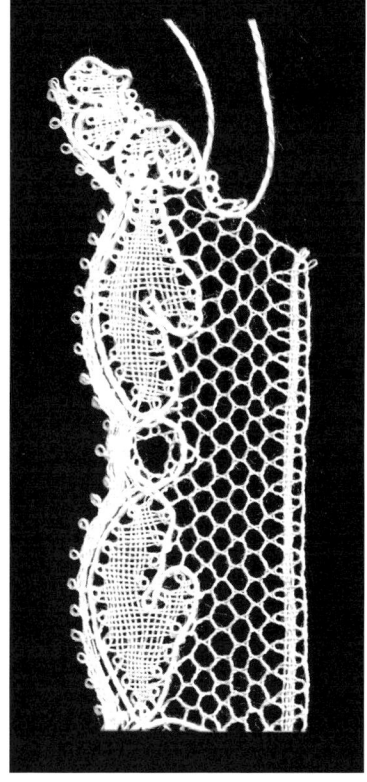

Figure 80 (left) Setting in at the corner

29

All about making—Floral Bucks Point Lace

Turning the corner
The corner for this edging is straightforward with just one extra pair of gimps added for the extra honeycomb ring.

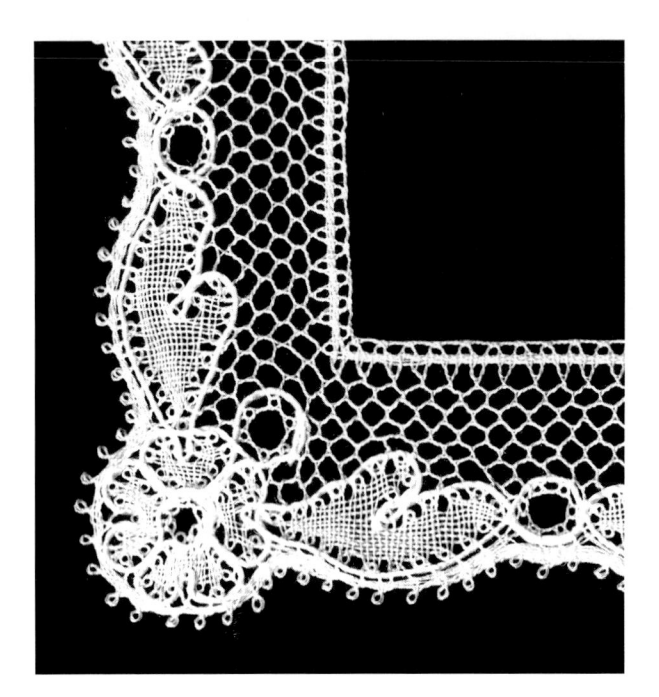

Figure 81 (left) The corner

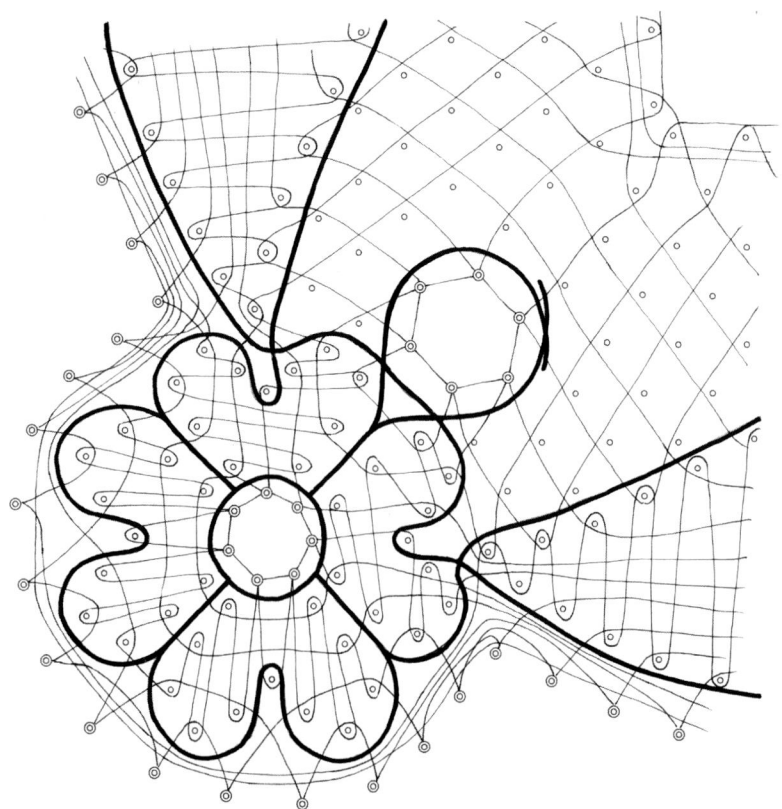

Figure 82 The corner

All about making—Floral Bucks Point Lace

END NOTES

1 Substituting threads
See Part 6.

2a Adding a new pair
A pair may be added at the end of a row by slipping it up the workers taking it round the pin and placing it next to the passives, the workers returning through this pair first. The new pair may remain in the clothwork or be left out of the clothwork to enter the ground or filling (figure 83).

Figure 83 New pair added and left out

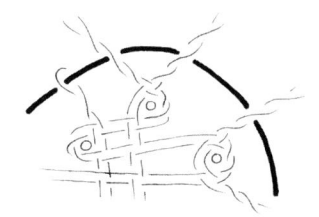

2b Adding a pair across a gimp
Sometimes the new pair is hung over a gimp and included as a passive pair at the start or end of a row or used as workers. figures 84 & 85).

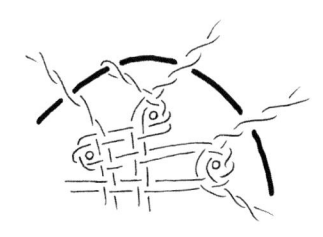

Figure 84 Passive pair added across the gimp   *Figure 85 Worker pair added across the gimp*

3a Nook pins
Nook pins occur when the gimp dips down into, rises up into or protrudes into the side of an area of clothwork with a pair passing round the pin in the nook. The pair passing across the gimp in the nook is pinned, twisted twice and crosses the gimp back into the clothwork; it is left untwisted. Usually there is no stitch at this pin and the pair passing round the nook pin may be workers or passives and may change function at this pin; a worker pair may become a passive pair (figure 53), a worker pair may continue as the worker pair (figure 55) or a passive pair may become a worker pair (figure 56). It would be very unusual for a passive pair working the nook pin to remain a passive pair.

3b By-passing the nook pin
If the gimp passes through one or more pairs of passives before encountering the workers, these pairs are not usually twisted before the gimp passes back through them, and these passive pairs are said to by-pass the nook pin (figure 86).

Figure 86 (right) Nook pin with a pair by-passing

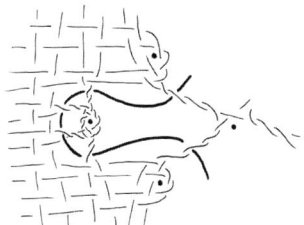

3b A stitch in the nook
Occasionally the nook pin is worked with two pairs at the pin in the 'nook', usually a worker with a passive making cloth stitch, two twists, cloth stitch, as in this case (figure 87). Compare with figures 55 and 86.

Figure 87 (left) A stitch in the nook

All about making—Floral Bucks Point Lace

3c Checking where to divide the clothwork at a nook pin
When the last full row of clothwork before the nook pin has been pinned, hold the working pair and lay the threads across the work to the pin on the other side of the area, loop them round the pin and bring them back to the pin below the end of the last worked row. If the pair crosses, or lies below the nook pin, the clothwork should divide at that point; if the workers lie above the nook pin then the clothwork is not ready to divide.

4 Twists between gimps
See *All about making*—Geometrical Bucks Point Lace, Alexandra Stillwell, Salex Publishing page 58, note no. 10.

5 Modified honeycomb stitch
Ibid., pages 75 & 80.

6 The church doll, also known as a 'plantation doll'
These dolls would be made for the little girls to keep them occupied during lengthy church services, some of which could last all day. These dolls have the advantage of not being seen when entering church and not making a noise when dropped. The alternative name of plantation doll may relate to their being made during the American Civil War.

7 Setting in point ground horizontally
Ibid., pages 21-22.

8 Carrying pairs along the gimp
When the lace narrows by the honeycomb ring the number of headside passive pairs increases and makes a wide band of clothwork. Personally I think that this spoils the appearance and prefer a maximum of four or five pairs. Any extra to these are laid next to the gimp and then are carried along the gimp, i.e. pairs crossing the gimp cross the surplus pairs at the same time (figure 88). The pairs carried along may be twisted with the gimp and an elastic band used to secure them together. Once the lace starts increasing in width these pairs can be taken off the gimp to enter the clothwork leaf or become headside passives again.

Figure 88 (right) Carrying pairs along the gimp, (carried pairs drawn just inside the gimp)

9 Whole stitch round a pin
Ibid., page 21.

10 False picot
Ibid., page 114.

11 Slipping on a pair when making a picot
Ibid., page 114.

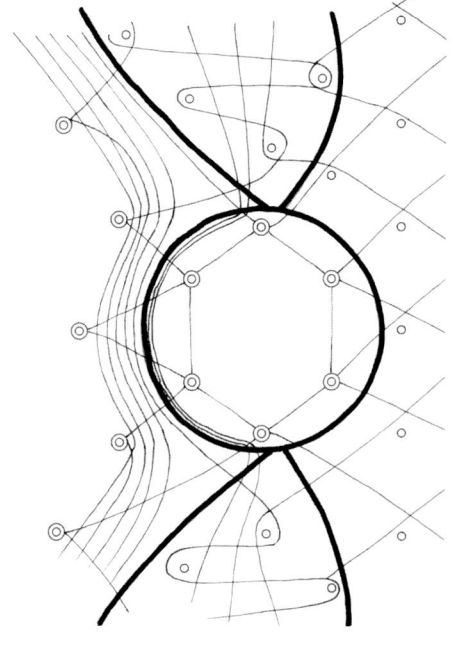

All about making—Floral Bucks Point Lace

12 Adjusting pins, angling and moving them
The final appearance of lace can be greatly improved by adjusting the slope and position of the pins. No one can prick 100% accurately and imperfections in a pricking can be compensated for by angling the pins. While making the footside keep checking the line of the edge pairs. If the line of the footside is not straight e.g. in figure 89, where the footside from pin A dips in at pin B and sticks out at pin C, lift pin B almost out of the pricking and angle outwards (figure 91) or pin C angle it inwards (figure 92) because the footside sticks out at that point. Compare the positions of the threads around the pins in figures 90-92. The first pin is shown vertical (figure 90) and the vertical lines through figures 91 & 92 indicate this position). Try this with any pin at the footside and notice how much difference these comparatively small movements can make. This technique may be used to correct the position of any pinhole in the pricking. Look along the footside as you angle the pin, and when you are satisfied with its position push the pin back in. Take care that you do not overcompensate. The pins may end up looking untidy - but the footside can be nearly perfect. There is no reason why pins cannot be moved if by doing so the lace will be improved, especially if the pinholes were uneven in the first place. Try adjusting the positions of pins by angling the pin or moving the pinhole slightly, particularly the footpins, nook pins and those along the clothwork. It is surprisingly easy to overcome bunching or spacing of the workers and/or passives and the size of unwanted holes.

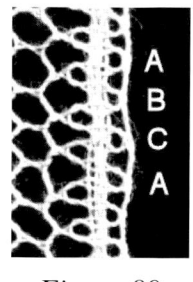

Figure 89

Figure 90

Figure 91

Figure 92

13 Casting off
Ibid., pages 115, 125, 126.

14 French knot
Fasten on the thread, take a small stitch under the fastening, wrap the thread round the needle two to four times (figure 93), pull the needle through and pass the needle through to the back adjacent to the original stitch. Fasten off immediately next to the knot.

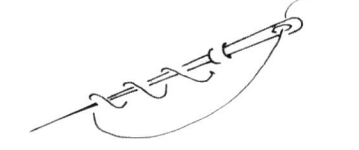

Figure 93 French knot

15 Back stitch
Fasten the thread on at one corner of the doll's mouth. Take a small stitch and pull through. *Insert the needle at the start of that stitch and bring out as far beyond the end of the stitch as the length of the stitch, and pull through (figure 94). Repeat from *. This doll has two rows of stitches starting and finishing together and slightly spaced in centre, giving her a slightly open mouth.

Figure 94 Back stitch

All about making—Floral Bucks Point Lace

CHAPTER 3

PROJECT 6: Bookmark with scrolls, hearts and vertical gimps through clothwork

Materials Required for Project 6
Egyptian cotton no. 100/2[1]
gimp D.M.C. perle no. 12
bookmark sleeve

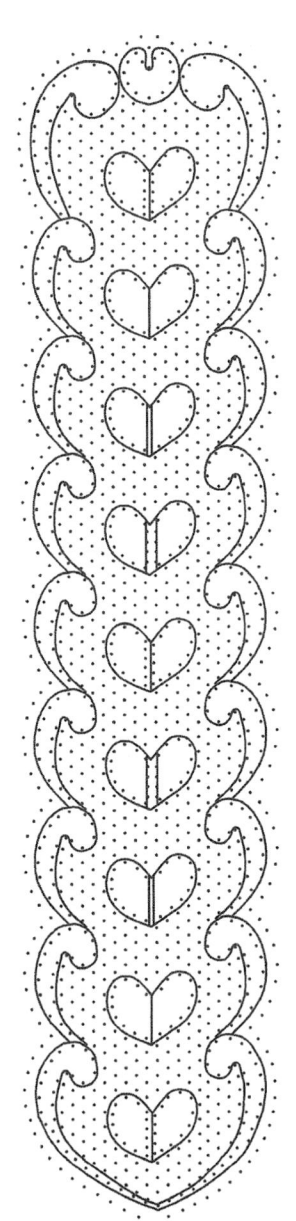

Figure 95 (left) Scrolls & hearts bookmark, pricking

Figure 96 (right) Scrolls & hearts bookmark

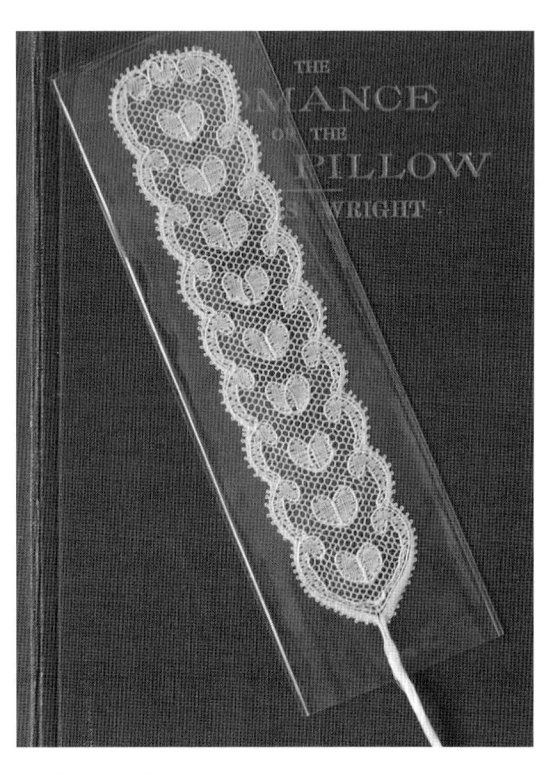

Setting in
Set in with a picot edge using false picots adding four pairs that travel in two directions for the headside passives and add pairs by slipping on as required. The central motif at the top and all the scrolls down the sides have nook pins.

Remember, this was designed as a learning piece and you will be left with working out the scrolls on the left for yourself so do not expect them to be perfect first time. Keep referring back to previous scrolls and trying different ways to improve them. You will have to be patient with yourself and accept that it takes time and experience to learn the judgement required. Your first pieces will not be perfect, they are the means to an end.

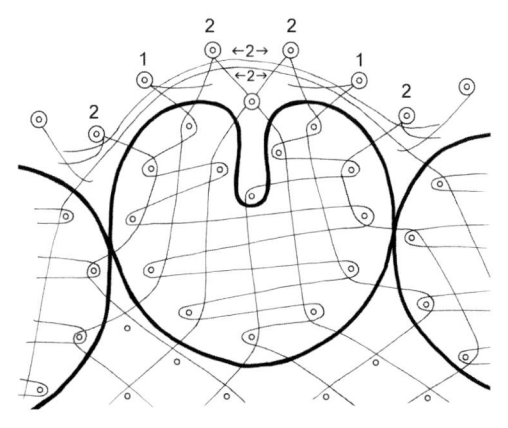

Figure 97 (right) Setting in the top motif (Key ←2→ new pairs travelling in two directions)

All about making—Floral Bucks Point Lace

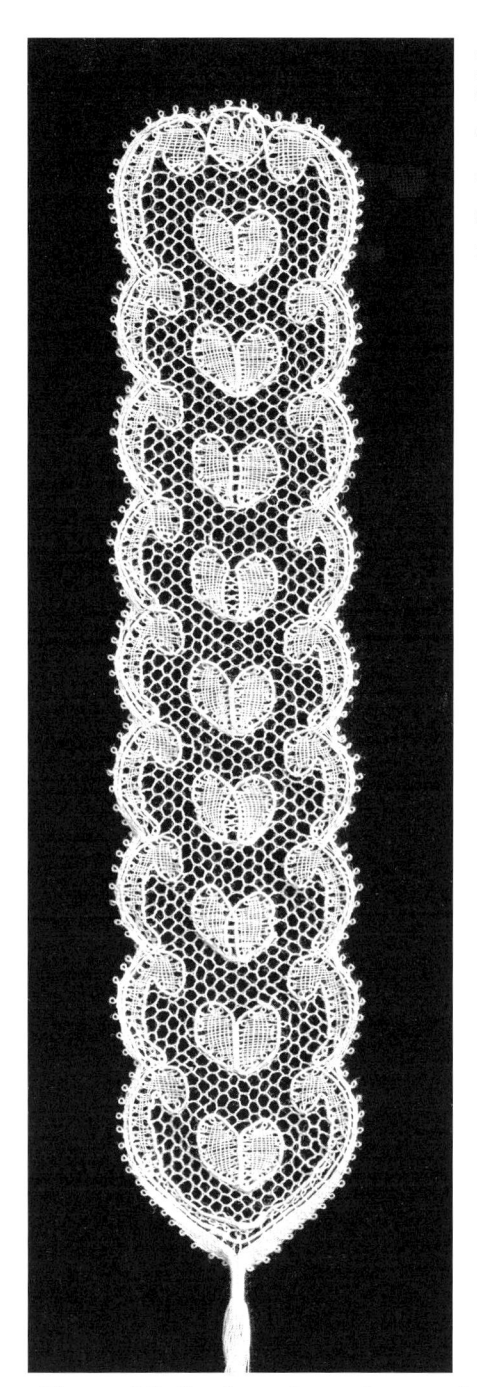

Headside
The edge passives from the top ring remain at the edge. The second headside passives enter the head of the scroll (figure 97) and the false picot in the valley provides a substitute. More pairs are added by slipping on or by making false picots.

First scroll on the right
This scroll started by working the head (figure 99) as far as row A-B when the passives were divided and the head continued as far as pin C. The left gimp was passed through the pairs left out from the head plus one more pair, and the nook pin, pin D, set up, the 'extra pair' becoming the workers for the stem.

The stem of the scroll narrows so the passives were reduced to one pair and then finally at pin E the narrowing of the stem made even this pair unnecessary, so it was left out to become a headside passive pair and the stem continued with pairs entering and leaving from both sides of the remaining pinholes.

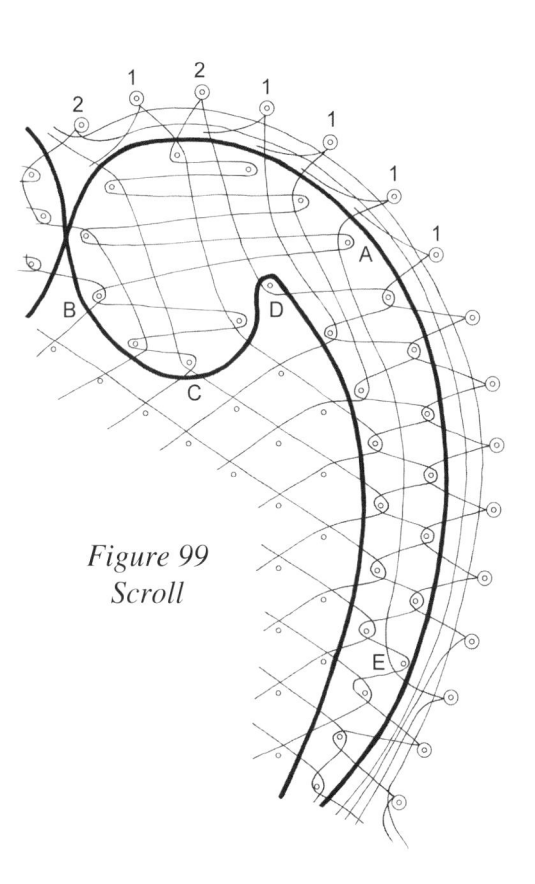

Figure 99 Scroll

Figure 98 Bookmark, made on pricking figure 97

First scroll on the left
This has the same pinhole arrangement within the gimps and for the picots as the one on the right, but not exactly the same relationship with the ground; the left side has a slight downward shift necessary because the left side of the heart is lower than its right side. This means that the left side cannot be worked as an exact mirror image of the right side and you may wish to add another pair. The smaller scrolls down each side are similar, but again will require slightly different working. Drawing your own working diagram on an enlargement of the pricking will be helpful.

All about making—Floral Bucks Point Lace

Vertical gimps through clothwork
Each heart contains a vertical pair of gimps and they have been worked in several different ways illustrating different techniques that can be used in this situation. In practice more than one of these techniques may be used when a pair of gimps passes down through an area of clothwork.

First heart with vertical gimps through clothwork (working the areas simultaneously)
When the two areas of clothwork are worked simultaneously a pair of passives repeatedly crosses to the other area after working two pins adjacent to the vertical gimp (figures 100 & 101). See also ninth heart (figures 110 & 111).

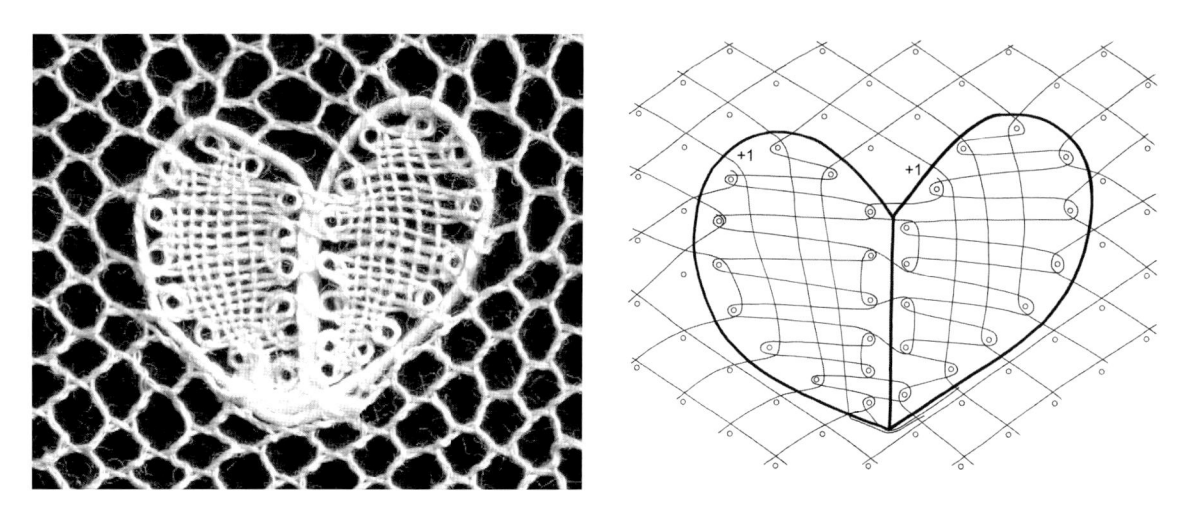

Figure 100 Working the areas simultaneously *Figure 101 Working the areas simultaneously*

Second and eighth hearts with vertical gimps through clothwork (rows crossing both areas)
When gimps pass vertically down through an area of clothwork a single pair of workers may pass across both areas of clothwork. As usual there are no effective twists when the workers cross to work on the other side of a gimp (figures 102 & 103) but twists are sometimes necessary to keep the weave going.

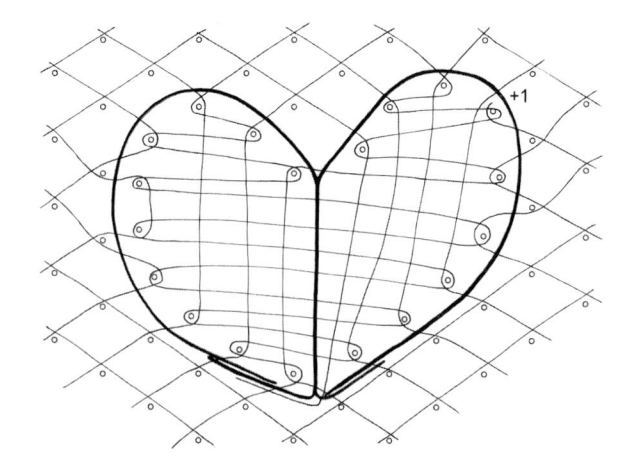

Figure 102 Rows crossing both areas 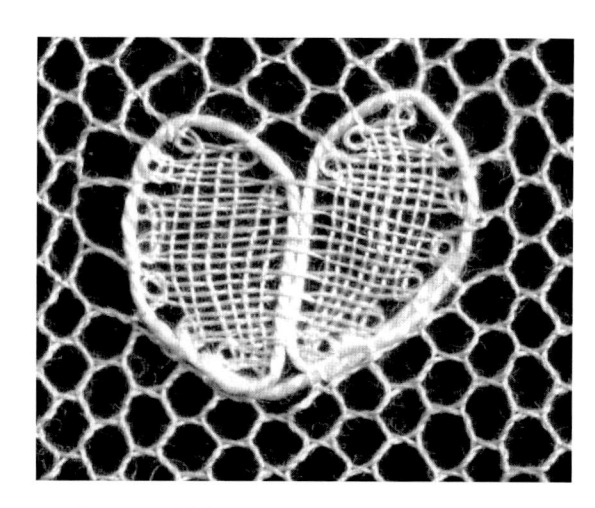 *Figure 103 Rows crossing both areas*

All about making—Floral Bucks Point Lace

Third and seventh hearts with vertical gimps through clothwork (rows crossing both areas without pins between the gimps)

When gimps pass vertically down through an area of clothwork two pairs of workers may pass across the area, one pair working from each side, with the two worker pairs making a cloth stitch when they meet between the gimps and then passing across the other side. There are no effective twists when the gimps pass through the workers but the workers continue the weave[2]. The gimps were not crossed at the top of the division for the third heart (figures 104 & 105) but were crossed for the seventh heart. The gimp is bound on at the fourth pin on the left side[3].

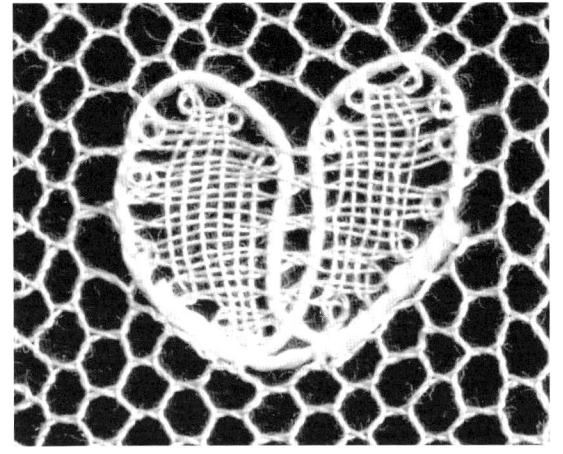

Figure 104 Unpinned workers crossing both areas

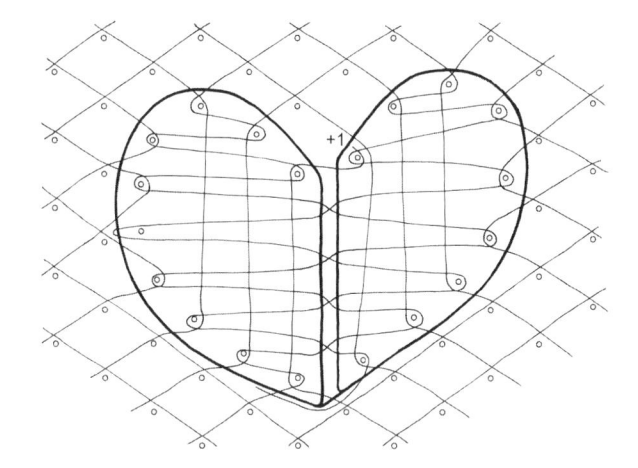

Figure 105 Unpinned workers crossing both areas

Fourth and sixth hearts with vertical gimps through clothwork (rows crossing both areas with pins between the gimps)

When gimps pass vertically down through an area of clothwork, two pairs of workers may pass across the area and work a cloth stitch when they meet between the gimps. Here they are pinned and twisted either side of the cloth stitch in between the gimps. The gimps were not crossed at the top of the division for the fourth heart (figures 106 & 107) but were crossed for the sixth heart.

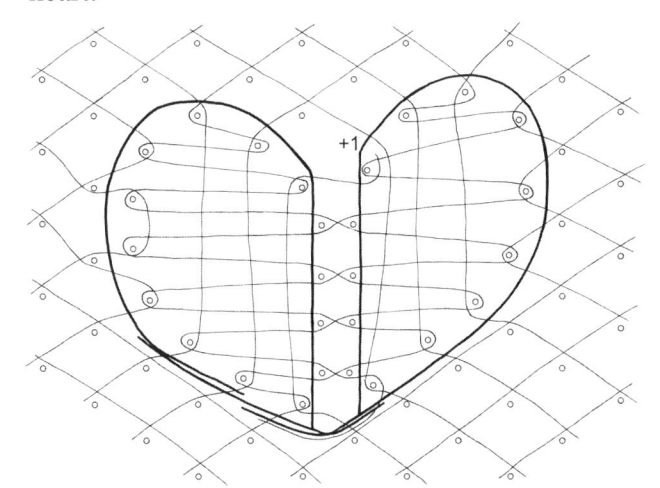

Figure 106 Pinned workers crossing both areas

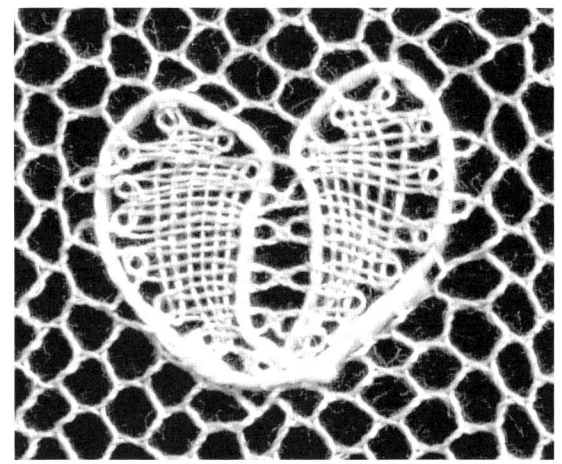

Figure 107 Pinned workers crossing both areas

All about making—Floral Bucks Point Lace

Fifth with vertical gimps through clothwork (working first one area, then the other)
When gimps pass vertically down between two areas of clothwork one side may be worked first with pairs added at the pins (+1) next to the vertical gimps providing pairs to cross the gimps. The pairs that have crossed the gimps are absorbed into the clothwork of the second side, thus linking the two areas. Pairs are thrown out (-1) to compensate[4] (figures 108 & 109). Only a single pair of gimps was necessary to make this heart. The left lobe was worked first, the gimps were doubled through the centre and then the right side was worked.

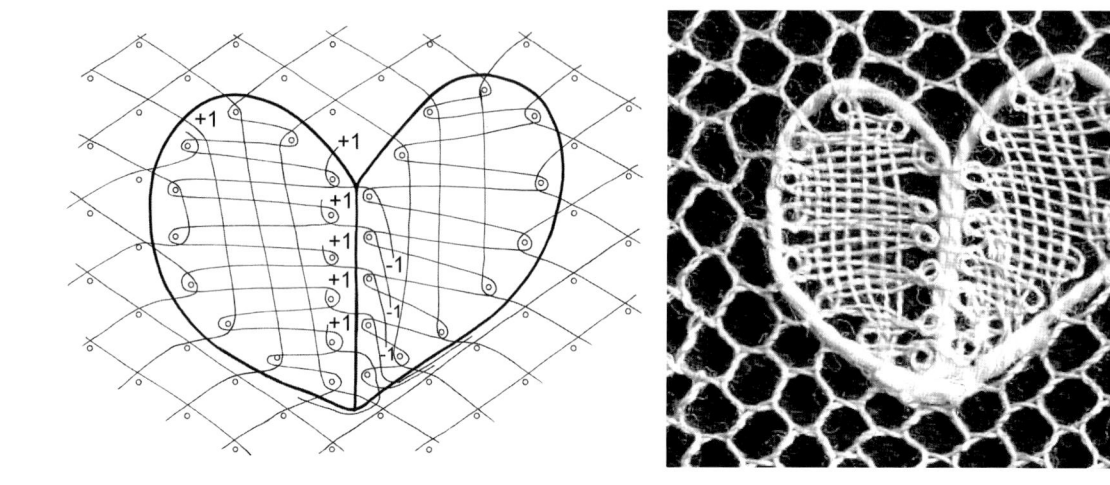

Figure 108 Working first one area, then the other

Figure 109 Working first one area, then the other

Ninth heart, clothwork divided by vertical gimps (working the areas simultaneously)
When the two areas of clothwork are worked simultaneously one pair of passives repeatedly crosses to the other area after each pin adjacent to the vertical gimps has been covered (figures 110 & 111). In practice it is more usual to pass the passives across after working two pins each side, see first heart figures 100 & 101.

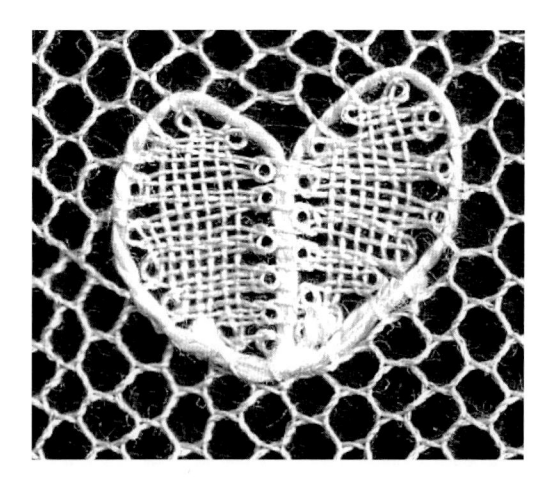

Figure 110 Working the areas simultaneously

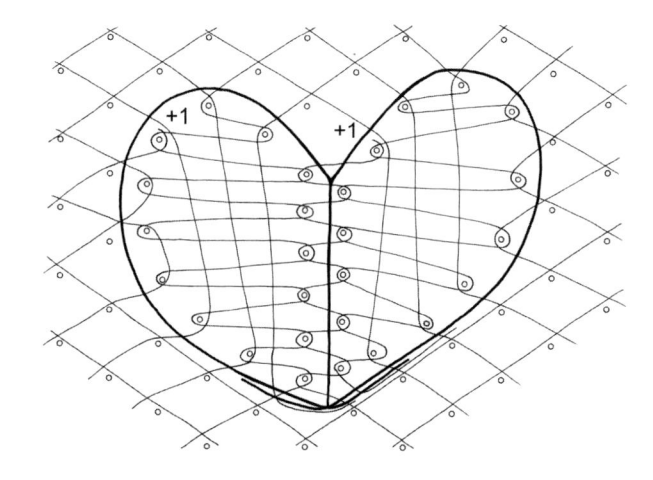

Figure 111 Working the areas simultaneously

38

Finish the bookmark either by tying off at a point[5] or by stacking[6] along a diagonal line of picots and making a tassel[5] or by casting off along a diagonal line of picots. Finally trim the sleeve to the required length and insert the bookmark[6].

END NOTES

1 Substituting threads
See Part 6.

2 Continuing the weave with the gimps
There is no effective twist between the clothwork and the gimps. However, to maintain the weave the workers are twisted as the gimps pass through (figure 112).

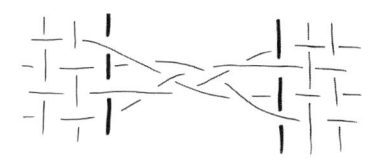

Figure 112 Continuing the weave

3 Binding on a gimp
See *All about making*—Geometrical Bucks Point Lace, Alexandra Stillwell, Salex Publishing page 154, 174, 180-182.

4 Throwing out
Traditionally pairs may be removed from the clothwork to prevent it becoming too choked by lifting out a pair and laying it back over the work, but sometimes lifting out a pair leaves a shadow hole at the point of departure. To avoid this shadow hole two threads, one from each of two adjacent pairs leaving a single thread between them may be lifted out and laid back. The laid back bobbins should be cut off before the pins are removed and the remaining ends trimmed off closely (figure 113).

Figure 113 Threads removed from clothwork indicated by 'x'

5 Casting off along a diagonal line of picots and finishing at a point
Ibid., page 115-116, 120, 125-126.

6 Stacking along a diagonal line of picots, making a tassel and inserting a bookmark into a sleeve
Ibid., page 160-161, 168-9.

All about making—Floral Bucks Point Lace

CHAPTER 4

PROJECT 7: A Birthday gift, more Nook Pins

Figure 114 A Birthday gift, an edging with a corner

Materials Required for Project 7
Egyptian cotton no. 100/2, gimp D.M.C. perle no. 12[1]
20 cm (8 in) x 20 cm (8 in) fine cotton lawn
'Happy Birthday' label (gilt sticker on card)
ribbon bow[2] and presentation box

Chapters 1, 2 & 3 contain very simple examples of Floral Bucks; for this one you will need to call on your previous knowledge to judge which technique to use and when to use it. Looking back through the techniques in this and other books you have on the subject may remind you of techniques you have not used for a while. I have explained a lot, but there will be times when you have to make your own choices, particularly where gimps are concerned; they are not easy in this pattern. Between two of the petals more than one method has been used for crossing vertical gimps; it's mix and match time, i.e. you can choose which techniques you think would work best for each pinhole independently; you do not have to use the same technique for corresponding pinholes in the pattern repeats. There is no ideal route for the gimps; add and take out gimps and pairs, experiment with different solutions and draw each of them as you work; it is surprising how similar most will look. You will make mistakes; treat each one as a challenge and enjoy the puzzle of making it work.

All about making—Floral Bucks Point Lace

Figure 115 Birthday Gift edging, pricking

Setting in
This design (figures 114, 115 & 117) corners very neatly (lacemakers' jargon for the way the pattern turns the corner) along the diagonal through the corner and this makes for a comparatively straightforward start. Since the pricking had to be modified slightly to accommodate the corner, the working for the motif adjacent to the diagonal is different from the rest of the edging. This piece has many problems for the lacemaker to solve and should be considered as a puzzle and learning piece rather than a piece to be made quickly for a gift. Experiment with different ways for working the petals, scrolls and gimps. Practice leaning the pins, especially the nook pins, and add and throw out pairs to keep the clothwork even.

Working diagram
Newcomers to Floral Bucks will find it very helpful to make an enlargement of the pattern, at least double size, on which to draw the line of the workers and the positions at which pairs enter and leave clothwork and grounds. However, as with any plan for making Floral Bucks, pattern repeats do not have to be made exactly the same. Do not hesitate to deviate from the basic plan or even change the position of a pin if the situation requires it.

Nook pin with a pair by-passing it
The first petal has a nook pin that is deeply indented and one or more pairs may pass across the doubled portion of the gimp where it passes in and out of the nook (figure 116).

Setting in the first petal
Add pairs in across a gimp and add support pins for the gimp[3] on either side of the honeycomb ring in the centre of the flower (figure 116). Modified honeycomb stitches[4] will be required when a worker from the clothwork makes the stitch and returns to the clothwork.

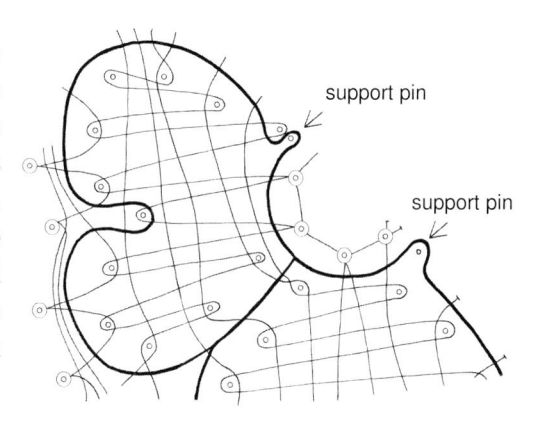

Figure 116 (above) First petal with support pins for the gimp (arrowed) and a nook pin with a pair by-passing

41

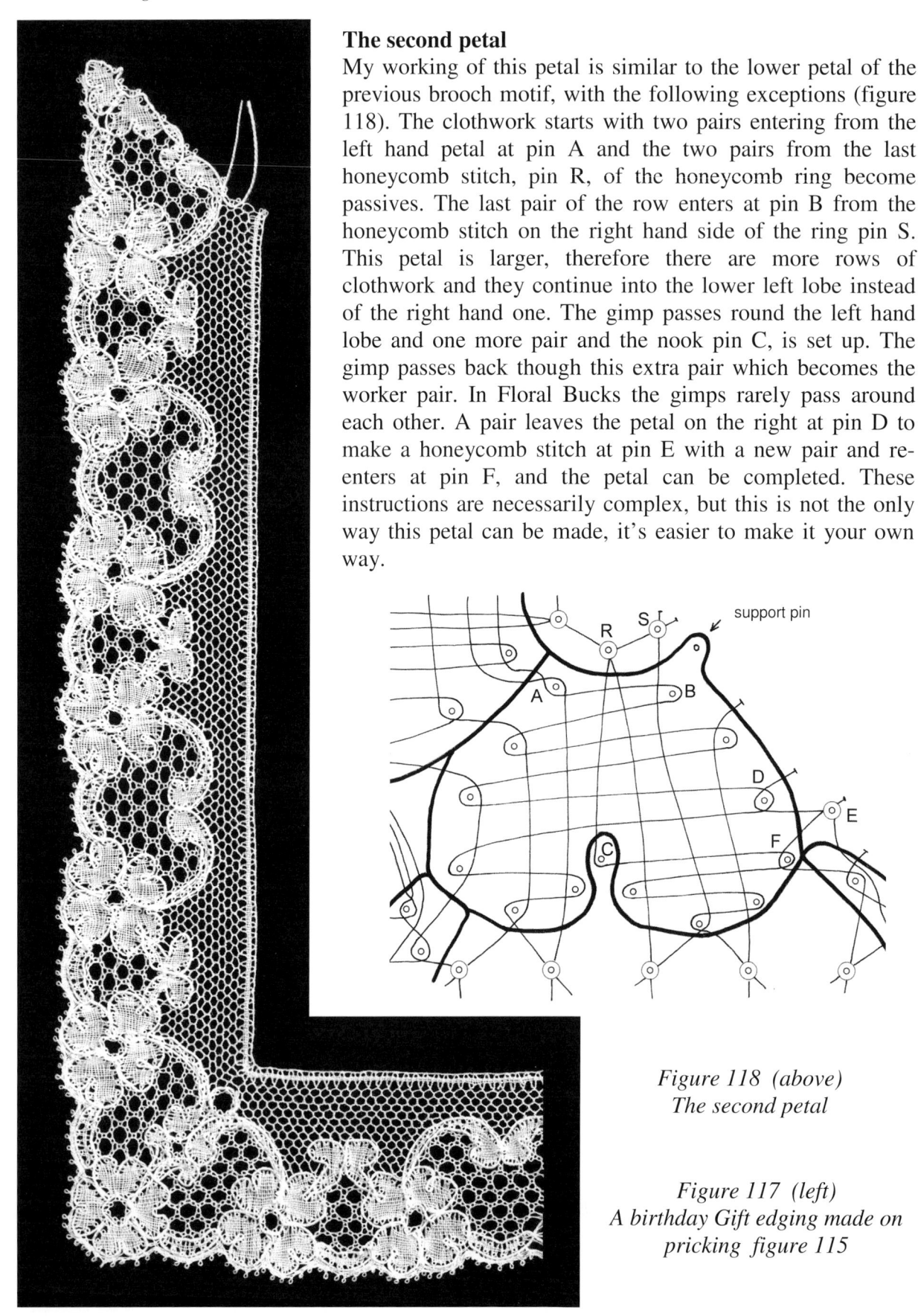

All about making—Floral Bucks Point Lace

The second petal

My working of this petal is similar to the lower petal of the previous brooch motif, with the following exceptions (figure 118). The clothwork starts with two pairs entering from the left hand petal at pin A and the two pairs from the last honeycomb stitch, pin R, of the honeycomb ring become passives. The last pair of the row enters at pin B from the honeycomb stitch on the right hand side of the ring pin S. This petal is larger, therefore there are more rows of clothwork and they continue into the lower left lobe instead of the right hand one. The gimp passes round the left hand lobe and one more pair and the nook pin C, is set up. The gimp passes back though this extra pair which becomes the worker pair. In Floral Bucks the gimps rarely pass around each other. A pair leaves the petal on the right at pin D to make a honeycomb stitch at pin E with a new pair and re-enters at pin F, and the petal can be completed. These instructions are necessarily complex, but this is not the only way this petal can be made, it's easier to make it your own way.

Figure 118 (above)
The second petal

Figure 117 (left)
A birthday Gift edging made on pricking figure 115

All about making—Floral Bucks Point Lace

Adding extra pairs into the clothwork
While researching Bucks Point I found comparatively few pieces containing extra pairs added into and removed from the clothwork. The patterns and thread size were carefully matched and the lacemaker workers were highly skilled in spreading the passives to fill the areas of clothwork. When they knew they would be making the same pattern repeat over and over again they would 'learn' their prickings and remember the routes of the different pairs so that they could avoid adding and removing pairs which takes time and time was money. Pieces designed and made to order for a particular person would be made by the highly skilled workers. These pieces were made 'by eye', and it is in these that we are more likely to find extra pairs added and removed.

Today we do not have the constraint of having to earn a living from our lacemaking and we prefer the ground to be more transparent. We now make lace for enjoyment and we are more concerned with its final appearance than the time it takes to make it. It is now common practice to add and remove pairs whenever it will improve the density of clothwork. This should never be solid. The threads should be spaced so that the background shows through. When the thread is a little fine for the clothwork we can compensate by adding pairs into it, and then removing them when there are too many. The skill of spreading passives to fill clothwork areas and managing the pairs, so that they are in the places where they will be needed, comes with experience.

Adding pairs when the clothwork becomes starved and removing pairs when it becomes too choked, or when they are not required for point ground or a filling, allows the less experienced lacemaker to achieve good results while gaining experience.

Moving pairs from clothwork into honeycomb or ground and vice versa
It is useful to plan the movement of pairs from clothwork to honeycomb or ground and vice versa on an enlarged pricking (figure 119). Draw the diagonal and vertical lines through the honeycomb pinholes and extend them until they nearly meet the gimp around the clothwork. In most cases it becomes obvious at which pin a pair needs to be left out from or absorbed into the clothwork; if the clothwork would be left starved an extra pair should be added and then left out[5]. Sometimes two pairs may leave or enter the clothwork at the same pin; sometimes the gimp may have to be bound on[6]. Sometimes a little creative thinking may be required to achieve a satisfactory result. Next time you are in this position on the pattern check your previous working to see if it can be improved.

Figure 119 Moving pairs from clothwork into honeycomb and vice versa

43

All about making—Floral Bucks Point Lace

First small scroll with nook pin protruding into the clothwork from the side

The first scroll starts with its stem worked in cloth stitch. Pairs are absorbed from the right with two entering at the first pin, pin A, the worker for this row being the second of the pairs added. The other pair making the first cloth stitch with the workers comes from the petal above (figure 120). The workers make a row to pin B, taking in a pair from the right. After covering pin B the workers pass through the passive pair into the honeycomb and this pair together with a pair released from pin A make a honeycomb stitch, at pin C. The other pair from the stitch covering pin B now acts as workers and makes a stitch with the next pair entering from the right. These workers cross the gimp immediately before the scroll's head at pin D making a nook pin and continue as workers, adding a pair at the end of the next row. Catch up working honeycomb so that you have the necessary pairs and work the head of the scroll. Two pairs will enter into the next row towards the left at pin E and the worker will bind on the gimp where there are no pairs entering or leaving at F.

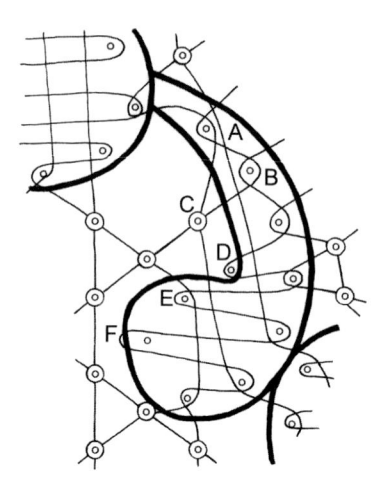

Figure 120 First small scroll with nook pin protruding into the clothwork from the side

First large scroll with nook pin rising up into the clothwork

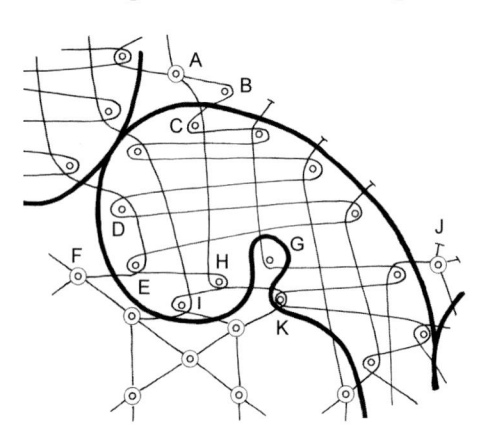

Figure 121 First large scroll with nook pin

This scroll starts with the head (figure 121). The worker comes from the left hand honeycomb stitch above it, pin A, and passes round the right hand pin, B, before entering across the gimp. This should be a honeycomb stitch but as only one pair is required from it the pair merely passes round the pin with two twists. When the edging is joined start to finish it will not show that it is not a honeycomb stitch. If preferred, sewings can be made to form a simulated honeycomb stitch[7]. Start the scroll at pin C and add a pair at the end of the next five rows. At the end of the following row, pin E, a pair is left out. When the lines for the honeycomb pairs are drawn in (figure 118) they indicate that a pair should be left out from pin D to work the honeycomb stitch F, but then the clothwork will look starved. I preferred to keep the pair in and release it after pin E. Of course, a pair can be added to be left out, but it will have no further use and a pair will have to be discarded. This is a case when neither choice is perfect. Try both and make your own selection. The next row aims across the nook pin G, so the head is completed by working through three pairs on this side and working pins H & I. Take the gimp through the pairs from the head and the next passive pair, the workers for the stem and set up the nook pin G. Here the nook pin rises up into the clothwork and the pair left out from the head at pin H, just below the nook pin, crosses both gimps to enter the stem to work pin K, thus forming the bump on the stem just below the head. Two new pairs are added at a honeycomb stitch, pin J, to feed the stem and the honeycomb ring on the right.

44

All about making—Floral Bucks Point Lace

Working the stem of the first large scroll
A pair is left out after pin K (figure 122) to work honeycomb stitch L (as suggested in figure 119). At pin M add a pair and use with a pair from the honeycomb stitch J in the honeycomb ring, then leave out a pair from this stitch to pass into the stem to work pin N. The gimp on the right side of the stem is now approaching the vertical so at pins N, Q and T a pair will leave the stem, work a stitch on the other side of the gimp and return. Leave out a pair after pin P to work the honeycomb stitch L. Pin R is too high to take in a pair from honeycomb stitch S, so bind on the gimp and then drop the pair from pin S in across the gimp. After working pin T take the workers across the gimp to make a honeycomb stitch at pin U and return a pair across the gimp to pin V. Now the working settles down. From each honeycomb stitch work a pair across the gimp and through the passives, set up a pin, cover it and release a pair to the ground. Since no pair enters at pin W, after covering the pin work back through one more passive pair, set up a pin,

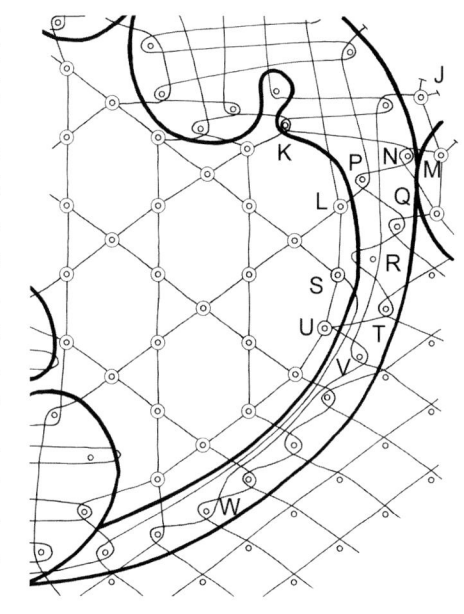

Figure 122 Large scroll stem

cover it and release a pair to the ground. The following large scrolls do not have quite the same pin formation so adapt these instructions using these and any other techniques that will achieve a suitable result.

Tricks of the trade, some techniques to play with when you are in trouble[8]
The following diagrams and their explanations are of one repeat. My repeats are all worked differently and you should try to follow my reasoning rather than the diagrams, so except perhaps for the first repeat do not try to follow my working diagrams exactly; it will be too frustrating and it is not the correct way to tackle Floral Bucks. Do not be concerned if you find you have a different number of pairs in a row or if you are travelling in the opposite direction from that indicated in my diagrams. These gimps are not easy. It is possible to work them without adding and removing any, but this involves having more than two doubling up; you may prefer to add and remove and again, it is your choice. There is no definitive answer. Be inventive and above all enjoy the challenge and the puzzle of working it out.

First petal of the complete flower
Starting at the top, pin A, the workers travel to the right taking in a single pair at pin B (figure 123). When they return to the left to pin C three pairs are added and the last of the three immediately left out. A pair is added in at the end of the following row at pin D, but because of the arrangement of the pins the gimp tended to be loose so I bound it on. A pair is left out at pin E to by-pass the nook pin F and is taken in again at pin G. The rest of the petal follows the regular rules quite well.

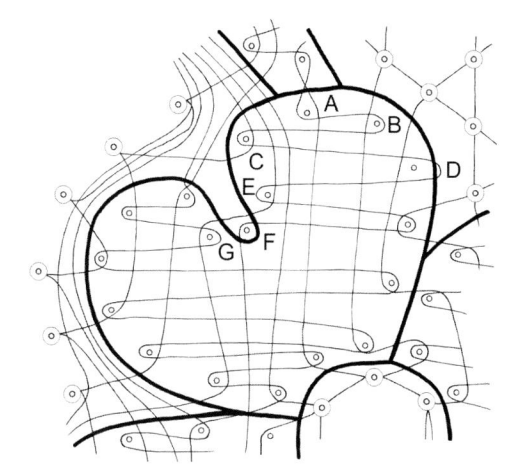

Figure 123 First petal

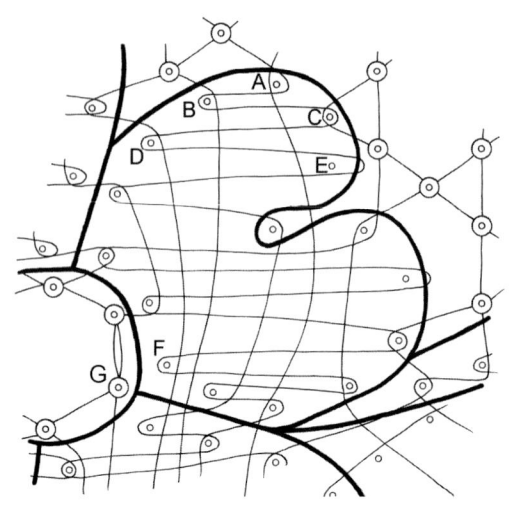

Figure 124 Second petal

The second petal of the complete flower

Starting at the top pin A the workers travel to the left this time taking in a single pair at the end of this row, pin B, and the next two rows pins C and D (figure 124), and leaving a pair out at the end of the first of these rows, pin C. (Take care with the spacing, you are rather low on pairs.) At the end of the row to pin E, there is no pair available for adding in. The pair left out to by-pass the nook pin would not hold the gimp securely in place by pin E, so the gimp required binding on. The pair from pin F will be required as a passive pair for the lower petal so a pin-stitch is made to the lower side honeycomb stitch of the central ring, pin G. The rest of the petal follows the regular rules.

Third and fourth petals

Starting the third petal (figure 125), the workers travel to the left from the top pin, A, taking in an extra pair in the first row. At the end of the fourth row, pin B, there are not sufficient passive pairs to leave one out to make the honeycomb stitch in the ring, pin B, so the workers cross the gimp to make a modified honeycomb stitch. At this point the honeycomb ring in the centre can be finished and the gimps may need to be removed. A blind spot is made at pin C. Pairs are left out from pins D and E to by-pass the nook pin F but the first row from the nook pin cannot be completed. There are now two areas of clothwork divided by vertical gimps.

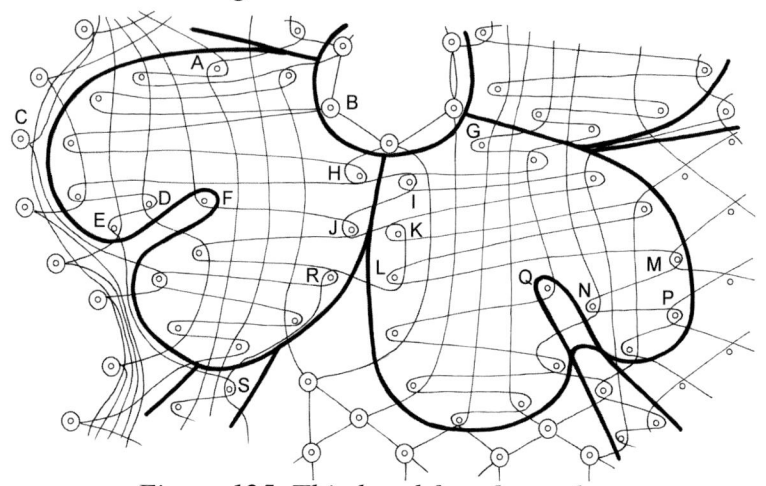

Figure 125 Third and fourth petals

The first row of the right hand petal travels from pin G to the right through three pairs and returns towards the left. The first pair left out from the left petal at pin H is included at the end of this row at pin I and immediately left out. The row from the nook pin of the left hand petal can now be completed taking in the pair just left out from the right hand petal at pin J and the pair is left out again to enter the right hand petal at K and used by the right hand petal for the next two rows. This right hand lobe continues with a pair left out for the ground at pin M, taken in again at pin P and left out. Two pairs are left out on the left after working pin N and the right lobe can be completed. The gimp passes round the nook pin Q and the left lobe can be completed. The pair left out from the right hand petal at pin L is used by the left hand petal as it is required to link the two, but since there are sufficient passives it must lie along the gimp until it is used in the bridge[9] between this and the next quatrefoil at pin S. The petal finishes with the spare pairs passing into the bridge or the headside.

All about making—Floral Bucks Point Lace

Small scrolls with nook pins either dipping down into the clothwork or rising up into it
The small scrolls start with the cloth stitch stem, then the nook pin, then the bulge of the head and finally the remainder across both two parts (figure 126). The second starts by working across the width of the clothwork, then the nook pin is set and finally the stem is worked (figure 127). The last pinhole of the first scroll may be used as a spacer[10] as illustrated, or the scroll may be finished as usual. The second scroll may be worked as a mirror image of the first with the centre pinhole at the top used as a spacer.

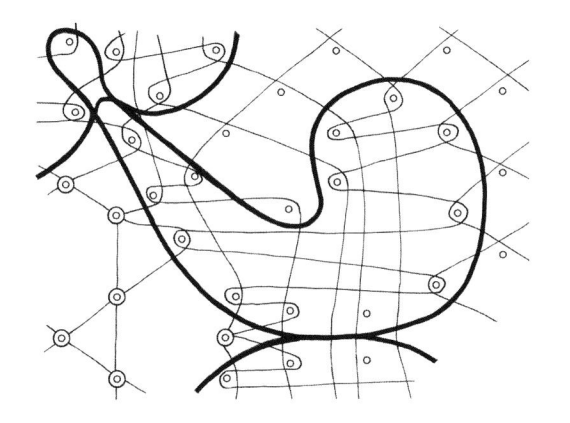

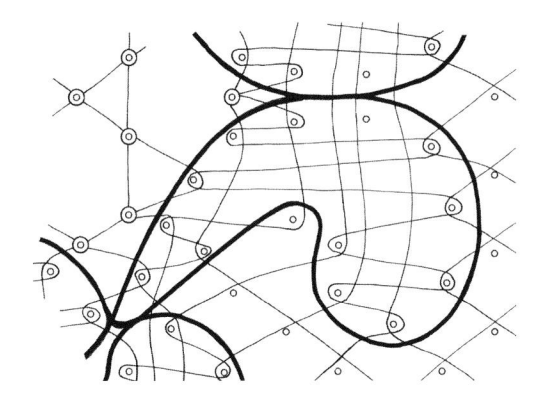

Figure 126 First small scroll of a pair with the nook pin dipping down into the clothwork

Figure 127 Second small scroll of a pair with the nook pin rising into the clothwork

Corner
The corner is fairly straightforward, but the pair that becomes the workers for the head of the large scroll should make a honeycomb stitch on the diagonal instead of passing around the pin; this may mean adding a pair when working into the corner and losing it after working out of the corner. Unlike Project 5, this corner has a single pin at the inner edge that will be first used when working into the corner and then reused[11] when working out.

Mounting
The edging was mounted to the fabric using four-sided stitch[12].

END NOTES

1 Threads
See Part 6.

2 Ribbon bow
See '*All about making*—Geometrical Bucks Point Lace' A. Stillwell, Salex Publishing, page 229, Making the bow.

3 Support pin
Ibid., page 74, Setting in - adding an extra hole 'P', figure 191.

All about making—Floral Bucks Point Lace

4 Modified honeycomb stitch
Ibid., pages 75 and 80.

5 Traditional method for adding pairs at this point
At the end of a clothwork row after twisting the workers and pinning them slip the new pair up the workers, pass them behind the pin and lay them next to the passives. The workers return through this pair first (figure 128). When there are insufficient pairs in the clothwork to enable a pair to be left out to pass into the ground, this method may be used to provide the required pair.

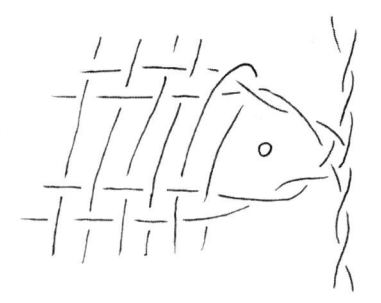

Figure 128 Adding a pair

6 Binding on a gimp
Ibid., pages 154, 174, 181-182

7 Simulated honeycomb stitch
Although sewings are not traditionally used in making Bucks Point there is no reason why we cannot borrow from other laces when we need to, especially if the finished result appears traditional. In this case we have a pair that looped round a pin at the start. In order to appear like a regular honeycomb stitch we can draw a loop through the original loop (figure 129) and pass its partner bobbin through this loop (figure 130) to make a sewing before the pin. Firm up, twist the pair twice and replace the pin below the pair (figure 131). Draw a loop through for the second sewing, this time below the pin (figure 132) and pass its partner bobbin through this loop (figure 133) and finally firm up (figure 134).

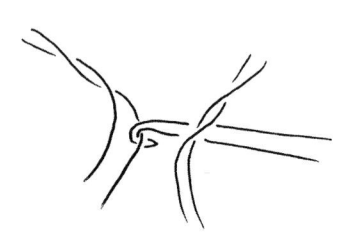

Figure 129 Draw through the first loop

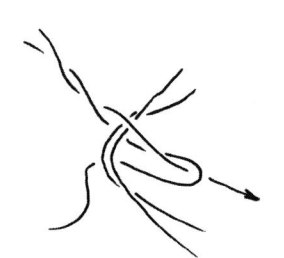

Figure 130 Pass its partner through the loop

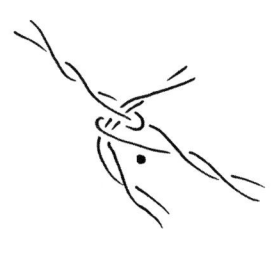

Figure 131 Replace the pin

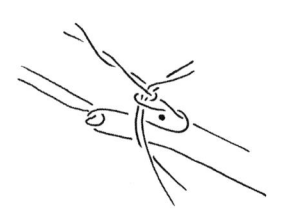

Figure 132 Draw through the second loop

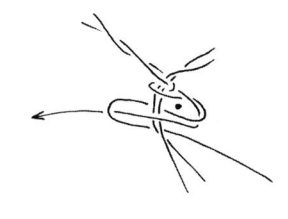

Figure 133 Pass its partner through the loop

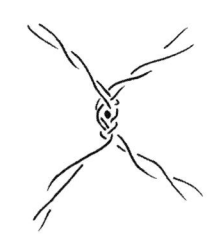

Figure 134 Simulated honeycomb stitch

All about making—Floral Bucks Point Lace

8 Up the creek without a paddle
These are *not* traditional methods (and don't do them when Teacher's watching), but these cheats can get you out of difficulties when you have forgotten to leave a pair out and it would take many hours of unpicking and remaking to correct the mistake.

8a Up the creek without a paddle (you forgot to leave out a pair for the honeycomb)
In the situation shown in figure 135 a pair should have been left out at A, (compare with pair left out above this pin B in figure 119) and therefore the honeycomb stitch at pin B cannot be made. To cheat, place a new pair over a support pin in any hole near the missing pair, in this case pin C, and work a honeycomb stitch with the new pair standing in for the missing pair and pin at B. Remove the support pin and the new pair merges into the ground or honeycomb, place a pair on a support pin in any convenient hole C and make a honeycomb stitch, pin B, (figure 135), release the new pair and allow it to settle down on the pin (figure 136).

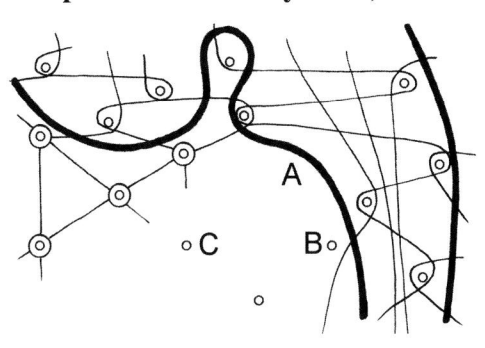

Figure 135 A pair should have been left out at A

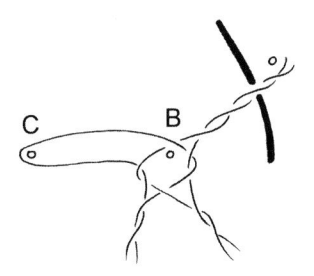

Figure 136 (left) Make a honeycomb stitch at pin B

Figure 137 (right) New pair let down

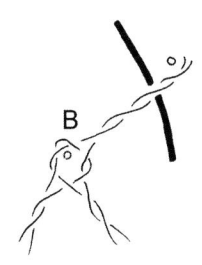

8b Up the creek without a paddle (you forgot to leave out a pair for point ground)
Figures 138 & 139. Follow the same process as for adding a missing pair for honeycomb see figures 136 & 137.

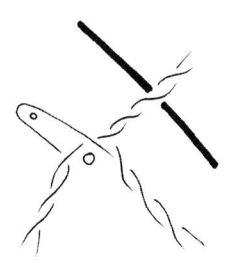

Figure 138 (left) Make a point ground stitch

Figure 139 (right) New pair let down

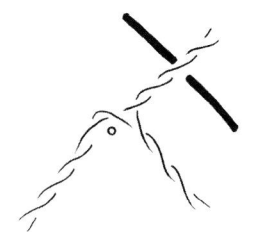

8c Up the creek without a paddle (you forgot to add a pair before making a picot)
Slip a pair on when the picot pair has been twisted (figure 140) and place on the pillow so that there is no weight on the picot pair. Complete the picot, lay the new pair as the edge passives and return through them first (figure 141).

Figure 140 (left) Slip a new pair on the picot pair

Figure 141 (right) Work back through the new pair first

49

All about making—Floral Bucks Point Lace

8d Back stitching the nook pin and nook pin worked twice
Some antique prickings have uncomfortably large gaps adjacent to the nook pin. If the gap is before the nook pin make the first half of the back stitch without crossing the gimp, it may require binding on; then work the pin as a normal nook pin the second time (figure 142).

When the gap is on the side following the nook then the nook pin can be worked twice.
1. Work down the first side, work the nook pin and take the gimp round the tip of the second side as normal (figure 143).
2. Work the second part until these workers make a cloth stitch with the original workers currently supported by the nook pin. Remove the nook pin, push the gimp up out of the way and replace the pin under the stitch reusing the hole in the nook (figure 144).
3. Twist the pairs, cover the pin and continue in the preferred direction. After a few rows remove the nook pin, push the threads up and replace in its original hole (figure 145).

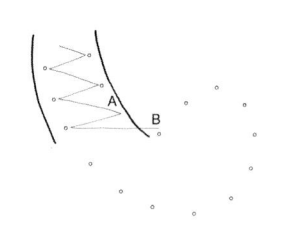

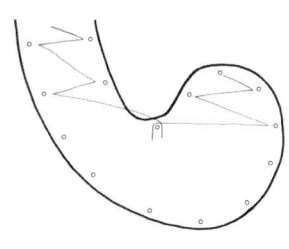

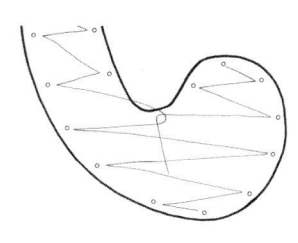

Figure 142 Back stitching the nook pin   *Figure 143 Nook pin worked twice*   *Figure 144 Nook pin worked twice*   *Figure 145 Nook pin worked twice*

9 Bridge
A design feature consisting of a narrow strip of clothwork, honeycomb stem etc. that links larger design motifs.

10 Spacer
A pin placed in a hole to control the position of the adjacent pairs although the pin itself is not worked, i.e. the pin is not placed after a stitch has been worked, nor is a stitch worked to cover it.

11 Reusing the inner pin at a corner
Ibid., 138-139

12 Four-sided stitch
Ibid., pages 41-43.

13 Designing a corner

13a Place a mirror on the lace, pricking or pattern draft at 45° to the footside. Keeping the mirror at the same angle slide it along the lace, pricking or pattern draft and watch how the corner in the mirror changes. Hopefully there will be at least one point when it looks possible to make a corner (figure 146). It is very unlikely that the lace will corner perfectly so imagine how the various design elements could be stretched or adapted to fit into the areas that are not working.

13b Make two copies of the pattern draft and on one draw a line corresponding to the chosen position of the mirror and cut along it (figure 147).

All about making—Floral Bucks Point Lace

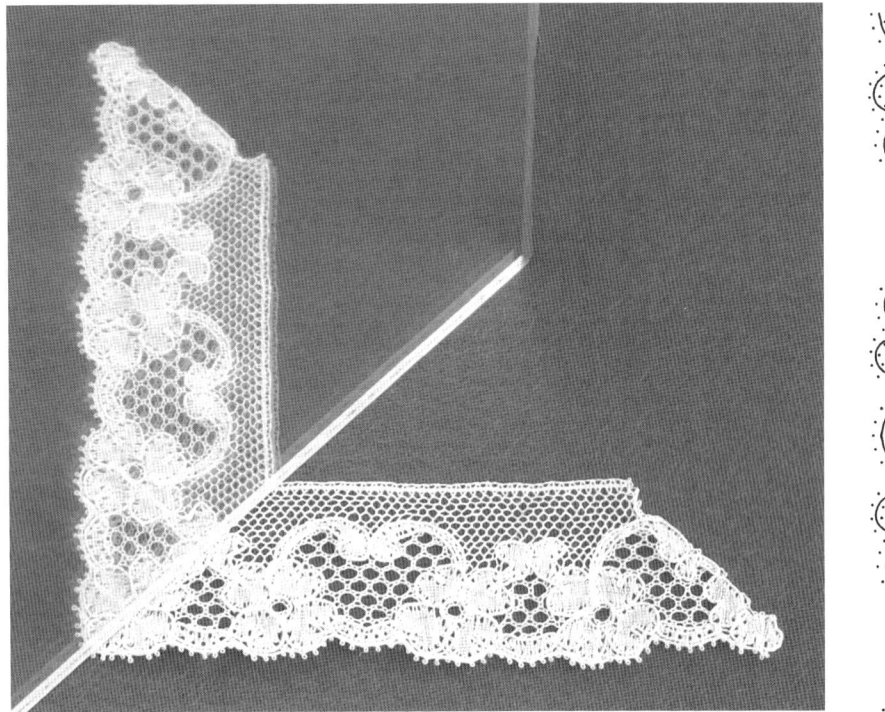

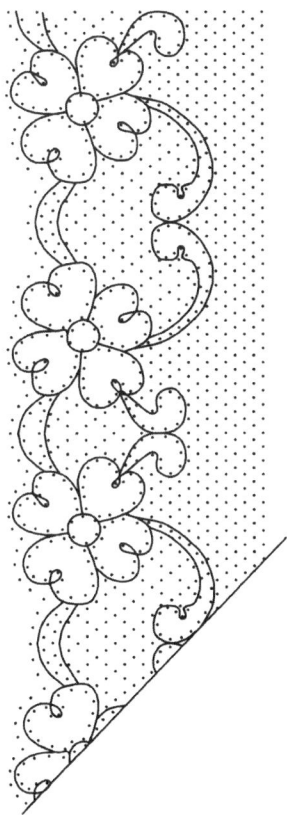

Figure 146 Using a mirror to plan a corner

Figure 147 Edging cut diagonally

13c Place the pattern draft cut at 45° across the corner on the other copy with the footsides at right angles so that they match along the diagonal through the corner (figure 148).

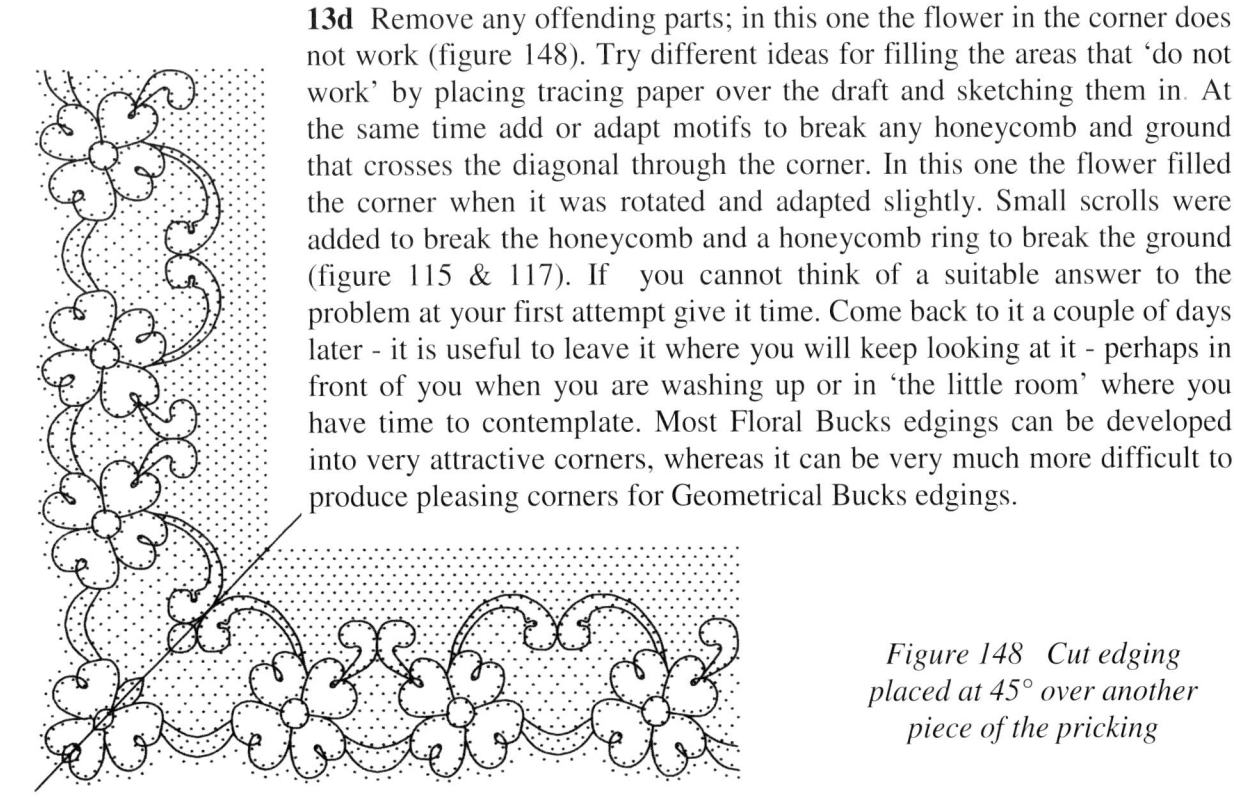

13d Remove any offending parts; in this one the flower in the corner does not work (figure 148). Try different ideas for filling the areas that 'do not work' by placing tracing paper over the draft and sketching them in. At the same time add or adapt motifs to break any honeycomb and ground that crosses the diagonal through the corner. In this one the flower filled the corner when it was rotated and adapted slightly. Small scrolls were added to break the honeycomb and a honeycomb ring to break the ground (figure 115 & 117). If you cannot think of a suitable answer to the problem at your first attempt give it time. Come back to it a couple of days later - it is useful to leave it where you will keep looking at it - perhaps in front of you when you are washing up or in 'the little room' where you have time to contemplate. Most Floral Bucks edgings can be developed into very attractive corners, whereas it can be very much more difficult to produce pleasing corners for Geometrical Bucks edgings.

Figure 148 Cut edging placed at 45° over another piece of the pricking

CHAPTER 5 PROJECT 8: Tablecloth edging with a reversing corner and side reverse

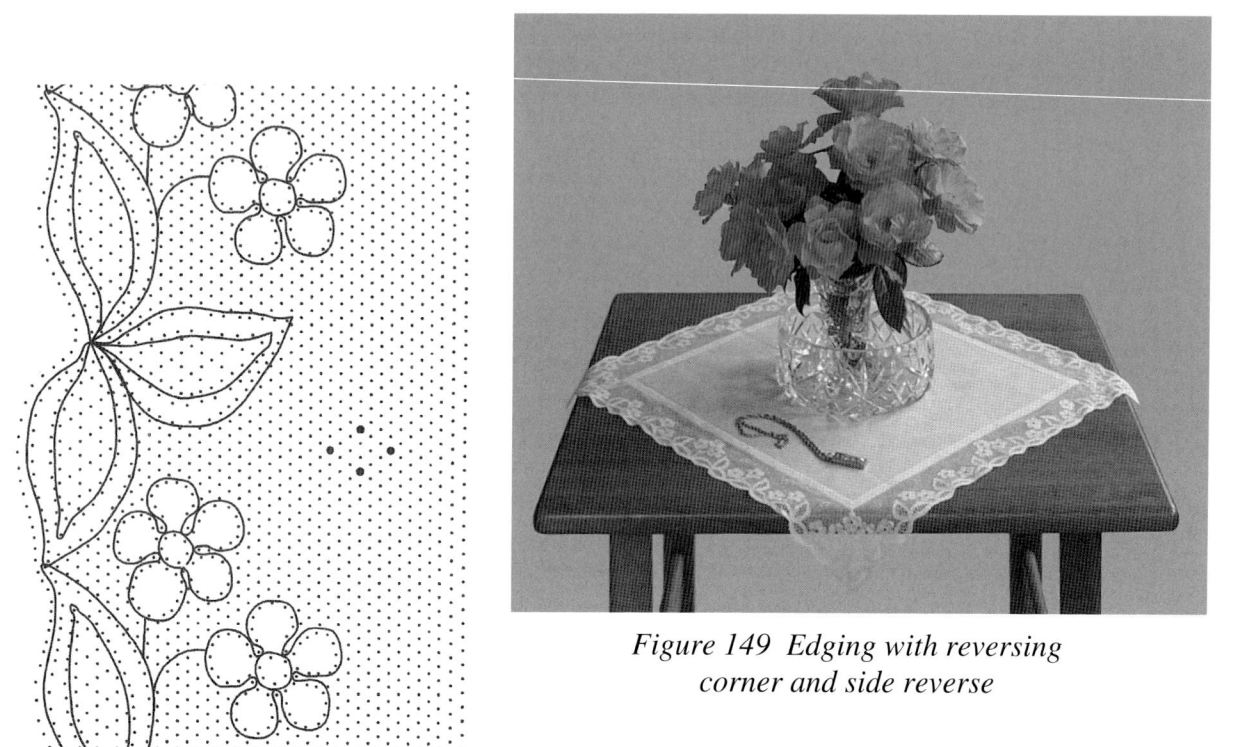

Figure 149 Edging with reversing corner and side reverse

Materials Required for project 8
Egyptian cotton no. 100/2[1]
gimp D.M.C. perle no. 12
50cm (20 in) x 50cm (20 in) fine cotton fabric
for edging with two repeats between each
corner motif and side reverse

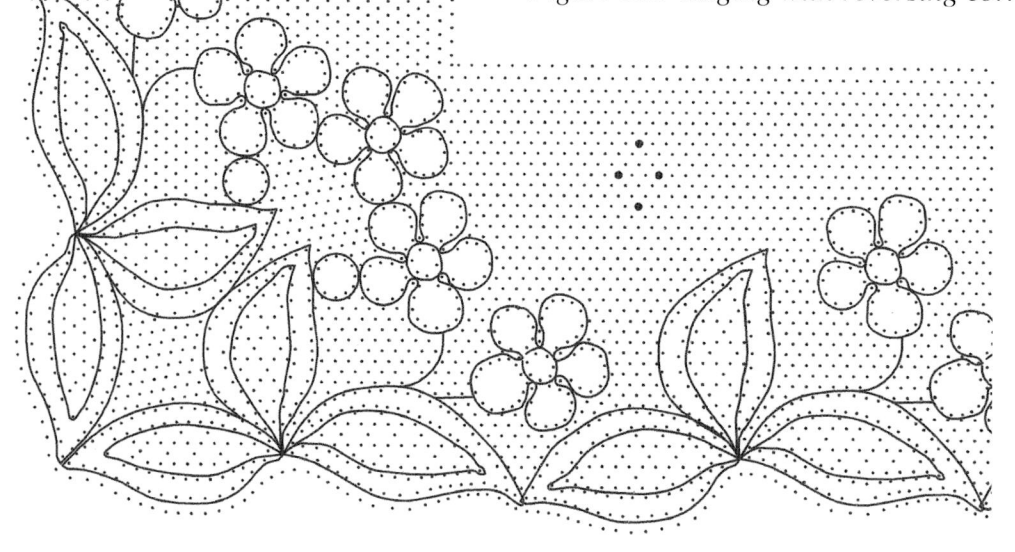

Figure 150 Edging with reversing corner, pricking

All about making—Floral Bucks Point Lace

Choosing a starting line[2]

Point ground is the hardest part of Bucks Point to join successfully and therefore setting in along a row of point ground is best avoided if the end of the work is to be joined to its start. The best starting line for this pattern occurs just before a corner[2] but this is not recommended if you are comparatively new to Floral Bucks and are practising the techniques. Setting in diagonally along rows of point ground from the footside and headside is much easier (figure 151). Being the easiest way, and because lace was made to be sold by the yard and cut to length for its purpose, the lace workers usually started along a diagonal. This became the accepted way to start and the practice has continued, the popular assumption being that this is always the correct place for setting in. However, it is not the best if you are joining the end to the start. Once you are comfortable working the edging try the corner and then try starting along my preferred line[2] for joining end to start.

Figure 151 (right) Edging worked on pricking figure 149

Grafting along the line

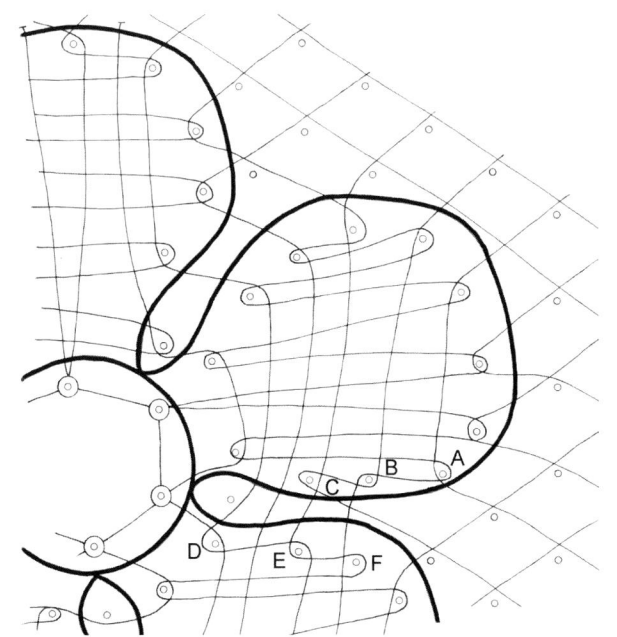

Figure 152 Grafting along the line

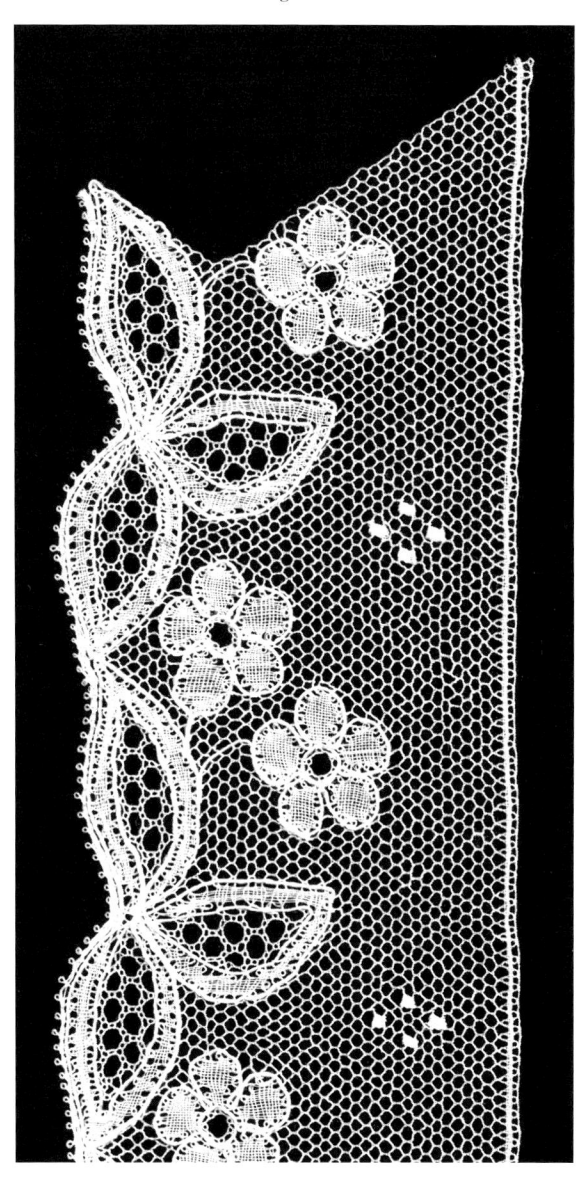

After the workers passed round pin A of the petal on the right (figure 152) I grafted the workers along the line of the lower edge of the petal by working back through two pairs and setting up a pin at B. Then I covered the pin and used a new pair of workers to work through another pair and set up a pin at C. I covered the pin and laid the workers across to the ground and saw that the pair from pin C made a better line for the ground than the one from pin B. In the next petal the workers from pin D worked to pin E. At pin D I exchanged workers and passives and took the new workers to pin E where I exchanged again before continuing to pin F.

All about making—Floral Bucks Point Lace

Using spacing pins

When the clothwork is started or finished along a wide shallow curve pins are often used as spacers (also called props) to keep the passives in the correct place, rather than to support the workers when they change direction. The top of the leaf (figure 153) starts along a nearly horizontal line. The first pin, pin A, is at one side of the top of the curve. Two pairs work a cloth stitch, pin A is set up and one pair passes to the left as the worker pair. The next four pins on the left, pins B-E, are spacers; the pairs entering either side of each of these pins may be previously connected by point ground stitches worked before they pass across the gimp or cloth stitches after passing across the gimp. The first row of cloth stitch turns at pin F and returns to pin K, pins G, H & J being spacers and two pairs are added, one at pin G and the other at pin J so that there would be sufficient pairs for the ground and the narrow clothwork strip starting with pins C and D. Rows are worked across to pins L, M and N. Pins P-U are set up as support pins to prevent the pairs drifting sideways, and the next row turns at pin V. The section continues to pin Z, pin Y being used as a spacer. Then the honeycomb centre was worked.

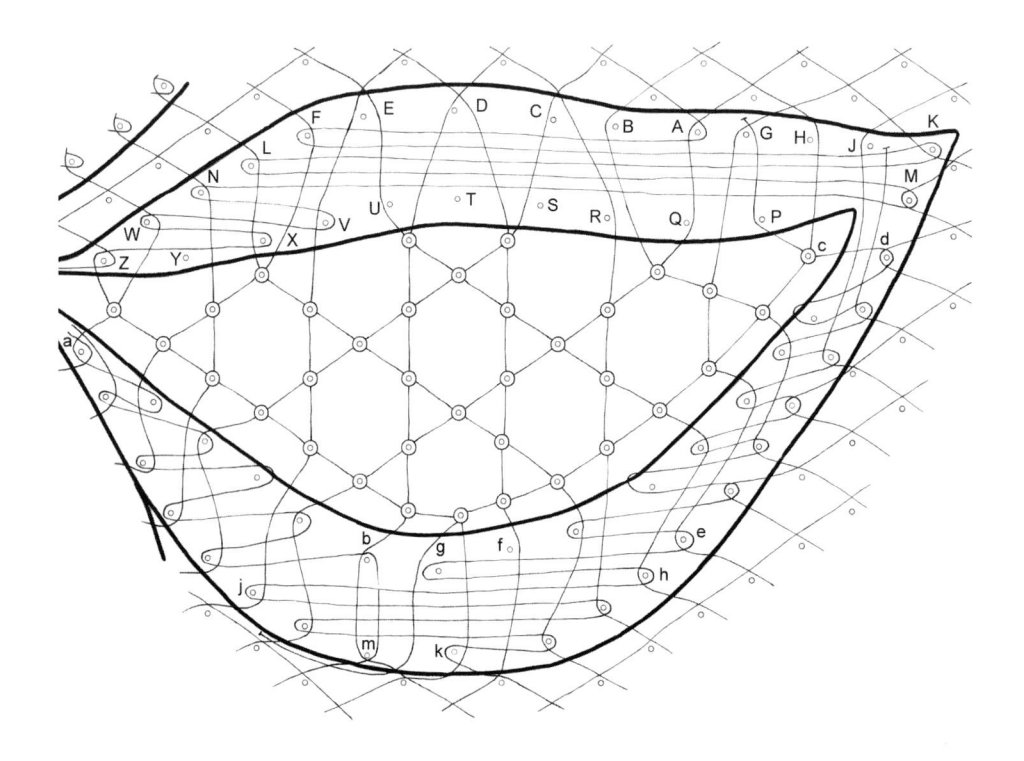

Figure 153 Using spacing pins

The lower part of the clothwork was worked in two parts. The part on the left side started at pin a and finished when the worker was supported by pin b, the pin was left uncovered. The workers for the part on the right side came from the honeycomb stitch at pin c and the first row worked to pin d and continued to pin e, pin f was set up as a spacer and the workers turned at pin g. From pin h the workers work across the full width of the area through remaining pairs from both parts to pin j and finished by covering pin k. Pin m was set up as a spacer and the pairs either side worked a cloth stitch. One pair was thrown out at this point.

All about making—Floral Bucks Point Lace

Figure 154 The corner

Turning the corner
To achieve an attractive corner some areas of the design, the innermost petal and two small areas of ground, ended up straddling the diagonal through the corner and this means that the working direction for these areas will need to be at right angles to this diagonal (figure 154), and new gimps will be needed. The second side is a mirror image[3] of the first.

All about making—Floral Bucks Point Lace

The ground area A and petal B continue to be worked in line with the current side (figure 155). Petal C can be started while working petal B but the workers must travel parallel to the diagonal through the corner. This usually requires pairs to be added to travel in two directions, i.e. into both petals B and C. The stitches for the flower centre D are worked when needed. Petals F and G leave out pairs for the ground area H which is worked diagonally across the corner and one or more pairs from petal G will approach petal F and probably need to be laid along the gimp to be discarded if necessary. The same happens along the gimp between petal E and the ground area H. The honeycomb ring J is worked in line with the current side. The leaf K and its honeycomb filling are made in line with the current side and pairs travelling in two directions may have to be added where the leaf K meets the ground area H. The same will happen where the leaf K and clothwork area M meet the ground area L. When all the pinholes on the current side of the diagonal through the corner have been used turn the pillow and start the second side from the outer point of the corner.

The second side is worked as a mirror image of the first. This time where pairs were added in two directions, when working the first side, they will meet 'head to head' and some will be thrown out. (Note: Leaf P is now up the other way, see figure 155.) When a corner is turned the lace is worked inwards from the outer point of the corner. However, it is usually easier to work in areas or blocks from the diagonal outwards towards the picot edge. Finish with the area of ground at V with the footside of the second side worked last of all.

Figure 155 Turning the corner, arrows indicate working directions

All about making—Floral Bucks Point Lace

After the corner
Once the diagonal through the corner has been crossed the pricking is inverted and has to be worked 'the other way up'. When working the first side the ground stitches settle on the upper sides of the pins as they approach a motif (figure 155). When the pricking is inverted the ground stitches again settle on the upper sides of the pins, but this time they are on the other sides of the pins relative to the pins of the motif and thus a mirror image of the working may not be suitable and the working diagram may have to be changed (figure 156). Also some Floral Bucks edgings will not work when inverted.

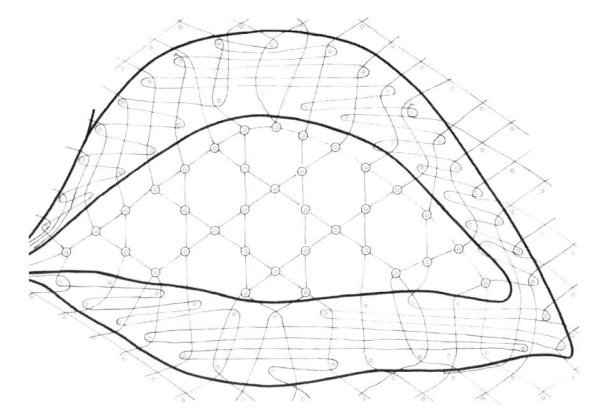

Figure 156 (left) The leaf after the corner, with shallow curves and spacing pins

Side reverse[4]
When the side reverse is reached the pattern inverts back to its original directions in preparation for working the following corner which will be the same as the previous one. (figures 157 & 158).

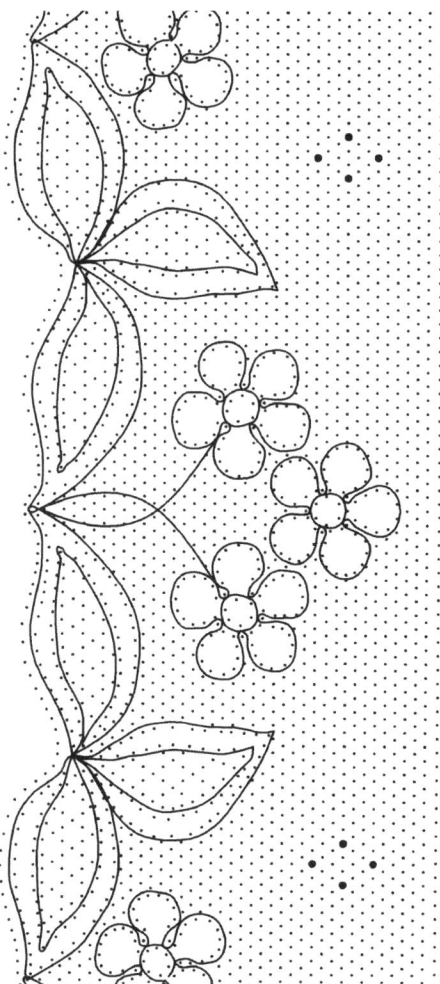

Figure 157 (left) Pricking for side reverse

Figure 158 (right) Side reverse, lace made on pricking figure 157

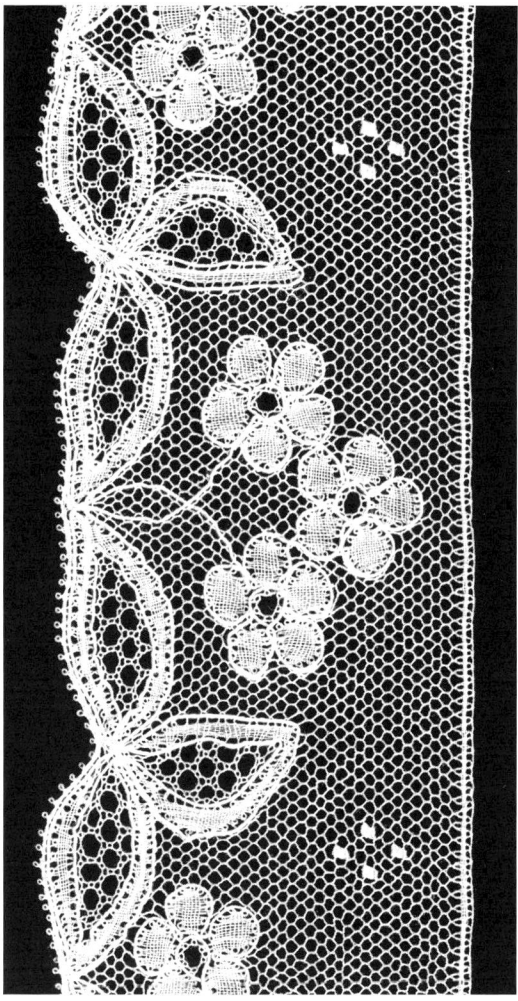

Mitred corner

The cloth was made using organdie and finished with a 1.5cm (0.6 in) hem mitred at the corners.

1 Check that the fabric is not distorted, i.e. that the threads lie at right angles. If necessary pull the fabric to correct any distortion and press. Then cut the fabric to size with a 3.5cm (1½ in) hem allowance all round.

2 Fold 2.5cm (1 in) of the fabric over to the wrong side for the finished size of the cloth and press. Then fold over 0.8cm ($^1/_3$ in) from the edge to make the turning and press (figure 159).

3 On the wrong side of the fabric draw a line at 45° across the corner (figure 160).

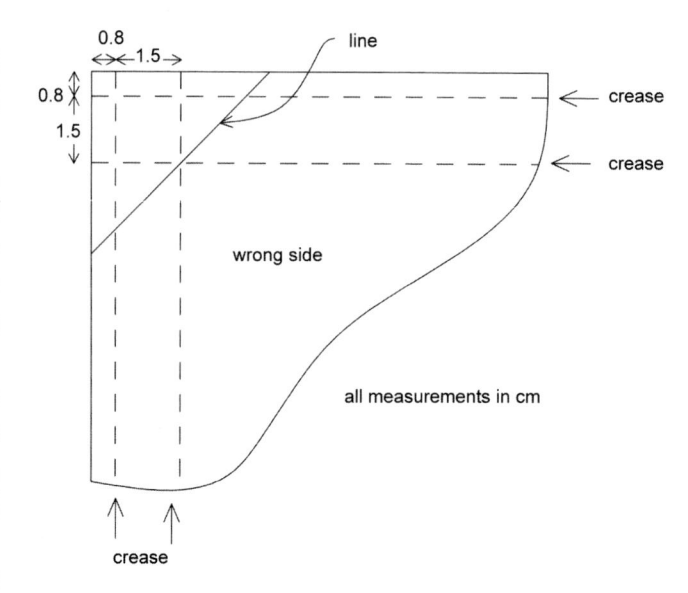

Figure 159 Fabric with creases and line

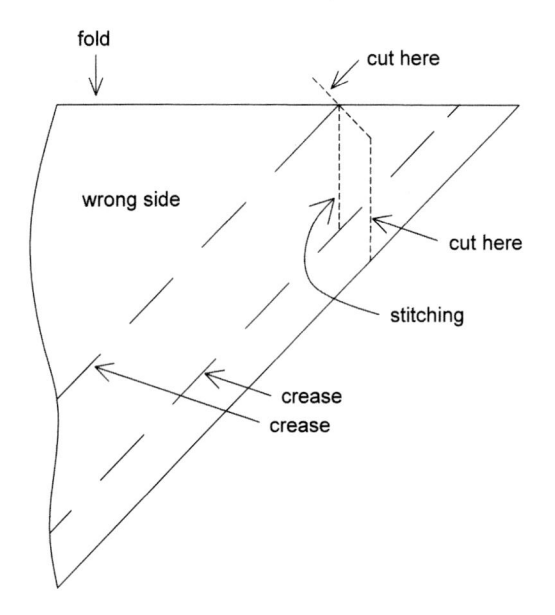

4 Fold the fabric right sides together diagonally though the corner, matching the two halves of the line (figure 160). (Do not press).

5 Machine or back stitch from the corner to the first crease.

6 Trim away the surplus fabric as indicated. Open the seam and crease it open by pressing along the seam line with your fingers.

Figure 160 (left) Corner stitched

7 Turn the corner through to the right side and fold the fabric along the original creases (figure 161). Check that the seam is open and press.

8 Secure the hem by slip stitching, hemming or hemstitching[5].

Figure 161 (right) Corner turned through

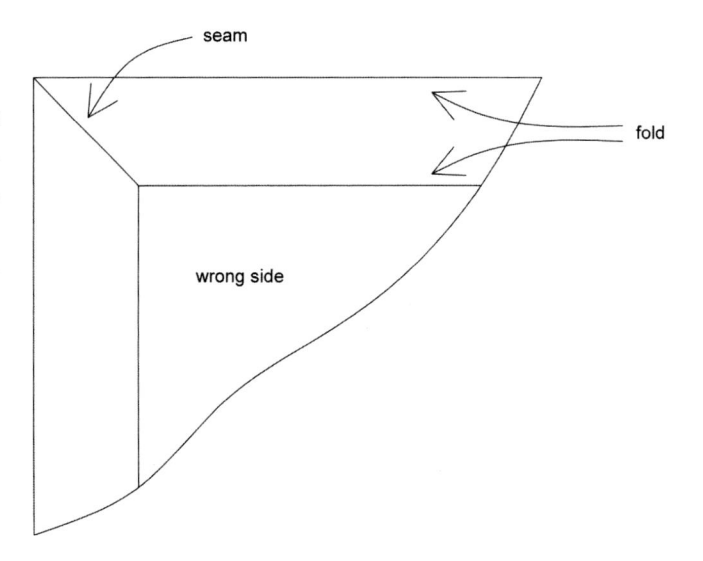

All about making—Floral Bucks Point Lace

END NOTES

1 Substituting threads
See Part 6.

2 My preferred starting line
Always try to avoid joining through an area of point ground, it is exceedingly difficult to neaten the ends so they do not show. Because it is also difficult to have more than a few rows of point ground turning a corner most Floral Bucks corners have gimps to break the ground so that it does not cross the diagonal through the corner. Hence it makes sense to set in the lace along these gimps. My preferred line (figure 162) started along the edge of a leaf. Technically two rows of point ground should have travelled across to the stem of the flower, but they were allowed to remain along the gimp. When the piece was joined end to start these rows were sewn in; not a traditional Bucks Point technique but creative use of techniques I know from other laces.

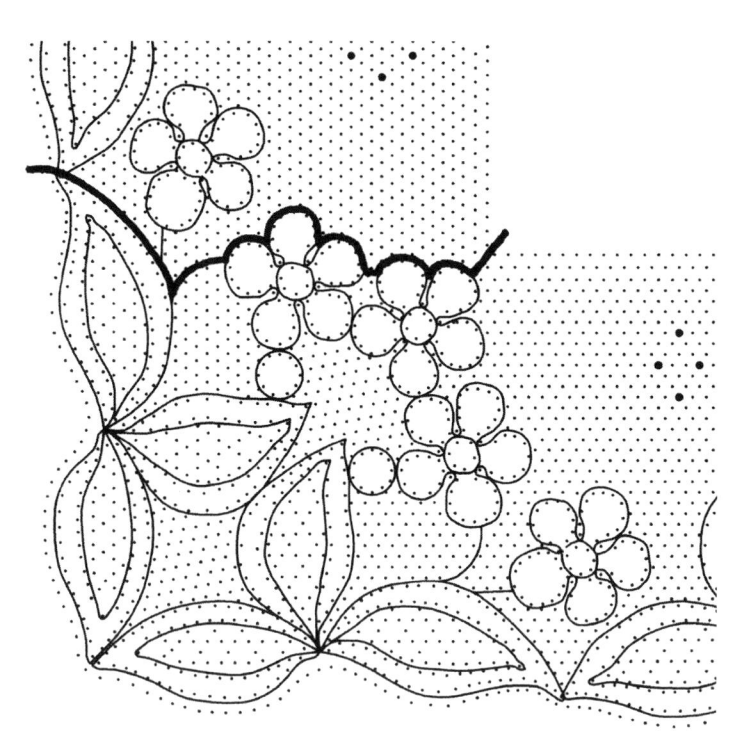

Figure 162 My preferred starting line

Figure 163 Chinese Folk Design by W.M. Hawley

3 Selecting and interpreting a design for making in lace
My designs come from many sources. Buttercup is a traditional pattern and it was selected for the first chapter because of the techniques required to make it. This time I have used a design from 'Chinese Folk Designs' by W.M. Hawley, pub. Dover 1949, No. 7 (figure 163). When choosing a design look at how the different areas can be interpreted in lace; which will be clothwork, ground or filling. Check that these areas are of a suitable size. Areas for clothwork require a reasonable number of pairs and rows to work successfully and should not be so

59

All about making—Floral Bucks Point Lace

large that the workers will sag and not firm up straight across the area. Fillings should have sufficient repeats so that the picture of the design shows and ground and fillings should not be so large that they become boring. From the Chinese design I discarded the leaf with the two curls and the seed head. The outlines of the three leaves are sufficiently wide and the petals are suitably sized for clothwork. The centres of the flowers are exactly right for honeycomb rings and I replaced the veined centres of the leaves with honeycomb. Curved areas like those of the petals are the easiest to make look good, pointed areas such as those of the clothwork section of the leaves are more difficult.

3a Drafting the edging
Unlike Buttercup which has a design that reverses in the centre, this one is a one-way design but it was still drafted as Chapter 1 End Notes 9.

3b Drafting corners
Corners are produced by turning a pattern through 90°. However, because point ground is not at 45° there will be problems that can be met by filling vacant spaces with features from the pattern. These features may be distorted or otherwise modified to make them fit. Since this is a one-way pattern the design will be inverted.

Use a mirror held at 45° to the footside and slide it backwards and forwards to enable you to decide on a position for the corner (see figure 145). Draw this line on a photocopy of the edging (figure 164) and then cut along this line.

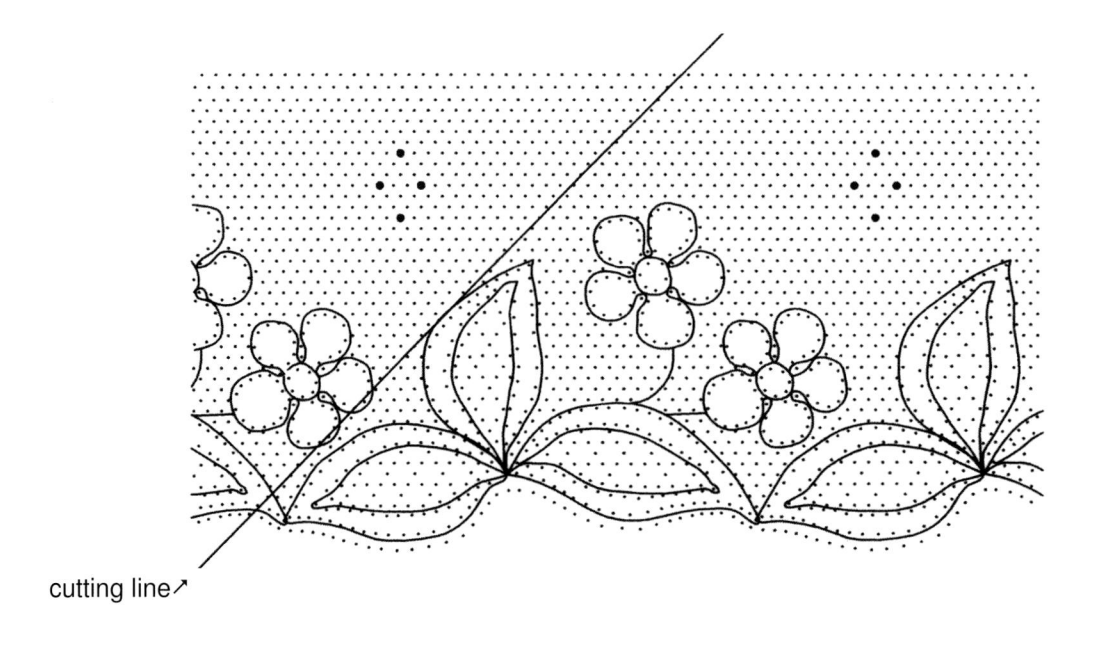

cutting line ↗

Figure 164 The diagonal line through the corner

All about making—Floral Bucks Point Lace

3c Matching the edgings through the corner
Make a photocopy that is a mirror image of the edging and place beneath the edging cut along the diagonal with the footsides at 90° and the cut edge matching the same points of the photocopy beneath (figure 165).

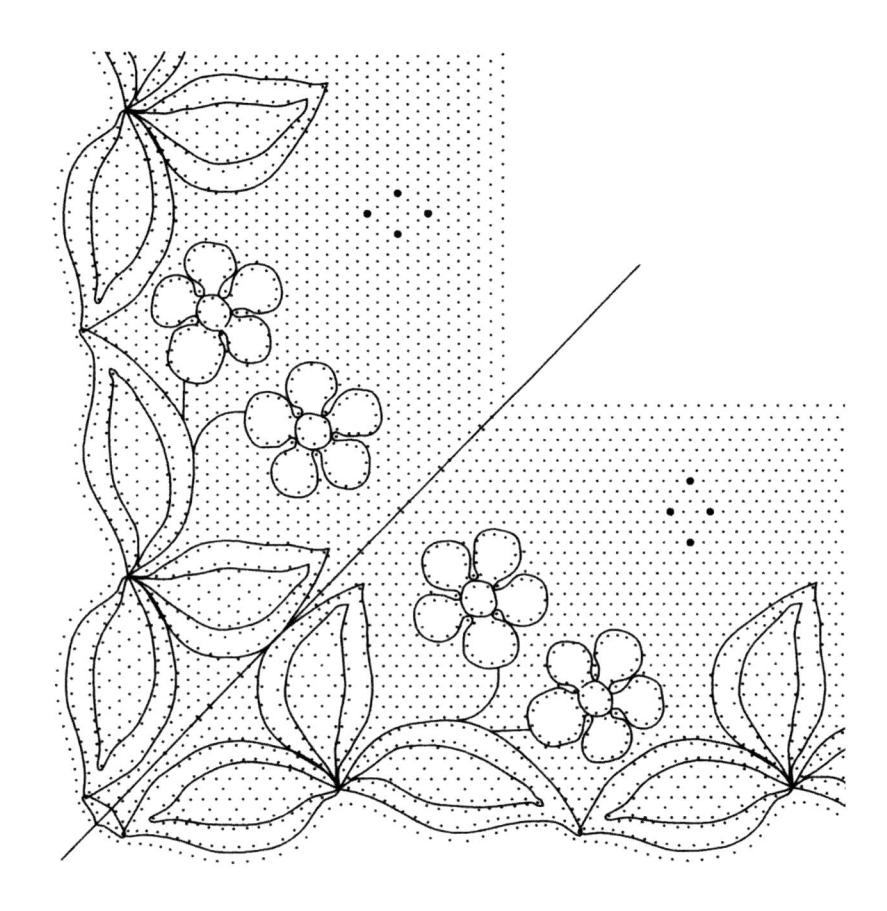

Figure 165 Matching the mirror image across the corner

3d Making the corner work
Corners rarely work perfectly, and this one (figure 165) has three major problems that need to be resolved.

1) There is a gap between the leaves where they do not quite meet at the outside of the corner, see End Note 3e, figure 166, where it is corrected.
2) There is an enclosed area of ground crossing the diagonal between the flowers, see End Note 3f for how it may be corrected.
3) There is a large area of ground crossing the diagonal between the leaves and the footside, see End Note 3g for how it may be corrected.

61

All about making—Floral Bucks Point Lace

3e Making the leaves meet at the corner

The diagonal was drawn along the edge of the centre leaf and when the two sections are matched the two leaves meeting at the outer point of the corner have a gap between them. This was resolved by realigning these two leaves so that they met at the point of the corner. Since this caused the leaves to rotate slightly the honeycomb had to be removed and replaced at the correct angle (figure 166).

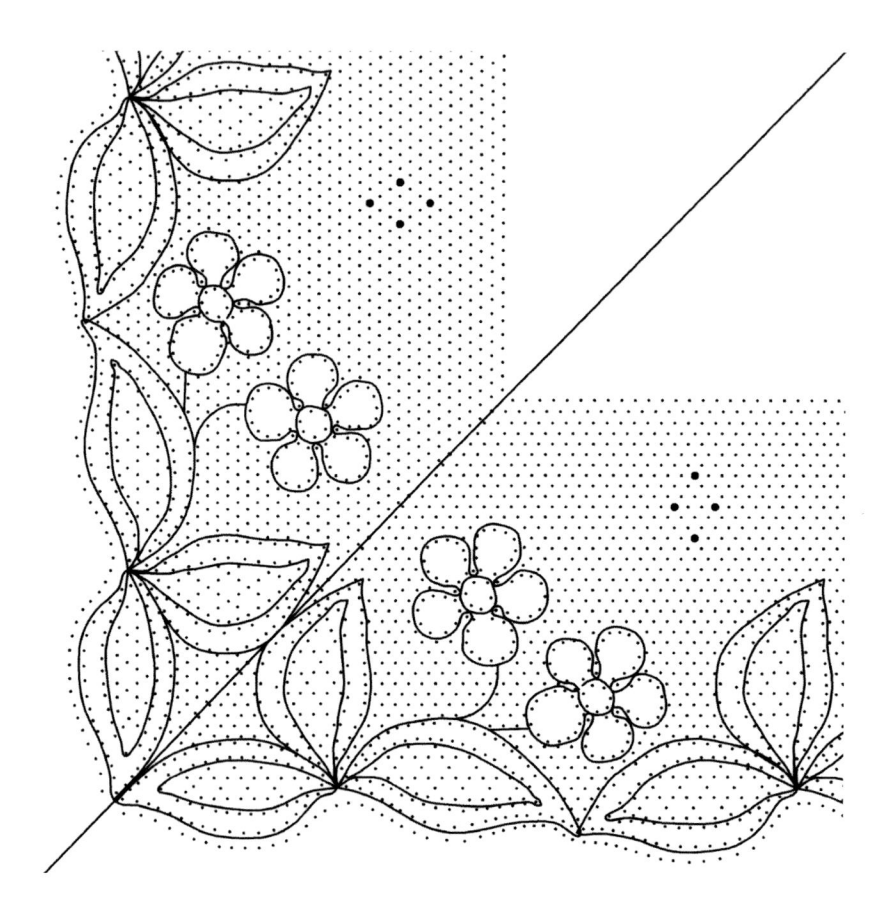

Figure 166 Leaves adjusted

3f Direction of work at the corner

For an item that is to be washed and pressed, ideally the clothwork workers should remain at 90° to the footside with the passives in line with the footside, so that there will be no stretching and distortion caused during pressing by the iron working diagonally across the direction of the work. However in this piece one small area of ground clothwork, the innermost petal, will be worked diagonally to the footside, but fortunately being small this should not cause a problem.

3g Breaking the ground from the motif to the footside and realigning the ground in the enclosed areas

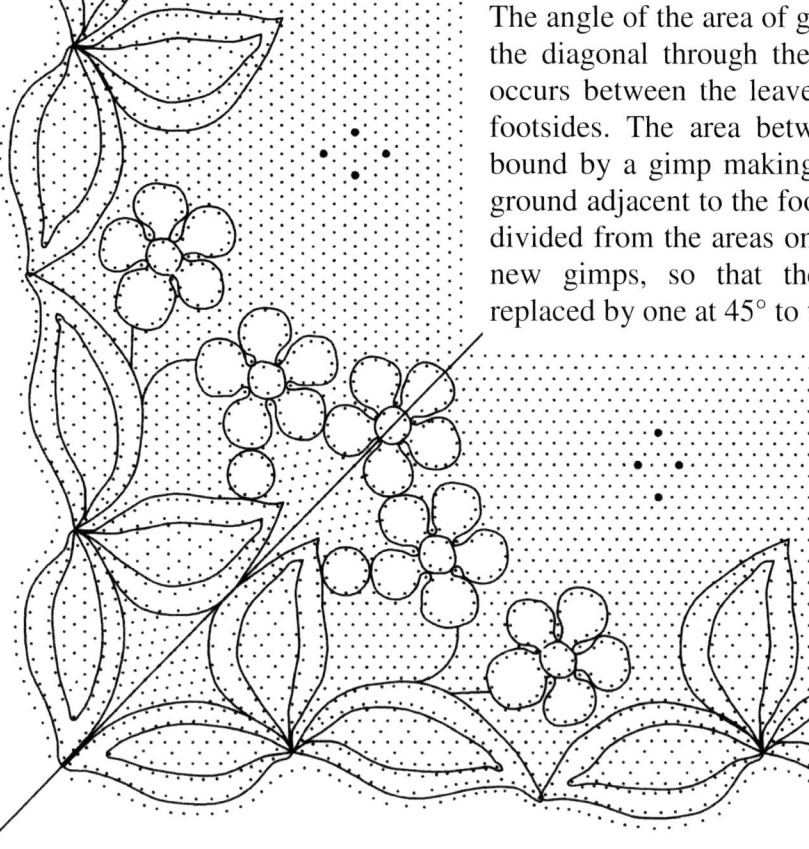

The angle of the area of ground changes as it crosses the diagonal through the corner (figure 167). This occurs between the leaves and also adjacent to the footsides. The area between the leaves is already bound by a gimp making an enclosed area, but the ground adjacent to the footside at the corner must be divided from the areas on either side by introducing new gimps, so that the ground inside may be replaced by one at 45° to the footside.

Figure 167 Flower across the corner

Honeycomb rings have been used to block the passages between the flowers and the leaves producing an enclosed area of ground.

Here a flower has been placed at the corner by the footside and the passages between this flower and the leaves were blocked using the honeycomb rings as used for the centres of the flowers. The pinholes within the petals and ground around them needed some adjustment (figure 165). The offending enclosed areas of ground can now be removed and replaced with the ground at 45° to the footside (90°) to the diagonal, the direction in which it is later worked. (Do a 'cut and paste'. Cut out the unwanted part, place the hole over an area of ground that is aligned in the required direction and attach the two parts together). Finally the catch-pin and footside rows of pins are adjusted (figure 150).

4 Reversing corner and side reverse

When a corner is designed by mirror the pricking is inverted; the second side is now the 'other way up'. Continuing in this way the next corner would have a different mirrored corner, and this in turn would result in the pattern reverting to the original 'way up' and the next corner will be the same as the first. If the corners are to be the same some modification to the design is required and this is called a side reverse (figures 157 & 158). This results in the edging approaching the next corner the 'original way up' and thus all sides and corners will be the same. The idea of having two different sets of corners does not appeal to me, so I reversed the pattern half way along each side.

All about making—Floral Bucks Point Lace

4a Side reverse

A side reverse is produced reversing the pricking, (i.e. inverting, mirror imaging or flipping it over).

1 Use a mirror held at right angles to the footside and slide it backwards and forwards along the footside to enable you to decide on the position where the pricking could reverse (figure 168).

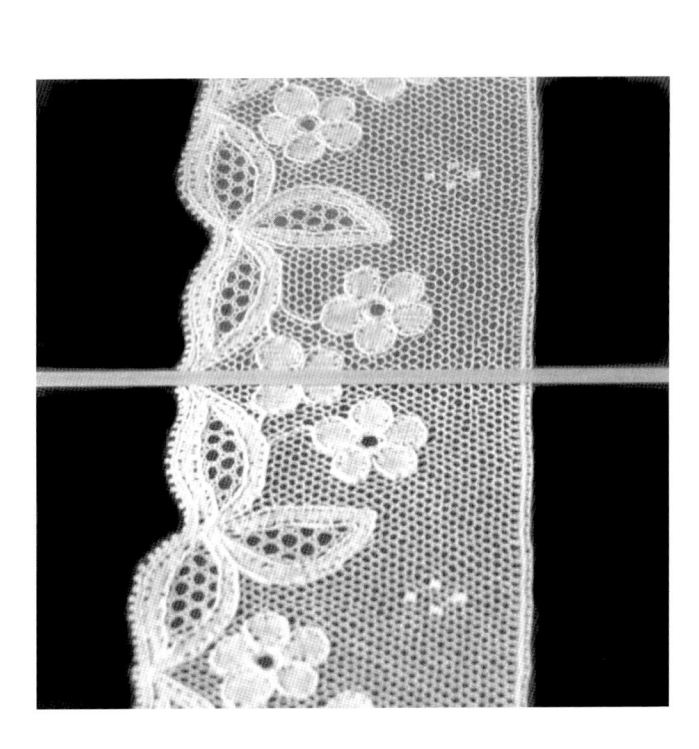

Figure 168 Using a mirror to find a suitable position for a side reverse

cut here →

2 Draw the line of the side reverse on a photocopy of the edging, making sure it passes through a line of holes (figure 169).

Figure 169 (right) The line of the side reverse on the pricking

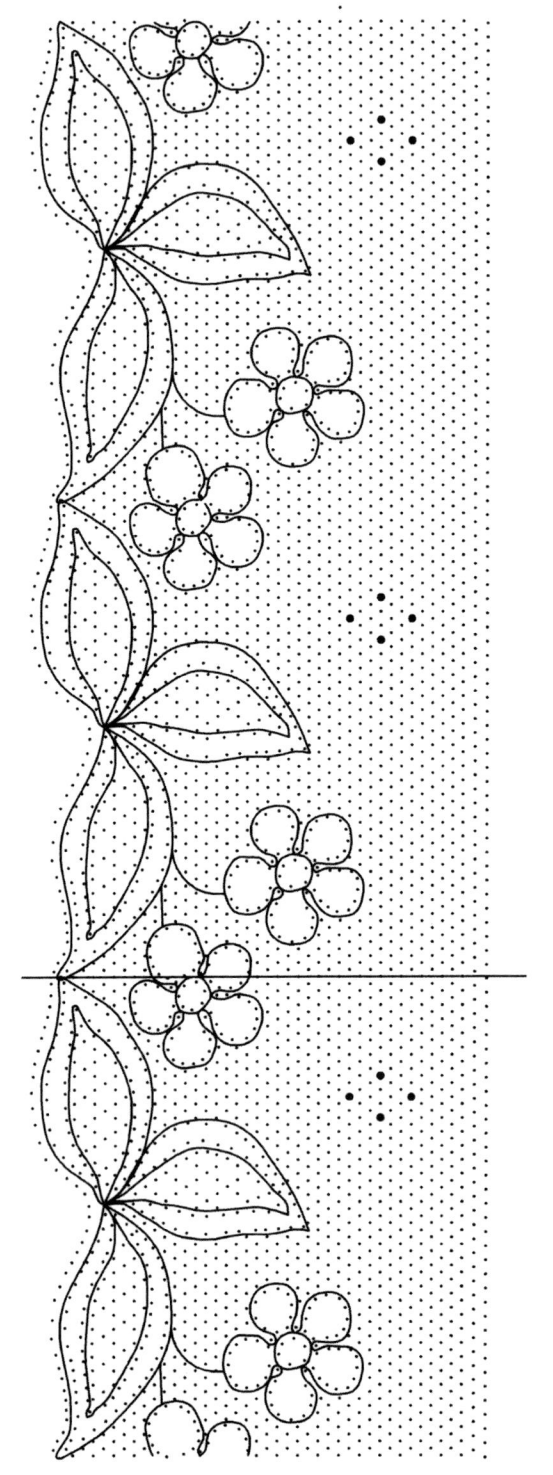

All about making—Floral Bucks Point Lace

3 Cut for the side reverse line (figures 169 & 170).

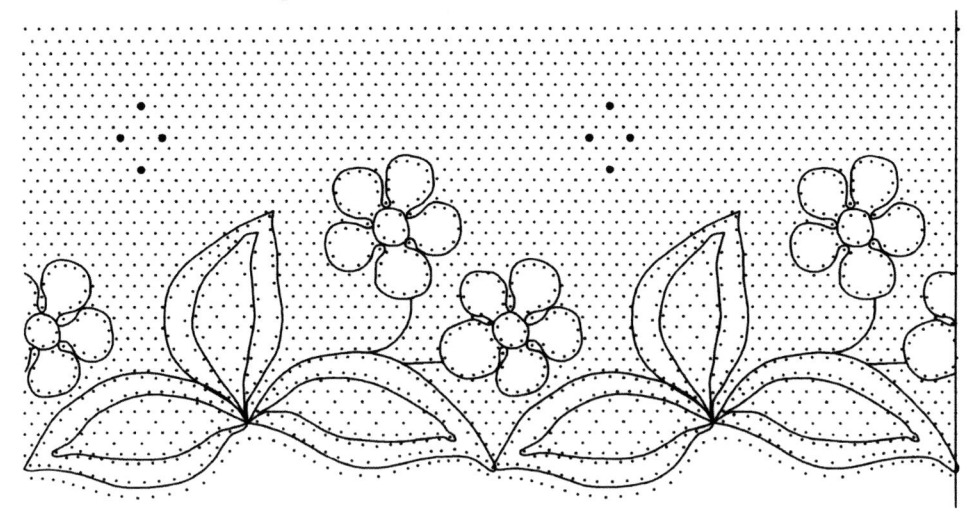

Figure 170 Pricking cut along the line of the side reverse

↑ cut edge

4 Make a photocopy that is a mirror image of the edging and place beneath the cut edging, matching pinholes with the footsides in line (figure 171).

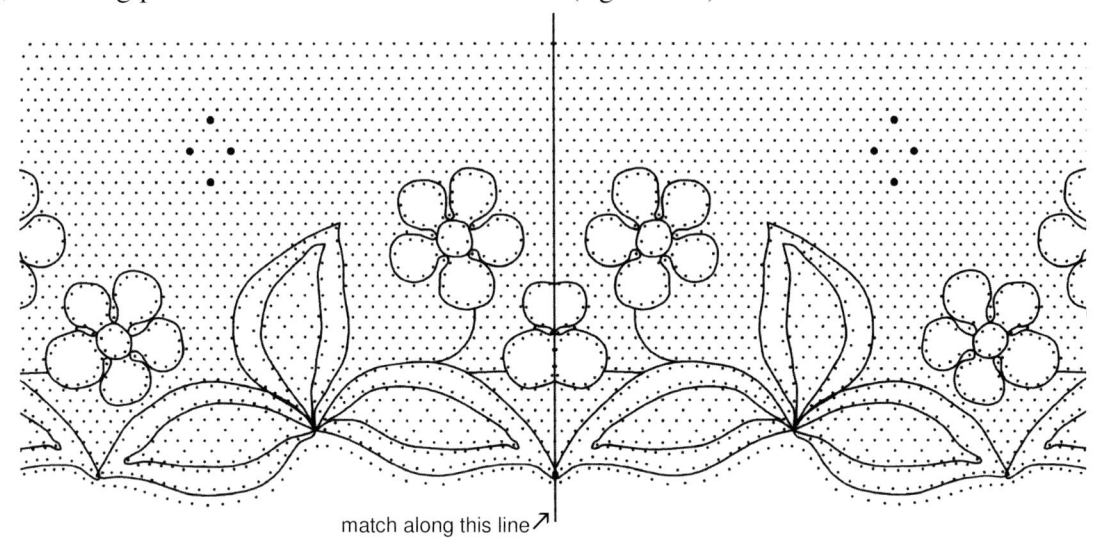

match along this line ↗

Figure 171 Prickings matched along the line of the side reverse

5 Adjust the design. Modify parts, add motifs (preferably from other parts of the design) and realign to make an attractive design. In this case the unwanted trefoil was removed. (Do a 'cut and paste'. Cut out the unwanted part, place the hole over an area of ground that is aligned in the required direction and attach the two parts together). Then a flower was added above and between the existing flowers and the gimps indicating their stems realigned to suit. Finally the catch-pins and footside pins were corrected (figures 157 & 158) (Inverting the pricking turns the footside 'up the wrong way'.

5 Hemstitching
See '*All about making*—Geometrical Bucks Point Lace' A. Stillwell, Salex Publishing page 142.

All about making—Floral Bucks Point Lace

CHAPTER 6

PROJECTS: 9 & 10 Working circular mats

Project: 9 An Anniversary present with the edge motifs worked radially and the point ground centre from top to bottom

Project 10-: An Anniversary present worked from top to bottom

PROJECT: 9 An Anniversary present with the edge motifs worked radially and the point ground centre from top to bottom

Figure 172 An anniversary present with the edge motifs worked radially and the point ground centre from top to bottom[2]

Materials Required for Project 9
Egyptian cotton no. 100/2[1], gimp D.M.C. perle no. 12
circular frame with 14.5 cm (5$^3/_4$ ins)
gold numbers

66

All about making—Floral Bucks Point Lace

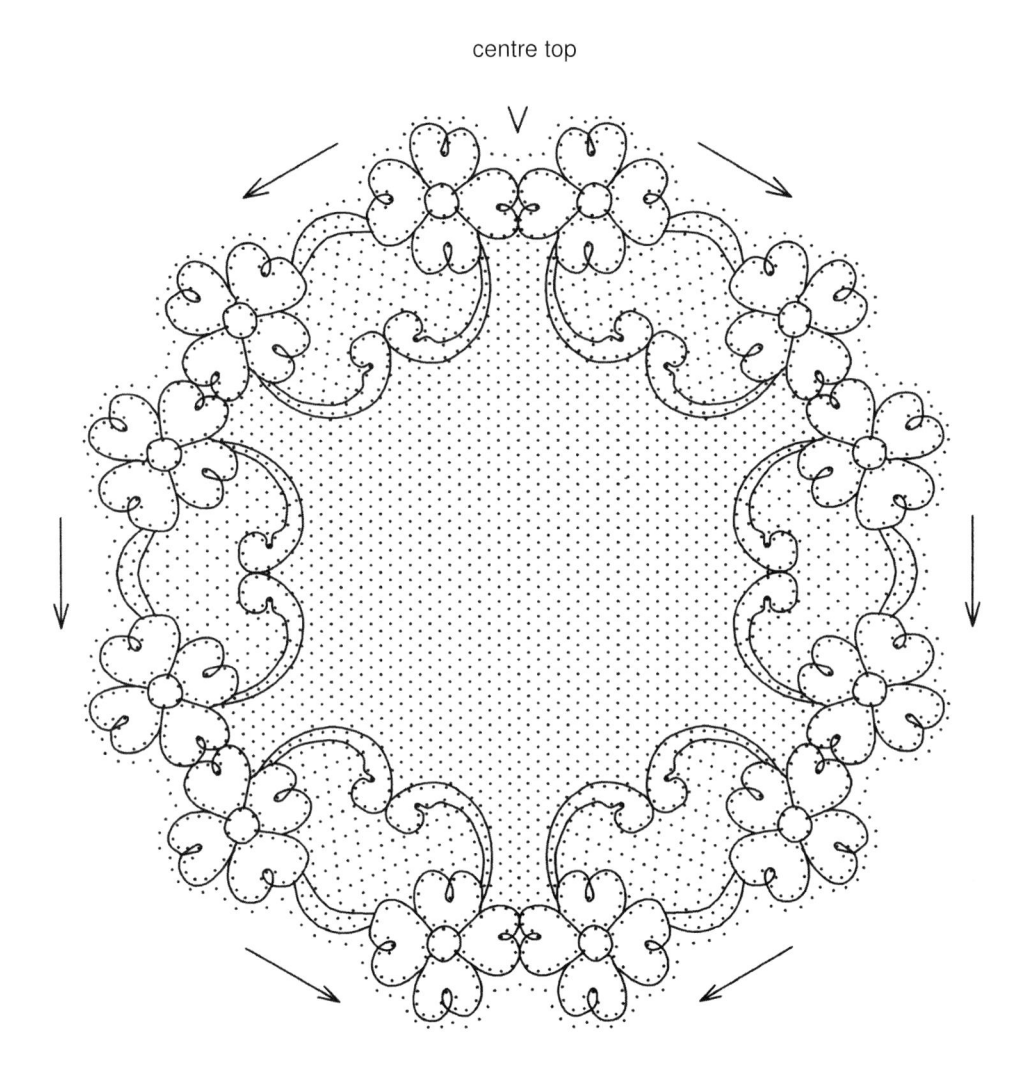

centre top

Figure 173 An anniversary present, pricking.

Each arrow indicates the direction of work for the adjacent edge motif.
The ground is worked from top to bottom.

All about making—Floral Bucks Point Lace

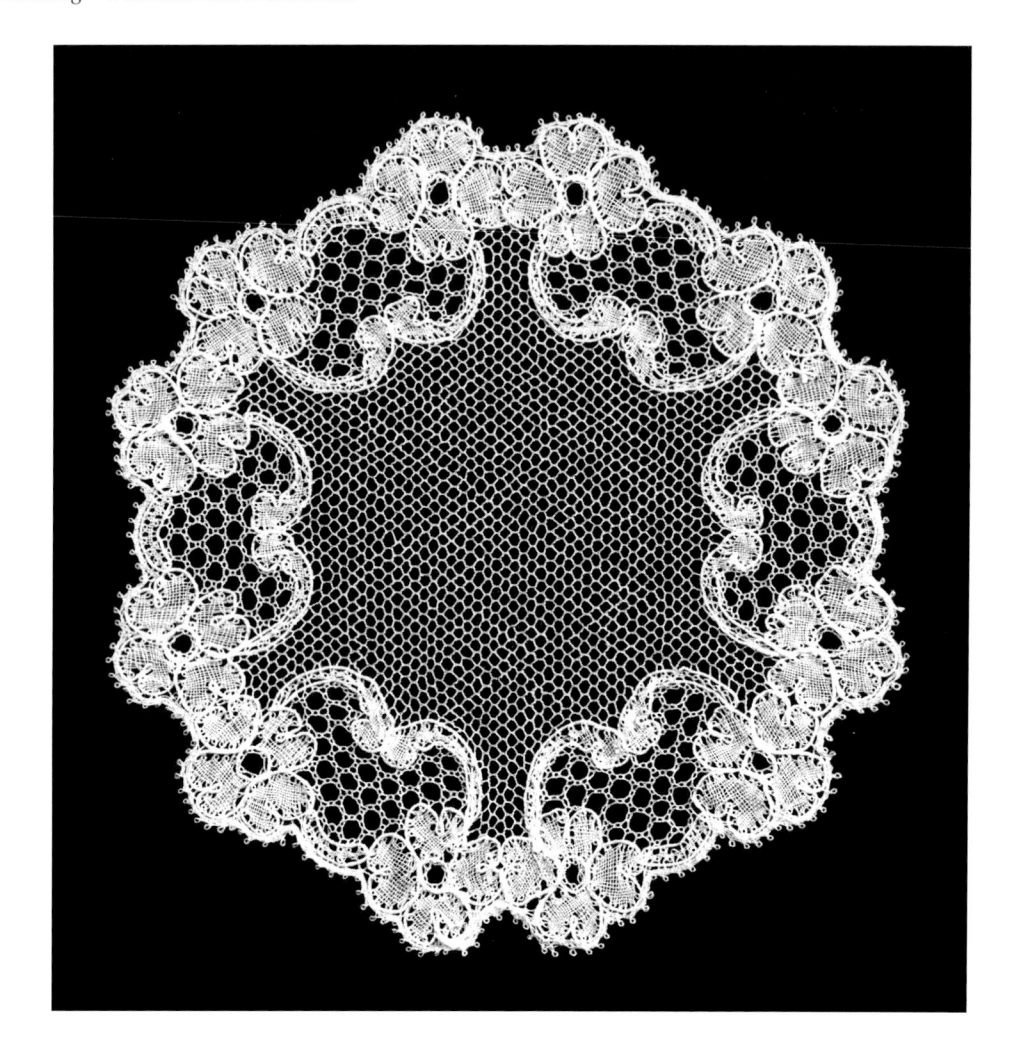

Figure 174 An anniversary present with edge motifs worked radially and the point ground centre worked vertically worked on pricking figure 173.

Set in the two motifs at the top, working one towards the left and one towards the right. These two motifs work radially from the centre, marked 'V' on the pricking (figure 173), and pairs are left out of and are absorbed into motifs from the ground which works from top to bottom.

Two cover cloths may be used, one each side, with each placed across the pricking so that the arrow on the pricking adjacent to the motif is vertical and at right angles to the cover cloth on that side. Later on you may wish to have a third cover cloth horizontally across the pillow when you work the ground. As with all radially worked pieces, the position of the cover cloth is crucial and different for every motif. It is an important factor in 'keeping your bearings' and knowing the direction in which to work.

Setting in the top left hand petal

Since the work will be proceeding in two directions pairs must be added so that they work in two directions, i.e. the bobbins are coupled but only one passes into this motif, the other is secured out of the way until it is used for the top right hand petal (figure 175). This left hand petal can be worked the same way as the motif of the edging (figures 114 & 115), then change the orientation of the pillow before setting in the right hand top petal. It is essential that the working cloth is in the correct position so that you can keep the workers horizontal for the motif currently being worked. Even so it will be difficult, and the occasional horizontal line drawn or scratched across the area can be very useful.

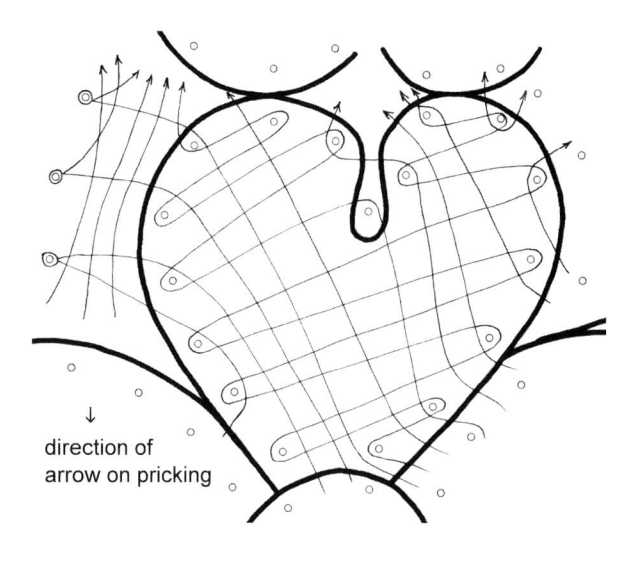

Figure 175 Setting in to work in two directions, arrowheads show the directions of the partner bobbins

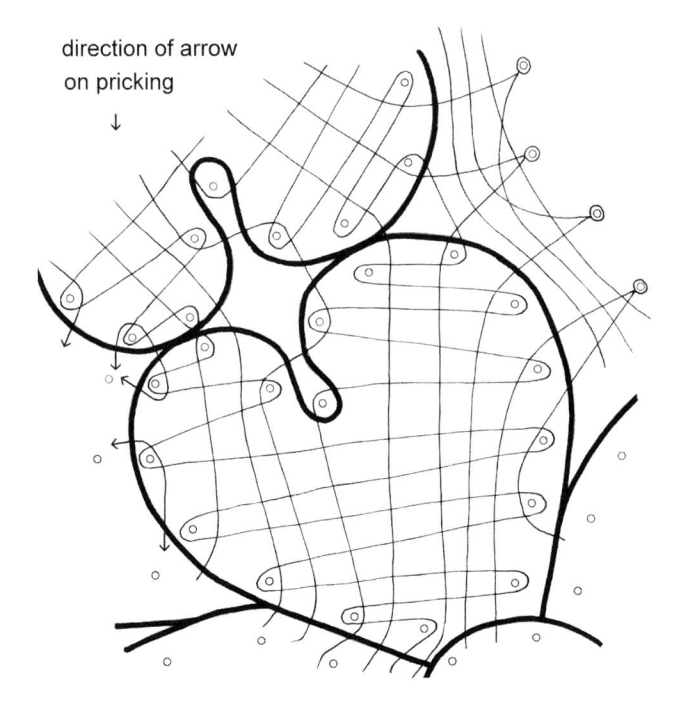

Setting in the top right hand petal

When the left hand petal is complete rotate the pillow so that the arrow by the top right hand motif is vertical, replace the cover cloth at right angles to it and remove the pins that secured the partner bobbins when the left hand top petal was set in. Check that these bobbins are untangled and work this petal. Pairs are required from the ground, but since the ground has yet to be started secure pairs to be worked in two directions and add these 'pairs' into the clothwork as required, leaving the other 'pair' to be used for the ground (figure 176).

Figure 176 Setting in the right hand petal using the bobbins originally secured out of the way. New 'pairs required' from the ground are indicated by arrowheads

All about making—Floral Bucks Point Lace

Starting the ground
When both top petals are complete rotate the pillow so that the vertical through the ground is vertical, place the cover cloth at right angles to it and remove any pins securing the partner bobbins when pairs have been started in two directions. Check that these partner bobbins are untangled and start working the ground; the first stitch being made using the centre two pairs, pin A. Then work the stitches either side, pins B & C, and the centre stitch between them, pin D. Now start the row from the left with the next two free pairs from the motif and work the row down through the pair from pin B ground stitch at pin E, then the stitch with the pair from pin D. Start the next row from the right with the next two free pairs from the motif then work the stitch at pin F with pair from pin C, work down the row to build a triangle of ground (figure 177).

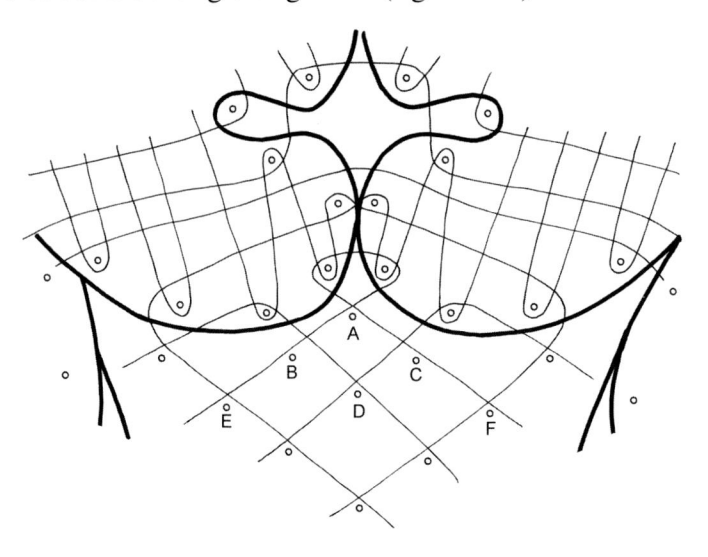

Figure 177 Starting the ground

Continuing
Rotate the pillow and continue the top motif on the left hand side, adjusting the cover cloth or using another one for that side. When new pairs should be available from the ground add them on in two directions. When a pair is left out from the motif add another cover cloth at right angles to the vertical line through the ground and work a row of ground, then remove before making the motif. Continue by moving from motif to ground to motif as required and keep building up the triangle of ground. Until you have plenty of experience it is wise, and in the long run a time saver, to keep moving cover cloths.

Side motifs
When the side motifs are reached the working returns to normal and the pairs pass from the motif to ground and vice versa as usual.

Centre
The ground in the centre can be almost completed while the side motifs are worked, but not all of it. There will be some point ground stitches that cannot be made until the lower motifs are worked.

All about making—Floral Bucks Point Lace

Working the lower motifs
After changing the angle of the pillow and cover cloths it is obvious that there will be times when there will be a pair that should be left out of the motif to enter the ground at the same time that there is a pair trying to enter (figure 178). Do not try to reproduce my route exactly, it will be too confusing and may not achieve the best results. Study my approach, shut the book and work the lace looking at the positions of the pinholes and the pairs you have to work with. There can be many routes for these pairs, most of which will not change the appearance of the lace. When I reached pin A, a pair would normally be left out but there is a pair entering from the ground. In this case I have taken in the pair from the ground and worked back through both pairs. Then I twisted both passive pairs twice, passed the nearest across the gimp and twisted it, then the second one across both and twisted it. Both these pairs were laid along the gimp and all worked together until three pairs had crossed them and then they were left out. The same method could be used at pin B, but instead I decided to use one of the pairs for the row of two ground stitches and threw a pair out of the ground to compensate for the other.

Two ground stitches
The row of two ground stitches C & D should work from right to left but that part of the pattern has not been worked yet. One or two pairs could be added to work these stitches, but we have too many pairs already and that would only compound the difficulties. Instead I chose to take a pair out of the clothwork and technically work the row 'uphill', i.e. in the wrong direction, pins C, D and a stitch without a pin at E. The thread flow works and I was using available pairs.

Scroll
Pairs will enter the scroll from both sides but only leave from the left and therefore they will accumulate. In this situation pairs can either be taken out again across the gimp and carried along the gimp until left out, as at pin A, they can be removed from the clothwork as pairs a-f or they can be brought in across the gimp and left lying along the gimp as pairs g & h. I used whichever method seemed best at the time.

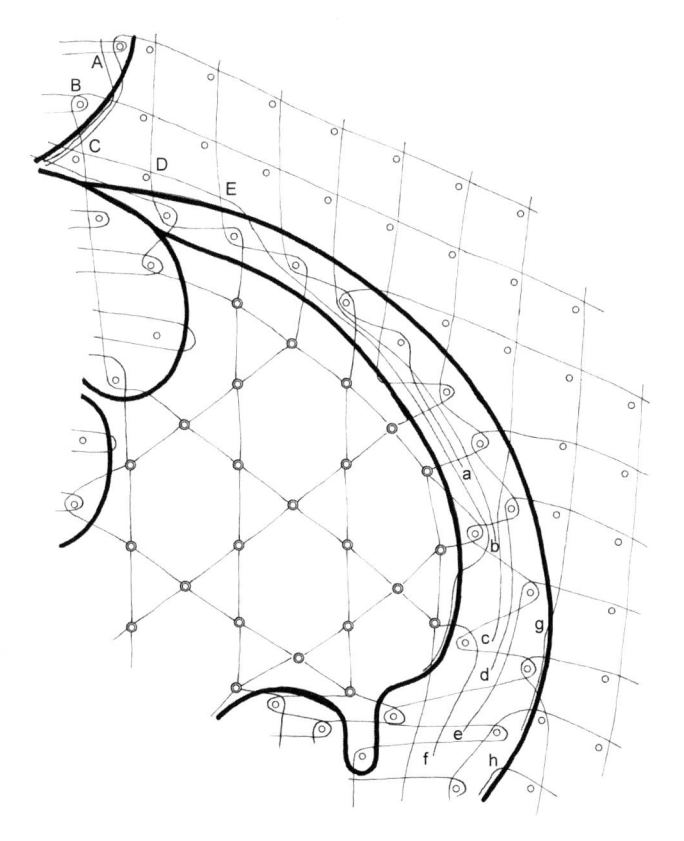

Figure 178 Removing pairs as the ground finishes

Finishing the petals and headside
The last pairs in the petals and the headside are joined 'head to head', i.e. one thread from one side ties a reef knot with the corresponding thread from the other side. Finally darn away the remaining ends.

All about making—Floral Bucks Point Lace

PROJECT 10: An Anniversary present worked from top to bottom

Figure 179 Anniversary present worked from top to bottom

Materials Required for Project 10
Egyptian cotton no. 100/2[1]
gimp D.M.C. perle no. 12
circular frame with 14.5 cm (5¾ ins) aperture
gold numbers

Working from top to bottom[3]
When the design is worked from top to bottom (figures 179-181), the motifs are all worked from the top of the design downwards and the actual working of the individual motifs will vary. Compare with figures 169-171 in which the motifs containing the honeycomb areas angle around the centre and each motif is made as for the Birthday Gift figures 114 & 115.

All about making—Floral Bucks Point Lace

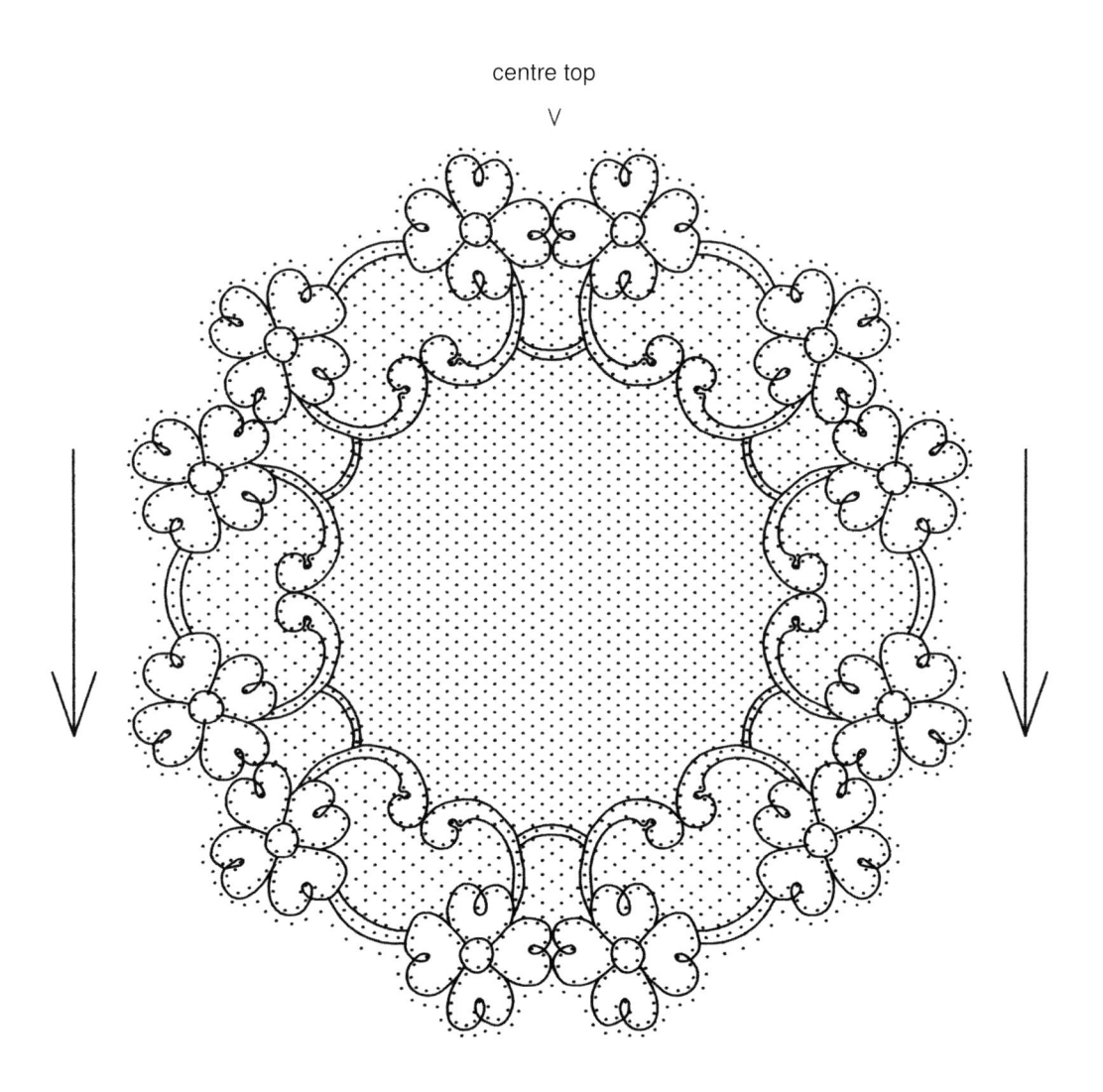

Figure 180 Pricking for an anniversary present worked top to bottom

73

All about making—Floral Bucks Point Lace

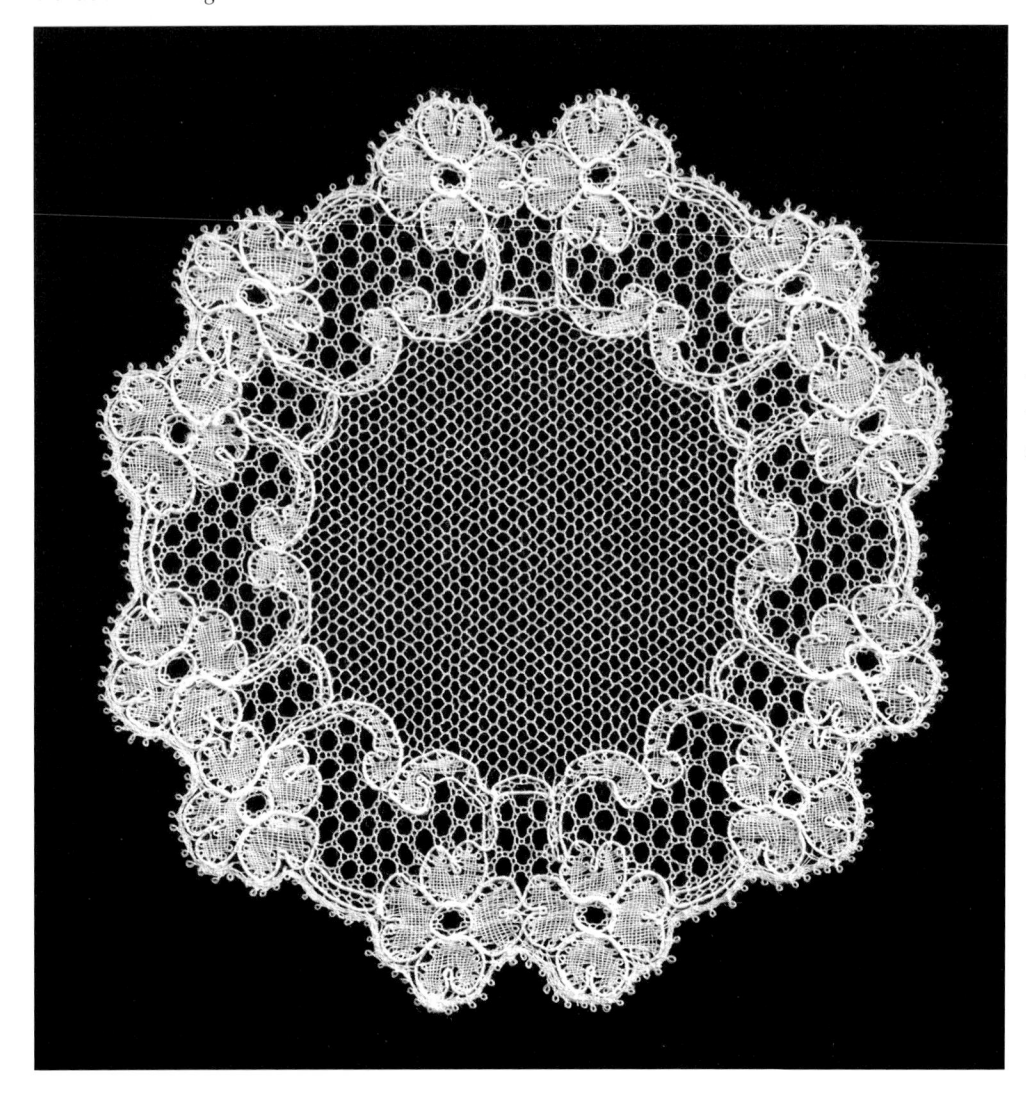

Figure 181 (left) An anniversary present worked top to bottom worked on pricking figure 180

Setting in for working the anniversary present top to bottom
This piece of lace is more advanced than Project 9 as every repeat around the edge is worked differently. In this piece set in the two top flowers independently using a mixture of false picots (F), with pairs slipped on (+1) and four pairs added effectively giving two pairs working in both directions (↓↓+2). (figure 182).

Figure 182 (right) Setting in the top petal on the left with false picots and pairs slipped on

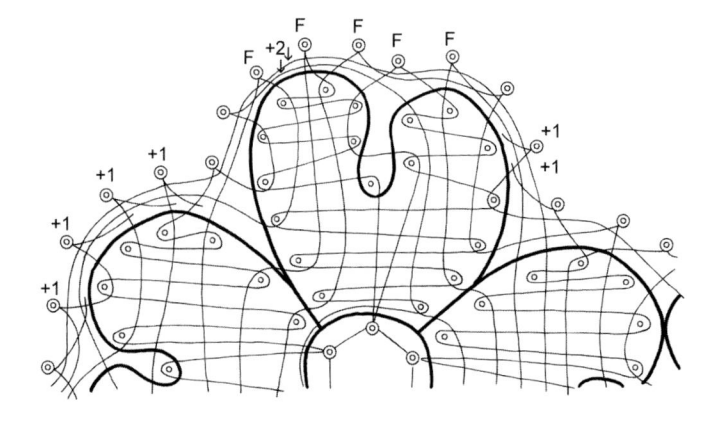

74

All about making—Floral Bucks Point Lace

Joining the top petals

Figure 183 shows just one way of joining the first petals but there are many other variations that work just as well. Look at the tricks I have used and start working, but it is not necessary to follow the diagram exactly. Although it was not common practice among the old lace workers we now add and remove pairs whenever it will improve the appearance, and with experience the need to do this becomes less. The flowers may be worked as mirror images, but not necessarily so. However, when the side petals meet and join together it looks neater if there is the same number of pairs crossing from each side to the other.

Fgure 183 (right) Joining the first two flowers.

F - false picot
+1 - slipped on pair

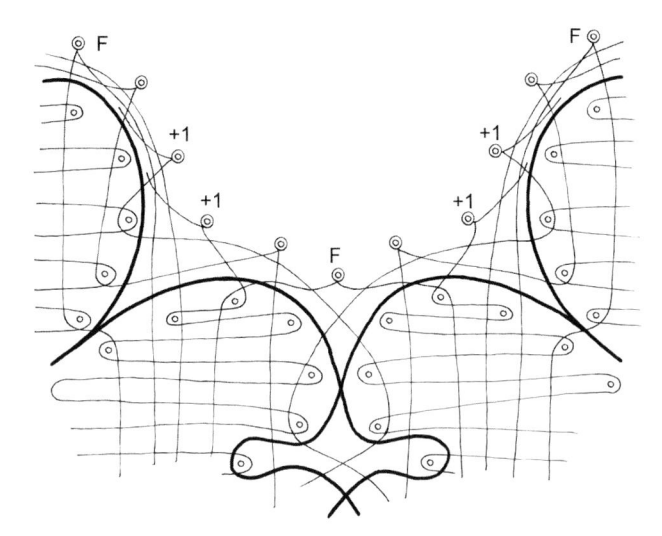

The scrolls

After working the stem as far as possible (figure 184) take the gimp around the head[3] (the nook pin, pin B, can be worked later using a long loop[4]). Work the first pin of the head. A pair will be required on the left to work pin A, but there is no pair available, therefore add a pair across the gimp (figure 185). Place a pair on any spare pin outside the gimp, pass the gimp through the pair, twist the pair and it is ready for use. Once the new pair has been used its support pin can be removed and take care to keep tensioning the gimp to prevent it becoming deflected by undue tension on the new pair.

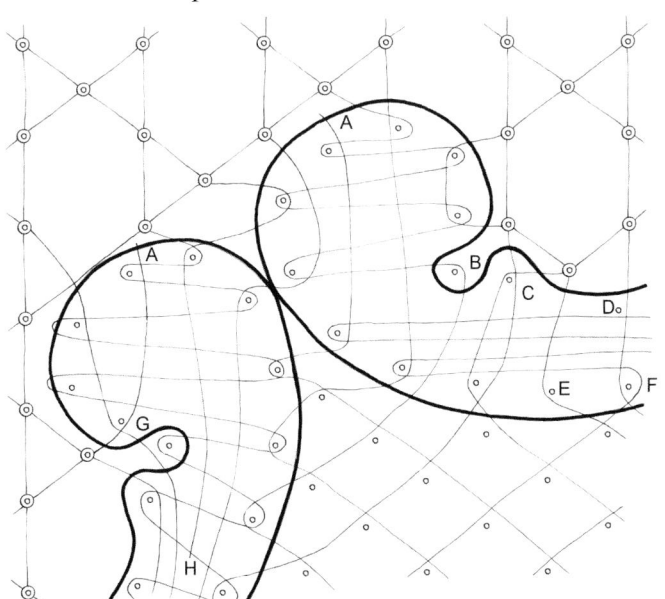

Figure 184 (left) The scrolls

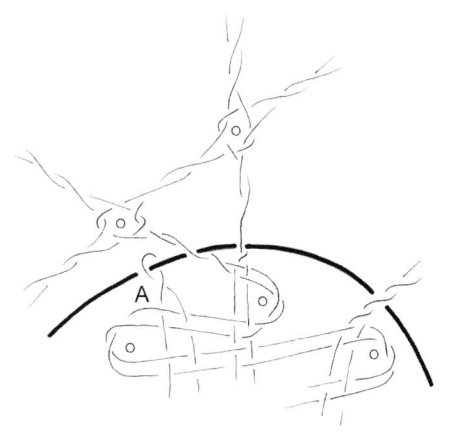

Figure 185 Adding a new pair across a gimp

75

All about making—Floral Bucks Point Lace

The first scroll of the last edge motif

This scroll poses several problems, in particular it has a wide curve above and below the clothwork.

Complete the head and work the nook pin, pin B, using a long loop. Two pairs enter across the gimp to pin C in the bump below the head, and this pin is better left uncovered (figure 186) so that these two passive pairs pass straight down. Pin D, to the right of the bump support pin, i.e. it is there to hold a pair in position; it does not support a stitch and pin E forms the same function as the pair leaves the stem. The clothwork in the scroll finishes at pin F and pin G is placed between two passive pairs and a stitch worked to cover it, the pairs then leave the scroll. In this case we have the same two pairs leaving without a stitch before the pin as we had entering at the bump without a stitch covering the pin, but this does not necessarily happen. Cross the gimps and work the second scroll (figure 187).

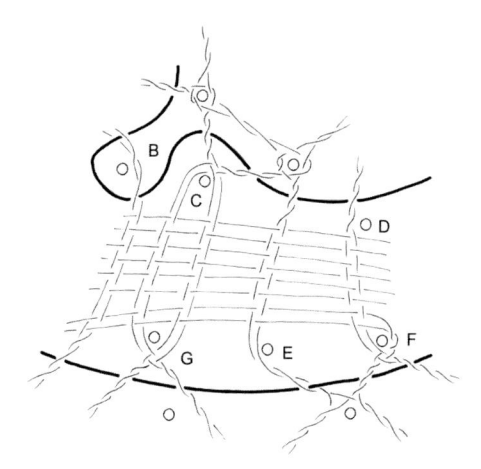

Figure 186 (left) Detail of the scroll

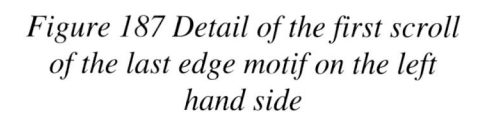

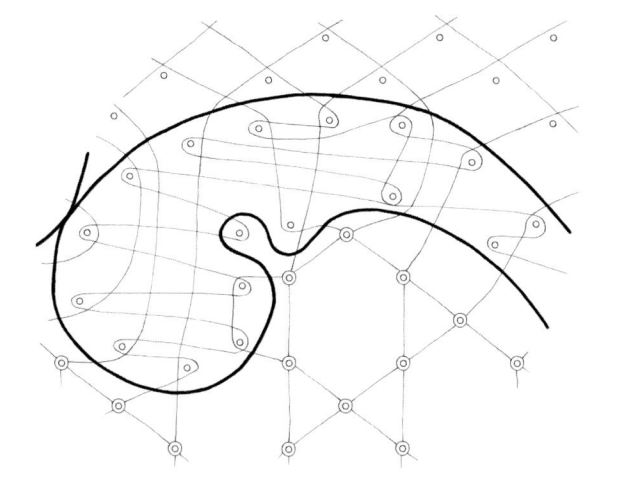

Figure 187 Detail of the first scroll of the last edge motif on the left hand side

END NOTES

1 Substituting threads
See Part 6.

All about making—Floral Bucks Point Lace

2 Working circular pieces
Circular Floral Bucks motifs may be worked in three ways. (1) The entire piece may be worked top to bottom as in the Anniversary Present Project No. 10 (figures 179 & 180) (2) The edging may be worked radially while the centre is worked top to bottom as in the Anniversary Present Project No. 9 (figures 172 & 174), or (3) the entire piece may be worked radially. Motifs worked radially[6] as type (3) require an angle of 60° for the ground and honeycomb and this angle is not appropriate for Floral Bucks, as traditionally the angle should be between 52° and 58° for ground and honeycomb; larger angles are usually used for kat stitch. When the edging is worked radially as type (2), while the centre is worked from top to bottom, the honeycomb areas align around the centre following the outer edge. When the piece is worked from top to bottom as type (1) all the honeycomb areas have that same alignment. The honeycomb areas lying across diagonals dividing the item into six sections can only be made when working entirely from top to bottom, not when the edging is worked radially even if the centre is worked top to bottom, because these areas would have to be divided with one half being worked in one direction and the other half worked another direction. This would not produce an acceptable design. Circular items worked top to bottom are said to gradually change shape with the circular shape becoming oval. I have not experienced this, even my piece made 25 years ago is still circular. Distortion may be a result of undue tension.

3 Working from top to bottom
When the lace is worked top to bottom (figures 179 & 180), the areas of honeycomb ground are all one direction; compare with figures 172 & 173 in which the honeycomb areas angle around the centre.

4 Awkward gimps and long loops
The traditional method of working is to add and remove gimps when necessary. For the scroll figure 181, the nook pin, pin B, cannot be worked until after the head has been made. Therefore a new pair of gimps is added and the head of the scroll made, then the nook pin can be set and the surplus gimp can be removed at a suitable time. Now that we no longer have the constraint of having to earn a living we have time for more time consuming techniques that produce improved results. In this case a long loop may be used for the nook pin.

5a Designing hexagonal mats
Place two plain rectangular mirrors fixed at 60° to each other on the edging so that the line through the centre of the 60° angle is at 90° to the footside and you will see a hexagon (figure 188). The mirrors are easier to handle if sticky tape is used to hinge them together.) The mirrors can be moved up and down and from side to side until a suitable design appears.

Figure 188 Designing with mirrors

All about making—Floral Bucks Point Lace

On tracing paper draw three lines that cross at the same point and have angles of 60° between them and crease these lines. Trace the gimps of the section of the pricking seen in the mirror and repeat in each section between the diagonals (figure 189). The equivalent footside for each tracing must be in parallel with one of the creases. Adapt or add motifs as required. In this piece honeycomb stem bridges have been added between the large scrolls.

Figure 189 Tracing with motifs in each section

All about making—Floral Bucks Point Lace

5b Developing the design into a hexagonal mat worked top to bottom
Choose a suitable grid and place so that all sections of ground and honeycomb will be worked top to bottom; the equivalent footside must be parallel to the vertical line through the mat. See Chapter 1, End Note 6 for adding ground and honeycomb. Draw the picot line (figure 190). The pinholes for clothwork and picots may be added at this stage or use a thin card for the pricking and prick 'as you go'.

Figure 190 Design with ground and honeycomb in the same direction and picot line added

All about making—Floral Bucks Point Lace

5c Developing the design into a hexagonal mat with the edge to be worked radially and the ground vertically.

Choose a suitable grid and place it in one section of the honeycomb so that the equivalent footside is at right angles to the horizontal line through that section. See Chapter 1, End Note 6 for adding ground and honeycomb or use a suitable section from the edging. Make photocopies of the motif and cut and paste in the other sections. The centre will be worked top to bottom so place the grid for this, which ideally should be the same scale and angle as the honeycomb in the motif, centrally with its equivalent footside parallel to the vertical line through the mat. Draw the picot line (figure 191). The pinholes for clothwork and picots may be added at this stage or use a thin card for the pricking and 'prick as you go'.

Figure 191 Design with ground, honeycomb and picot line added

6 Working a hexagonal shape in six sections with a point ground centre
Ibid., page 217.

CHAPTER 7

PROJECTS 11 & 12: Inserts with Floral fillings

Project 11: Book cover insert with mayflower filling
Project 12: Card insert with honeycomb and pin chain filling

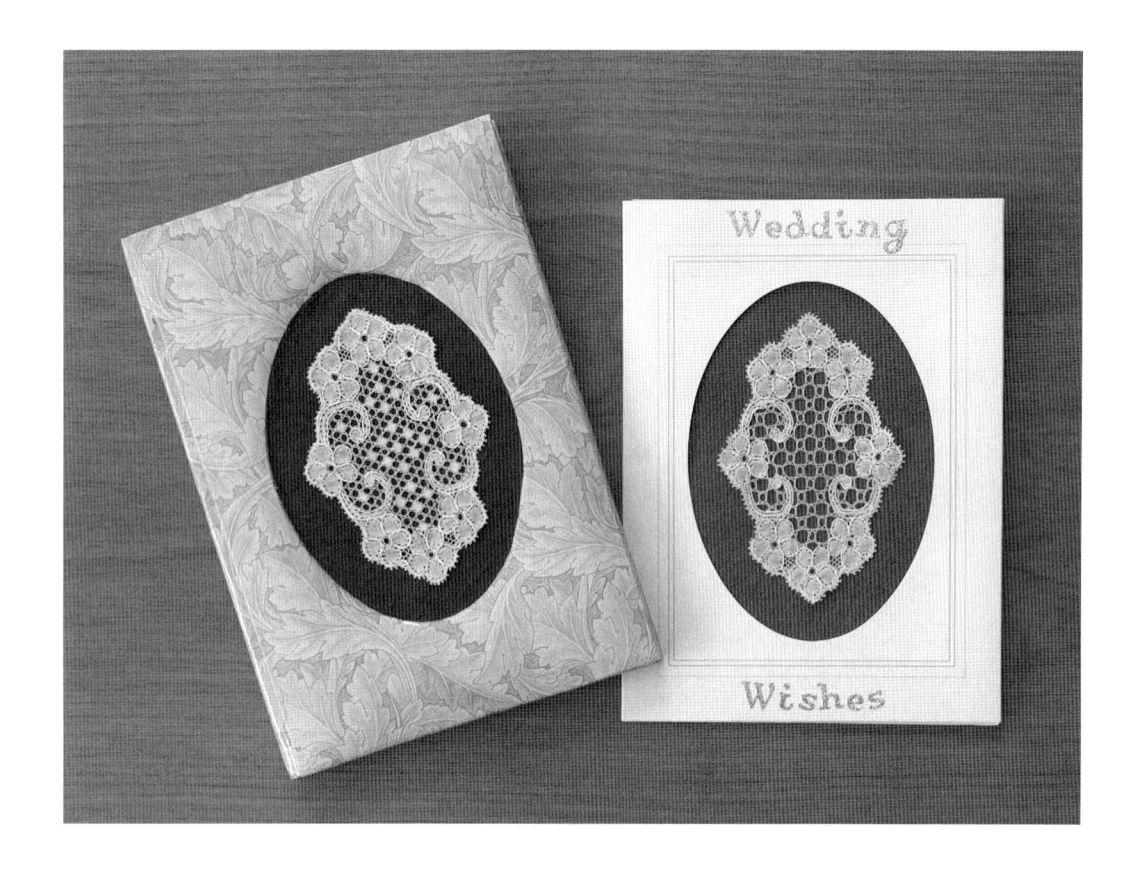

*Figure 192 (left) Book cover insert containing old mayflower filling
(right) Card insert containing honeycomb and pin chain filling*

Materials Required for Projects 10 & 11
Egyptian cotton no. 100/2[1], gimp D.M.C. perle no. 12
book or card with oval aperture 9.7cm (3¾ in) x 13.7cm (5³/₈ in)

Fillings
There are some Bucks Point fillings[2,3&4] that are more appropriate for use in Floral Bucks than in Geometrical Bucks. These include fillings that do not have all their pinholes placed true to the grid and those that result in a pattern of large holes that do not allow the pairs to pass in and out from the surrounding areas as required for Geometrical Bucks.

All about making—Floral Bucks Point Lace

PROJECT 11: Book cover insert with mayflower filling[2]

Materials Required for Project 11
Egyptian cotton no. 100/2[1]
gimp no. 12 perle
book with oval aperture
9.7cm (3¾ in) x 13.7cm (5³/₈ in)

Figure 193 (right) Book cover insert with old mayflower filling made on pricking figure 194

Figure 194 (below) Pricking for book cover insert figure 192

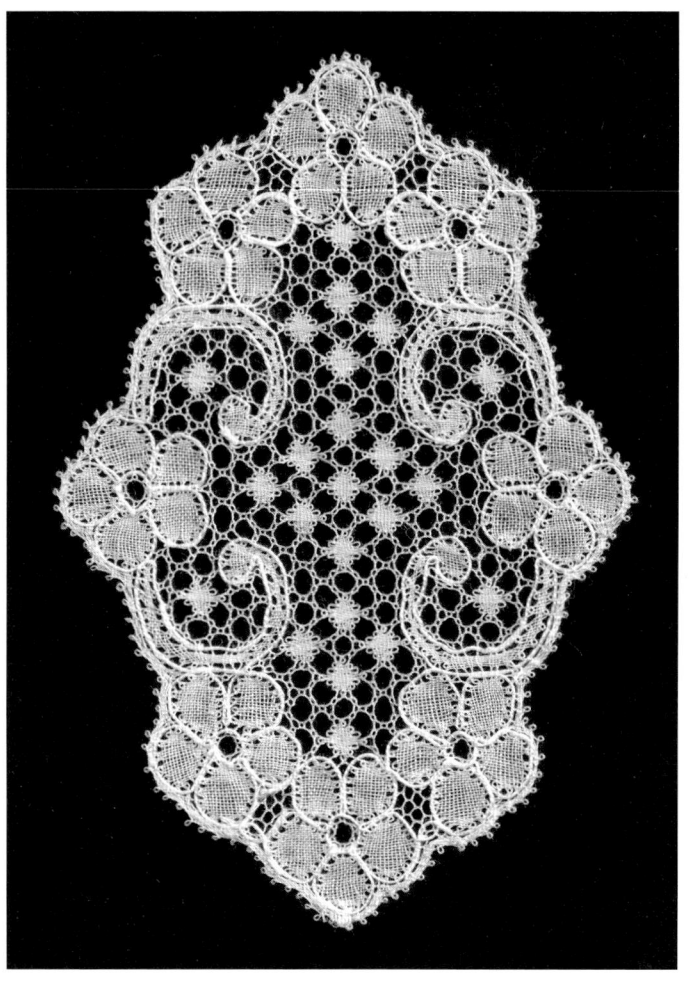

There are nook pins between the petals surrounding the honeycomb centre of the flower. Unfortunately due to the limitations of my computer and the printing these may be difficult to see.

Pattern repeats in Floral Bucks do not have to be made exactly the same and the same applies to the two sides of items such as this. Work the sides individually; they do not have to be mirror images of each other.

All about making—Floral Bucks Point Lace

Old mayflower filling
This honeycomb filling has a regular pattern of cloth stitch diamonds each having four pins per side (figures 195 & 196) and the traditional indicator, a cross, placed in the centre of each honeycomb ring that has been replaced by a cloth stitch diamond. These cloth stitch diamonds do not have pairs added at the third pin each side or left out at the pins following the widest point of the diamond. When a diamond overlaps a design motif it is not modified, instead the remaining area is filled with honeycomb stitches. As in this piece, mayflower diamonds may be grouped as a shape within the honeycomb filling.

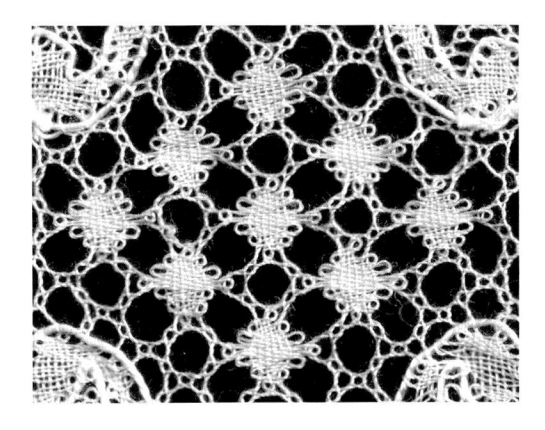

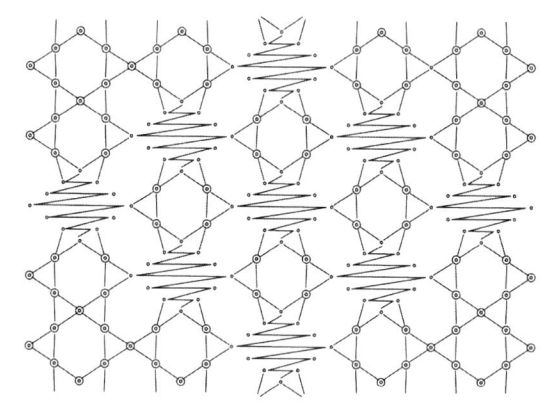

Figure 195 Old mayflower filling

Figure 196 Old mayflower filling

All about making—Floral Bucks Point Lace

PROJECT 12: Card insert with honeycomb and pin chain filling[3&4]

Materials Required for Project 12
Egyptian cotton no. 100/2[1]
gimp D.M.C. perle no. 12
card with oval aperture
9.7cm (3¾ in) x 13.7cm (5³/₈ in)
acetate window to protect lace
self-adhesive silver letters

Figure 197 Card insert containing honeycomb and pin chain filling, pricking

Figure 198 (right) Card insert containing honeycomb and pin chain filling made using pricking figure 197

Honeycomb and pin chain filling[3&4]

This honeycomb filling has a single pin chain on each side of each ring. (figures 197 & 198) and this filling will need to be modified when incomplete units overlap the edge of the clothwork. Traditionally there is no indicator for this filling but I have found that placing a ring in the centre of each honeycomb ring makes it easier to follow. Because this filling has unusually large holes there will be times when there will be no pairs available to enter or leave the design motifs. When this happens the gimp may need binding on or pairs may need to be added to or removed from the clothwork.

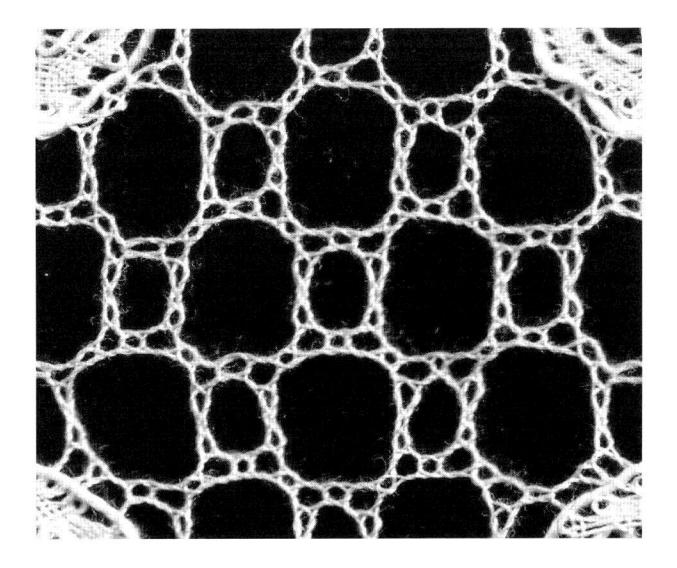

Figure 199 Honeycomb and pin chain filling

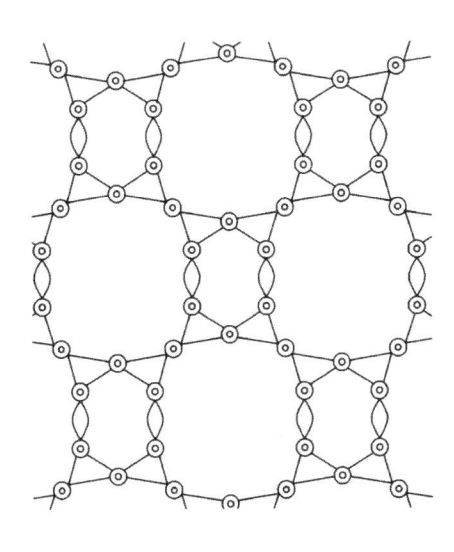

Figure 200 Honeycomb and pin chain filling

key () - pin chain

Substituting fillings
This is easy. Photocopy the pricking and cut out the area of filling along the gimp lines. Choose a filling with a similar angle and similar spacing between the pins. Place under the hole in the pricking checking that it is in line vertically, is symmetrically placed and the pins around the edge are in the best positions. Secure the two pieces of paper together and photocopy. Pins of the filling adjacent to the gimps may be moved slightly to avoid gaps or balance the space between stitch and gimp; this is accomplished more easily when making the lace than when preparing the pricking.

END NOTES

1 Substituting threads
See Part 6.

2 Old mayflower filling
The term 'mayflower' is considered by some to be a pattern of diamond shaped cloth stitch blocks each with four pins per side and set in honeycomb ground, as opposed to the variation which has only three pins each side of the diamond. It is also considered by some to apply to the honeycomb with a pattern of diamond shaped blocks with four pins each side and not to a single cloth stitch block. However, the majority of lacemakers now use this term for a single diamond-shaped block with either three or four pins per side as well as a filling of diamond-shaped blocks in honeycomb with either three or four pins per side. I have called the version with four pins per side 'old mayflower filling' to distinguish it from the newer version with three pins per side. See '*All about making—Geometrical Bucks Point Lace*' A. Stillwell, Salex Publishing, page 153, 162 figures 413-415.

All about making—Floral Bucks Point Lace

2b Drafting old mayflower filling
The cloth stitch diamonds usually replace alternate honeycomb spaces along alternate rows of honeycomb.

1 From an area of honeycomb filling for each mayflower remove the dot in the centre of each side of the diamond (ringed) (figure 201).
2 Then each dot that was removed is replaced by two equally spaced dots. Add the indicators (figure 202).

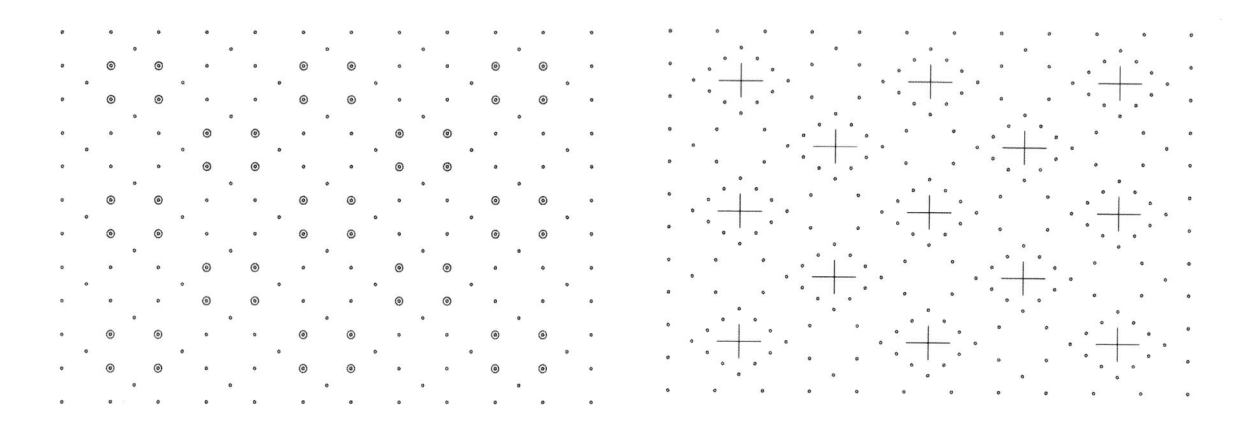

Figure 201 Centre dots along the sides of the diamond, ringed, removed

Figure 202 Each dot removed replaced by two dots equally spaced along that side

The two new dots replacing the single dot of each side no longer fit the geometrical grid, hence the filling fits the definition of Floral Bucks. However, when the boundary of the filling is honeycomb, the filling may comfortably be used in a Geometrical Bucks pattern.

3 Pin-chain
Ibid., P 99, 110.

4 Drafting honeycomb and pin chain filling
Using the same point ground grid as the rest of the pricking draw honeycomb rings around every third pinhole along a horizontal row. Then a row of rings below with their centres between the rings of the first row and their upper pinholes on the row below the lower pinholes of the first row (figure 203).

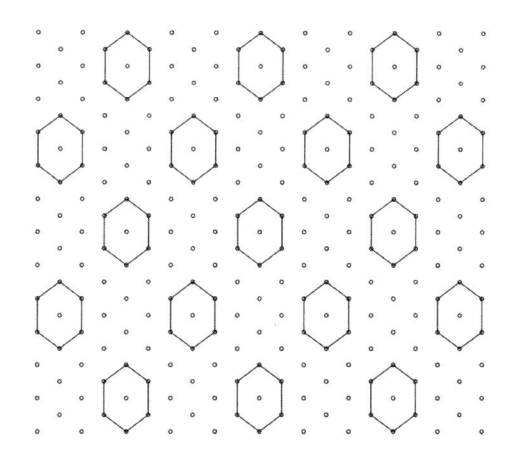

Figure 203 Honeycomb rings

86

All about making—Floral Bucks Point Lace

Remove all the dots except those of the honeycomb rings (figure 204). Draw construction lines connecting the lower pinholes of the honeycomb rings of one row with the upper pinholes of the row below and then add a pinhole at the mid-point of each construction line (figure 205). These pinholes do not match the original grid therefore this is by definition a Floral Bucks filling, also this filling is not suitable for use in Geometrical Bucks since the large holes between the honeycomb rings do not allow for pairs to be available for surrounding design motifs.

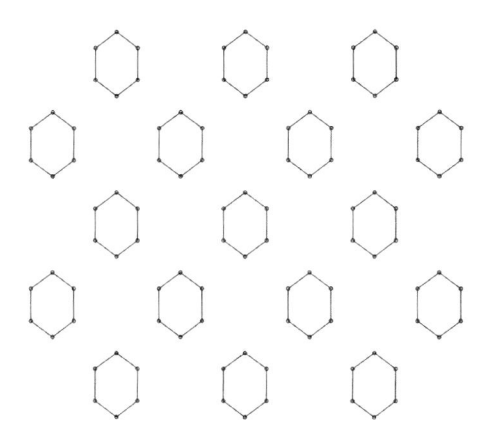

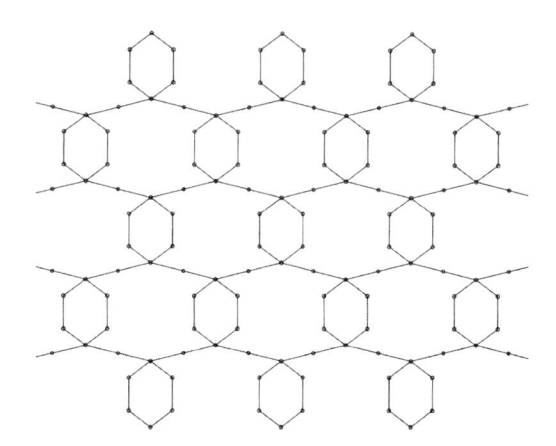

Figure 204 Honeycomb rings

Figure 205 Connecting lines added and pinholes placed at the mid-points of these lines

Finally remove the construction lines and, if you wish, insert circular indicators within the honeycomb rings (figure 206).

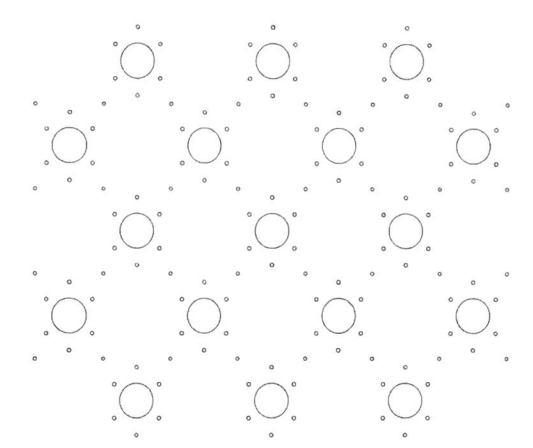

Figure 206 Construction lines removed and indicators added

CHAPTER 8

PROJECT 13: Designing a shaped jabot

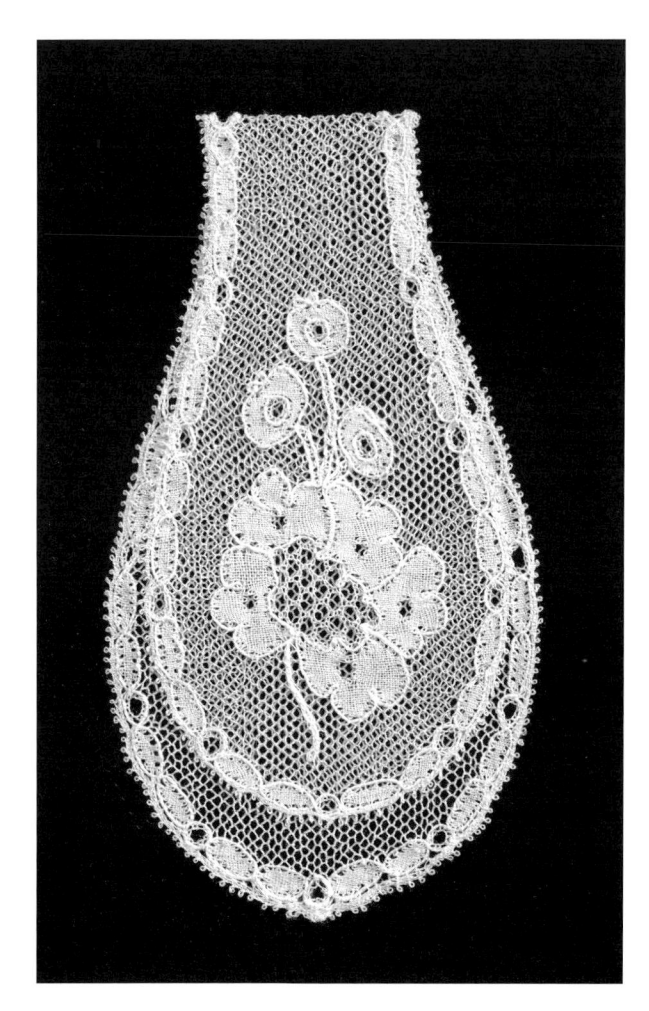

Materials Required for Project 13
Egyptian cotton no. 60/2[1]
gimp D.M.C. perle no. 8
cotton net 15cm X 30cm
to match lace thread

Figure 207 (left) Shaped Jabot.

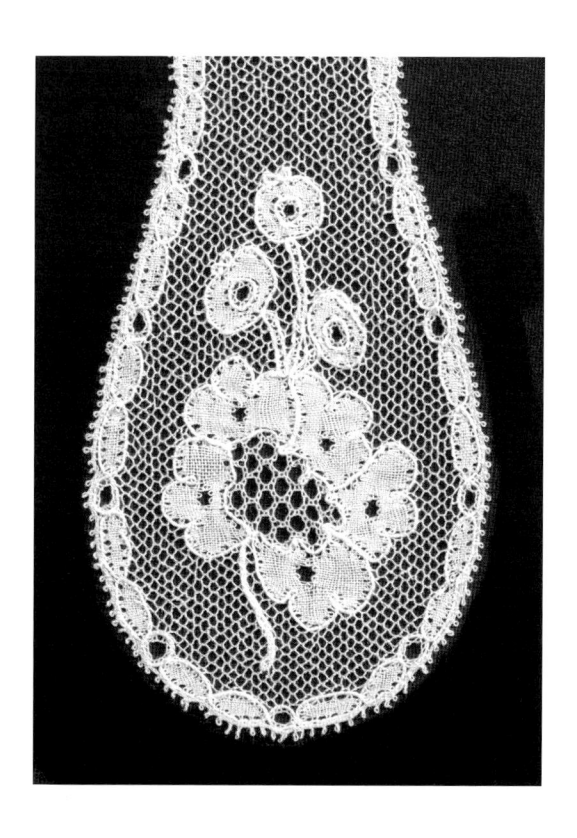

When the jabot is folded and the motif of the top layer overlays the layer beneath (figure 207) there is interference between the honeycomb and the underlying ground. This interference produces a pleasing effect no matter how the two parts are aligned.

Figure 208 Shaped Jabot, detail

The chosen thread [1] is the thickness that would have been used by the lace workers so that the jabot can be made without adding or throwing out pairs and the final piece will be strong and wear well. However, we now make lace for our own enjoyment and prefer finer thread than would have been formerly used, even if it means adding and throwing out pairs; we have the time. If you prefer to use a finer thread and add and leave out pairs it is your choice.

All about making—Floral Bucks Point Lace

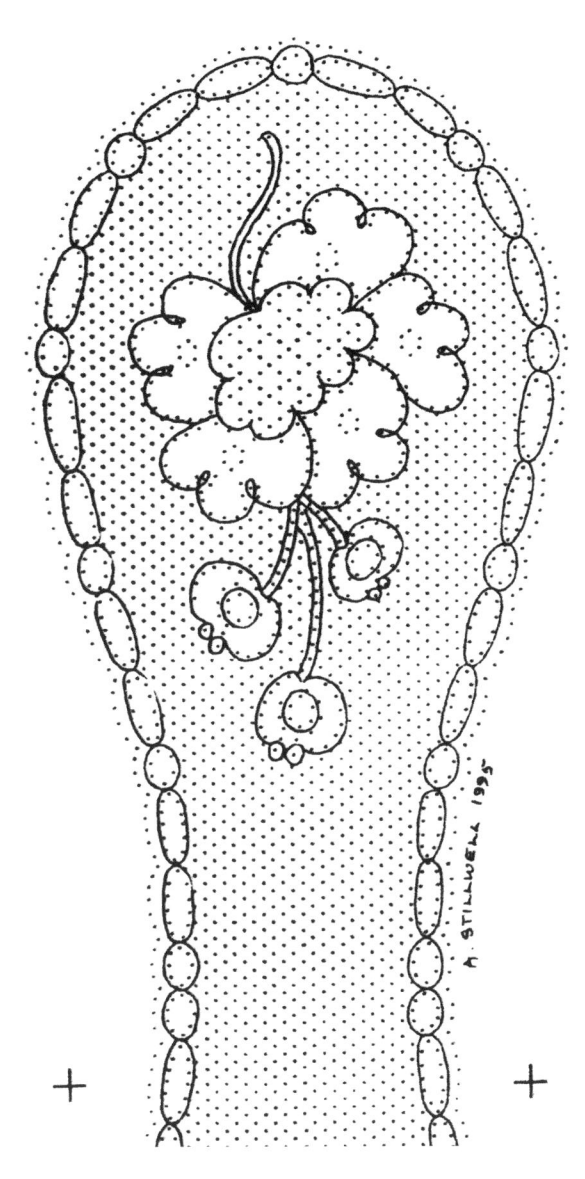

Figure 209a (left) Jabot, pricking

Figure 209b (below) Jabot, pricking

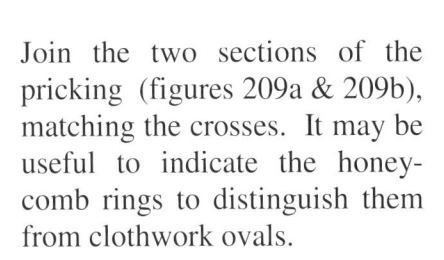

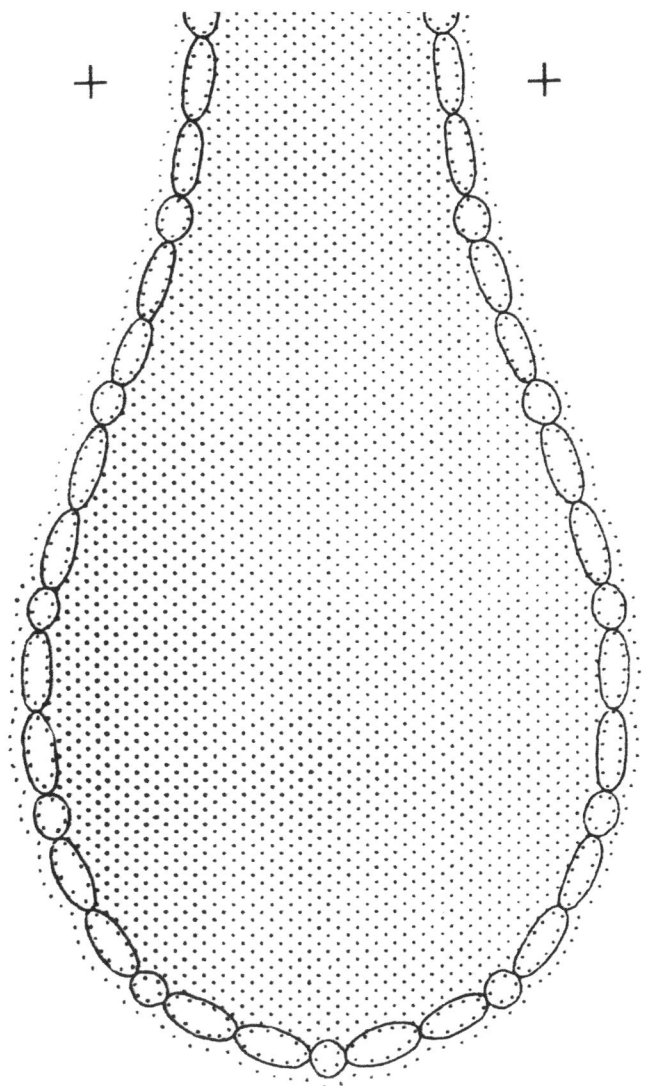

Join the two sections of the pricking (figures 209a & 209b), matching the crosses. It may be useful to indicate the honeycomb rings to distinguish them from clothwork ovals.

89

All about making—Floral Bucks Point Lace

Setting in
Set in using the techniques previously described. Note that I made a pin-chain at the left side of the honeycomb ring (figure 210) and added two pairs working in two directions between the lower two honeycomb stitches.

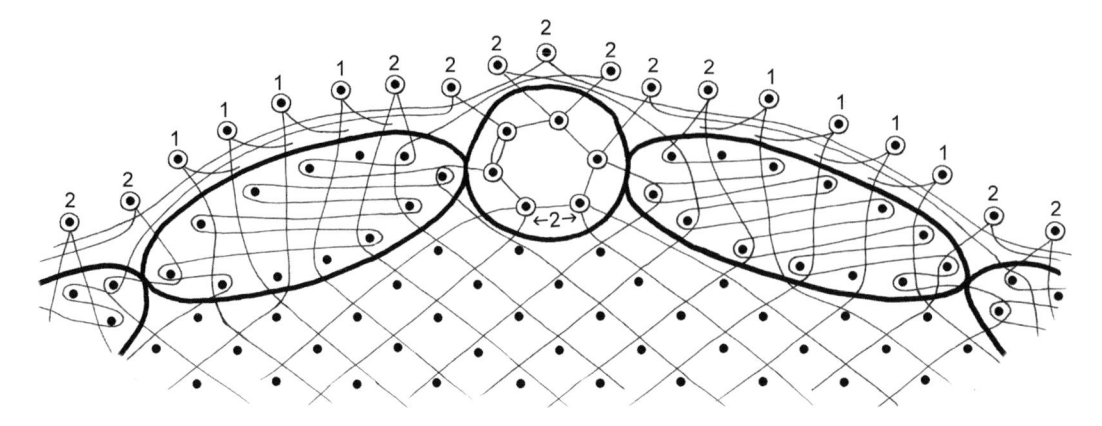

Figure 210 Setting in

Continue making the jabot using techniques explained in the previous chapters, and add any ideas you have that will achieve the result you are looking for. Now is the time to take the plunge. Work without any instructions, use your own judgement and make this Floral Bucks Point jabot as it should be made.

Designing the jabot
I started by preparing a paper pattern of the item (figure 211) and then cutting out the shape in net (or other soft fabric) (figure 212) and trying it on to make sure it looks and fits properly. Paper does not move the same way as net or fabric and this stage is especially important when designing a collar.

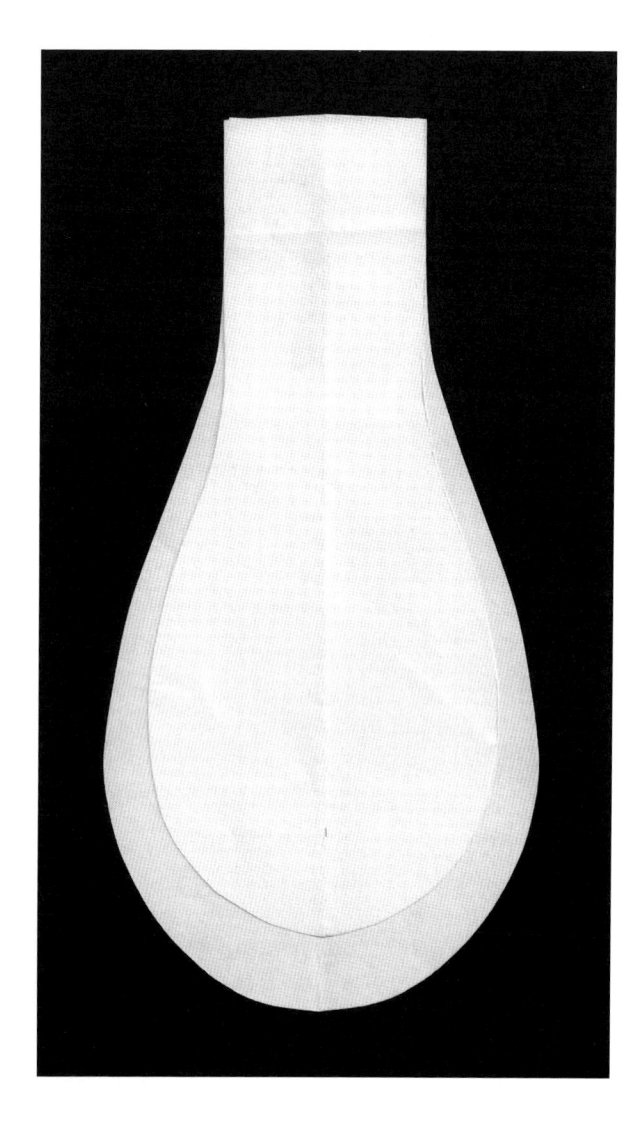

Figure 211 Paper pattern (reduced)

All about making—Floral Bucks Point Lace

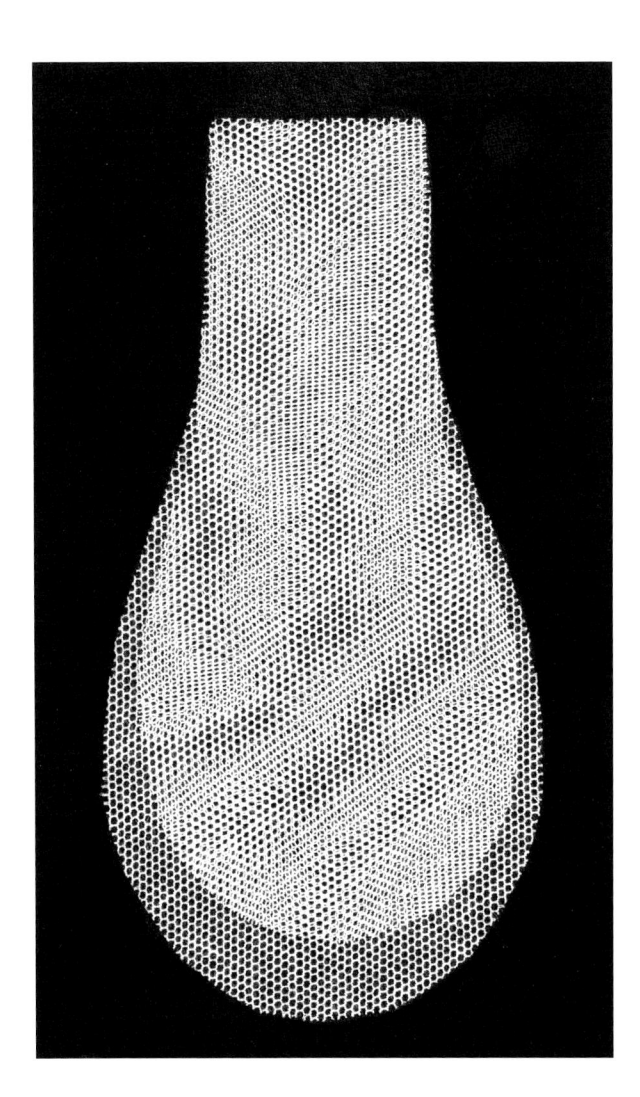

Figure 212 (left) Pattern cut out of net (reduced)

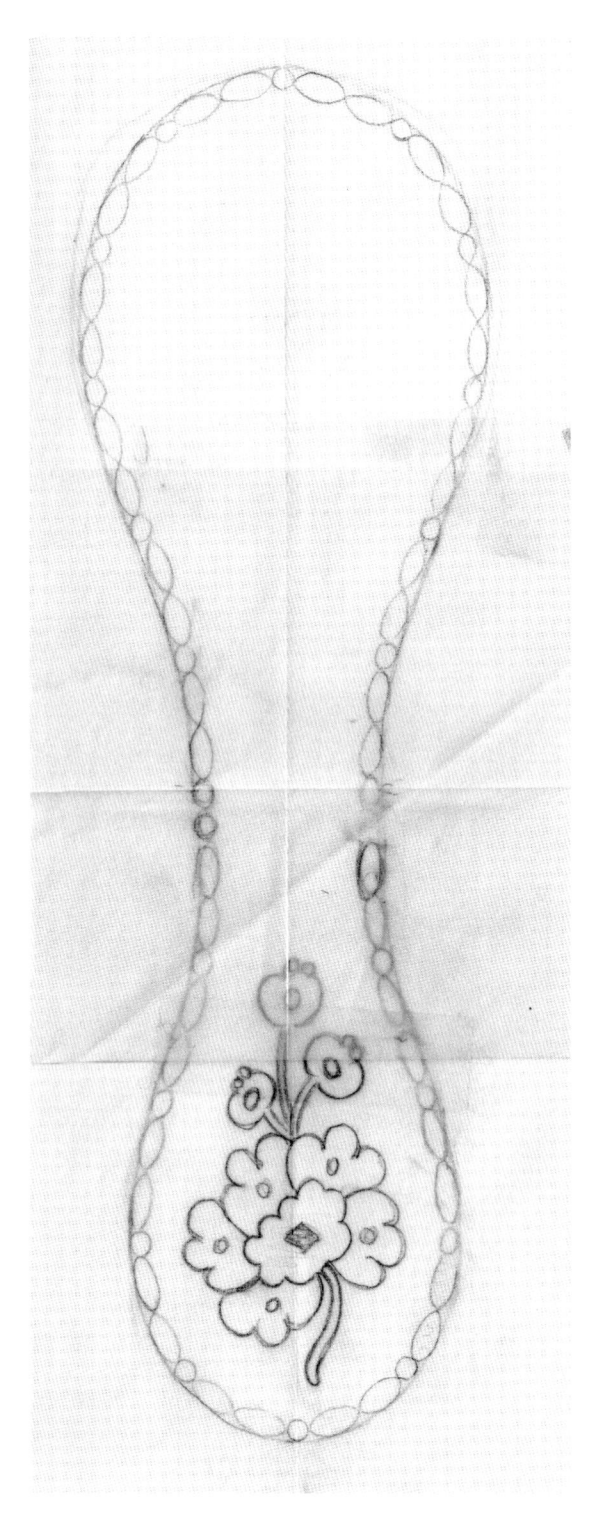

I drew rather more than half the shape on one piece of paper, rather more than the other half on another piece and attached them together using repositional tape (i.e. tape with weak tack that would allow me to separate the tracings and move them against each other to reposition them). I drew some simple shapes to form an edging using a combination of honeycomb rings and clothwork ovals. Then I started from the two ends and using two tracings allowed me to adjust the shapes where they met (figure 213).

Figure 213 Jabot tracing with edging of honeycomb rings and clothwork ovals and flower motif (reduced)

All about making—Floral Bucks Point Lace

My chosen design was the Flower, page 220 'Chinese Folk Designs' by W.M. Hawley, pub. Dover 1949 (figure 214). But the fruits were not in the best position for my jabot shape so I traced the flower (figure 215) and fruits (figure 216) separately, rearranged them under the tracing of the jabot edging and then carefully drew them on the jabot tracing (figure 213).

I retraced the edging and flower, tidying them up, went over the tracing with a fine felt tipped pen and erased the pencil lines (figure 217).

Then I chose a grid with a suitable angle and spacing for my chosen thread and placed the penned tracing of the border and flower over it (figure 218).

Figure 214 The flower

Figure 215 Flower, (reduced)

Figure 216 Fruits, (reduced)

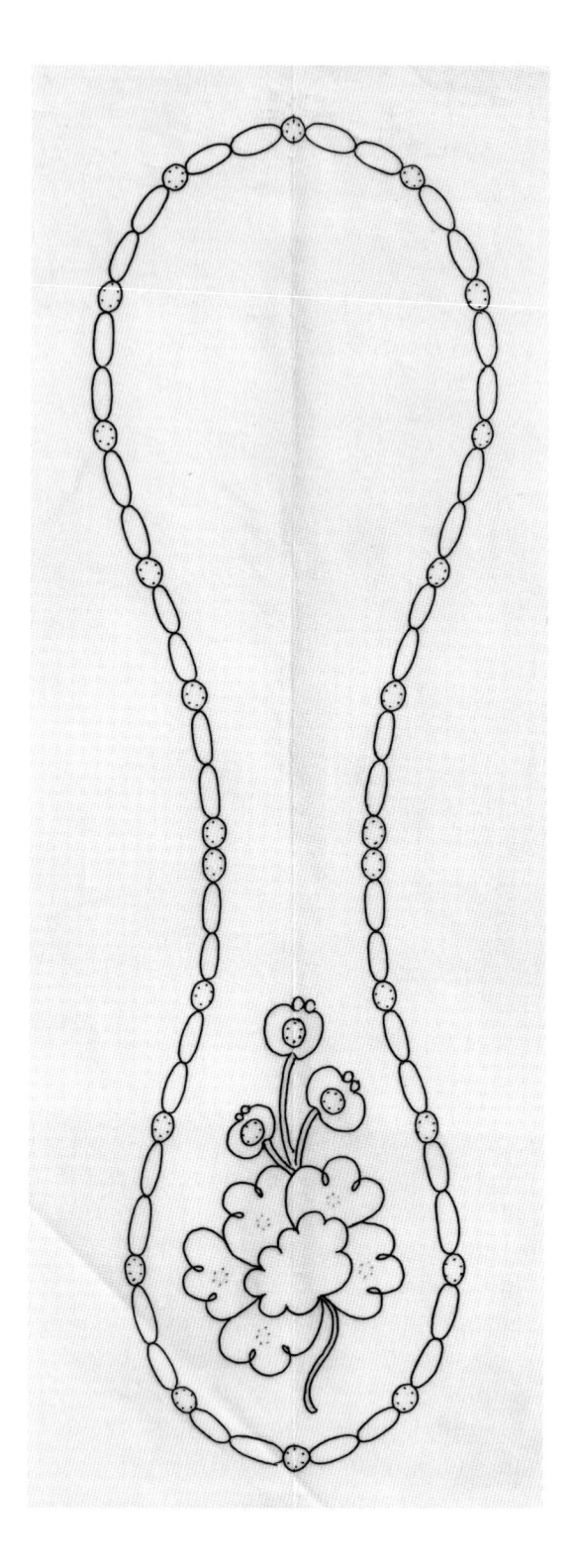

Figure 217 Tracing of the edging and flower redrawn in pen, (reduced)

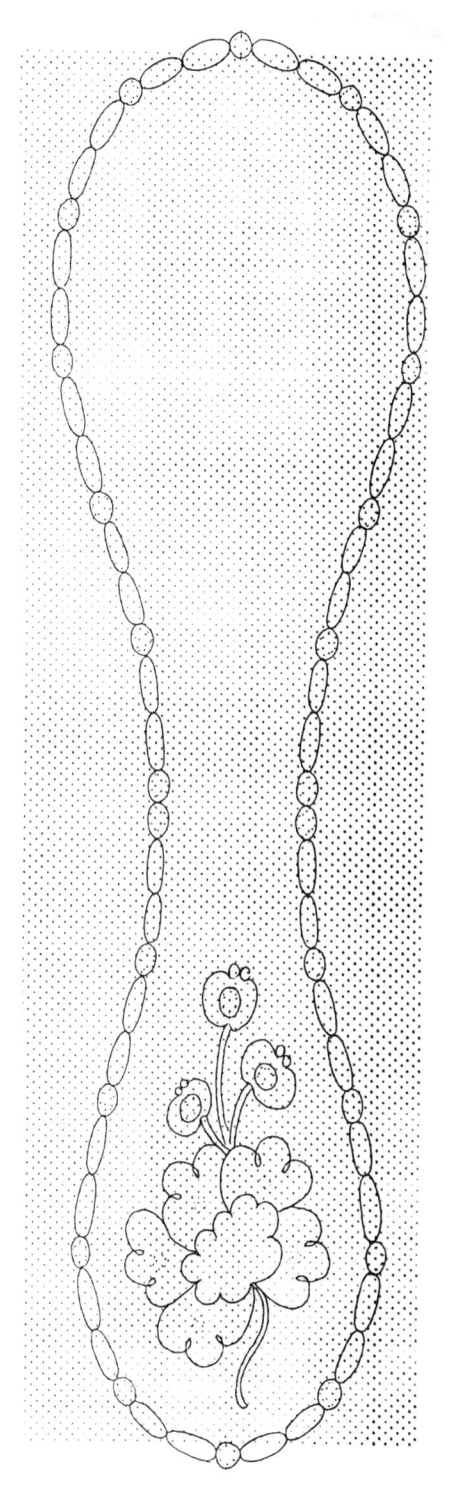

All about making—Floral Bucks Point Lace

I made a photocopy of the tracing and dots (figure 218), removed the dots within the motif using Tippex and trimmed away the dots from around the edging. I used a template of honeycomb filling adapted from the ground and placed it in the best position within the flower (figure 219).

Figure 218 (left) Tracing of the edging with the flower and fruits flower placed over a grid, (reduced)

Judging the positions of the dots within the motifs is not easy and they may be moved as required when making lace. This does not mean that the original positions are necessarily incorrect, you may simply be using a different thread, working from a different direction, or using a different technique.

Finally write your name along the edge of the pricking and add the symbol © and year if you wish to protect your copyright (figure 209).

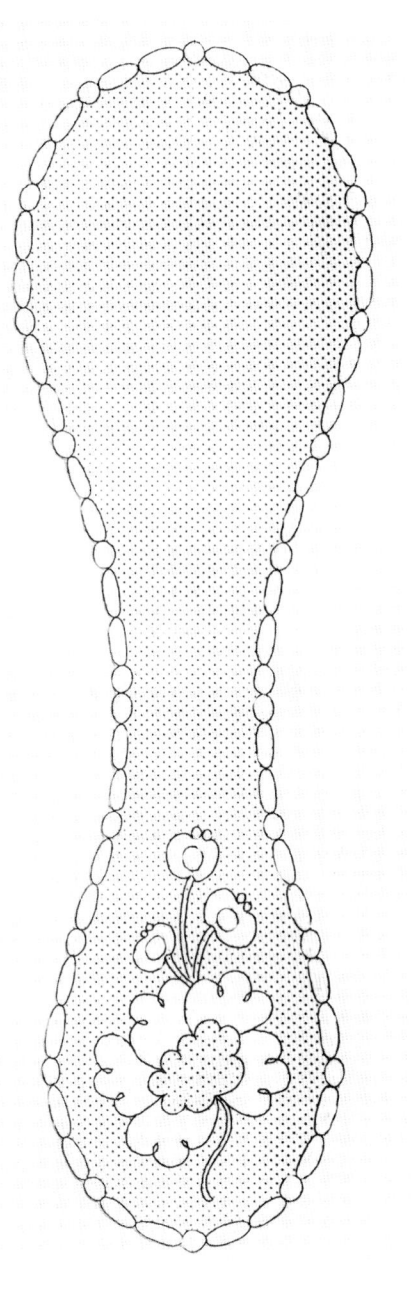

Figure 219 Photocopy of the tracing of the edging and flower with unwanted dots removed and honeycomb filling added, (reduced)

END NOTES

1 Substituting threads
See Part 6.

All about making—Floral Bucks Point Lace

CHAPTER 9

PROJECT 14:   Tray insert made in three strips connected by fine joining

Figure 220 Tray with lace insert

Materials Required for Project 14
Egyptian cotton no. 120/2[1]
gimp D.M.C. perle no. 12
two fine tapestry needles (nos. 26 or 28) or ball-ended needles
tray with 28.5cm (11 in) x 16cm (6¼ in) aperture

Wide pieces of lace take large numbers of bobbins which create logistical problems; they take up time to move them around and when they are layered or bundled they can cause the lace to rise up off the pricking. To avoid these problems the lace workers would make the lace in strips and join them with fine joining[2] or raccroc stitch[3], and these joins may be noticeable as irregularities looking like 'flaws' passing through the ground (figure 222). Also, for some reason, maybe the tension on the joining thread is greater or the friction of the thread passing through the eye of the needle may damage the thread, these joins frequently weaken allowing the strips to part company along all or part of the join.

The pricking for this tray insert (figure 221) has two vertical lines of pinholes through the ground that are missing. This allows the bobbins to be divided and the lace worked in three separate sections, each with a manageable number of bobbins. Later on the three sections come together again and the lace is completed. Finally the strips are connected by fine joining.

Figure 221 Tray insert made in three strips connected by fine joining, pricking

All about making—Floral Bucks Point Lace

Figure 222 Tray insert made in three strips connected by fine joining made on pricking figure 221
Note: There are two vertical 'flaws' where the strips have been joined. In the past a highly skilled specialist would have sewn the joins.

All about making—Floral Bucks Point Lace

The pinholes adjacent to the join
The pinholes for the loops along the edge of the strips need adjusting to allow for thickness of the pins[4].

The loop edge of the ground adjacent to the join
Only one thread arrives at, passes round the pin at the edge of the strip and returns. For practice make a pricking (figure 223). Work a row of ground[5] as far as setting up pin 1. Take a single new thread, T, make a cross with this thread and the nearest one from the adjacent pair and twist the new thread three times with the other thread of the pair; set up pin 2 under the cross. Set up pin 3 under the new edge thread (figures 223-225). When the loop edge is on the other side of the strip ensure that the edge thread makes a cross when it works with the ground pair. Work two strips to practicing joining.

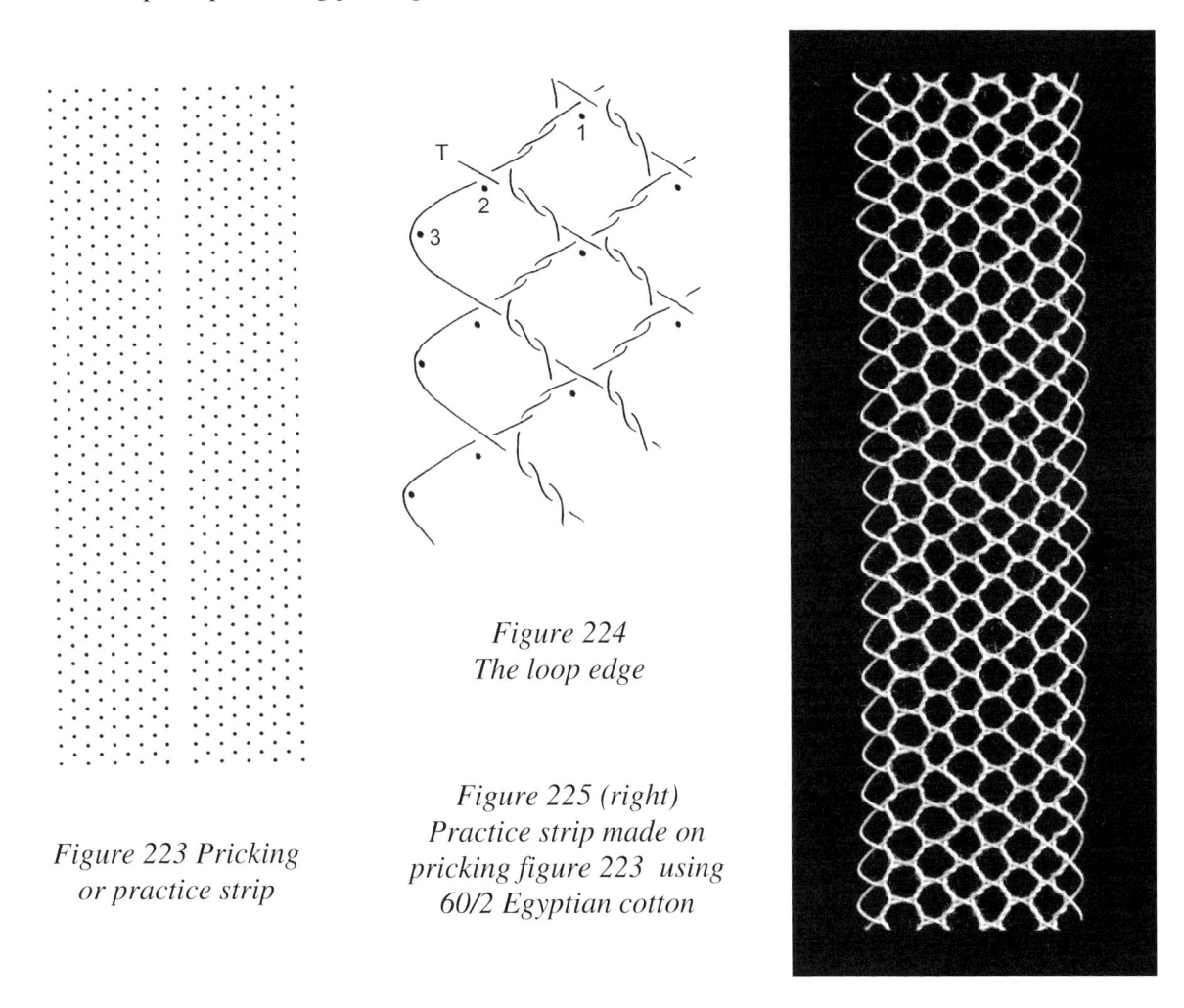

Figure 224
The loop edge

Figure 223 Pricking or practice strip

Figure 225 (right) Practice strip made on pricking figure 223 using 60/2 Egyptian cotton

Fine joining
Complete both strips that are to be joined and remove all but a row of pins 5-6 rows from the inner edge of each strip. It is easier for right-handed workers to progress upwards and left-handers to progress downwards. Pin a cover cloth over the pins; as you progress you may need to insert other pins to steady the work.

All about making—Floral Bucks Point Lace

Lacing two strips together
Thread two fine tapestry or ball-ended needles each with a length of lace thread and attach to the lace at the lower end of the opening. Pass the right thread over left at 1 (figures 226 & 227). Pass the current left hand needle up through the next two loops on the left, loops 2 & 3. Leave this needle and pass the current right hand needle down through the next two loops on the right, loops 4 & 5, pass this needle thread over the other needle thread at 6 and pass this needle up through the previous one used on the left, loop 3, action (7), and up through the following one on this side, loop 8. Return to the current right hand needle and pass it down through the previous loop used on the right, loop 5, action (9), and down through following loop on the same side, loop 10. Pass this needle thread over the other needle thread at 11. Continue for the length of the lace and fasten off both threads securely.

Tensioning the lacing
Tension each mesh as it is made so that the holes of the lacing become the same size as the rest of the work by gently pulling up the needle threads while holding the free strip between thumb and forefinger of the other hand and gently pulling it sideways away from the other strip to balance the tension on the needle threads. Do not rush this stage; it will take practice to get the work even.

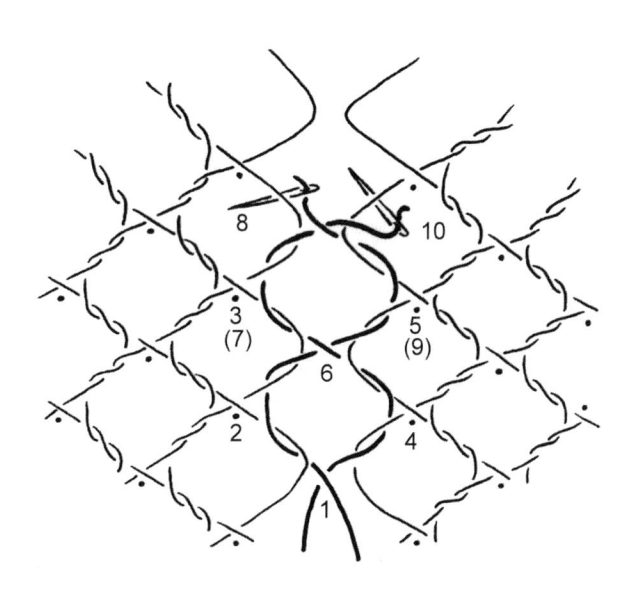

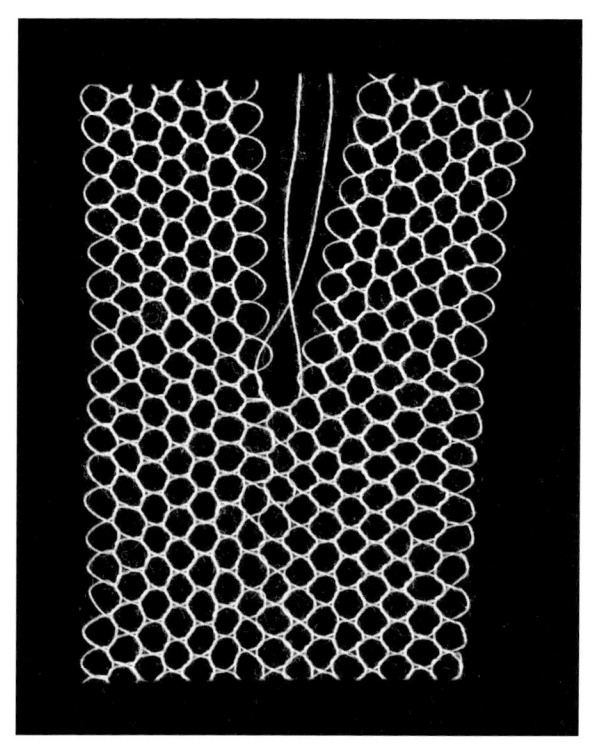

Figure 226 Lacing two strips together

Figure 227 Lacing two strips together

All about making—Floral Bucks Point Lace

Making the tray insert.
Set in at the top as usual and work as far as the gaps in the ground. Separate the bobbins into three groups, those for the central strip of the ground and a group on each side. Secure each side group into a bundle and pin out of the way. Continue working the central strip, making loops each side for the fine joining. When the lower ends of the gaps are reached secure these bobbins out of the way. Return to one of the side groups and continue working down, making loops at the inner edge and adding pairs at the outer edge as required and then throwing them out as the work narrows. Work as far as the end of the gap, secure this group out of the way and repeat for the other side group. Then amalgamate the three groups and finish as usual. Finally lace the sections together (figures 222). Assemble the tray, including the lace insert, according to the manufacturer's instructions.

END NOTES

1 Substituting threads
See Part 6.

2 Fine joining
Fine joining is the almost invisible join between two strips of lace, each with a loop edge, that make large pieces of lace possible. When one piece has a loop edge and the other twisted loops, the needle lace raccroc stitch (point de raccroc) is used for joining the strips. This name is now sometimes used for fine joining.

3 Raccroc stitch
Using a strip with a loop edge and another with six twists at the edge and place side-by-side on a pillow with the single loops on the left of the gap. Replace a vertical row of pins 5-6 rows from the left edge of the right hand strip and pin a cover cloth over the pins. As you progress you may need to insert other pins to steady the work. Thread a fine ball-point needle with a length of lace thread and fasten on. Starting from the lower edge pass the needle up through the first loop on the left, loop 1 (figure 228). Pass the needle down through the first six-twist two loop of the right strip, loop 2, so that it exits the loop below the thread coming from loop 1, at 3. Pass the needle up through loop 1 again (action 4), and up through the following one on this side, loop 5. Pass the needle down through the next six-twist two loop of the right strip, loop 6 so that it exits the loop below the thread coming from loop 5, at 7. Pass the needle up through loop 5 again (action 8). Tension the join carefully as you go. Continue for the length of the strips and fasten off the thread securely.

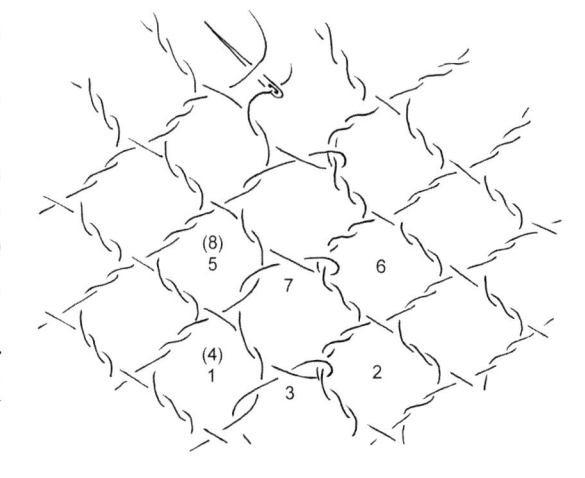

Figure 228 Raccroc stitch

All about making—Floral Bucks Point Lace

4 Positions of the loop pins along the edges of the strips

The point at which the cross of a point ground stitch occurs is directly above a pin. When a row is removed and the adjacent rows used for the loops just as they are, pins 1-4 (figure 229) then, since the join will occur at the side of the pin not at the actual position of the centre of the pin, the loops will be slightly larger than required. To compensate for this the pins need to be moved very slightly so that the edge of the loop just reaches the centre of the original pinhole, pins 5-8.

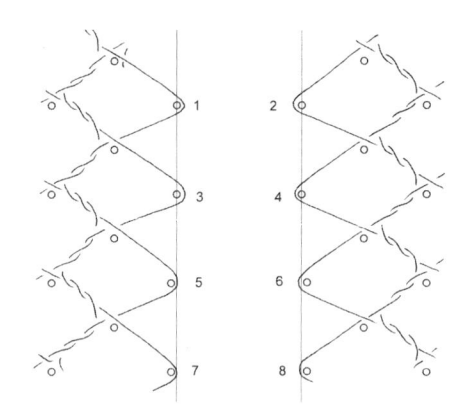

Figure 229 Adjusting the loop pins. The vertical lines are through the standard pin positions, pins 5-8 are adjusted

5 Ground with two twists

When the joins are examined the 'pairs' of threads involved in the join have the appearance of only two twists between the pins and there are some pieces of antique lace that have been made with all the ground made with only two twists between the pins[6] so that they match the join. However, the majority of pieces of antique lace that I have studied have the standard three twists. Using a pricking for point ground work each stitch as half stitch, twist, pin (cross, twist, twist, pin) (figures 230 & 231). As you can see from the illustration of the lace I find that this version of point ground is very difficult to get even and, although I have a very light tension, 24 hours after my sample was taken off the pillow it had shrunk 20% across its width. This cannot be called a 'two-twist ground'. The machine-made ground made as standard point ground was called 'two-twist net from the lace workers' definition 'half stitch and two twists'.

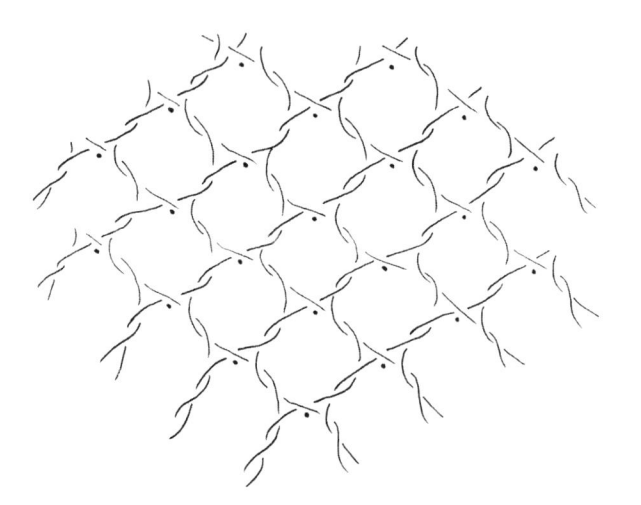

Figure 230 Point ground made with only two twists between the pins

Figure 231 Point ground made with only two twists between the pins

6 Antique lace with point ground made with only two twists

See Point de Raccroc, Ann Day, Lace 45/36-46/36

All about making—Floral Bucks Point Lace

PART 2

KAT STITCH

also called French Ground and Wire Ground

This ground, developed in the Flemish laces of the mid 17th century, the modern version being Point de Paris, is quicker to make than the same area of point ground. It is coarser in appearance than point ground and has a different 'feel' when making it. Widely made in Victorian times it was frequently made in black with half stitch for the 'clothwork' (figures 232 & 233) but it was also made in white and with cloth stitch areas. Some prickings have wording on them indicating that they are to be made in kat stitch and some that they are to be made in black thread.

Figure 232 Lace with kat stitch ground worked in white thread

There are certain differences between a pricking intended for point ground and those for kat stitch. Point ground prickings have pinholes in the clothwork corresponding to most pinholes of the ground surrounding it, but most prickings for kat stitch have approximately twice that number[2]. When the number of pins within the clothwork is similar to that of the pinholes in the ground surrounding it then two pairs will usually be left out or added at a pin. When there is a comparatively larger number of pinholes for the clothwork a fine thread compatible with the clothwork should be used, even though the footside pins are comparatively widely spaced. The angle to the footside is usually greater than that for point ground prickings, with 60° to 65° being the most popular. Areas of point ground and fillings are usually spaced closer than those of the kat stitch area and they usually have a different angle. The footpins are not usually off-set, although this may improve the final appearance. Not all these characteristics are present in every kat stitch pricking, but if there are some of them in a pricking it is a fairly reliable indication that kat stitch may have been intended.

All about making—Floral Bucks Point Lace

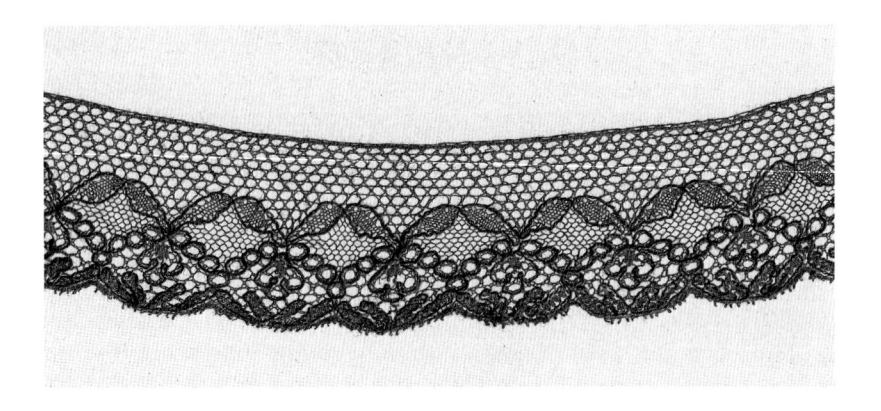

Figure 233 Lace with kat stitch ground worked in black thread

All about making—Floral Bucks Point Lace

Materials Required for
Kat stitch ground and footside sample
Egyptian cotton no. 60/2 or 80/2[1]

Starting line
The easiest starting line is along a diagonal working downwards from the footside. Kat stitch has an arrangement of continuous and gap rows similar to honeycomb filling and it is usual to start with a continuous row.

Setting in along a continuous row
Place a number of linked pairs on support pins above the pricking and starting from the right work a whole stitch round the pin at the footpin and twist both pairs, adding an extra twist to the edge pair to make two twists on this pair.

Figure 234 Pricking for kat stitch ground and footside

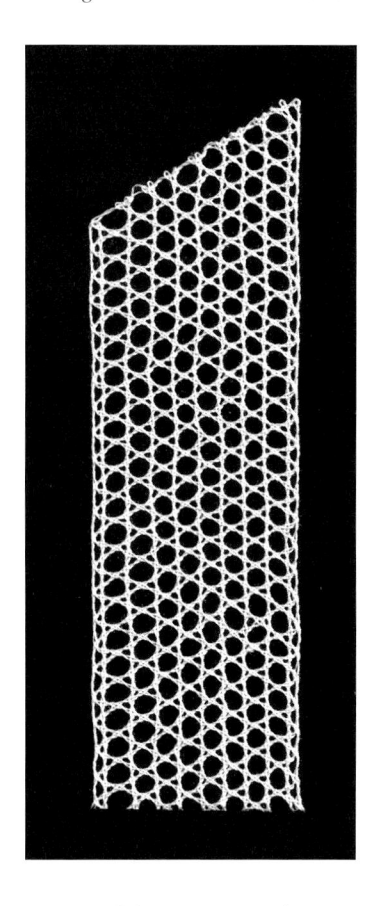

Figure 235 Lace made on pricking figure 229 using Egyptian cotton no. 60/2

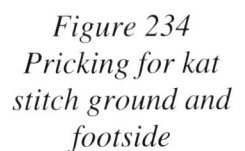

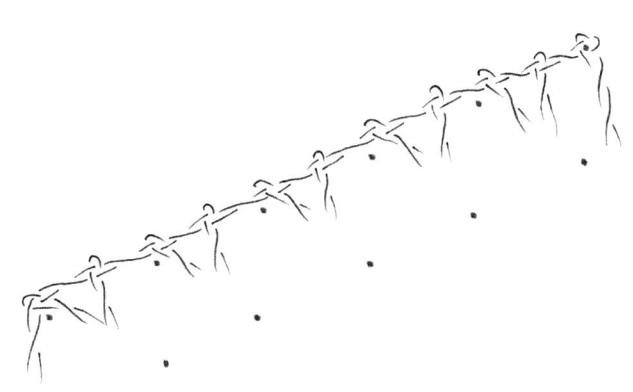

Figure 236 First continuous row

The kat stitch footside may have one or two passive pairs worked cloth and twist, this sample was made with one footside passive pair each side. With the left hand pair work a continuous row towards the left making cloth and twist with each new pair, but pinning only after each second stitch[2] (figure 236). The pins are left uncovered.

103

All about making—Floral Bucks Point Lace

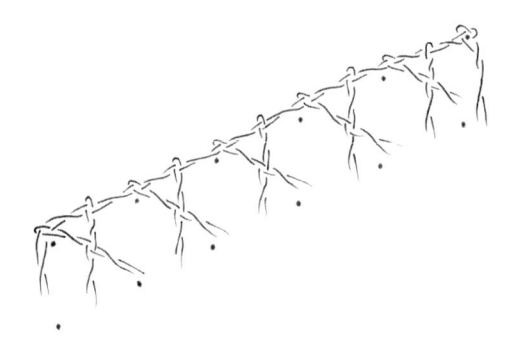

Figure 237 The first gap row

Gap row
Work cloth and twist with each set of two pairs that are separated by the pins; no pins are set and the pins are not covered (figure 237).

To continue
Starting from the footside work the next continuous row. Using the third pair from the right, cloth and twist through the next pair on the right and pin under the right pair. Cloth and twist the two edge pairs, making two on the new edge pair. With the other pair from the edge stitch work cloth and twist through two pairs and pin to the left of the two pairs. Continue working cloth and twist with each pair down the row pinning only after each second stitch (figure 238). The pins are left uncovered. Then work a gap row (no pins). Continue making alternate continuous and gap rows, pinning only the continuous rows, until you are completely comfortable making the ground.

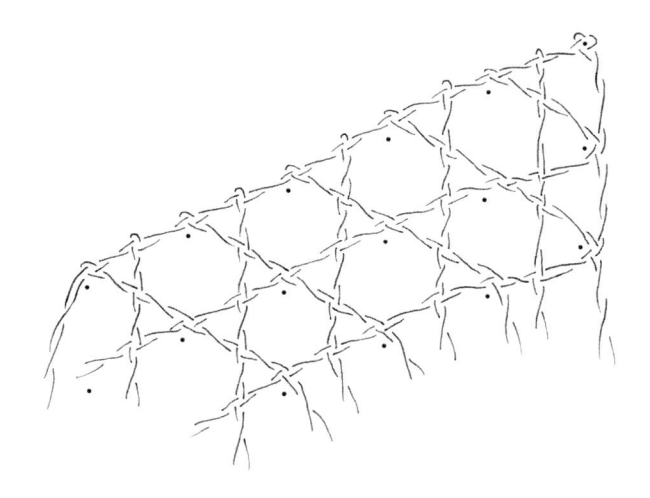

Figure 238 Kat stitch ground

1 Substituting threads
See Part 6.

All about making—Floral Bucks Point Lace

CHAPTER 10

PROJECT 15: Matching edging and insertion

Project 15a: Edging
Project 15b: Insertion

PROJECT 15a: Edging

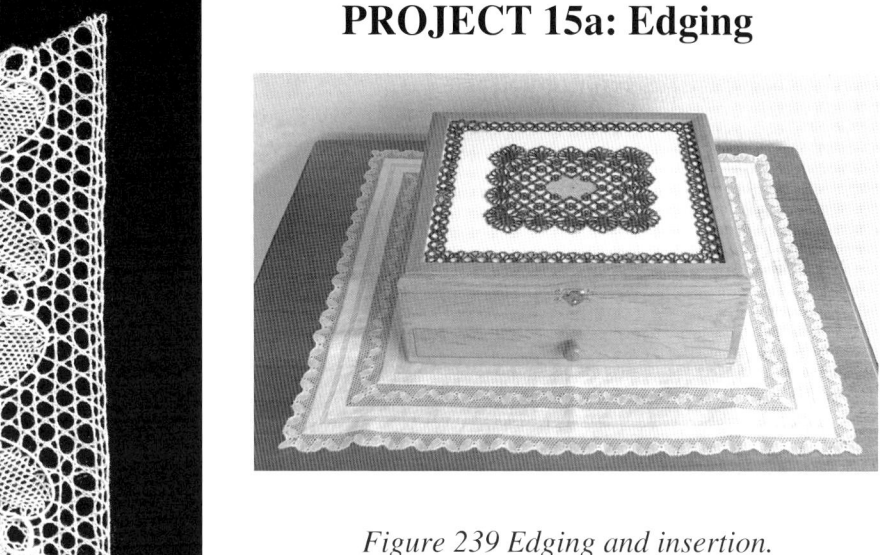

Figure 239 Edging and insertion.

The pricking (figure 242) has approximately twice the number of pinholes within the clothwork compared with the number of corresponding pinholes for the ground surrounding it^3. This edging was made with half stitch motifs, but may also be made with cloth stitch motifs.

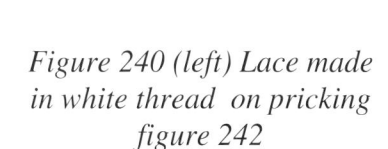

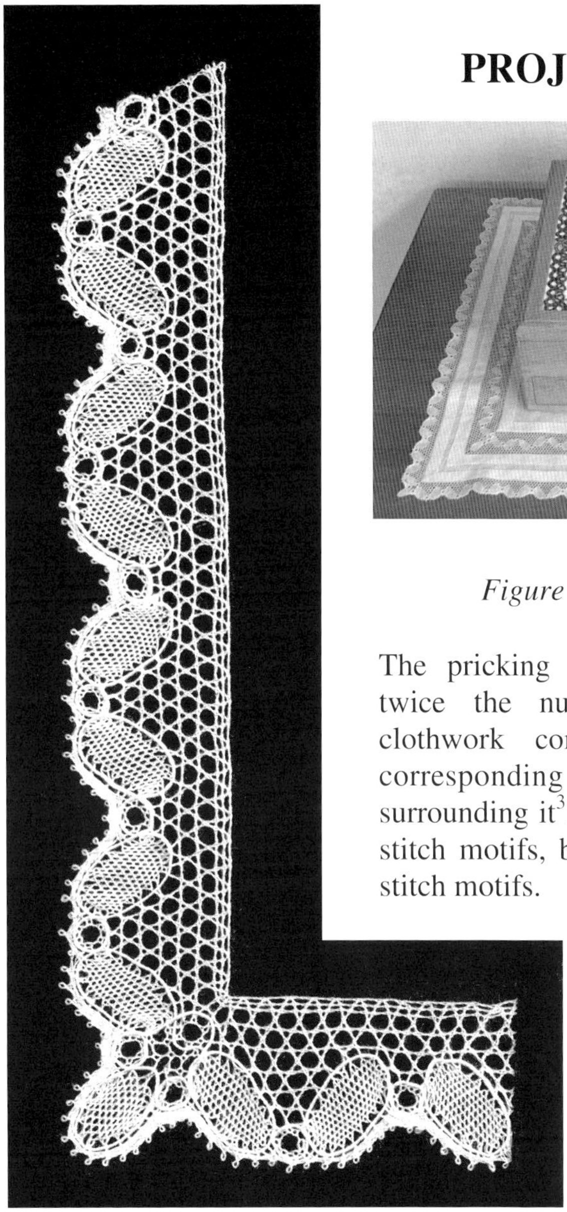

Figure 240 (left) Lace made in white thread on pricking figure 242

Materials Required for Edging Project 15a
Egyptian cotton no. 80/2^1
gimp D.M.C. perle no. 12
cotton fabric for centre

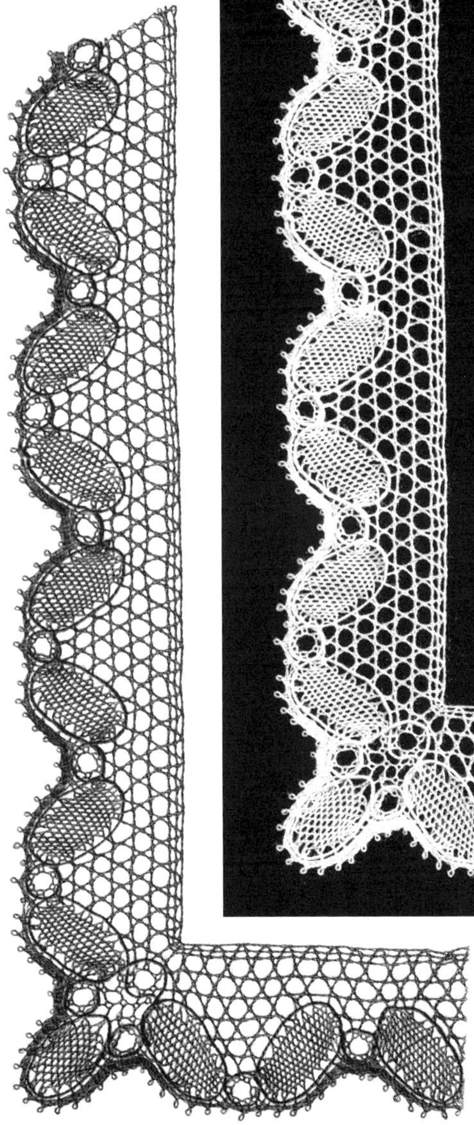

Figure 241 (far left) Lace made in black thread on pricking figure 242

105

*All about making—*Floral Bucks Point Lace

Starting line

The easiest starting line along a diagonal travelling down from the footside has been used for this sample but, when making an edging that will be joined end to start my preferred starting line is through the corner so that most of the joining will be along the gimps. I also used half stitch for the oval as would have been used when worked in black and also frequently found in kat stitch worked in white, although much of the black lace was originally made in white and then dyed.

The edging (figures 240 - 242) and insertion (figures 248 - 250) have two footside passive pairs. When starting a continuous row from the footside use the fourth pair from the right and cloth and twist through the next two pairs (the footside passives) to the right then pin after the second stitch. Cloth stitch and twist the two edge pairs, making up the twists to two on the new edge pair. With the other pair from the edge stitch work cloth stitch and twist back through three pairs and pin to the left of the third stitch. Continue working cloth and twist with each pair down the row pinning only after each second stitch (figure 243).

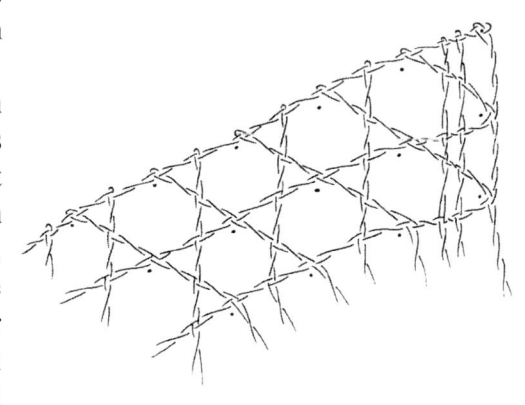

Figure 243 Kat stitch with two pairs of footside passive pairs

Start and work the six-pin honeycomb ring (figure 244) before working the last pin of the kat stitch row. The pair leaving the ring from pin A will work that last pin, pin C, of the kat stitch row before re-entering the ring to work the second pin on that side of the ring, pin B. Note that I show a pair lying along the gimp down the right side of the ring. This need not be introduced until the oval of half stitch is started but may lie along this gimp in later repeats. There are approximately twice as many pinholes along the side of the oval as pins in the kat stitch row adjacent to it, allowing one pair at a time to be taken into the oval. After completing the last continuous kat stitch row start the gap row, pins D-F, stopping where the oval swings away from the row to allow a new row to start. Work the oval of half stitch until the pair that can enter from the gap row has been taken in at pin G. This pair is immediately left out and works through two pairs from the gap row stitch and one from the next continuous row approaching from the right, pin I. Continue working the oval taking in pairs at pins J and K and adjusting the angle of pin K to give the best line.

Figure 242 (left) Kat stitch edging, pricking

All about making—Floral Bucks Point Lace

Then leave out a pair after each of the following pins L, M and N. Work the gap row stitches under the gimp and continue the continuous row from the right to pin P.

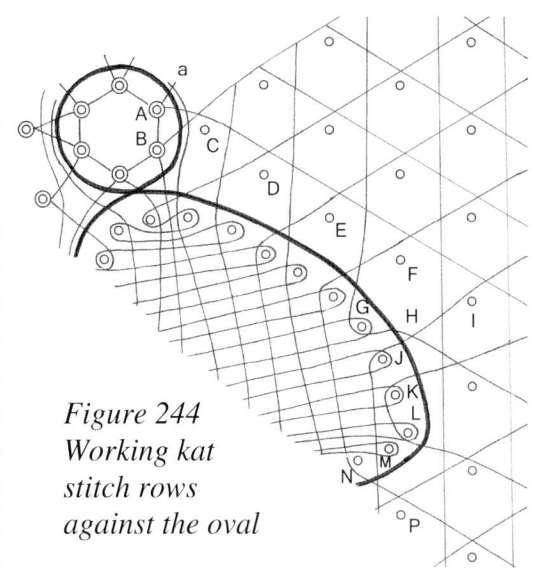

The next oval (figure 245) starts with a pair from the last honeycomb stitch of the ring and one from the ground, pin A. The latter does not appear to be the correct one at first glance but is necessary to preserve that line of the ground. There are two pairs on the right from the ring, one that has travelled down the gimp and one from its lower side pin. I took the one from the gimp to work the next row of half stitch to pin B, the one from the lower pin of the ring and I took along the gimp to be used later. Continuing the half stitch the next pair to enter is a vertical pair at pin C, then a diagonal pair at pin D. This pair is immediately left out to work a gap row stitch with a vertical pair and then a continuous row stitch with the next diagonal pair which is pinned at E. There are no pairs entering or leaving at F and the pair lying on the gimp can be taken in here. A gap row stitch is worked with the diagonal pair approaching from pin E and the pair is taken in at G. The half stitch continues with a pair being left out after each successive pin. A gap row is worked under the oval starting with the pair from pin G working with the vertical pair that just missed the end of the oval, stitch H, then each two pairs leaving the oval are worked together in turn, stitches I-K.

Figure 244 Working kat stitch rows against the oval

Figure 245 Working kat stitch rows

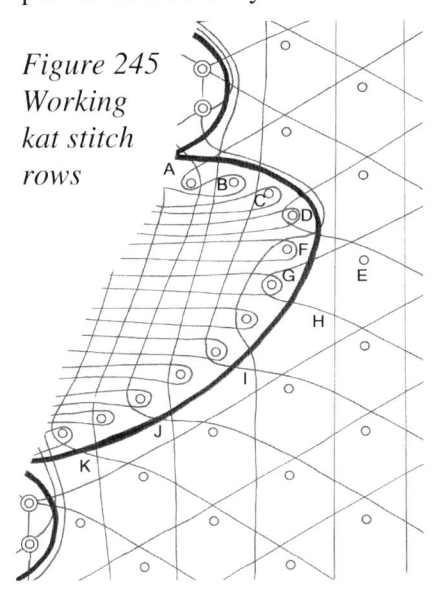

Corners in kat stitch are similar to those for point ground patterns. For this pricking the last row, pins A, B & C (figure 246), ends with a footside at pin D, the first use of the corner pinhole. The row leaving the half stitch area and starting the row at pin E works one stitch, pin F, of a row with the pair leaving the footside at pin D. The pair working from pin D to pin F enters the honeycomb ring and makes a honeycomb stitch at pin G with the vertical pair entering from its left. The vertical pair on the left of pin E enters the ring to make honeycomb stitch H, the other pair from pin G is left to cross the diagonal and work the other side of the ring. The left pair from pin H leaves the ring to make a honeycomb stitch at pin I with a pair left out from the point of the half stitch oval. The right pair from this stitch returns to the ring to make the stitch at pin J. The right pair from pin J is left to cross the diagonal and work the other side of the ring. The left pair leaves the

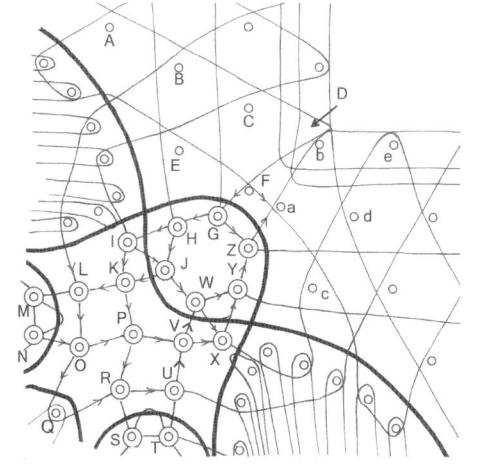

Figure 246 Working the corner

107

ring to work the stitch at pin K with the remaining pair from pin I. The left pair from pin K works a stitch with a pair from the oval at pin L. The left pair from pin L enters the honeycomb ring and makes a stitch with a pair from the oval at pin M and the right pair from this stitch binds on the gimp and the same pairs make the next stitch on this side at pin N. Make a honeycomb stitch at pin P on the diagonal using pairs from pins K and O, and finish the honeycomb ring.

The oval at the corner of the edging (figure 247) does not require any extra pairs and is worked across the diagonal, i.e. the workers run parallel to the diagonal through the corner, so rotate the pillow through 45° so that the diagonal through the corner is parallel to the cover cloth. Work out of the valley and make picots at pins A-E. The inner two passive pairs enter directly into the corner oval and are replaced by two pairs from the honeycomb ring. Pairs from picots at pins A & B enter the oval and start the half stitch at pin F, with the left hand pair becoming the workers. Because the first three pins lie almost horizontally if rows were worked from pin F to pin H to pin K to pin I they would be so close that the result would be

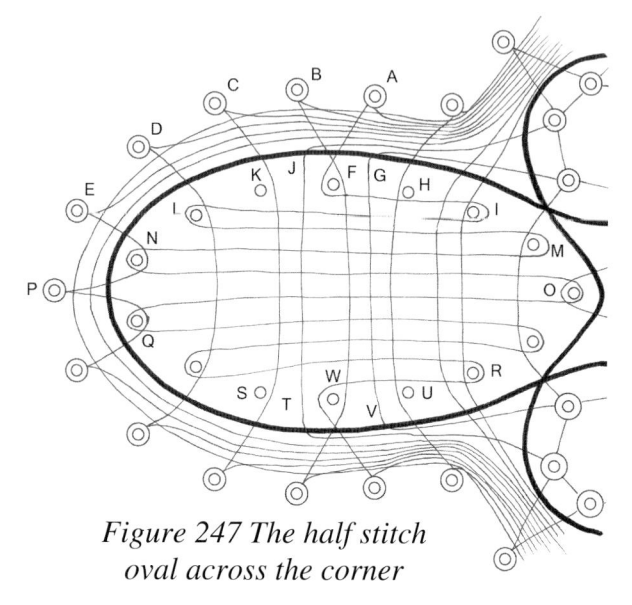

Figure 247 The half stitch oval across the corner

unsightly. To avoid this take the workers through two pairs, the second one pair G being the inner passive pair, and set up a pin support pin, pin H; then the workers continue through two more pairs and pin at the end of the row, pin I. Return the workers through these five pairs and continue through two pairs, the first being the next inner passive pair entering across the gimp, pair J, and set up a support pin, pin K to control the second pair; then continue the workers through another pair and set up the pin at the end of the row, pin L. Work rows setting up pins M and N and add a pair from the honeycomb filling before setting up pin O. Take a pair out of the half stitch to make the picot at pin P and return it into the next row pinning at Q. The second half of the corner oval is a mirror image of the first half.

Now return to figure 246 and continue the honeycomb ring at pin S bringing in a pair from pin R, bind on the gimp and use the same pairs to work the next pin, pin T, on this side and take a pair out of the ring and work stitches U and V using pairs from pins R and P respectively. A pair from pin V enters the ring to make a stitch at pin W with the pair crossing the diagonal from pin J, then a pair leaves the ring to work the stitch at pin X with the remaining pair from pin V. A pair from this stitch returns into the ring to work the stitch at pin Y and continues to make the stitch at pin Z with the pair crossing the diagonal from pin G. These pairs leave the ring, the right pair making a kat stitch with the pair from pin F at pin a and continuing to make the footside, pin b, the edge pair from the first stitch about the pin worked at this pin is untwisted. At this point the pin is removed from the corner pinhole, pin D, and replaced in the same pinhole. Complete the oval and continue the kat stitch on this side with the row of pins c, d and e. After completing the corner oval rotate the pillow through 45° and continue down the following side.

All about making—Floral Bucks Point Lace

PROJECT 15b: Insertion

Materials Required Insertion Project 15b
Egyptian cotton no. 80/2[1]
gimp D.M.C. perle no. 12

Figure 248 (centre) Insertion with kat stitch ground, pricking

Figure 250 Lace worked in black thread on pricking figure 248

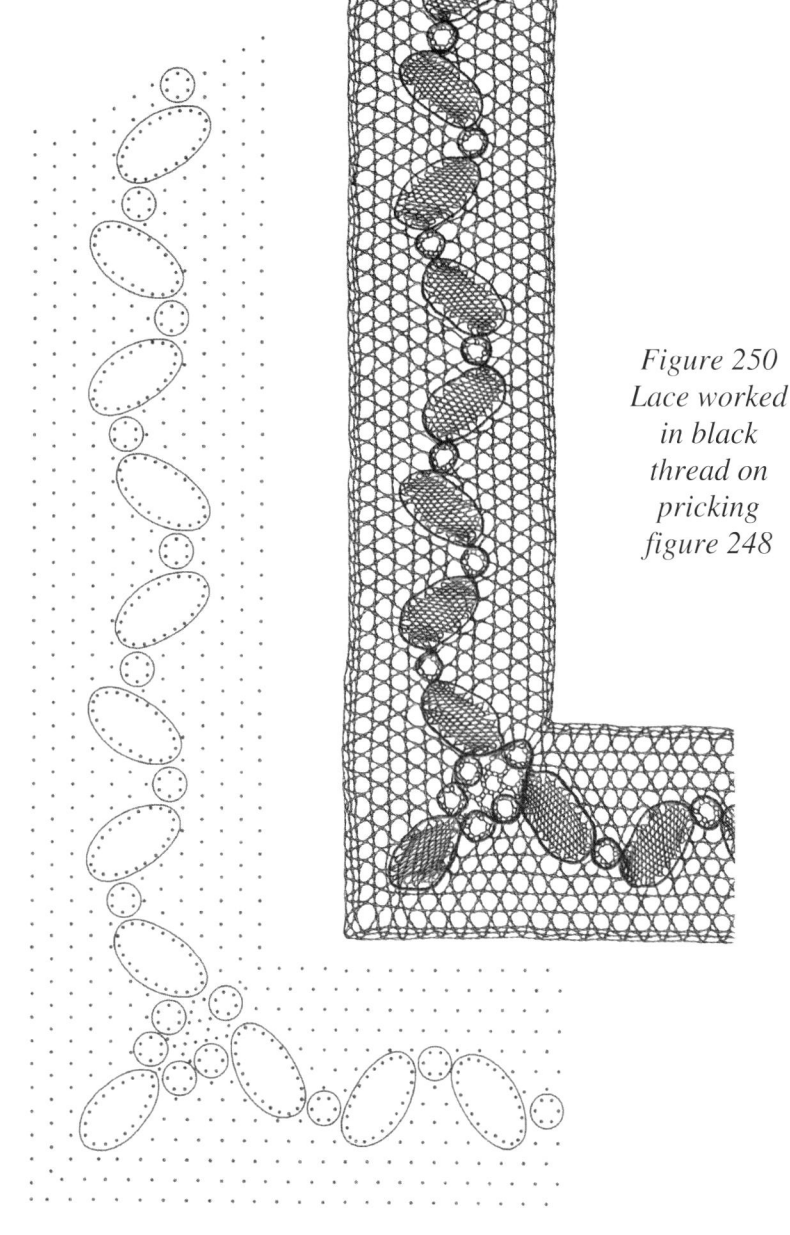

Figure 249 (left) Lace worked in white thread on pricking figure 248

Being an insertion there is a footside on the left as well as the right. Thus the working of the right side of this insertion motif (figures 248-250) is similar to the right side of the edging (figures 240-242) and the working of the left side of the central motifs is similar to those on the right.

109

Like the corner for the edging this one (figure 251) does not require any extra pairs either. This honeycomb ring is closer to the inner corner so there is no pair crossing the diagonal between the ring and the footside.

When the outer footside approaches the corner work the last continuous row leaving the oval from pin A to reach the pin before the corner pin, pin B, and make up the edge. Now cloth stitch and twist the two passive pairs at C, and with the one nearest the edge work cloth stitch and twist across the pair returning from pin B and make up the edge at the corner pin, pin D, and return across the next pair, the one from pin B and the remaining passive pair at E. Make gap row stitches with the two pairs nearest the oval and the next two pairs. With the outer three pairs make the footside at pin H and work a continuous row to pin I in the oval. Make the following row and then finish the oval.

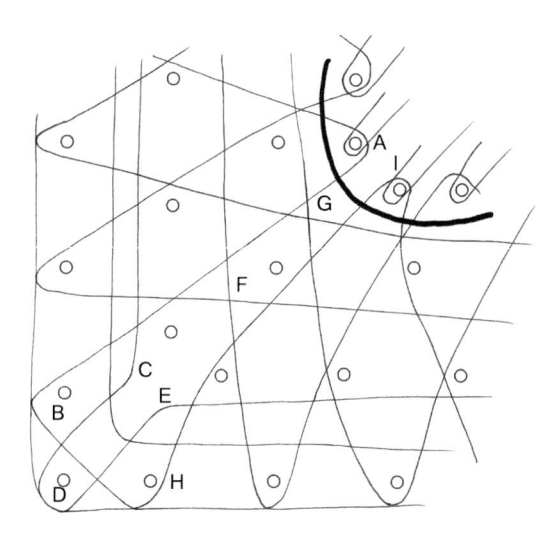

Figure 251 The outer corner of the insertion

Mounting the edging and insertion

My insertion and edging were mounted using a mitred corner[4]. However, where the outer corner of an insertion meets the fabric the hem requires reinforcement.

1 Trim the fabric leaving the required hem allowance (figure 252)
2 Machine or back stitch along the required finishing line.
3 Cut through the corner of the hem allowance A-B.

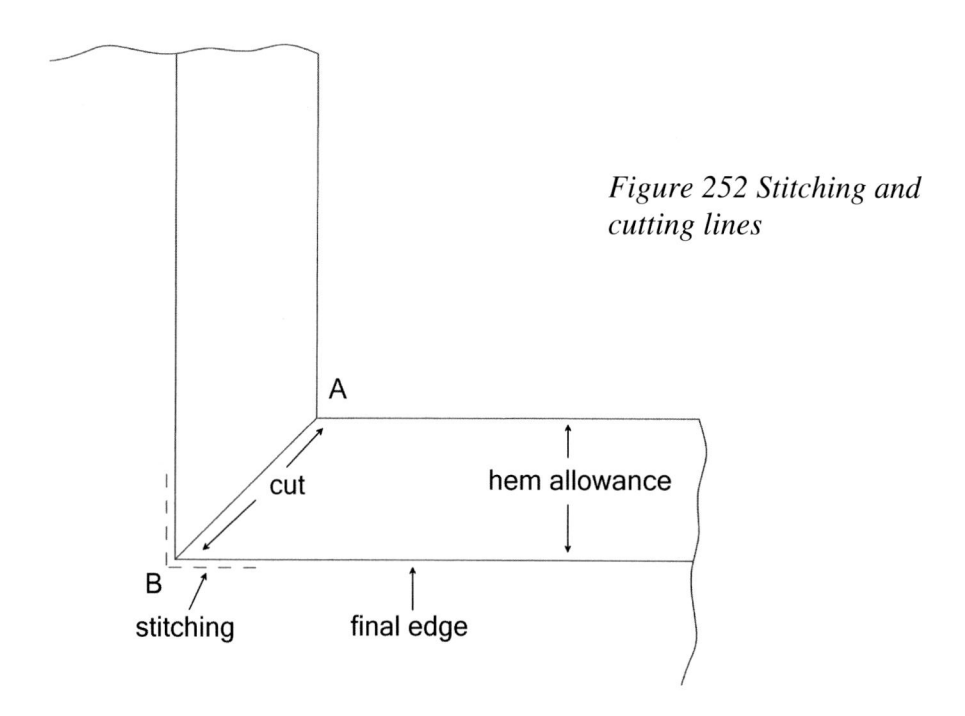

Figure 252 Stitching and cutting lines

All about making—Floral Bucks Point Lace

4 Open out the cut so that its two sides form a straight line ABA (figure 253), place a reinforcement triangle of fabric along ABA with right sides together and machine or back stitch close to their edges.

5 Fold along the final edge, turning the hem and reinforcement triangle over to the wrong side, (figure 254) and stitch the hem in place.

Figure 253 Reinforcement triangle stitched in place (wrong side)

Figure 254 Reinforcement triangle (wrong side)

Figure 255 (left) Hem with reinforcement triangle, (right side)

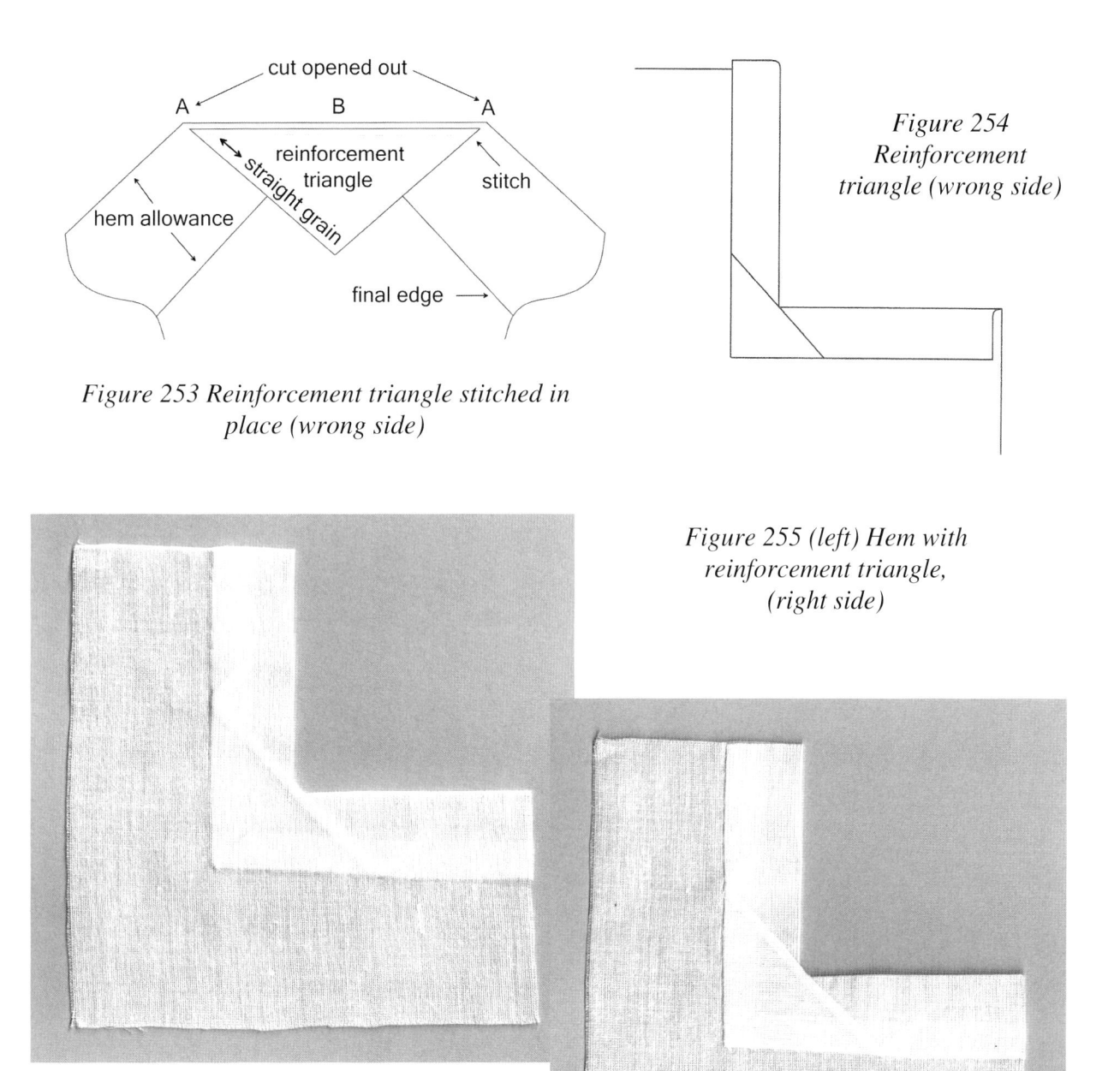

Figure 256 (right) Hem with reinforcement triangle, (wrong side)

All about making—Floral Bucks Point Lace

END NOTES

1 Substituting threads
See Part 6.

2 Kat stitch ground
The ground is usually made as continuous or long rows of cloth and twist pinned after every second stitch alternating with gap or short rows where each two pairs between the pins of the previous continuous row work cloth and twist (figures 257 & 258). In an alternative method the ground has continuous or long rows worked half stitch, pin, half stitch, cloth and twist alternating with gap or short rows where each vertical pair works cloth and twist with the following pair (figures 259 & 260). The gap row is not pinned. The first method produces a much tighter stitch than the second and the hole created by the pin by the second method never quite disappears.

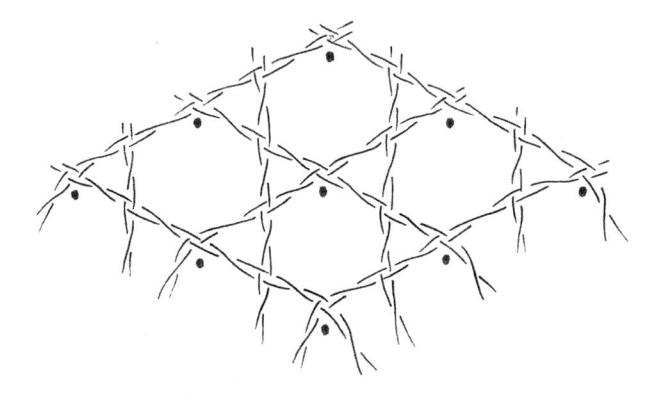

Figures 257 (above) & 258 (right) Kat stitch, continuous rows pinned after each two cloth and twist stitches

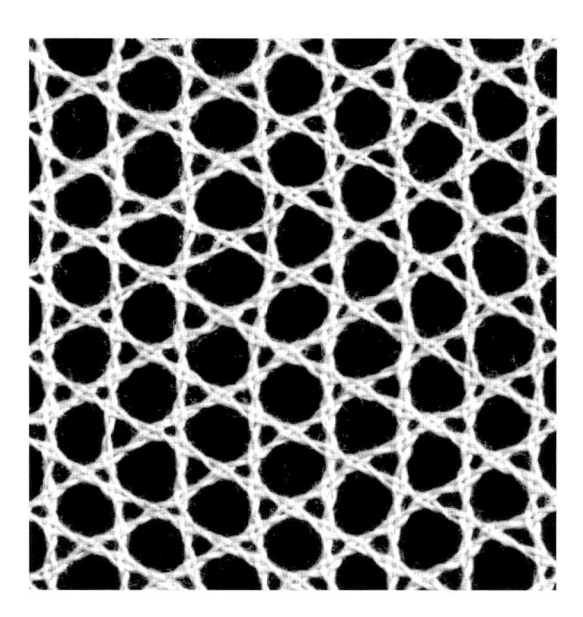

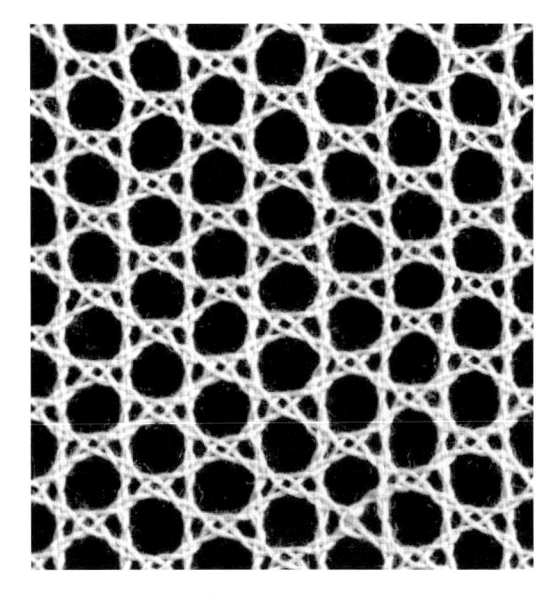

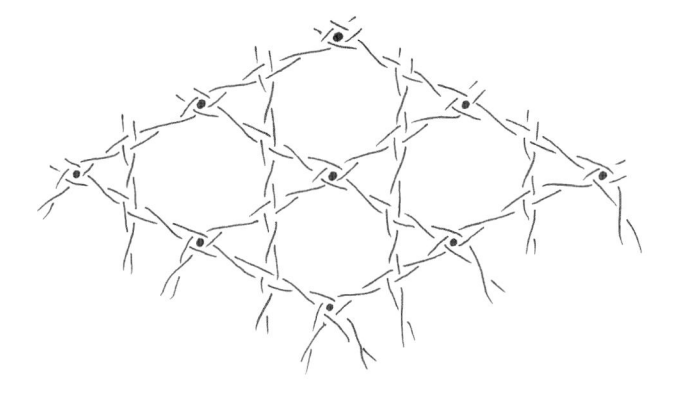

Figure 259 (above) and 260 (left) Kat stitch, continuous rows of half stitch, pin, half stitch, cloth and twist

All about making—Floral Bucks Point Lace

3 Kat stitch edging with the spacing of the pins around the clothwork similar to the spacing of the pinholes in the ground surrounding it

Compare figures 261 & 262 with figures 240-242 and the working diagrams for the two pieces figures 263 & 264 with 244 & 245. In this piece (figures 263 & 264) two pairs are left out or brought into the oval at most of the pins, one being a vertical pair the other a diagonal pair. In most, but not all cases, there will be a gap row stitch made by these two pairs immediately after being left out or before being brought in.

Since there is approximately half the number of rows in the half stitch area a thicker thread must be used to prevent it looking starved, but unfortunately nothing can be done to prevent large holes appearing around its edge.

Figure 262 (left) Lace made on pricking figure 261 using Egyptian cotton no. 60/2

Figure 261 (far left) Pricking with the spacing of the pins around the clothwork similar to the spacing of the pinholes in the ground surrounding it

113

All about making—Floral Bucks Point Lace

The two pairs making a gap row stitch are left out of or added into the half stitch areas at adjacent pins (figures 263 & 264), compare with the working diagrams for the project (figures 244 & 245). Adding two pairs at a pinhole makes it more difficult to gauge when to add or leave out a pair and also results in large holes appearing along the gimp.

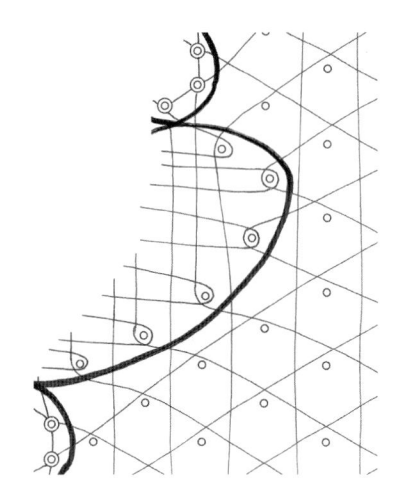

Figure 263 Pairs entering and leaving a half stitch oval

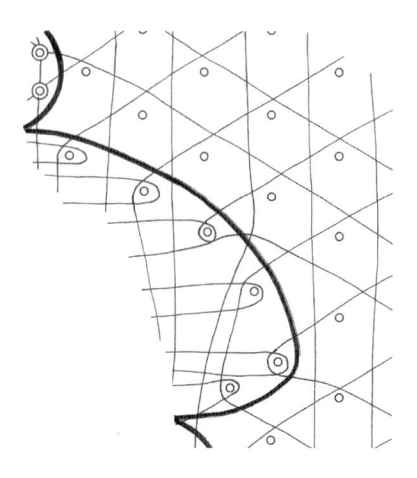

Figure 264 Pairs entering and leaving a half stitch oval

CHAPTER 11

PROJECT 16: Tray insert with a non-reversing corner and pin chain bars

Figure 265 Kat stitch and pin chain bars tray insert with a non-reversing corner

Materials Required for Project 16
Egyptian cotton no. 120/2[1], gimp D.M.C. perle no. 12
tray with 33.5cm (13 in) x 22.5cm (8¾ in) aperture
gold numbers and stars

This edging with a non-reversing corner[2] (figure 265) was taken from an old parchment with a corner designed by Miss Catherine Channer (figure 266). The ground of the parchment has an angle of 65° which indicates that kat stitch was probably intended. The edging has been trued up but has been kept as faithful as possible to the original. The gimp lines and the pinholes of the clothwork have been smoothed out and all repeats are now identical. The ground has been replaced with an accurate grid having the same angle and spacing as the original, and pinholes near gimps have been adjusted as required. Since the original parchment had become distorted the pinholes around the motifs in the trued up version are not in exactly the same positions along the motifs as those of the original. I was not comfortable with Miss Channer's corner as the ground passes through from one side to the next causing some ground pairs to make unsightly changes of direction, so some parts of the corner have been redesigned.

All about making—Floral Bucks Point Lace

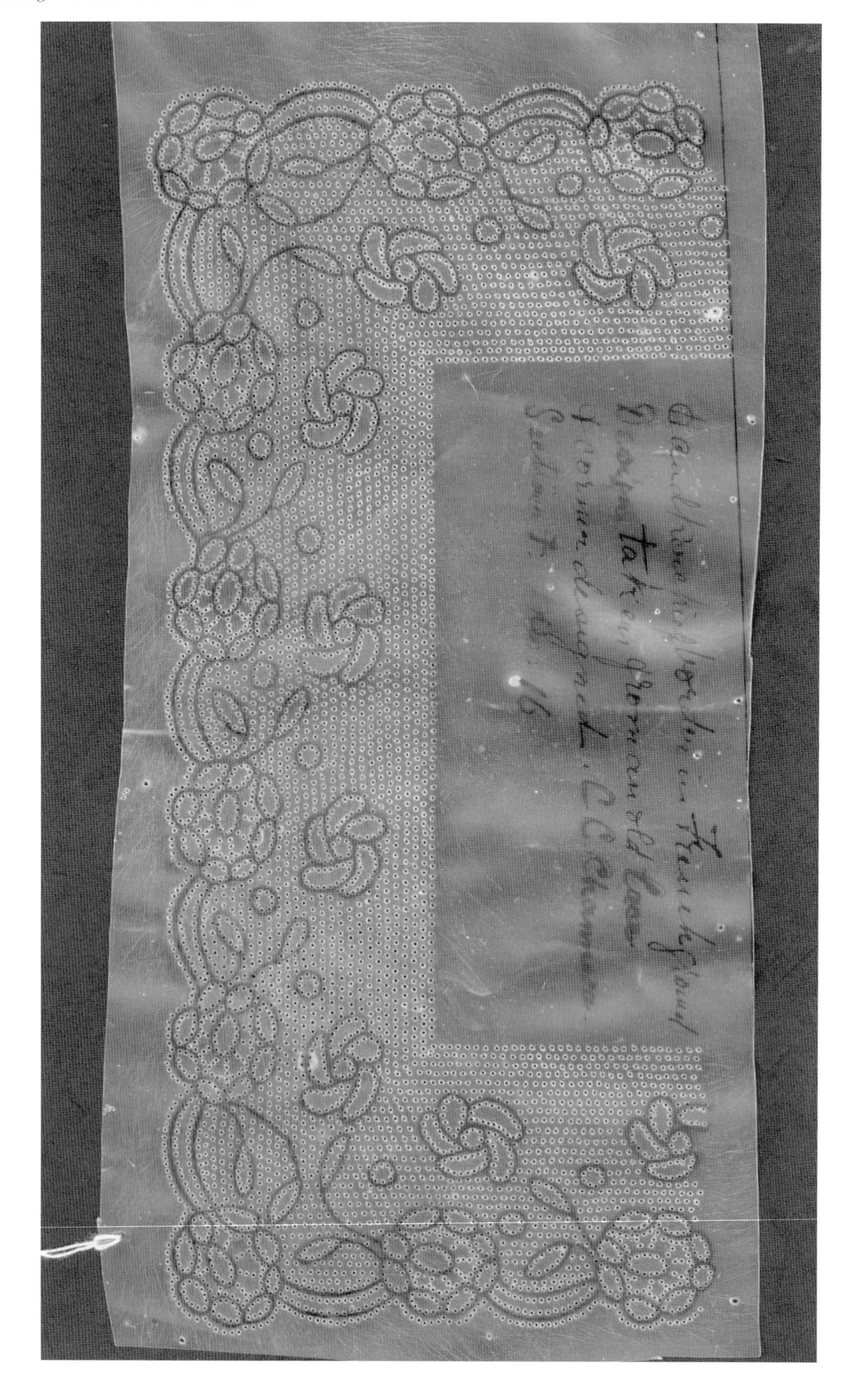

Figure 266 The original pricking with Miss Channer's corner. The size has been reduced slightly to fit the page. It was originally the same scale as figure 267

All about making—Floral Bucks Point Lace

Figure 267 (below) Kat stitch edging with non-reversing corner, pricking

Figure 268 Kat stitch edging with non-reversing corner made on pricking figure 267

All about making—Floral Bucks Point Lace

Pin chain bars
There are a number of patterns from the second half of the 19th century containing areas where the motifs are connected by pin chain bars instead of a regular filling. These areas usually have some or all of the area lined with a row of honeycomb stitches, sometimes called the rim. In this case (figure 269) the outer edge of the area is lined with a row of honeycomb stitches, whereas the central clothwork motif does not have a row of honeycomb stitches surrounding it.

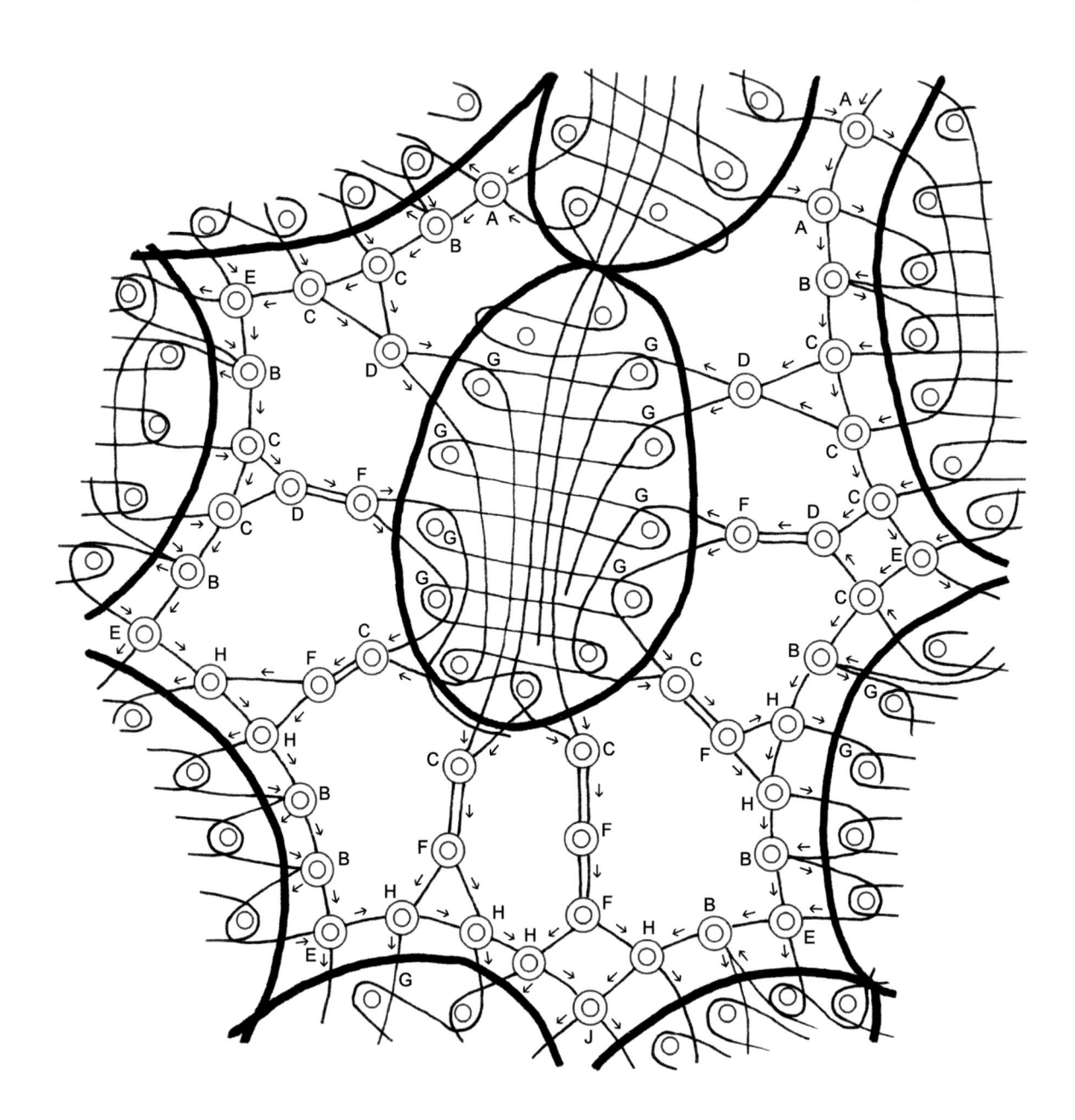

Figure 269 Pin chain bars with honeycomb stitches lining the area and a central clothwork motif without honeycomb stitches outlining it.

All about making—Floral Bucks Point Lace

Working the pin chain bar area (figure 269)
The letters in the diagram do not indicate the order of work. Each of the following techniques is represented by a different letter and this letter is used to mark each and every pinhole where I used this technique.

1 Two pairs enter the area, one pair leaves, the other continues the honeycomb rim
At pin A at the upper left of the area two pairs have entered from the right from the upper central clothwork motif. The two pairs make a honeycomb stitch, the left pair exits across the gimp into the clothwork motif on the left and the right pair continues as the rim pair.

2 Two pairs enter the area, one pair from a clothwork area, the other from previous honeycomb
At pin A on the right of the area one pair has entered from the left from the upper central clothwork motif and the other pair has entered between the clothwork motifs from a previous honeycomb stitch. The pairs make a honeycomb stitch, the right pair exits across the gimp into the clothwork motif on the right and the left pair continues as the rim pair.

3 Continuing the rim
At pin B there is no second pair available within the area to make a stitch with the rim pair so a pair is brought in across the gimp from the clothwork area to make the stitch, and then a pair exits across the gimp back into the clothwork area after the stitch has been made. The remaining pair continues the rim.

4 Pairs leave the rim to feed the central clothwork motif
A pair crosses the gimp from the clothwork area to make a honeycomb stitch at pin C. One pair continues the rim, the other remains within the area to work a bar.

5 Honeycomb stitch and pin chain bars
When two pairs are available to make a bar they work a honeycomb stitch pin D, and may continue to make pin chain bar of one or more pins F. Finally these pairs work individually with the rim pair, pins H, not necessarily at consecutive pins as at pin J, and then exit the area to enter the clothwork at pins G.

6 Rim changing direction
When the row of rim following a gimp meets another gimp it may terminate and a new row of rim starts and follows the new gimp. The honeycomb stitch at pin E, where two rows of rim stitches meet, is made with the current rim pair and one entering the area. This new pair should be in line with the new rim and becomes the new rim pair; the other exits across the new gimp, thus completing the line of the previous row of rim.

7 Closing the rim
The last pin of the area is worked using the last two rim pairs at pin J with both pairs exiting the area.

All about making—Floral Bucks Point Lace

The corner

As this edging does not corner exactly along the diagonal, a number of pairs will have to be added and ultimately removed (figure 270).

1 Work as far as the corner pin but do not work the circle of clothwork at A.
2 Continue making the lace, working areas B, C and D and starting the honeycomb ring E.
3 For each row indicated by a double arrow add two pairs so there is one pair travelling in each direction.
4 Work round the corner motif, changing direction and continue working down the new side, throwing out pairs as required.
5 Continue by working areas F, G and H, completing the ring E, then area J and the clothwork circle A.

As usual it is easier to work diagonally inwards from the gimp through the corner rather than outwards, and my starting line was around the corner motif, down the gimp then clothwork motifs F, G, and H, under the ring E, and clothwork motif C (these are all worked in the same direction, not as when turning the corner), then motif A and then the footside.

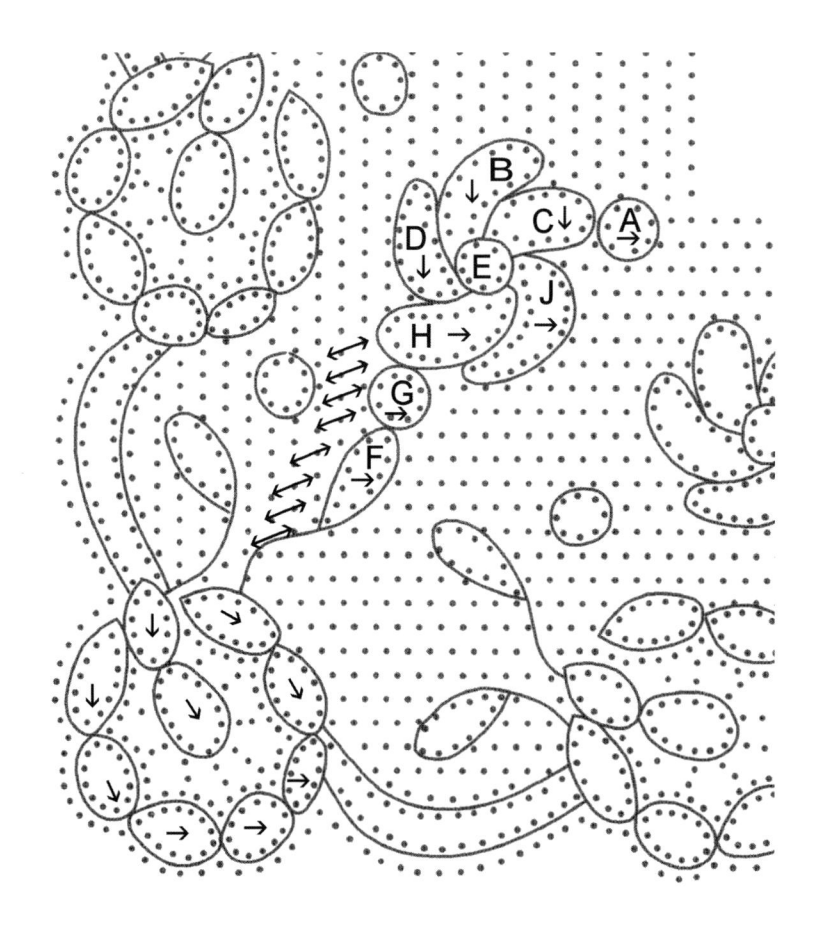

Figure 270 Working the corner

Mount the lace in the tray according to the manufacturer's instructions.

All about making—Floral Bucks Point Lace

END NOTES

1 Substituting threads and colour
See Part 6. When the edging is made in black the cloth stitch areas become very heavy (figure 271), hence kat stitch usually has these areas worked in half stitch.

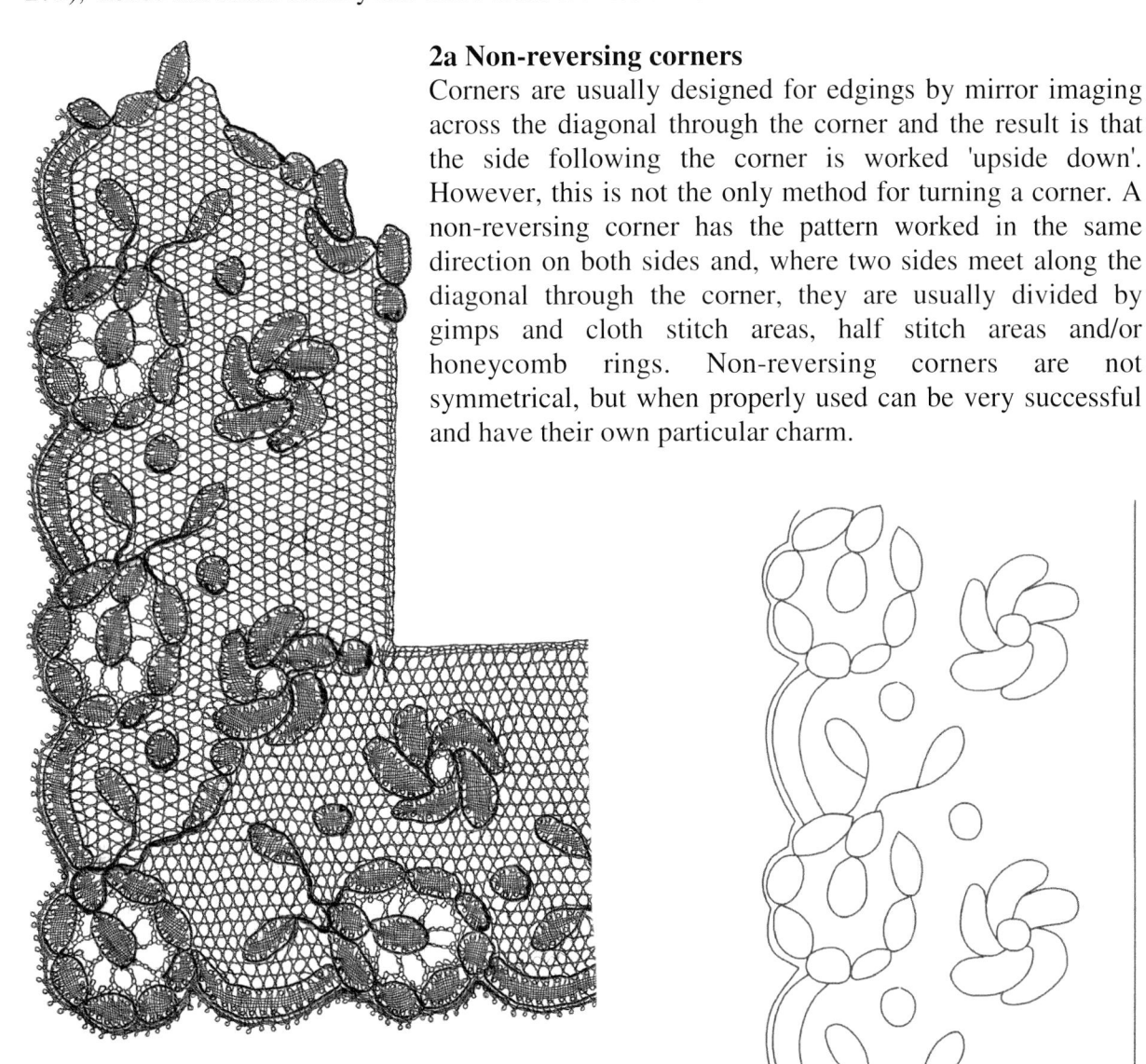

2a Non-reversing corners
Corners are usually designed for edgings by mirror imaging across the diagonal through the corner and the result is that the side following the corner is worked 'upside down'. However, this is not the only method for turning a corner. A non-reversing corner has the pattern worked in the same direction on both sides and, where two sides meet along the diagonal through the corner, they are usually divided by gimps and cloth stitch areas, half stitch areas and/or honeycomb rings. Non-reversing corners are not symmetrical, but when properly used can be very successful and have their own particular charm.

Figure 271 Edging with non-reversing corner made in black thread on pricking figure 263

2b Designing a non-reversing corner
A non-reversing corner is necessarily asymmetrical.

1. Trace three pattern repeats indicating the positions of the picot edge, gimps, footside and any other features that make up the picture (figure 272).

Figure 272 Tracing gimps and picot lines

All about making—Floral Bucks Point Lace

2. Turn the tracing through 90° but do not turn over. Slide it up and down and sideways (do not rotate) over the original and imagine a modification of the design that would fit into the corner, (squared paper attached to the footside of the pattern helps to keep two pieces meeting at the corner at right angles) and trace the new side as far as it is useful. Erase the parts of the initial tracing that are no longer required (figure 273).

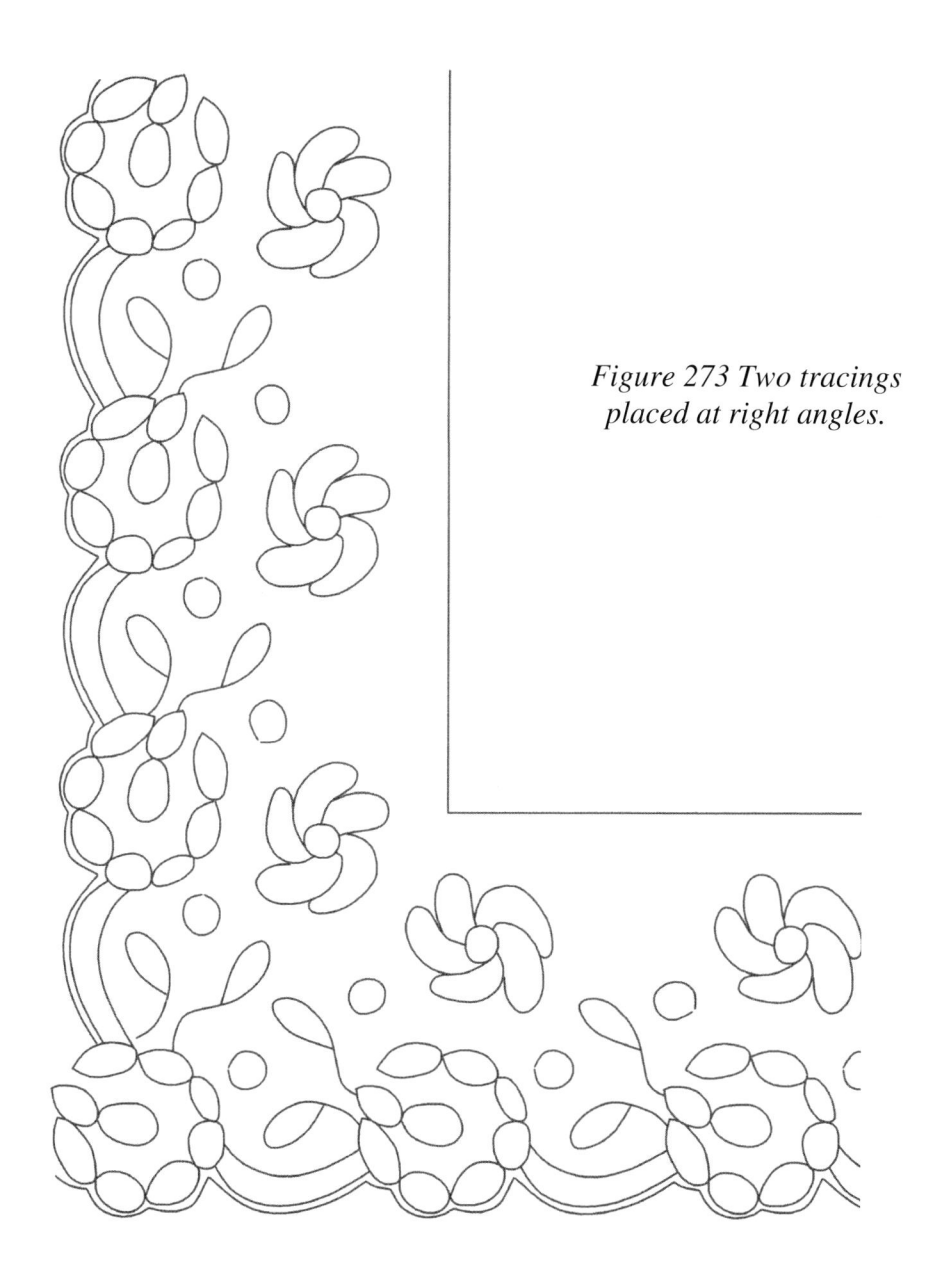

Figure 273 Two tracings placed at right angles.

All about making—Floral Bucks Point Lace

3. Draw the gimps, motifs and picot lines to complete the corner (tracing when possible). Add heavy lines to indicate the boundaries of the original pattern, preferably along a gimp that has broken the ground through to the footside (figure 274).

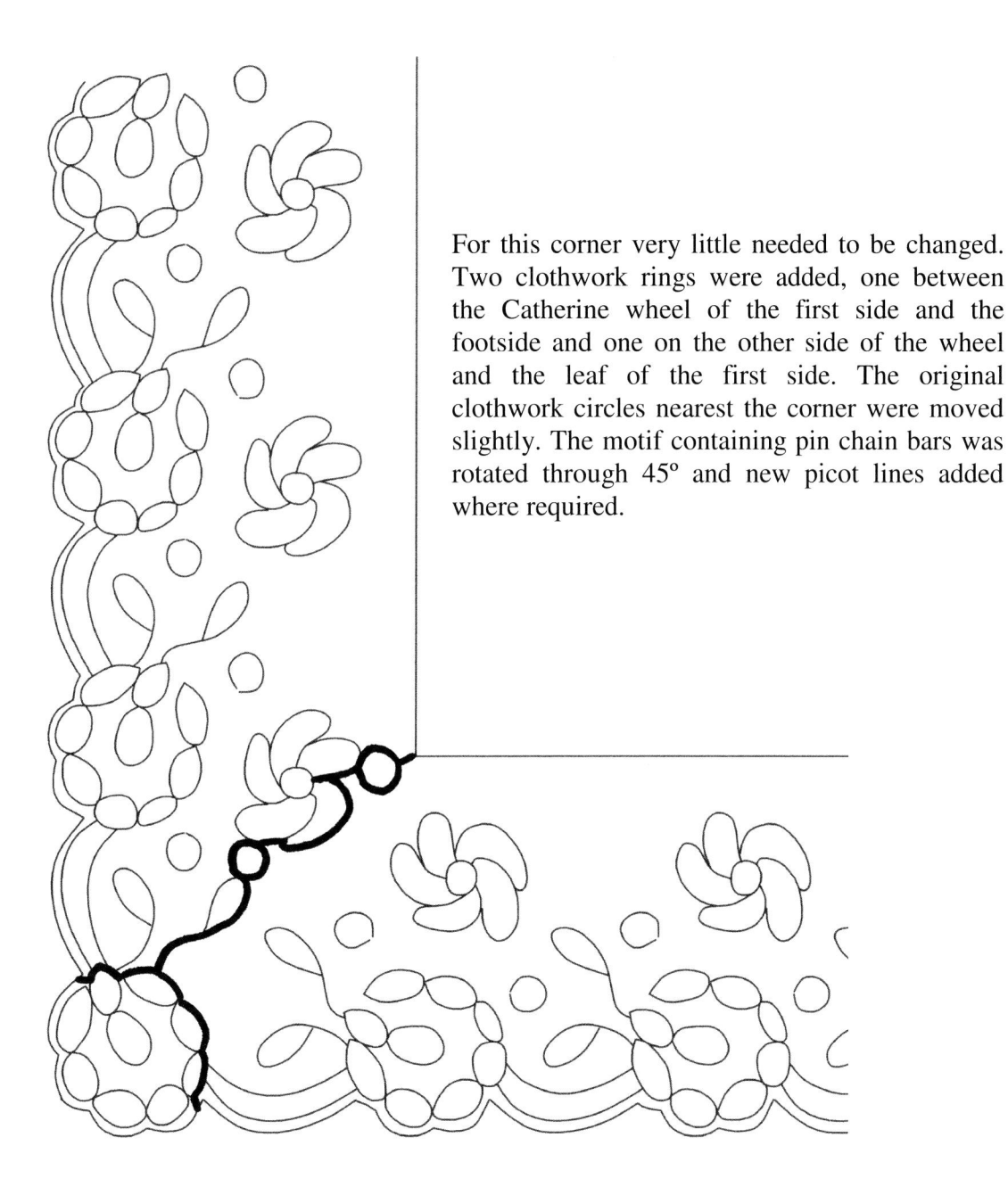

For this corner very little needed to be changed. Two clothwork rings were added, one between the Catherine wheel of the first side and the footside and one on the other side of the wheel and the leaf of the first side. The original clothwork circles nearest the corner were moved slightly. The motif containing pin chain bars was rotated through 45° and new picot lines added where required.

Figure 274 Gimps and picot lines

All about making—Floral Bucks Point Lace

4. Make two copies of the pricking and trim them along the heavy lines, one for before the corner and one after. Then, using the tracing (figure 273) as a guide, stick the trimmed patterns onto white paper (figure 275).

6. Draw the picot line and the gimps for motifs required to complete the corner either by freehand or by transferring from the tracing. Add any ground or filling as required; these areas may be in line with one or other of the sides or at right angles to the diagonal through the corner*.

5. Add pinholes by eye within the cloth or half stitch areas, and for the picots. These may be in line with one or other of the sides or at right angles to the diagonal through the corner.

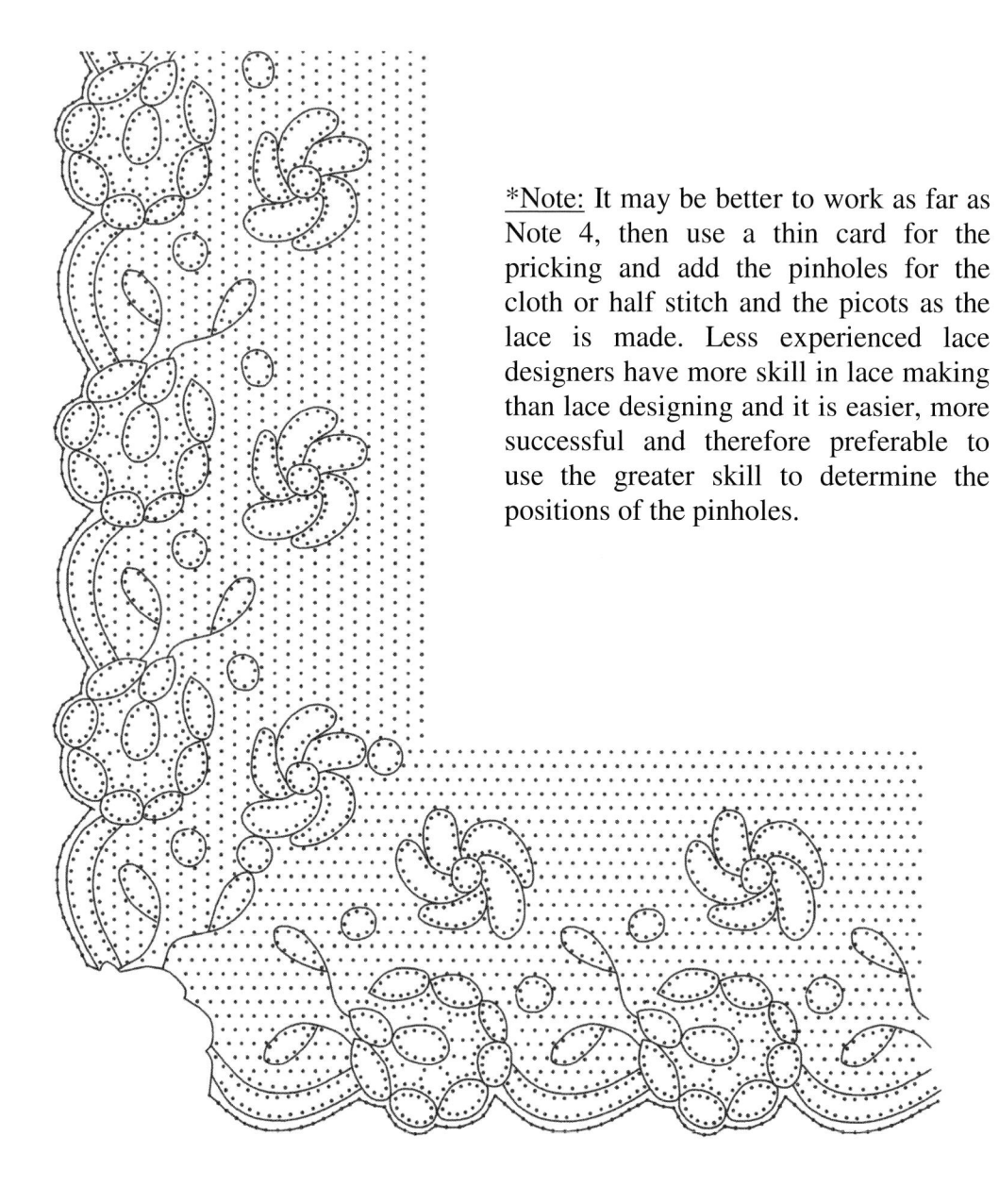

*Note: It may be better to work as far as Note 4, then use a thin card for the pricking and add the pinholes for the cloth or half stitch and the picots as the lace is made. Less experienced lace designers have more skill in lace making than lace designing and it is easier, more successful and therefore preferable to use the greater skill to determine the positions of the pinholes.

Figure 275 Two pattern pieces placed at right angles and gimps drawn in

All about making—Floral Bucks Point Lace

CHAPTER 12

PROJECT 17: The Willow Pattern, an exercise in designing

Figure 276 The Willow Pattern Picture mounted in a frame

Materials Required for project 17
Piper's silk floss
gimp four strands of the silk floss, loosely twisted
picture frame with 40cm ($15^5/_8$ in) x 30cm (11¾ in) aperture
mount 33cm (13 in) x 23cm (9 in) aperture

The Willow Pattern Picture
This picture was inspired by Pipers blue silk which made me think of the Willow Pattern (figure 277). The blue of the silk is not the rich royal blue used for Willow Pattern crockery but a deep saxe blue that suits this purpose better since lace, unlike the plates, has ground and the more brilliant colour would be overpowering.

We now design and make lace for our own pleasure and this piece is about interpreting a picture from one of my favourite stories.

All about making—Floral Bucks Point Lace

Figure 277 Willow Pattern platter

All about making—Floral Bucks Point Lace

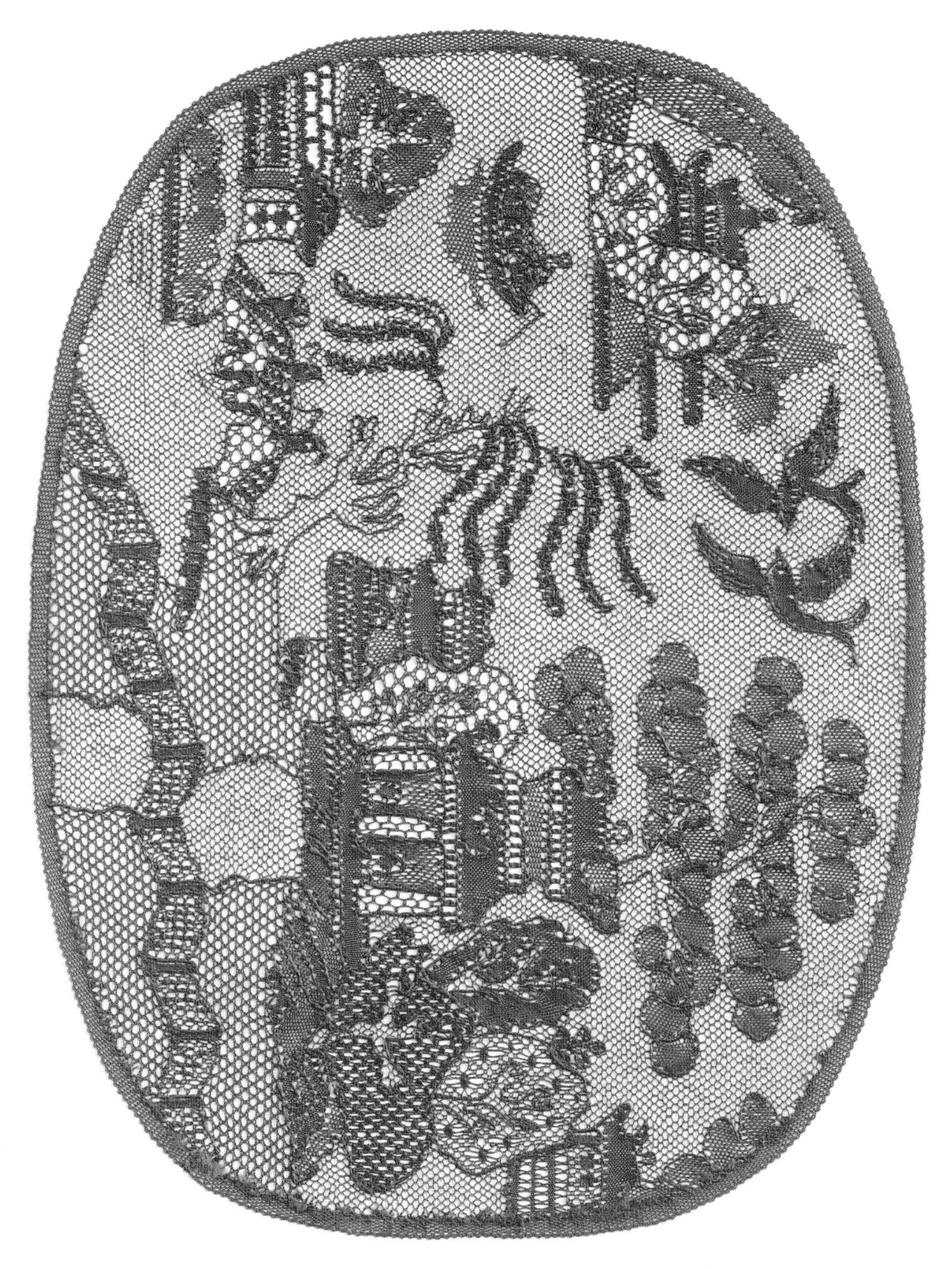

*Figure 278 The Willow Pattern Picture slightly reduced.
The original measures 25.7 cm from side to side and took 448 bobbins including gimps.*

All about making—Floral Bucks Point Lace

This design was traced (figure 279) from a Willow Pattern platter (figure 277). As this was to be made as a picture the selection of stitches was governed by the effect they would produce, so occasionally a technique not normally associated with Bucks Point was used as it was considered the best way to produce the desired result. You are allowed 'artistic licence' when designing your own lace.

The picture was made from the left side to the right as less pairs would be needed than if it had been worked top to bottom. The bracketed numbers in the following list match the numbers in figure 279.

(1)   The background is point ground.
(2)   The main grassy area of the island is kat stitch.
(3)   Cloth stitch for the birds, the dark tree and parts of the buildings and ground.
(4)   Half stitch for lighter areas and its shading effect was used to advantage for the foliage of the large tree behind the house.
(5)   Half stitch without a surrounding gimp makes it less obtrusive—the tree in the distance and the reflection of the boat in the water.
(6)   Gimp fingers with honeycomb stitches within them for the willow tree foliage.
(7)   Honeycomb stitch for the bridge, its texture representing the stones which would have been used to build the bridge, and also some trees.
(8)   Tallies in honeycomb for the fence to give a more solid appearance. These tallies were made very shallow to give the impression of height (the piece was worked from side-to-side).
(9)   Three-pin mayflowers are used for some of the windows.
(10) Spiders in honeycomb stitch squares[2] for the blossom for one of the trees.
(11) Spiders holding hands for the denser tree[3].
(12) Decorative bands on buildings are represented by bars of cloth stitch connected by tallies.
(13) Decorative bands on another buildings are represented by cloth stitch bars connected by kisses[4].
(14) Honiton no-pin filling[5] to give the impression of bricks in the wall on the left.
(15) The pillars of the large building are worked in cloth and twist ground[6].

The tracing was attached to a piece of pricking card and the grounds pricked using a transparent template. The holes along the lines were pricked as the lace was made; artistic licence is allowed here too.

The oval border of half stitch with cloth and twist edges was made first and joined end to start. Then, with the left side of the picture at the top, pairs were sewn in and the main part of the lace was made. When a pair touched the border at the side of the work (the upper and lower edges of the picture) it was sewn in and the pair returned into the work. When the piece was nearing completion and the borders started curving in towards each other pairs were sewn out and knotted. Finally, when all the pairs had been sewn out and knotted (right side of the picture) the ends were sewn through to the wrong side of the picture and trimmed.

Finally the piece was stiffened using a non-perfumed hairspray, so far (25 years) without any disastrous results, but who knows what the results will be if a different brand is used.

All about making—Floral Bucks Point Lace

↑ Top when working
the main part of
the lace

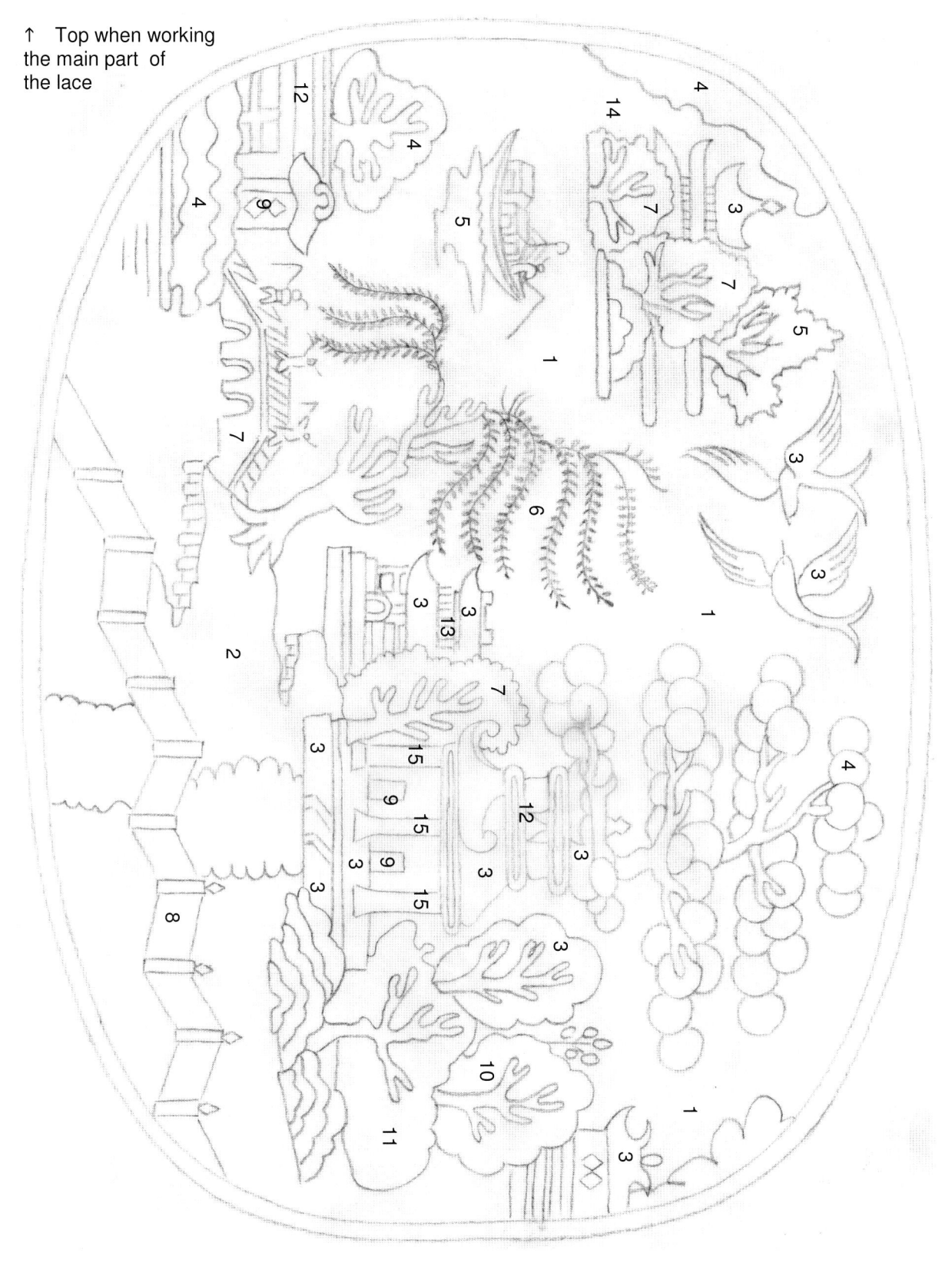

Figure 279 The tracing

Sew out the centre as the borders down the sides of the work start curving towards each other.

129

All about making—Floral Bucks Point Lace

END NOTES

1 Substituting threads
See Part 6.

2 A spider in a honeycomb stitch square
Spiders can be found in many traditional Bucks Point patterns. Because of the limitations of the area available and the space required for each spider this design has two rows of honeycomb stitches between the spiders (figure 280).

Figure 280 Spider in a honeycomb stitch square

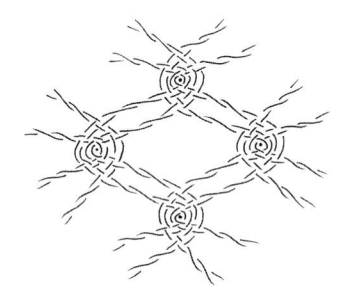

3 Spiders holding hands
Although this arrangement of spiders with two legs on each side, each leg being twisted twice is not traditional in Bucks it seemed appropriate for one of the bushes. (figure 281).

Figure 281 (left) Spiders holding hands

4 Clothwork bars and kisses
Kisses are made by crossing the worker pairs from two adjacent bars of clothwork by twisting and working cloth and twist and the workers change then bars. This is traditionally a Bedfordshire technique but is right for the picture (figure 282).

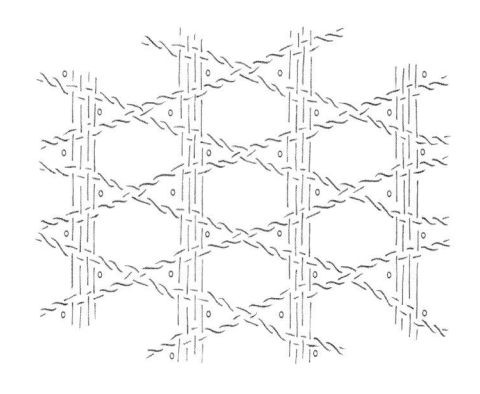

Figure 282 (right) Clothwork bars and kisses

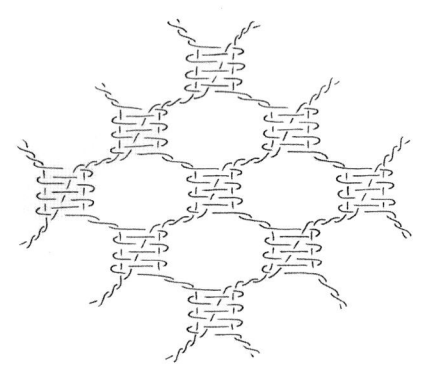

5 Honiton no-pin filling
A traditional Honiton filling consisting totally of tallies that are unsupported by pins (figure 283). After completing a tally always stabilize the passive pair without the working bobbin first, either to make the next tally or to sew out. Then use the pair with the working bobbin. Always use working bobbin from one tally as the working bobbin for the following tally. The passives should be firmed up before sewing out.

Figure 283 (left) Honiton no-pin filling

6 Cloth and twist ground
A variation on a traditional ground producing yet another texture for the picture (figure 284).

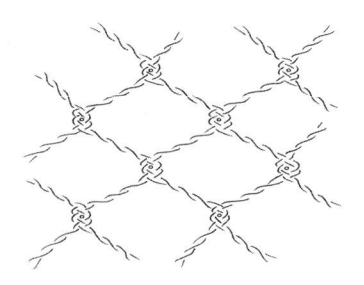

Figure 284 (right) Cloth and twist ground

All about making—Floral Bucks Point Lace

CHAPTER 13

PROJECTS 18 & 19: Designing and working fans

Project 18: Fan leaf worked with no changes of direction
Project 19: Fan leaf worked with four changes of direction

PROJECT 18: Fan leaf worked in one direction

Figure 285 Fan leaf Project 16 made in one direction prickings figures 286a-c

Materials Required for Project 18
Egyptian cotton no. 120/2[1], gimp D.M.C. perle no. 12
fan sticks 16.5 cm (6³⁄₈ in) radius, mine has 13 inner sticks
adhesive (see page 137)

Fan leaves, Projects 18 and 19 both contain point ground, honeycomb filling and kat stitch[2]. Project 18 (figure 285, prickings figures 286a-c) is worked in a single direction i.e. from the tip of the right hand guard to the tip of the left hand guard. Project 19 (figure 292, prickings figures 293a-c) has the working direction changed four times. Changing the working direction may reduce the number of bobbins required but is more difficult to make. The decision whether to design a fan to be made in a single direction or with changes of direction may be influenced by features within the design.

131

All about making—Floral Bucks Point Lace

Fan leaf (worked in one direction)

Figure 286a Fan leaf pricking to be worked in one direction

Join the three sections of the pricking (figures 286a-c), overlapping as required to match A-A and B-B. It may be useful to indicate the honeycomb rings to distinguish them from clothwork rings.

Figure 286b Fan leaf pricking

All about making—Floral Bucks Point Lace

working direction →

C

D

Figure 286c Fan leaf, pricking

All about making—Floral Bucks Point Lace

Figure 287 Fan leaf made on prickings figures 286a-c and worked with no changes of direction

All about making—Floral Bucks Point Lace

Making the fan leaf
Pin the pricking to the pillow so that the lace will be worked straight down from the point on the right to the one on the left (figure 288). Starting at the top where the right guard will be attached add pairs as the width increases towards the left. When the lace curves to the left, away from the vertical, pairs will be thrown out along that edge, then when it curves back towards the right pairs will be added again. At this point the outer edge will start curving to the right and pairs will be thrown out.

There are no changes in the working direction.

Mounting a fan leaf[4]
Draw a full size plan of the fan leaf showing the positions of the inner sticks and place on a sheet of pin board or cork. Place the fan leaf on top (face down) and arrange the sticks on top of the leaf (again face down) with the front guard on the left, the inner sticks in their order and the back guard on the right according to the plan. Use pins to hold the sticks in place. The lace should protrude just slightly above the guards when the fan is closed.

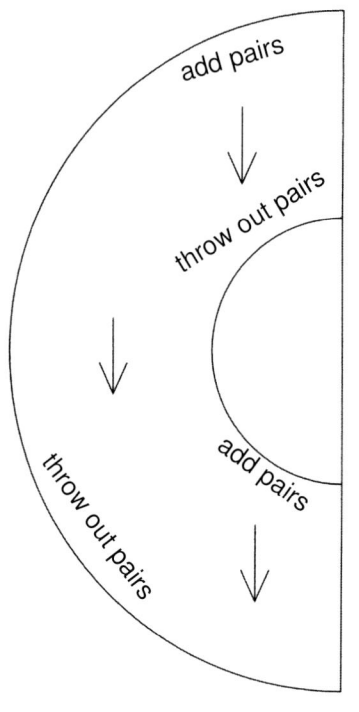

Figure 288 Working direction

1 Attaching to perforated sticks
Some fans have a line of small holes down the inner sticks so the leaf may be attached by stitching. One way of attaching is to take the needle down through the end hole in the stick, hole A (figure 289), and straight down through the lace, then up through the lace immediately to the side of the stick and tie a reef knot. With the same thread move to the next hole of the stick, hole B, repeat sewing through stick and the lace and secure with a half hitch (figure 290).

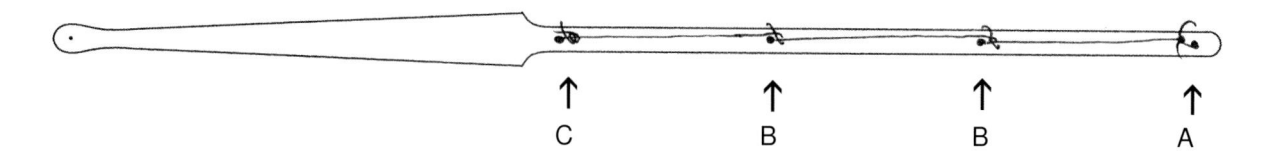

↑ ↑ ↑ ↑
C B B A

Figure 289 Fan leaf stitched to an inner stick

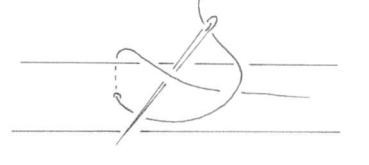

Figure 290 (left) Making a half hitch at hole B

Repeat at each hole down the stick until you reach the last hole, C. At this one sew through the stick and lace and fasten off with a double half hitch (figure 291).

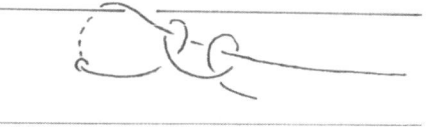

Figure 291 Making a double half hitch at hole C

All about making—Floral Bucks Point Lace

Use a separate thread to attach the lace to each stick. If the sticks have many perforations the fan leaf may not need attaching at every one and if the inner sticks do not have holes close to the inner edge of the leaf use a separate thread, pass it round the stick taking a small stitch through the lace and tie a reef knot. Since the guards are not perforated, attach them by following the instructions in item 2 below 'Attaching to sticks without perforations'.

2 Attaching to inner sticks without perforations
When the fan sticks do not have perforations the lace will have to be stuck to them. It is advisable to use a water soluble glue so that the lace can be removed for any necessary cleaning, also it should not discolour with age.

Some wallpaper paste is suitable and usually contains fungicide which may be useful in combating fungi but its long term effect on thread is uncertain. Paste without fungicide is available. Mix in the proportion of -

1 part paste : 10 parts water

Water soluble PVA glue, the type intended for childrens' use, may be suitable but check that it will wash out after it has dried. Again, its long term effect on thread is uncertain. The A in PVA is short for acetate, sometimes its odour can be detected indicating its presence. Although probably in very small quantities it may have long term adverse effects. Dilute slightly if necessary so that the glue can be painted onto the sticks.

Make sure the surface of the stick is clean and use a paint brush to brush on a thin layer of your chosen glue. Allow the glue to partially dry, and when it is tacky press the lace in position. Practice using similar materials so you can gauge the amount of tackiness required to get sufficient attachment, and this will vary according to the weight of the lace. Allow to dry thoroughly.

Finally fold the fan[4], with the folds evenly spaced, and keep closed using elastic bands. Leave closed for at least a month to allow the creases to set. Unless displayed open store the fan closed, preferably in a special fan box or rolled in white fabric in a cardboard tube. There should be just a slight pressure to keep the fan closed and creased.

All about making—Floral Bucks Point Lace

PROJECT 19: Fan leaf worked with four changes of direction

Figure 292 Fan leaf worked on pricking figures 292a-c with four changes of direction

Materials Required for Project 19
Egyptian cotton no. 60/2[1]
gimp D.M.C. perle no. 12

All about making—Floral Bucks Point Lace

TOP

working direction ↓

←C

C→

working direction ↓

C↗

Figure 293a Fan leaf pricking to be worked with four changes of direction

C→   change direction across here

working direction →

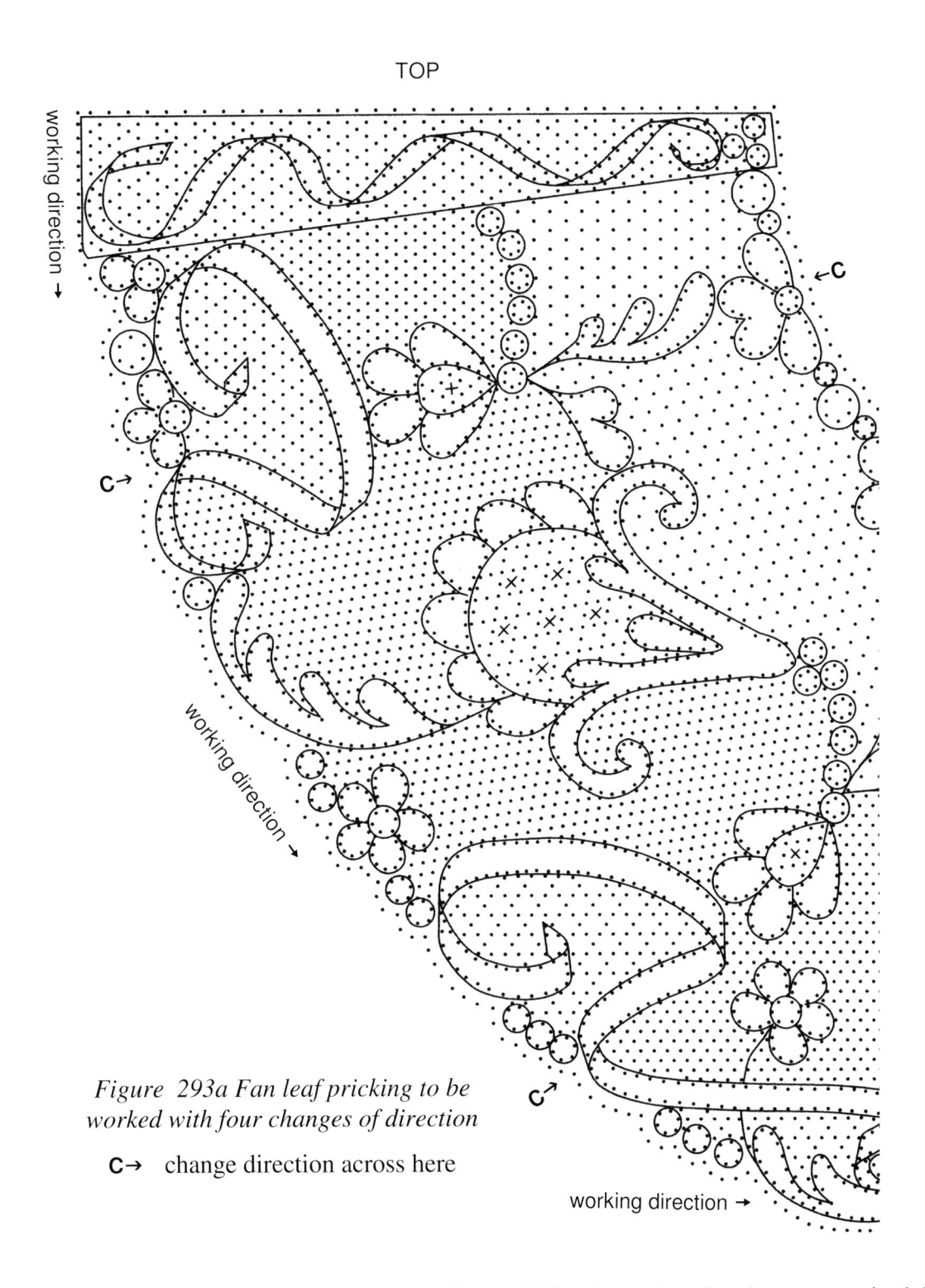

Join the three sections of the pricking (figures 293a-c), overlapping them as required. It may be useful to indicate the honeycomb rings to distinguish them from clothwork rings.

139

Figure 293b Fan leaf pricking

C→ change direction across here

All about making—Floral Bucks Point Lace

Figure 293c Fan leaf pricking

working direction →   C→   change direction across here

141

All about making—Floral Bucks Point Lace

Figure 294 Fan leaf worked on prickings 293a-c with four changes of direction

All about making—Floral Bucks Point Lace

Making the fan leaf
Set in horizontally with false picots, six passive pairs and a pair of gimps all seven pairs of bobbins working in two directions (figure 295). This will give a single gimp and three pairs of passives working each way, the number of passive pairs required to cast off securely along the horizontal picot edge when completing the fan leaf.

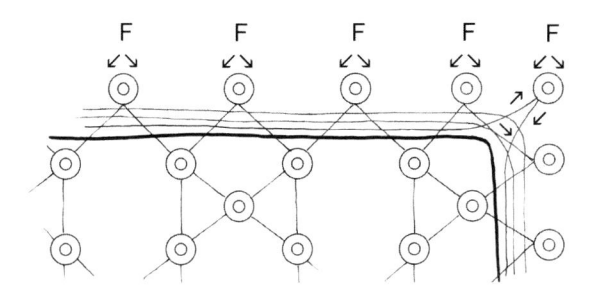

Figure 295 (left) Setting in along a horizontal picot edge

Figure 296 Working directions

After setting in along the picot edge work as far as the first heavy line (figure 296) where the motifs connect across from the outer edge to the inner edge. From the lower edges of these motifs, indicated by the heavy line, the works changes direction[3]. Continue in the new direction until the next heavy line is encountered. Again the motifs connect from the outer edge to the inner edge and the working direction changes. There are two more changes of direction indicated by heavy lines. The clothwork workers may be kept horizontal to the direction of work or, using artistic license, they may complement the fan outline and be worked radially, i.e. at right angles to the inner and outer edges at that point. Either will work. Finish by casting off horizontally along the picot edge.

143

*All about making—*Floral Bucks Point Lace

Casting off along the horizontal picot edge

The last picot of the outer edge is made using the inner passive pair which then works back through one pair (figure 297). From the inner corner work towards the last corner by taking the first of two pairs leaving a honeycomb stitch and working out through the passives, twist the workers once and leave as the edge passive pair. Work the second pair from the same honeycomb stitch out through all the passives, make a picot and return through all the passives leaving the pair as inner passives. After finishing all the honeycomb stitches next to the final gimp along the lower edge with each pair from the honeycomb stitch reduce the number of passive pairs to three.

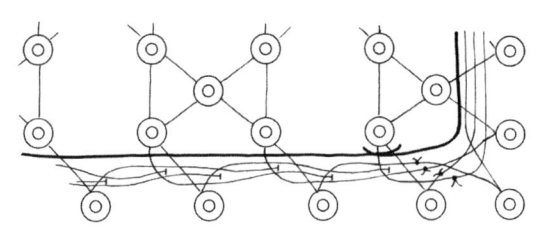

Figure 297 Casting off along a horizontal picot edge

END NOTES

1 Substituting threads
See Part 6.

2 Kat stitch ground used in conjunction with point ground and honeycomb
These prickings (figures 286a-c & 293a-c) contain areas of point ground, honeycomb and kat stitch and when these three grounds are used in the same piece of lace the point ground and honeycomb grids should have about twice the number of pins per 10cm (4in) than in the kat stitch ground, or to put it another way the kat stitch ground should have about half the number of pins per 10cm (4in) than the point ground, clothwork and honeycomb.

3 Designing a fan[4]
Draw a plan of your fan by placing your fan sticks on a piece of paper on a pricking board, space them evenly and mark the positions of the sticks and the inner and outer edges of the fan leaf. Then draw the design, bearing in mind the positions of the sticks; the picture of the lace when it is attached to the guards will not be seen properly and should not be an important part of the design. Different design elements may be traced on separate pieces of paper and moved under the main sheet of tracing paper until a pleasing design is produced. Trace the design onto the main sheet. Grids for the grounds can be placed and then attached underneath. If the fan leaf is to be made in one direction all the grounds will be in the same direction (figure 298). If the design breaks the ground from the inner to the outer edge the grids can be rotated and the lace worked radially. If the design has three changes of direction the grids will rotate by 60° at each break (figure 299), but the grounds do not need to be 60° to the footside, usually 52°-56° for point ground and honeycomb and 60°-64° for kat stitch.

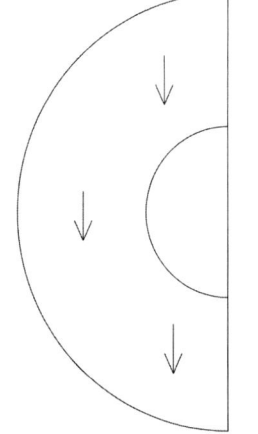

Figure 298 (left) Fan with no changes of direction

Figure 299 (right) Fan with two changes of direction

All about making—Floral Bucks Point Lace

In the fan worked with changes in direction (figures 293a-c & 294), the design dictated that there should be four changes with the grids changing direction by 45° each time. However, many antique prickings were designed to be worked in a single direction from point to point (figures 286a-c & 287)

Changing direction invariably involves adding and throwing out pairs along the breaks where the direction changes, whereas working in a single direction involves adding pairs as the lace increases in width from the vertical and then throwing them out as it decreases in width from the vertical.

It is much easier to design and work a fan that is worked in one direction.

4 Designing and mounting fans
For further information about all aspects of designing and making fans see Designing and Mounting Lace Fans by Christine Springett 1985.

All about making—Floral Bucks Point Lace

Blank page.

PART 3
REGENCY BUCKS

This form of Floral Bucks (figure 300) was at the height of its popularity during the 1820s and 1830s and its main characteristic is the placement of the gimp within the clothwork rather than surrounding it. There is at least one pattern signed by Thomas Lester so it is not surprising that some of the designs are similar to some of the Bedfordshire lace patterns; the gimped veins and clothwork not being surrounded by a gimp are found in both. Regency Bucks Point, frequently abbreviated to Regency Bucks or Regency Point, uses the same ground as Standard Floral Bucks and honeycomb and other fillings were frequently used. In the pieces I examined the angle to the footside varied from 51° to 64°. In the prickings I studied the footside was not always off-set and all variations for working the Standard Floral Bucks footside are suitable for Regency Bucks; one piece I studied had cloth stitch catch-pin stitches. Many pieces of lace and prickings that were studied were found to contain elements made using Standard Bucks alongside those worked using Regency techniques.

Figure 300 Regency Bucks

The techniques used to make this form of Floral Bucks are generally those used for making Standard Floral Bucks, but the techniques are less well defined. Periwinkle, the third skirt insertion was a very popular design and many examples of the lace and prickings can be found. While researching I was surprised to see how many very different ways the pricking had been interpreted. I found many cases of pins shown in the pricking not being involved in making the lace. This suggests that the designers had insufficient knowledge of this branch of Floral Bucks to enable them plot the pinholes successfully. Alternatively, since the lace workers had to contend with new situations they used their ingenuity to devise new methods of coping with the problems they came across and, since the popularity of this lace was short lived, the techniques did not become as standardised as Standard Floral Bucks.

All about making—Floral Bucks Point Lace

Although I found that lace workers rarely added pairs when making Standard Bucks I found many cases of pairs being added and thrown out from the clothwork in the Regency pieces I studied. This form of Bucks Point tends to use very fine thread and the finest pins obtainable. The finer the thread and scale of the pricking the less exacting the size of the thread and a wider variety of techniques are used. Anomalies that would show in an enlarged version are not so easily apparent; the pattern repeats may be more varied, yet still look the same since the fine detail cannot easily be seen without a lens.

For those who are not comfortable working with very fine threads enlarged pickings are included for use with Egyptian cotton no. 100/2 and as with Standard Floral Bucks the number of pairs in the clothwork may be adjusted as required. However, the shortcomings of the techniques will be more apparent (see Part 6).

The edgings in this section all have the footside off-set, some more so than others enabling you to assess the results.

All about making—Floral Bucks Point Lace

CHAPTERS 14-17

PROJECTS 20-24 : Christening set for Emily, a 43 cm. (17 inch) doll

Figure 301 Emily's christening gown

Figure 302 Emily, a 43cm (17 in) doll made by Elaine Woodhams of Becky Dolls

Materials Required for Projects 20-24
Egyptian cotton no. 170/2[1], gimp no. 12 perle
commercial pattern for christening gown for 43cm (17 in) doll
fabric for the underdress and gown calculated according to the pattern
narrow heading (sometimes known as an engrêlure[2]) sufficient
for around the lower edge of the underdress and around the skirt panel
slightly wider heading to take a 2mm threaded ribbon for around the sleeves of the gown
1m (1 yd) 2mm ($^1/_{12}$ in) ribbon
6 small buttons
card with 6.5cm (2½ in) aperture and sticky letters in silver

The order of working the different parts of the set has been arranged according to the difficulty of making the lace. Thus making the lace for Project 21 the underdress is described between Projects 20a & b the gown bodice and Projects 20d & e the gown skirt panel.

All about making—Floral Bucks Point Lace

CHAPTER 14

PROJECT 20: Bodice insertions and sleeve edgings

Project 20a: Bodice insertion and sleeve edging
Project 20b: Heading used as an insertion

PROJECT 20a: Bodice insertion and sleeve edging

Materials Required for Project 20a
Egyptian cotton no. 170/2[1]
gimp no. 12 perle
fabric according to pattern
narrow heading[2] for around sleeves
3 small buttons

Figure 303 Christening overdress bodice

This insertion for the bodice (figures 303-305) has the usual point ground and a footside on both sides. The edging for the sleeves (figures 303, 304 & 306) has the usual point ground, a footside and a headside with two passive pairs. The clothwork in Regency Bucks is not surrounded by gimps and there are the usual two twists[3] when the worker passes round the pin at the end of the row. Some pieces of antique Regency Bucks were made with the passives tightly packed in the clothwork and others with them well spaced so that an underlying colour shows through, thus the density is one of personal choice. This piece has such small areas of clothwork that I have chosen to keep them fairly dense. Start and finish the sleeve edgings so that they can be finished by joined end to start.

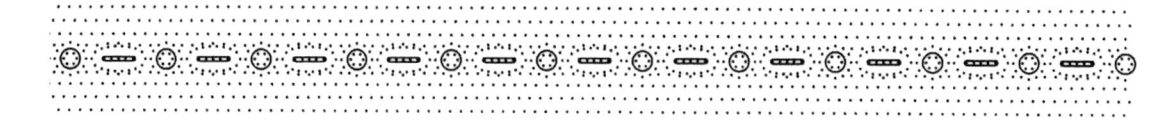

Figure 304 Pricking for the insertion for the overdress bodice and the edging for the sleeves to be made using Egyptian Cotton no. 170/2, gimp no. 12 perle

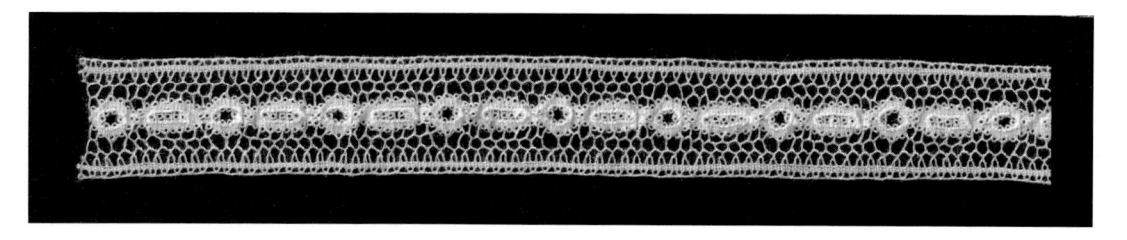

Figure 305 Lace for first insertion of the overdress made on pricking figure 304 using Egyptian Cotton no. 170/2, gimp no. 12 perle

All about making—Floral Bucks Point Lace

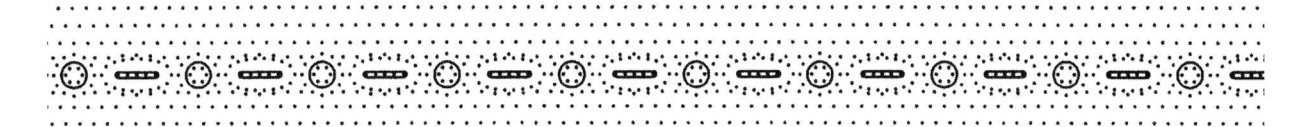

Figure 306 Enlarged pricking for the insertion for the overdress bodice and the edging for the sleeves to be made using Egyptian Cotton no. 100/2, gimp no. 12 perle

Figure 307 The narrow edging used around the sleeves made on pricking figure 304 made using Egyptian Cotton no. 170/2, gimp no. 12 perle

Regency ring[4&5] and Regency gimped beetles

The gimped rings have the gimp at the inner edge of the clothwork surrounding the pins of the hole; the outer edge of the clothwork has no gimp. The beetles are the oval areas of clothwork with a central gimped division or vein[6]. Again there is no gimp around the outer edge of the clothwork.

Regency ring[5], winkie pins at the sides and starting and finishing with cloth and twist

When the pricking was drafted some of the pinholes very close to the sides of the clothwork were left in; they may be too close for pins but I found them as a useful guide for making stitches without pins. It is your choice; when you do not have room for the ground pin leave the stitch unpinned.

Set in the ring at pin A (figure 308) and work rows across the top to pins B & C. The decision regarding when to divide the passives and start the centre depends on the number of pins down each side. (Thinking backwards from the centre pin at the side, pin G, you find that the top pin of the ring, pin D, follows pin C, but some prickings may have more rows before the dividing pin). Once the passives are divided work the stitch at the top ring pin, pin D, with the odd pair of passives if there is one; otherwise choose one of the centre two pairs. Pass the gimp through the workers and the chosen passives, usually without twists between the workers and the passives[4], and work cloth and twist twice, pin, cloth and twist twice at pin D; both pairs are now workers.

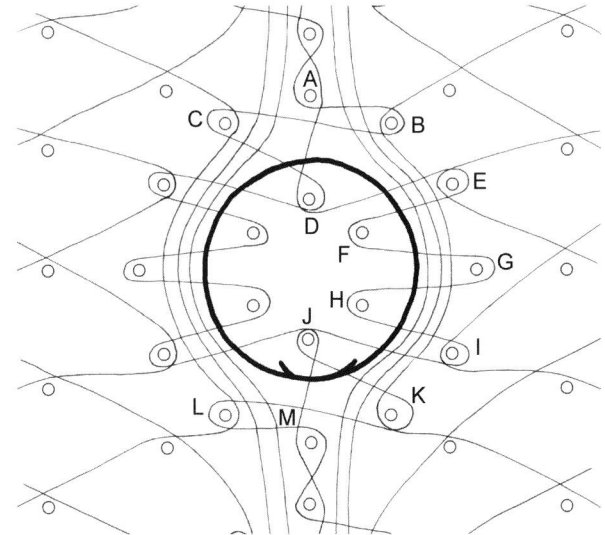

Figure 308 Regency gimped ring, winkie pins at the sides and starting and finishing with cloth and twist

151

All about making—Floral Bucks Point Lace

Pass each of these workers out across the adjacent gimp. Work down one side of the ring giving the workers three twists as they pass round the winkie pins, pins F & H, and two twists as they pass round pin G where there is no pair entering or leaving the clothwork. Repeat for the other side. When both worker pairs re-enter the ring work cloth and twist twice, pin J, cloth and twist twice. The sides now combine and, unless the number of pinholes following the pinhole dictates otherwise, make up the half row before the division (from pin C to pin D) by working from pin J to pin K. Finish by working the remaining rows to pins L and M. Any remaining passive pairs continue to lie either side of the final pin of the ring, pin M.

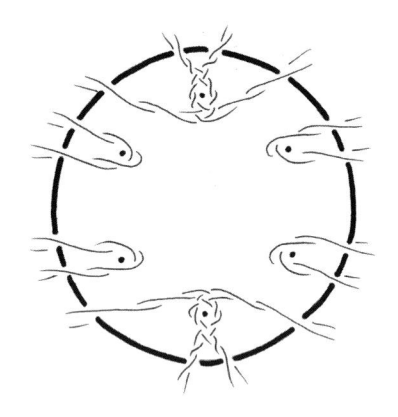

Figure 309 (left) Regency ring, winkie pins at the sides and starting and finishing with cloth and twist

Figure 310 (right) Regency ring, winkie pins at the sides and starting and finishing with cloth and twist

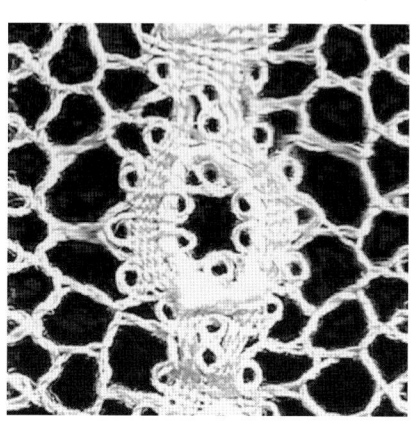

Regency beetle[6]

A beetle is an oval of clothwork with a gimped central vein. This particular one starts immediately below a ring which has two passive pairs remaining either side of the final pin. After covering the final pin of the ring, pin M, (figure 311) twist the pairs twice and set up the first pin of the beetle, pin N. Cover the pin and continue as for the Regency gimped ring, pins P-S. However, this time there are more rows as dictated by the arrangement of pinholes down the sides of the beetle, and there is a slight bowing upwards of the last full row, pins R-S; which is typical of Regency Bucks Point. The clothwork divides for the central division at pin T, as for the gimped ring, and the sides are worked simultaneously. When the workers meet between the gimps[6] they work twist, cloth and twist, pin, cloth and twist (figures 309 & 310). The division closes at pin U as for the gimped ring and the beetle finishes at pin V. There are now two pairs of passives either side of the finishing pin ready for the following gimped ring. Again, there will be more rows than for the ring and the first rows of clothwork may bow downwards slightly. Finish the beetle the same as finishing the ring. The pinholes for the ground at the sides of the beetle (the ones containing 'x') are really too close for use, but I found them useful indicators for making stitches without pins.

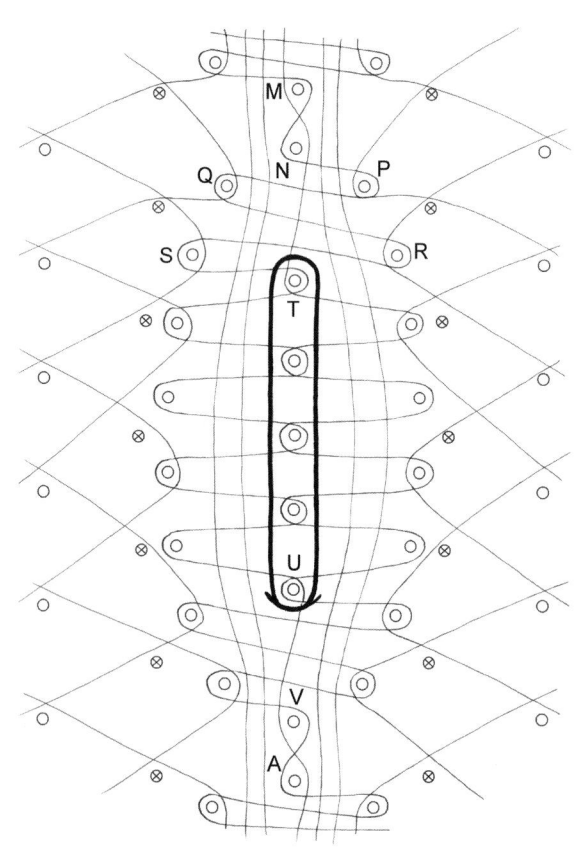

Figure 311 Beetle with cloth and twist vein

All about making—Floral Bucks Point Lace

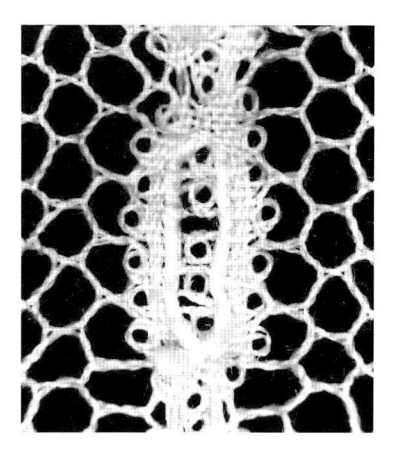

Figure 312 (right) Beetle with cloth and twist vein

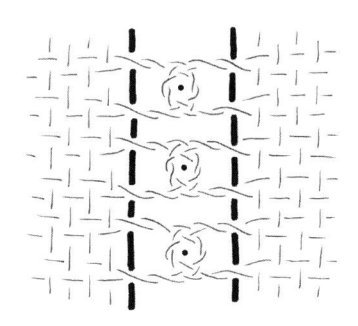

Figure 313 (left) Cloth and twist vein

153

All about making—Floral Bucks Point Lace

PROJECT 20b: Bodice, heading used as an insertion

Heading or Engrêlure[2]

Although not containing Regency Bucks techniques, the original hand-made version of the machine-made heading was used as an insertion down the centre front of the bodice (figures 314 & 315). Reminiscent of the cucumber foot[7], this is probably its precursor and is made with the footside of the cucumber foot down both sides.

Materials Required for Project 20b
Egyptian cotton no. 170/2[1]

Figure 314 Heading to be used as an insertion, pricking for use with Egyptian cotton no. 170/2

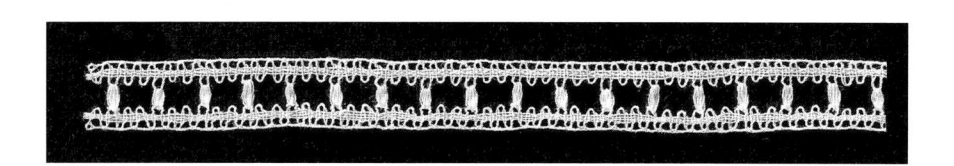

Figure 315 Heading to be used as an insertion, made on pricking figure 314, using Egyptian cotton no. 170/2

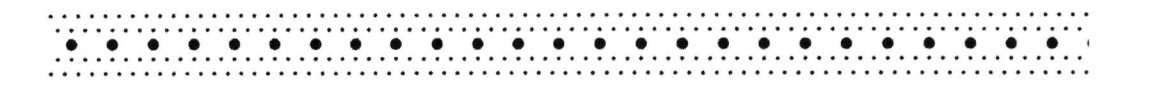

Figure 316 Heading, enlarged pricking, for use with Egyptian cotton no. 100/2

All about making—Floral Bucks Point Lace

Making up the bodice
The bodice (figure 303) has the narrow hand-made insertion (figures 314 & 315) down the centre front and narrow insertions (figures 304 & 305) at a small distance away on either side, all are attached to the fabric using four-sided stitch before the bodice was cut out as per the pattern.

The bodice was made up and lined as per the pattern with the lower edge left open for attaching to the skirt panel.

Making up the sleeve frill
The edging was stitched to the sleeve frill strip using four-sided stitch[8] and the free edge of the fabric was gathered. The surplus fabric was trimmed from one side of the machine-made heading, a narrow strip of machine embroidery resulting in a line of squares through a narrow strip of fabric (figure 317) and this edge was attached to the lower edge of the made up sleeve while rolling the edge at the same time (figure 316). The edge of the sleeve frill was rolled, the needle placed under the roll until it touched the fabric at the edge of the roll by the heading and then the point slid against the edge of the fabric in the direction of the arrow A where it was pushed through the fabric at arrow B (figure 318 & 319).

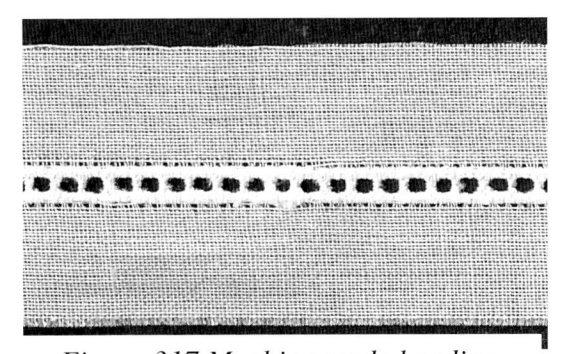

Figure 317 Machine made heading.

Figure 318 Attaching the heading to the sleeve

This narrow heading was used when attaching the lower edge of the underdress skirt; a wider one with a narrow ribbon threaded through was used for the sleeves.

Figure 319 (right) Machine made heading attached to sleeve frill

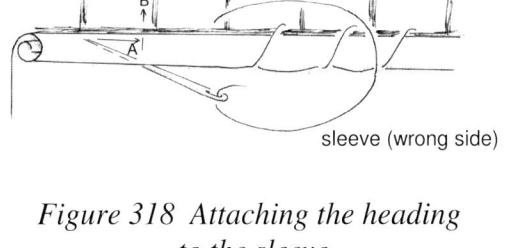

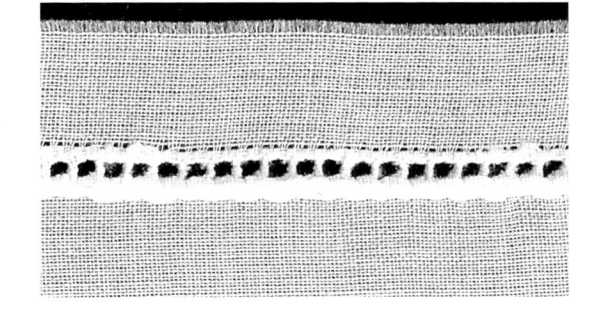

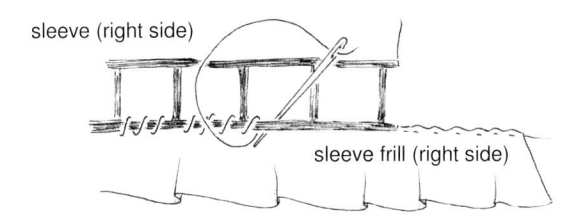

Figure 320 Attaching the frill to the heading

The remaining surplus fabric of the heading was trimmed, each sleeve frill was gathered to fit and the gathered edge of the right side of the frill was placed to the wrong side of the free edge of the heading. Then the two were oversewn closely together with the needle passing through the holes of the heading (figure 320).

155

All about making—Floral Bucks Point Lace

END NOTES

1a Substituting threads
Standard Floral Bucks is very demanding regarding the size of thread used and the use of substitute threads may not give the same results. However, this form of Floral Bucks has facilities for adjustment, the tendency for the clothwork to look starved or choked may be easily compensated for by adding or removing pairs, also see Part 6.

1b Adding pairs
Although in the past pairs were only occasionally added to thicken the clothwork of Standard Floral Bucks, much of the Regency Bucks I have studied made good use of this technique, pairs usually being slipped on at the end of a row of clothwork.

1c Throwing out pairs
Since there is no gimp around the clothwork for surplus pairs to lay along before being thrown out, the surplus pairs are then thrown out of the clothwork and cut off.

2 Heading/Engrêlure
Antique lace, particularly the early lace, often had a very narrow insertion stitched to the edge of the lace with the other side of the insertion attached to the garment. I have not used the term 'footside' for the edge of the lace to which the narrow insertion would be attached as this is frequently missing, many of these pieces possibly being too early for the technique. These very narrow insertions are usually referred to as headings. Their function was to protect expensive lace from being damaged during the removal of the lace from the garment for cleaning and reattaching, as the heading would remain attached to the lace and any damage occurring would be to the heading. Machine made versions of these headings, often known as engrêlure, can be purchased from good haberdashers, or a handmade one may be used. The machine made version has a strip of fabric along each side and this is removed before the heading is attached. Have another look at the handmade heading and compare it with a cucumber foot. Could the heading be the precursor of the cucumber foot?

3 Twists round the pin
There may be from one to three twists when the worker passes around the pin at the end of a row of clothwork.

4 Gimps and twists
It is not usual to have twists between the gimp and the clothwork. Sometimes the gimp continues the weave (figure 321); sometimes the adjacent passive thread parallels the gimp (figure 322). However, whether there are or are not twists is at the discretion of the lacemaker as is the way the gimp passes through the pair. The number of twists from clothwork to point ground may be two or three.

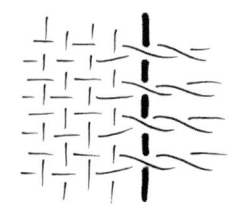

Figure 321 (left) Weaving the gimp through the workers

Figure 322 (right) Passing the gimp through the workers to parallel the passive thread

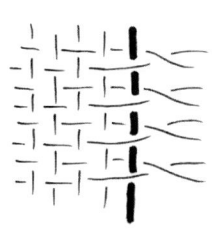

All about making—Floral Bucks Point Lace

5a Regency honeycomb ring and Regency cloth and twist honeycomb ring
Regency rings can also be made as regular honeycomb rings (figure 323) or as honeycomb rings with cloth stitch, twist twice, pin, cloth twist twice at each pin (figure 324). The two pairs entering to make the top pinhole may be a worker and a passive pair or two passive pairs according to the requirements of the pattern. If they are both passive pairs another passive will enter from the side away from the original workers and they then continue as workers for that side.

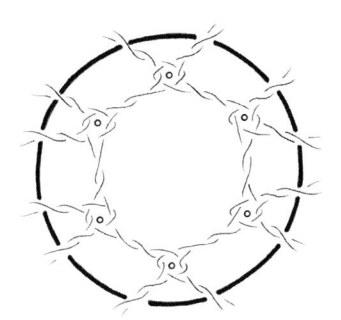

Figure 323 (left) Honeycomb ring

Figure 324 (right) Cloth and twist honeycomb ring

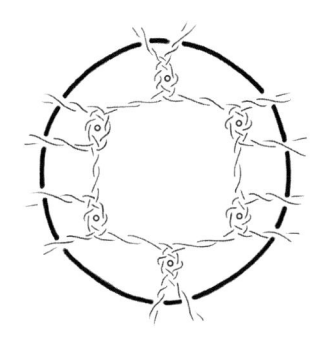

5b Regency ring starting and finishing with winkie pins
Work until the last row of clothwork is just above the top pinhole inside the gimp and bring the workers back across the gimp, stopping just before the passive pair that is in line with this pinhole (figure 325). (Here the workers are approaching from the right). Pass a new gimp through the workers and this passive pair. Pin, then twist the passive pair and pass it out across the gimp towards the left to become the other pair of workers. (Here they are working towards the left). Pin under the original workers, twist them and pass them back across the gimp to continue as workers for this side. Each worker makes a winkie pin at the following two pins within the ring. At the last pinhole one pair of workers passed across the gimp, is pinned, twisted and passes out across the gimp to be left as passives. This part row balances the part row that was made when the ring was started unless the pinholes dictate otherwise. The remaining pair of workers continues the clothwork.

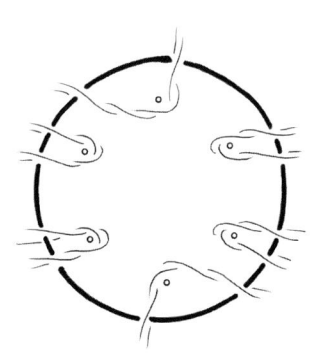

Figure 325 Regency gimped ring starting and finishing with winkie pins

6 Gimped veins
These may be worked in several ways. After passing the gimp through both workers it may be left untwisted or twisted once or twice. Then work cloth and twist (one or two twists), pin, cloth and then twist as before (figure 326). They may also be worked in honeycomb stitch (figure 327). The cloth and twist version is the one most commonly used in Regency Point.

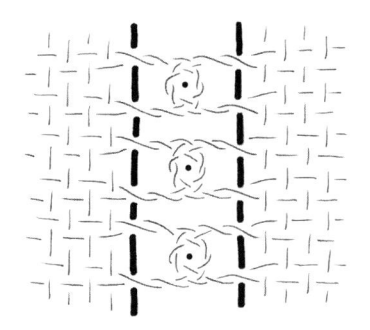

Figure 326 (left) Cloth and twist vein

Figure 327 (right) Honeycomb stitch vein

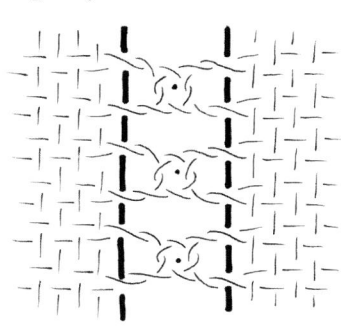

All about making—Floral Bucks Point Lace

7 Cucumber foot
See '*All about making*—Geometrical Bucks Point Lace' A. Stillwell, Salex Publishing, page 108.

8 Four-sided stitch
Ibid. page 41

9 Corners
Although not used for the christening gown here are some corners for the insertions and edgings.

Figure 328 (left) Corner pricking for the very narrow insertion and edging, to be made using Egyptian cotton no. 170/2, gimp D.M.C. perle no. 12

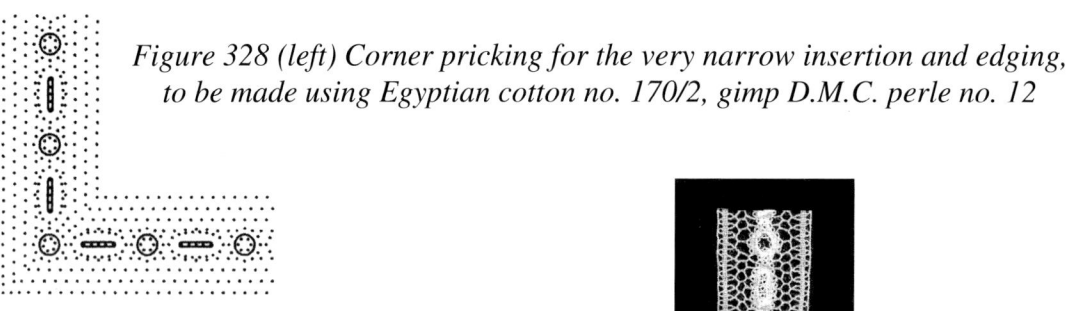

Figure 329 (right) Insertion corner made on pricking figure 328 using Egyptian cotton no. 170/2, gimp D.M.C. perle no. 12

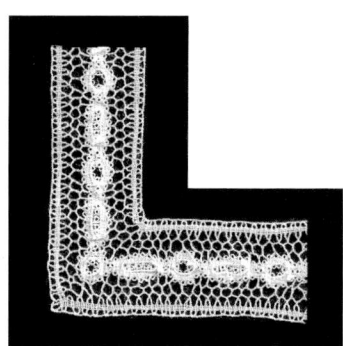

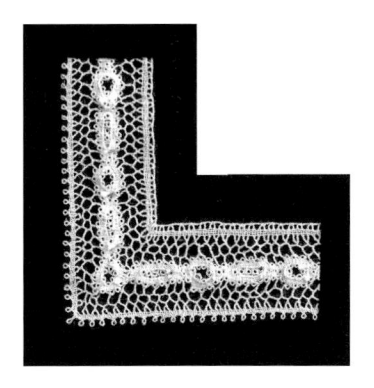

Figure 330 (left) Edging corner made on pricking figure 328 using Egyptian cotton no. 170/2, gimp D.M.C. perle no. 12

Figure 331 (right) Corner for the very narrow insertion and edging, enlarged pricking to be made using Egyptian cotton no. 100/2, gimp D.M.C. perle no. 12

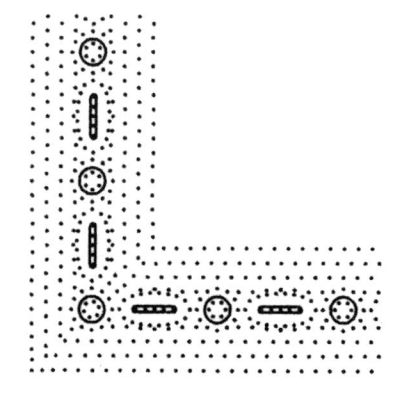

All about making—Floral Bucks Point Lace

CHAPTER 15

PROJECT 21: Underdress

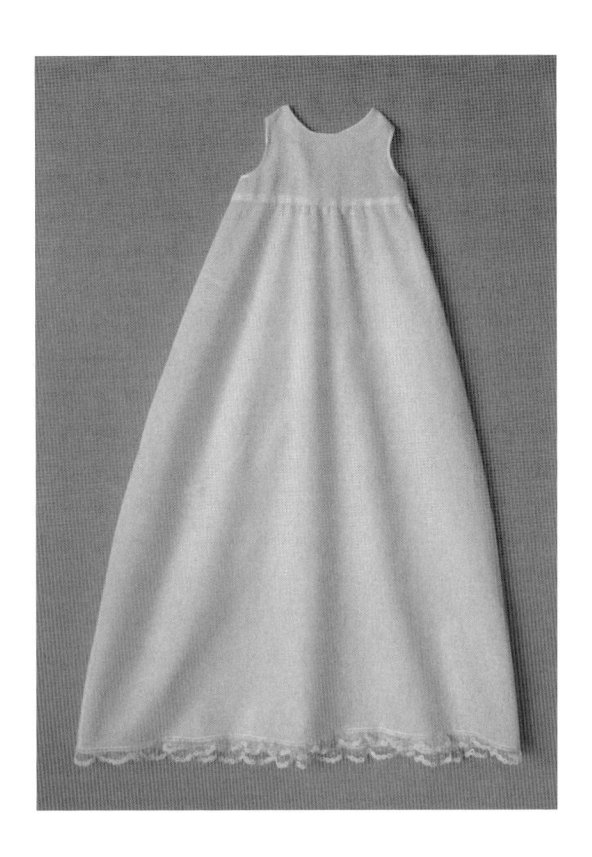

Materials Required for Project 21
Egyptian cotton no. 170/2[1].
gimp no. 12 perle
fabric according to pattern
2 small buttons

The underdress (figure 332) has a plain bodice and a gathered skirt. The neckline and armholes have rolled hems and the skirt has French seams at the sides and is gathered into the lower edge of the bodice. The underdress was made up first so that the length of lace required for around the lower edge could be estimated. Allowance was made for slight gathering and the lace was joined end to start.

Figure 332 (left) Underdress

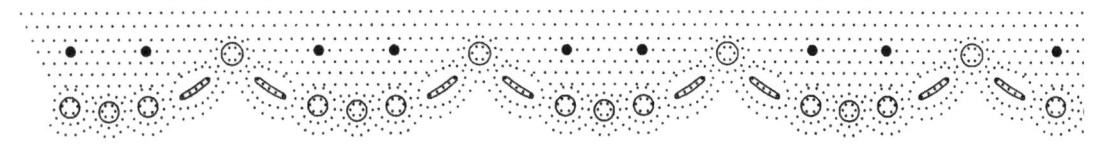

Figure 333 Edging for the underdress, pricking for Egyptian cotton no. 170/2, gimp no. 12 perle

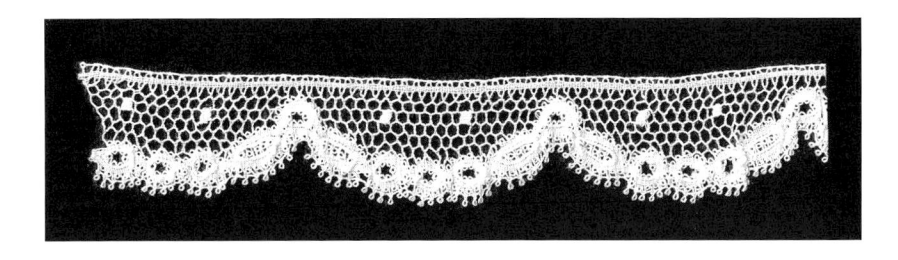

Figure 334 Edging for the underdress made on pricking figure 333 using Egyptian cotton no. 170/2, gimp no. 12 perle

159

All about making—Floral Bucks Point Lace

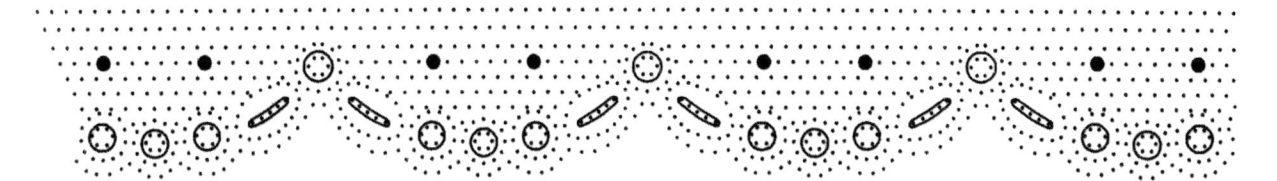

Figure 335 Edging for the underdress, enlarged pricking for using Egyptian cotton no. 100/2, gimp no. 12 perle

Regency headside
The Regency headside usually has a picot edge with a single twisted pair of passives. There may be two or three twists between the edge passives and the clothwork and two or three twists on the edge pair between the picots (figure 336).

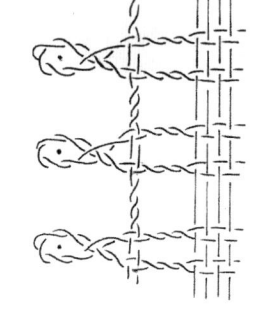

Figure 336 (right) Regency headside with a single passive pair twisted three times

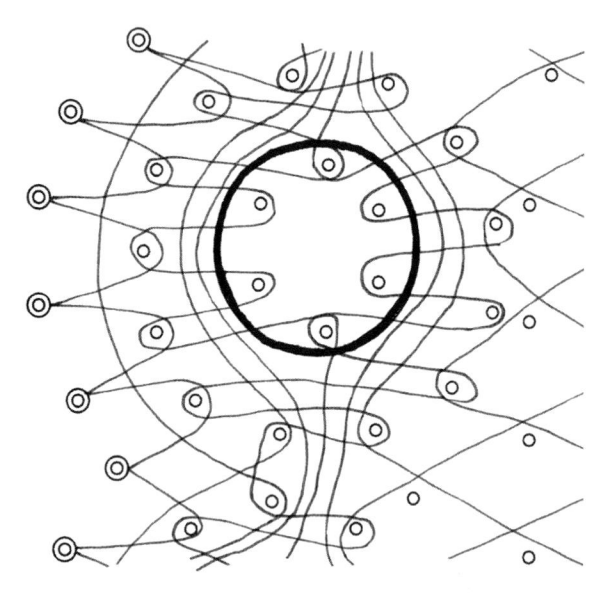

Setting in the edging
Start by working diagonally down the ground from the footside to the top of the upper ring. Although this is the easiest place to start, it not the best if the piece is to be joined end to start. Note the way the Regency edge bounding the circle exchanges with a new twisted edge pair in the valley while a picot is made (figure 337). There are twists on the edge passives before and after entering the clothwork, but there are no extra twists between the picot and the twisted edge pair.

Figure 337 (left) The first of the outer three circles of the underdress edging

Stitches without pins
The following figures show pairs drawn across some of the pinholes. Technically these pinholes should have been omitted as the stitch should be made without a pin, but they assist in working out where to absorb and leave out pairs.

Regency valley
The pairs do not stack in the valley as they do in Standard Floral Bucks. Invariably there is only a single twisted passive pair along the headside that usually exchanges with another pair in the angle of the valley. The edge clothwork typically contains a vein or circle of clothwork and the number of passive pairs between this gimped motif and the Regency edge usually remains constant from when they start following the gimp through the vein until they stop following it. Instead of stacking the pairs in the valley, the pairs enter and leave the clothwork on the other side of the gimped motif (figure 338).

160

All about making—Floral Bucks Point Lace

The gimped ring in the valley starts with the workers from the beetle and a pair from the ground (figure 338). After working back through these pairs the workers make two twists round the pin and return through four pairs to make the upper stitch inside the gimp with the next pair of passives. This time there are more passive pairs and in lieu of stacking them they are divided so that four pairs pass each side of the gimp motif (figure 339). Another pair enters from the ground making five on this side for a short time. The apparent gaps at the left side of the ring do not show in the lace, only in the diagram. Note the arrangement of the pinholes along the clothwork in the valleys and the way the edge of the clothwork ring interacts with the footside. Pairs then pass to the next beetle (figure 340).

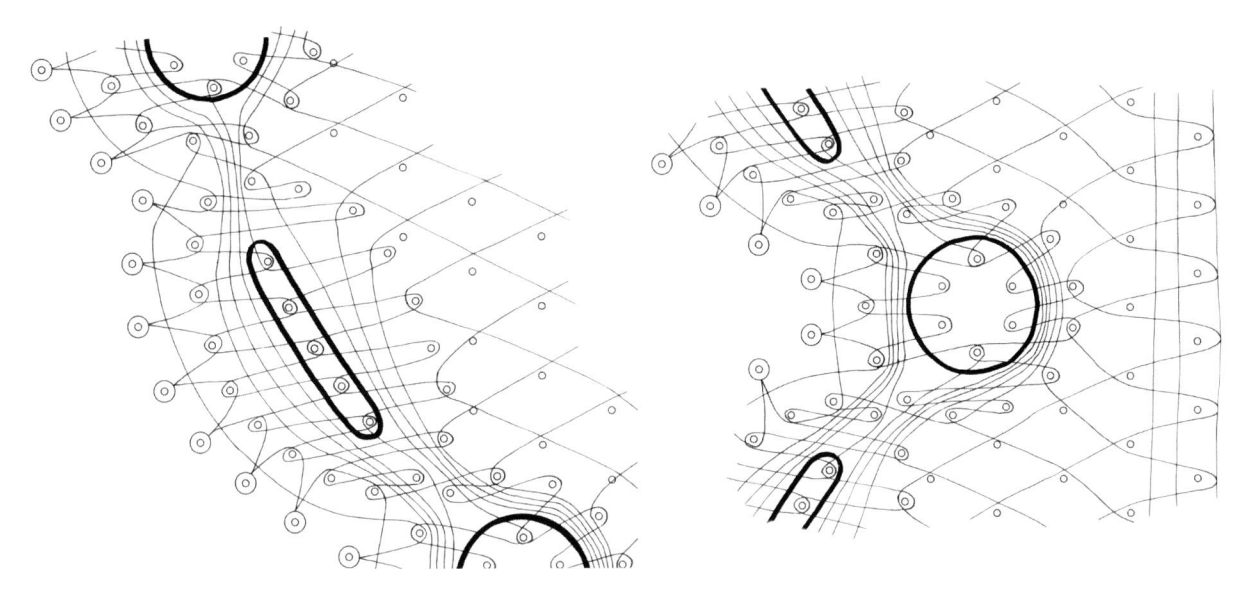

Figure 338 (left) Passing into a valley along a beetle with gimped vein

Figure 339 The ring in the valley

Figure 340 (right) Passing from the circle in the valley to the next beetle

Making up the underdress
The underdress has a sleeveless bodice with a rolled hem around the armholes and neckline and the skirt is trimmed with a lace edging attached with a machine-made heading, the heading being attached at the same time as rolling the hem. The lace edging is gathered slightly and oversewn to the remaining edge of the heading. Buttonholes were made and buttons attached at the neck edge and waistline.

END NOTES

1 Substituting threads
See Part 6.

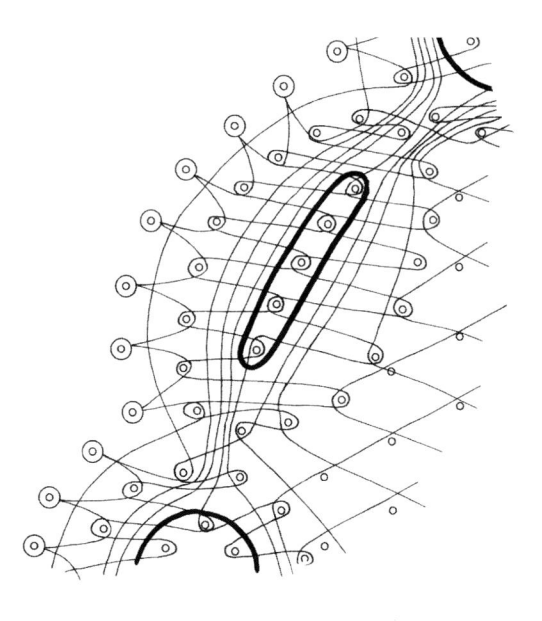

All about making—Floral Bucks Point Lace

CHAPTER 16

PROJECT 20c: Gown, Skirt panel upper insertion

Materials Required for Projects 20c
Egyptian cotton no. 170/2[1]
gimp no. 12 perle
fabric according to the pattern
narrow heading sufficient for around
the skirt panel

The christening gown overdress has a skirt panel with three insertions across it and an edging the same as the underdress down both sides and across the lower edge.

Skirt panel
None of the pieces of lace for this panel needs a neat start or finish as all ends will be sewn into a seam. The insertions lengthen as you progress down towards the hem so estimate the length for each individual insertion prior to making it.

Figure 341 Skirt panel

Skirt panel upper insertion

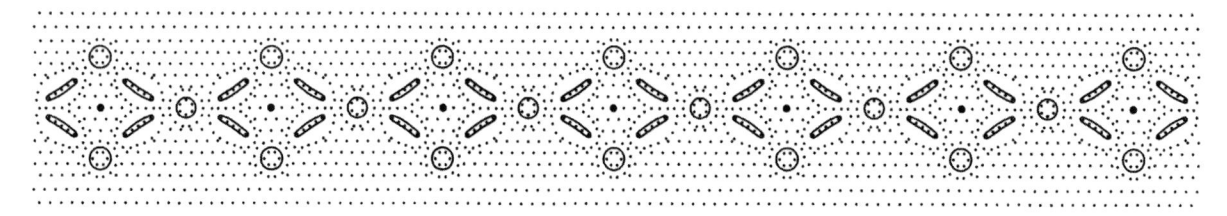

Figure 342 Christening gown upper insertion, pricking for use with Egyptian cotton no. 170/2, gimp no. 12 perle.

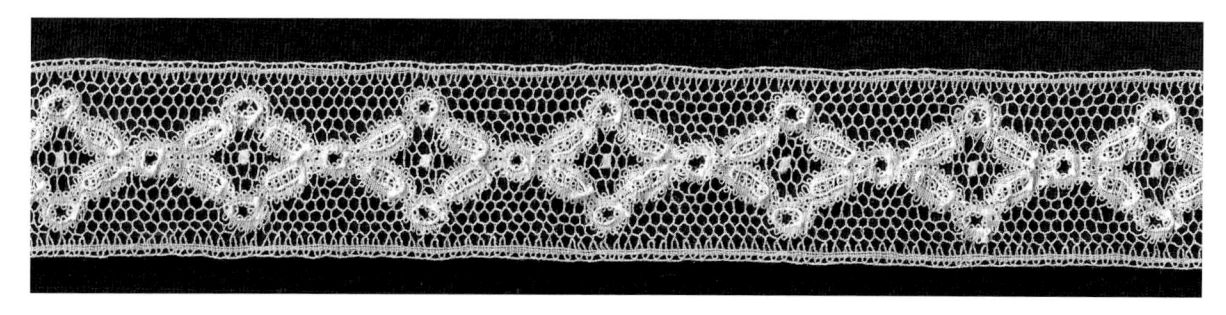

Figure 343 Christening gown upper insertion[2] made on pricking figure 342

162

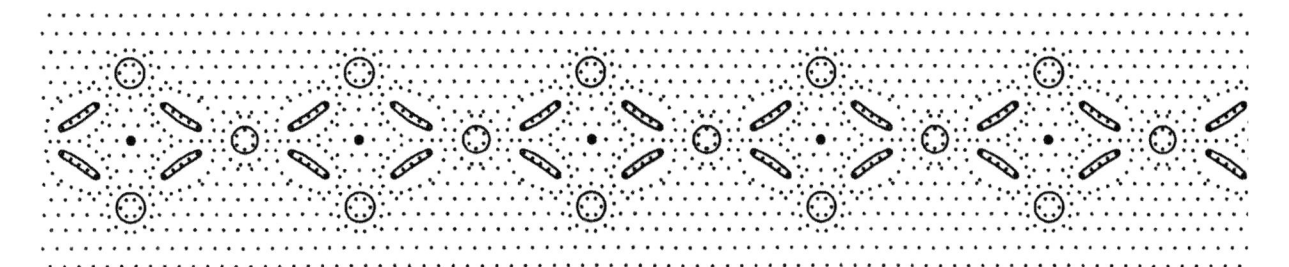

Figure 344 Upper insertion, enlarged pricking for use with Egyptian cotton no. 100/2, gimp no. 12 perle.

Regency ring starting and finishing with two pins side-by-side

The number of holes within the ring will vary according to the surrounding work.

When the top two pins of the ring lie side-by-side they are usually worked as winkie pins, one being made by the worker, in this case the one on the right, and the other using a passive pair which becomes the worker pair for the remaining side, in this case the left (figures 345 & 346). When the last two pins of the ring have been worked it is usual for the pair that was previously a passive pair to continue as the workers, the previous workers becoming passives thus making the sides even, but the positions of the following pinholes may require working differently.

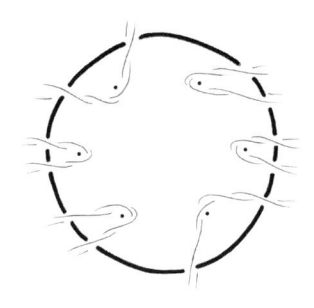

Figure 345 Regency ring starting and finishing with two pins side-by-side

The Regency ring (figure 346) starts at A with the centre two pairs, then the workers pass through two more pairs on one side to B, then back through two more pairs to C on the other side. Two more pairs enter the clothwork from the ground at the ends of each of the next two rows, pins D and E, with each having a third pair entering from and then leaving to work the ground. The ring opens by the worker returning through half the passives and a new gimp pair to pin F and back across these pairs to pin G. In this case there is an odd number of passive pairs.

Not counting the pairs entering from and leaving at pinholes, the motif is completed by discarding two pairs at the end of the following three rows, pins N, P and Q, and covering the last pin, pin R. The discarded pairs lie against the sides of the motif.

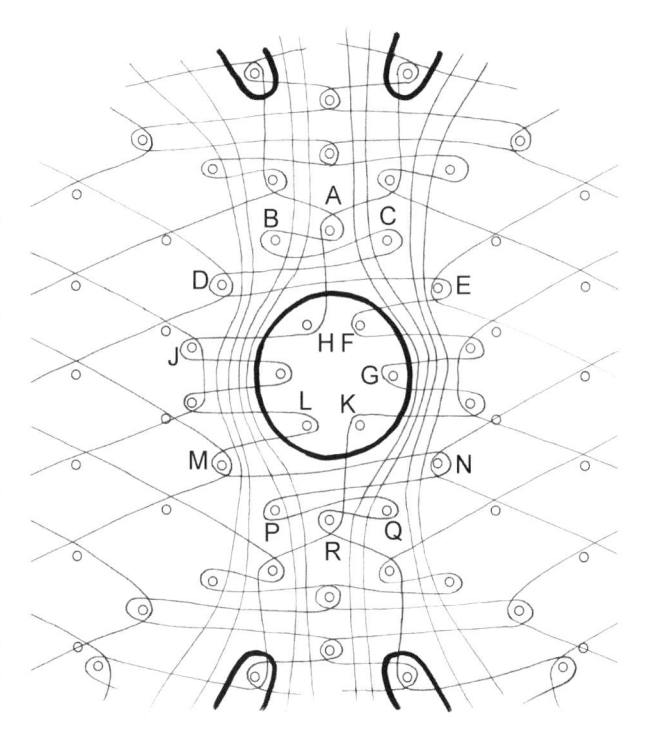

Figure 346 Regency ring starting and finishing with two pins side-by-side

163

All about making—Floral Bucks Point Lace

Passive pair crossing a gimped vein
The beetles in this pattern lie diagonally within the ground and therefore pairs will enter into it from the ground on one side and leave from it to pass into the ground on the other, thus one side will become starved and the other side choked. To avoid this, and keep to an approximately constant number of pairs in their respective sides, a passive pair may be passed across the vein (figure 347). When both workers have passed out from the stitch in the vein and worked a row out to their respective sides, pass both the gimps through the adjacent passive pair on the side that is becoming choked, twisting the passives once or twice between the gimps. There are no twists on the clothwork side of the gimps. Return to the working pairs and continue. Passing a passive pair across the vein may occur more than once across long veins, and if the vein changes direction then one or more passive pairs may cross back in the opposite direction.

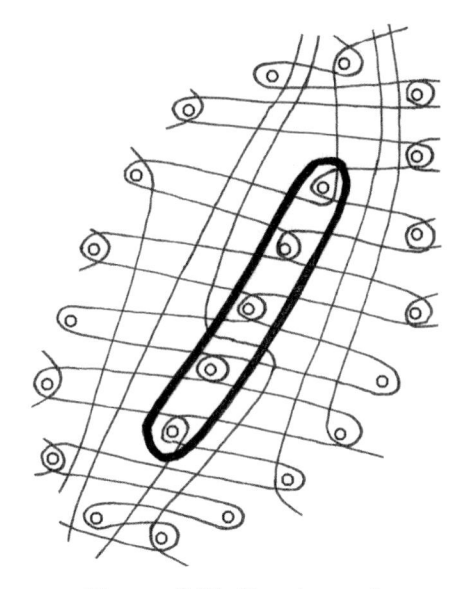

Figure 347 Passive pair crossing a gimped vein

END NOTES

1 Substituting threads
See Part 6.

2 Design variations
Tallies can make a lot of difference to a design. The first insertion (figures 341 & 342) can be made without any tallies (figures 348 & 349).

The following prickings are for use with Egyptian cotton no. 170/2. To use Egyptian cotton no. 100/2 adapt pricking figure no 344 by replacing the large dots indicating tallies with small dots for point ground..

Figure 348 Variation without tallies, pricking

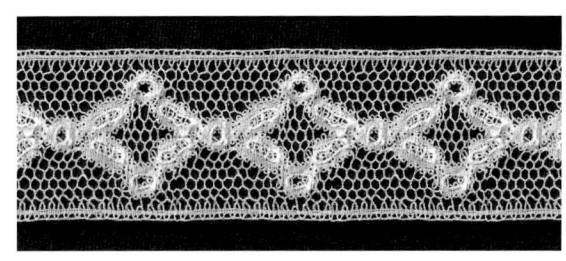

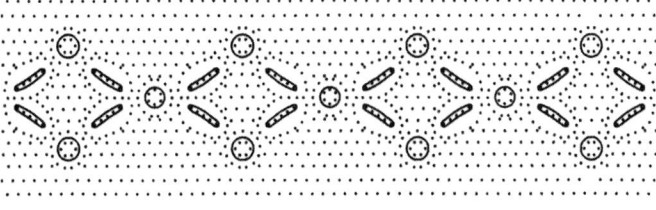

Figure 349 Variation without tallies, lace made on pricking figure 348

164

All about making—Floral Bucks Point Lace

Note the difference when a single tally is placed in the centre of each enclosed space (figures 342 & 343) and how the design changes again when a tally is added on each side of the central motif (figures 350 & 351).

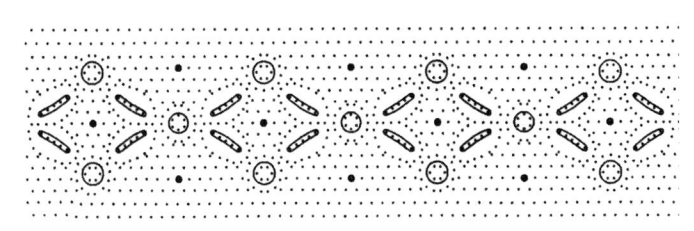

Figure 350 Variation with a single tally each side, pricking

Figure 351 Variation with a single tally each side, lace made on pricking figure 350

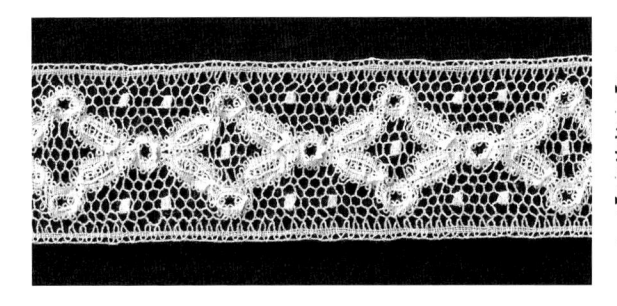

Figure 352 Variation with two tallies each side, lace made on pricking figure 353

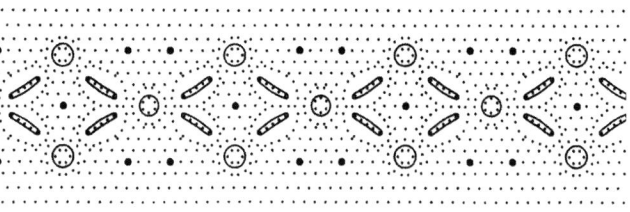

Figure 353 Variation with two tallies each side, pricking

When two tallies are worked on each side of the motif the design becomes cluttered (figures 352 353).

165

All about making—Floral Bucks Point Lace

CHAPTER 17

PROJECT 20d: Gown, Skirt panel lower insertion

Lower insertion 'Periwinkle'
Estimate the length for each insertion separately as the panel widens and the insertions lengthen as you progress downwards towards the hem.

This design was popular with the lace workers and the leafy sections were tackled in many completely different ways; some pieces were made ignoring some of the pinholes; indicating that perhaps the pricking was drafted by a designer rather than a laceworker.

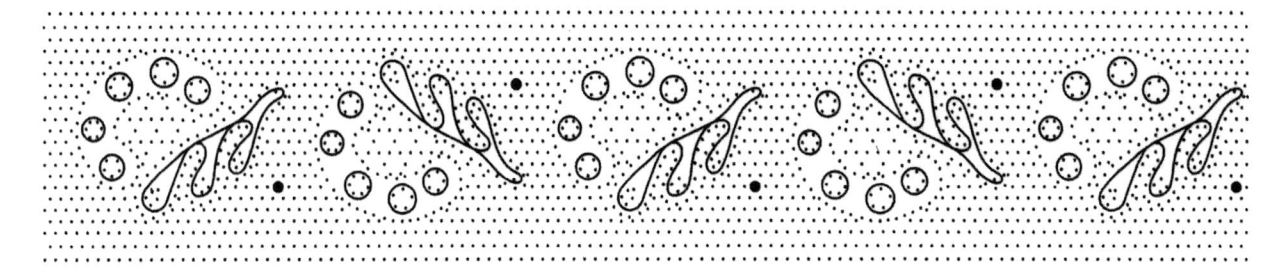

Figure 354 'Periwinkle' with whole stitch honeycomb filling. The lower insertion, pricking, to be made using Egyptian cotton 170/2[1], gimp D.M.C. perle no. 12

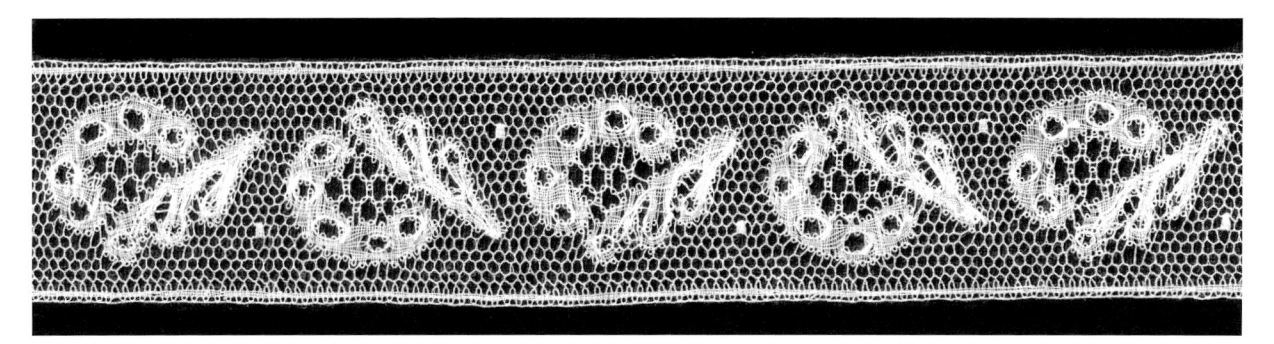

Figure 355 Lace made on pricking figure 354 using Egyptian cotton 170/2, gimp no. 12 perle

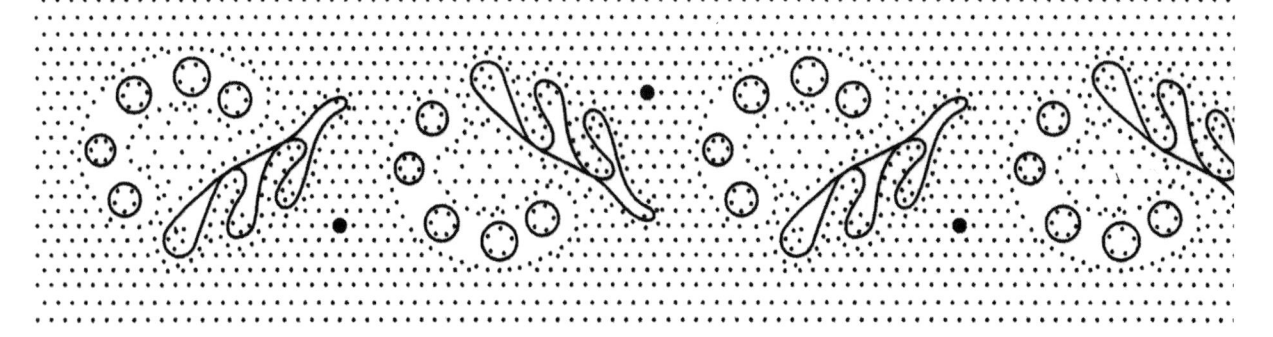

Figure 356 'Periwinkle' with whole stitch honeycomb filling. The lower insertion, pricking, to be made using Egyptian cotton 100/2, gimp D.M.C. perle no. 12

166

Clothwork crescent with rings

The crescent of clothwork with Regency rings (figures 354 & 355) is made using the standard techniques as previously described, and traditionally these more complex Regency patterns have pairs added in and thrown out. This piece requires an extra pair to be added in at the first pin of the clothwork and extra pairs may need to be added and thrown out while working the crescent to avoid the sections between the rings looking starved or choked. Some of these extra pairs may pass out into the leafy section on the lower left of the first repeat. The whole stitch variation of honeycomb^2 was used for the filling.

Leaf with three leaflets

The leaf starts using standard techniques and a gimp is added when the group of five pins is reached (figure 357). The diamond of four pins is for a Regency ring and when the gimps are crossed the fifth pin, pin A, is set up between the gimps.

Figure 357 (right) Gimp within the leaf. (The workers finishing the crescent may have worked in the other direction)

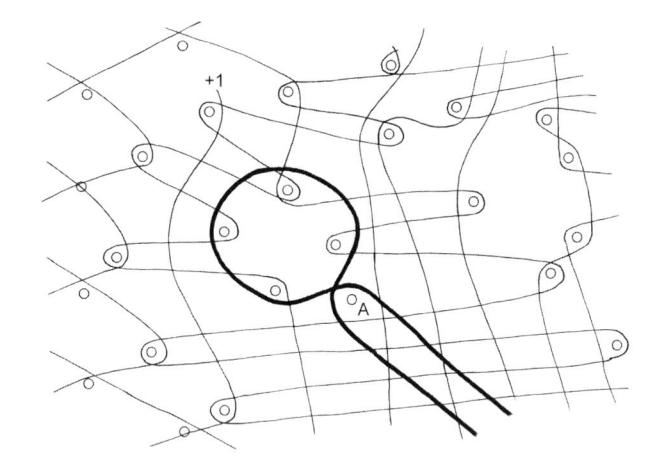

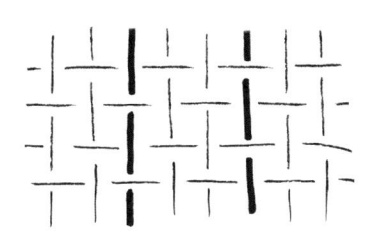

Figure 358 Two rows of clothwork crossing passive pairs and gimped vein

Gimped veins without central pins

The two new gimps pass down the leaf to form a vein (figure 358) and when there are no pins between the gimps of a vein the standard method of working the gimps and threads between them changes. At first glance everything looks normal, but a closer look reveals that the gimp passes over the left worker thread and under the right worker thread. The passive threads lying inside and next to each gimp have become that gimp's fine partner and the worker and it's fine partner work as any other pair to make a cloth stitch. The two rows illustrated show four cloth stitches per row. Additional pairs between the gimps are worked normally.

Passives entering a gimped vein without central pins

Passives entering a gimped vein without central pins do so as a pair (figure 359, pair A); the gimp passing over the left passive thread and under the right one of the pair. The new passive thread, B, lying inside and next to the gimp becomes its fine partner, the former fine partner pairing up with the remaining thread of the passive pair that entered.

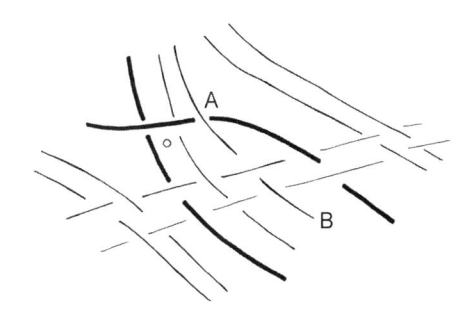

Figure 359 Passives entering a gimped vein without central pins at pin A

All about making—Floral Bucks Point Lace

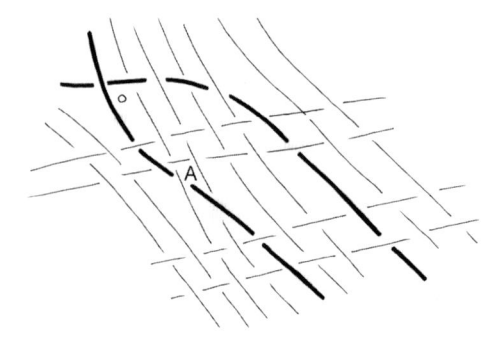

Figure 360 Passives leaving a gimped vein without central pins

Passives leaving a gimped vein without central pins
Passives leaving a gimped vein without central pins do so as a pair (figure 360, pair A); the gimp passing over the left passive thread and under the right one of the pair. If there are pairs remaining within the gimped vein the passive thread now lying inside and next to the gimp becomes its fine partner. If there is more than one pair between the gimps the other thread of the passive pair will pair up with the passive gimp on the other side of it and the thread on the inner side of the other gimp becomes that gimp's partner.

The leaflets
The working described here is my version of working the leaflets taking into account the many different methods that I have seen, and as usual my motifs have all worked up slightly differently. It is not necessary or even advisable to follow figure 360 exactly, it would be too frustrating. It may help to make an enlargement and draw over some of the lines in colour. Once you understand the approach then make the lace, adding in and throwing out when necessary. You may have a different number of pairs from mine at the end of the first leaflet and you may wish to remove pairs.

The clothwork starts at pin A, the workers travelling towards pin B and then two more rows are worked adding a pair at the end of each. The worker only works through half the pairs in the following row (figure 361). Support the pairs entering the frond using pinholes C and D. The gimp travels up the frond through the supported pairs and the workers at the tip of the frond passing under the right thread of each pair and over the left. The workers from the leaf, now at pin E, work up through all these pairs and work cloth and twist, pin, cloth and twist at pin F with the workers that started the leaflet. These same workers then return back down through the passives to pin G, the pinhole below pin E, then back up to the diamond pinhole on the right, pin H then back down to pin J, the pinhole below pin G. The original leaflet workers start working down the remaining underside of the motif, making winkie pins at pins of the diamond, pins K and L. The gimp passes down the frond through the passives, passing under the left and over the right threads to continue the weave.

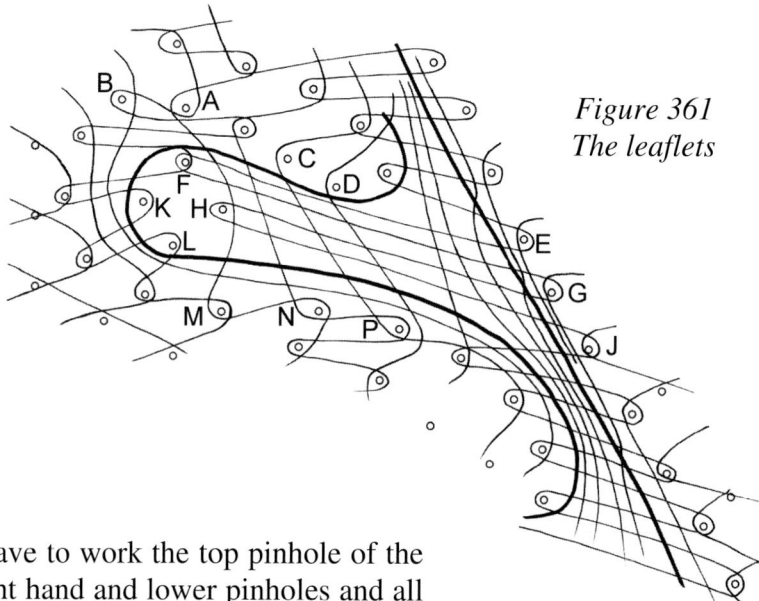

Figure 361 The leaflets

The workers do not necessarily have to work the top pinhole of the diamond, they could work the right hand and lower pinholes and all the pinholes may be winkie pins. The rules for working Regency Bucks Point are even less rigid than for Standard Floral Bucks.

All about making—Floral Bucks Point Lace

Along the underside of the leaflet graft pairs along the line at pins M, N and P until the workers that went down the leaflet, now at pin J will be able to continue at a suitable angle. Rows made exchanging workers for passives can be alternated with grafting out, it's your choice. The angle of the workers when setting up the pinhole in the angle between leaflets is important as it sets the angle of the workers travelling up the second leaflet.

Casting off at the end of the stem
Throw pairs out as the end of the stem is approached then, after working the pinhole at the end of the stem, cross the gimps each with its fine partner, if present, and throw them out (figure 362). Throw out the remaining passives and make the final cloth stitch at *. Unfortunately from this pinhole there is only one pair required to work the ground stitch with the one from the row approaching from the left. Traditionally surplus threads were simply cut off[3], but I twisted each pair many times and used them as single threads as when doubling up to join a thread. After working them double for a few stitches one thread from each of these pairs was thrown out. This adaptation was prompted by our current desire to make lace that is as perfect as possible, and we have the time in which to do it.

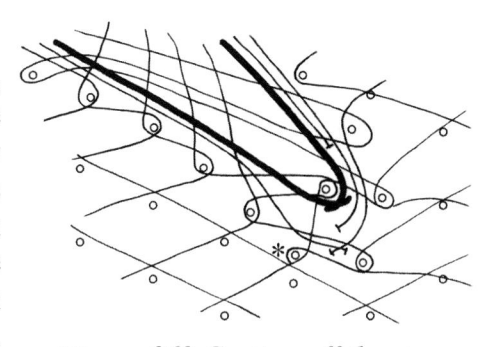

Figure 362 Casting off the stem

END NOTES

1 Substituting threads
See Part 6.

2 Whole stitch honeycomb
Using the standard honeycomb arrangement of pinholes work cloth stitch, twist, pin, cloth stitch, twist, instead of the usual half stitch and twist, pin, half stitch and twist (figures 363 & 364).

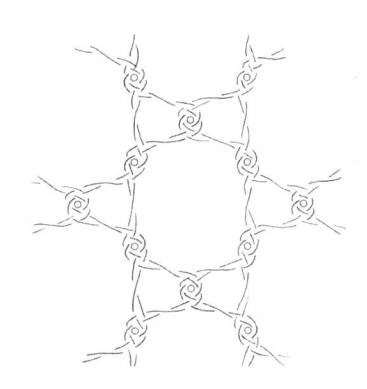

Figure 363 Whole stitch honeycomb

Figure 364 Whole stitch honeycomb

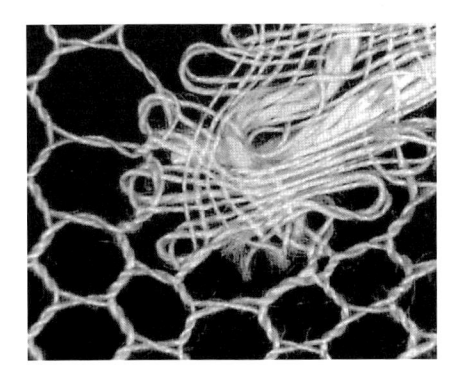

3 Cutting off pairs
Traditionally the surplus pairs at the end of a clothwork motif were merely cut off with no effort being made neaten them (figure 365).

Figure 365 (left) Antique lace with pairs cut off at the end of a clothwork motif

169

All about making—Floral Bucks Point Lace

CHAPTER 18

PROJECT 20e: Gown, Skirt panel central insertion

Materials Required for Project 20e
Egyptian cotton no. 170/2[1]
gimp no. 12 perle

Estimate the length for each insertion separately. The panel widens so that the insertions lengthen as you progress downwards towards the lower hem.

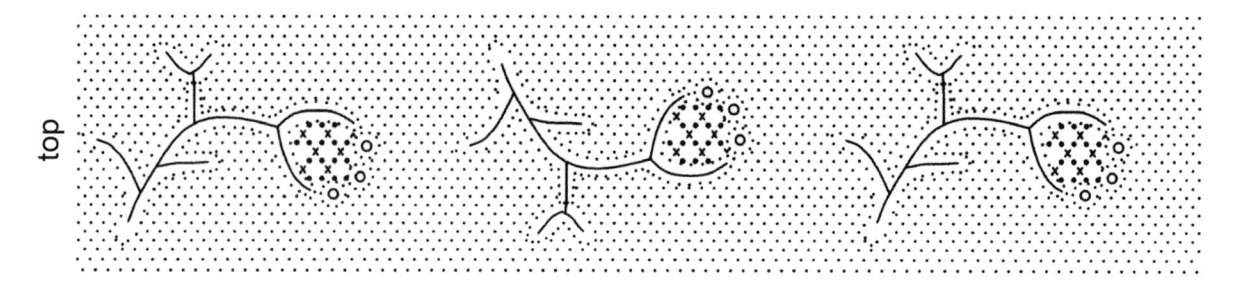

Figure 366 The central insertion, pricking, for use with Egyptian cotton no. 170/2[1], gimp D.M.C. perle no. 12, containing five-stitch filling[2] and closed Regency rings[3]

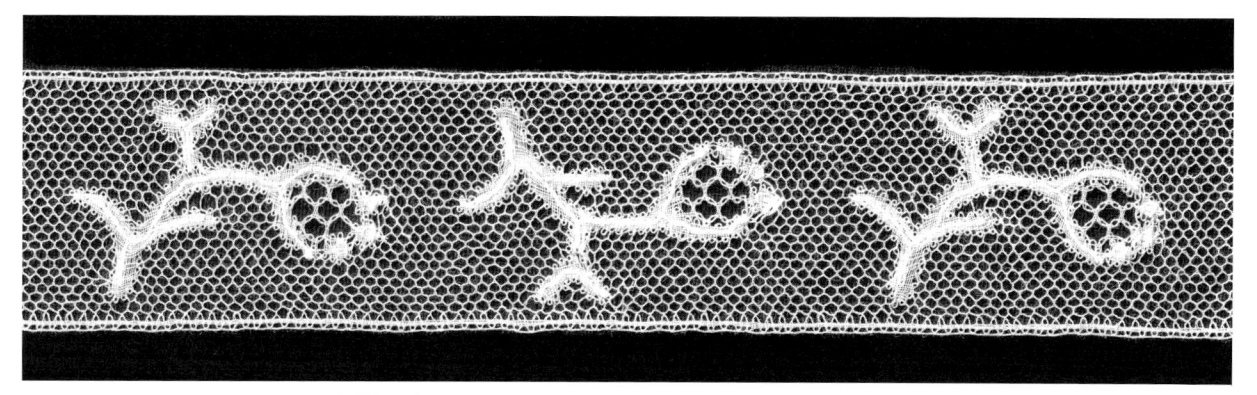

Figure 367 The central insertion made on pricking figure 366 made in Egyptian cotton no. 170/2, gimp D.M.C. perle no. 12

Figure 368 Insertion, pricking, for use with Egyptian cotton no. 100/2, gimp D.M.C. perle no. 12, containing five-stitch filling and closed Regency rings

170

All about making—Floral Bucks Point Lace

Setting in the motif
Using a comparatively finer thread results in the clothwork requiring more pairs than are provided by the ground. The first row of the clothwork requires five pairs of passives, but has only two pairs approaching it. Therefore four extra pairs must be added. (Do not forget the workers, they make the sixth pair.)

Adding multiple pairs at the first pin and adding two pairs into the row
Straddle two new pairs over the first pin, pin A (figure 369), twist them twice and make a cloth stitch with the left pair and the pair from the ground on its left. Using the pair on the right of the pin as workers, cloth stitch through the pair from the ground then the other half of the straddled pairs. Straddle the two new pairs, B, over a support pin placed to the left and twist the pairs once. With the current workers continue working through these pairs and include another ground pair at pin C. Remove the support pin at B and let down the pairs.

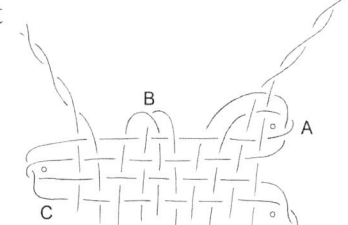

Figure 369 Adding two pairs at the first pin and two more pairs into the row

Folded gimp
The gimp veins in this insertion look like single thread, but in reality they are double and have been started by folding a pair of gimps over the workers, a passive pair or existing gimps. The two gimp threads may be twisted loosely in sympathy with their spin to make them look like a single gimp and, for the most part, they are worked as a single gimp thread without any pairs or twists separating them. A folded gimp may be passed under the left thread of a pair and over the right as for most Bucks Point or may be passed over the left thread of the pair and under the right as found in much of the Regency Point; in both cases one of the passive threads adjacent to the gimp will pass over and under the working threads parallel to the gimp. As usual it is advisable to be consistent.

Hanging in a folded gimp
In this piece the folded gimp is hung in half way along the fourth row so, when the workers return from pin A (figure 370) the pair of gimps is slipped over the workers between the two central pairs of passives (figure 371) and the workers continue the row. Providing the bobbins are lightly spangled and tension is kept light the gimps should not require a support pin.

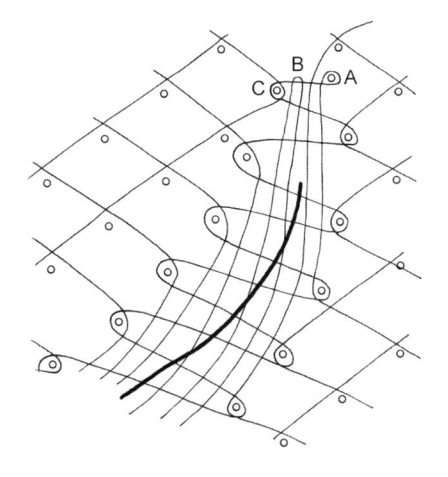

Figure 370 (left) Starting a vertical folded gimp

Figure 371 (right) Starting a vertical folded gimp

All about making—Floral Bucks Point Lace

Working a folded gimp through a side branch
When the work starts to level out for the side branch at pin A^4 (figure 372) graft along towards the tip of the branch to pin B and then work three rows to pin C. Remove any twists on the pair of gimps and weave one gimp through the side branch passives until the fourth pair of passives from the tip is reached, fold the gimp around this pair and return it to its original position next to its partner gimp by passing it under and over the same threads it passed through on its outward journey. Work three rows across the branch below the gimp. Grafting out will be necessary at some, but not all of the pinholes when working back along the underside of the branch.

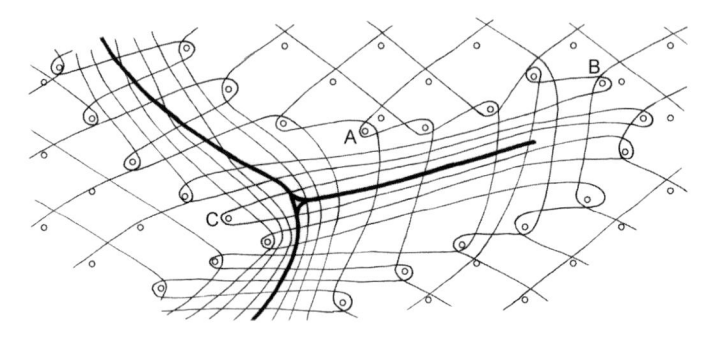

Figure 372 Folded gimp through a side branch

Dividing a folded gimp
When a main stem divides a folded gimp continues down each new stem (figure 373). To achieve this, at an appropriate position above the pin where the stem divides, a pair of gimps is introduced, one to partner each gimp forming the current folded pair. Several rows are worked, with each new folded gimp passing out through one or more of the passive pairs, so that when the pin at the division is reached there will be sufficient passives on each side of the folded gimp for each new stem.

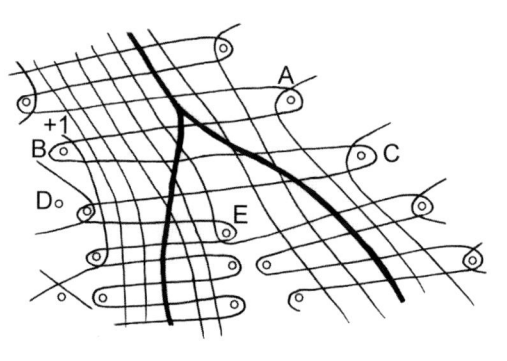

Figure 373 Introducing a new pair of gimps when dividing a folded gimp stem

Figure 374 Introducing a new pair of gimps

Half way along the row from pin A to pin B, (figure 373), a new pair of gimps (figure 374) is placed over a support pin and laid between the current folded gimps making two pairs of folded gimps and, in the following row new gimp pairs are treated as an ordinary pair with the workers cloth stitching through them. The row is completed and the support pin removed. In this insertion the passive pairs need to be adjusted so that there will be nine passive pairs in the row pin C to pin D (not counting the pairs entering and leaving the clothwork) thus providing two pairs on either side of the folded gimp in each new stem and another pair of workers. Each folded gimp is passed outwards through a pair of passives and the row to pin D is worked. One gimp is passed outwards through one more pair before the row towards pin E is started. There are now five pairs of passives between the folded gimps and two pairs outside each folded gimp. Work the half row from pin D through three of the central five passive pairs, set up pin E, twist and cover the pin. Both these pairs continue as workers, one pair working down each stem. When the gimps are no longer needed lay them back and trim.

All about making—Floral Bucks Point Lace

Corner

Being narrow, the corner for the edging around the skirt panel, figures 375 & 376, does not need extra pairs. This time (figure 378) the pairs for the new rows that appear along the diagonal are accommodated by working a short row 'uphill' from the beetle towards the tally. The tally is worked at 45° to the footsides. A matching short row is worked towards the beetle on the other side of the diagonal.

Figure 375 (left) Corner for the skirt panel, pricking, for use with Egyptian cotton 170/2 , gimp D.M.C. perle no. 12

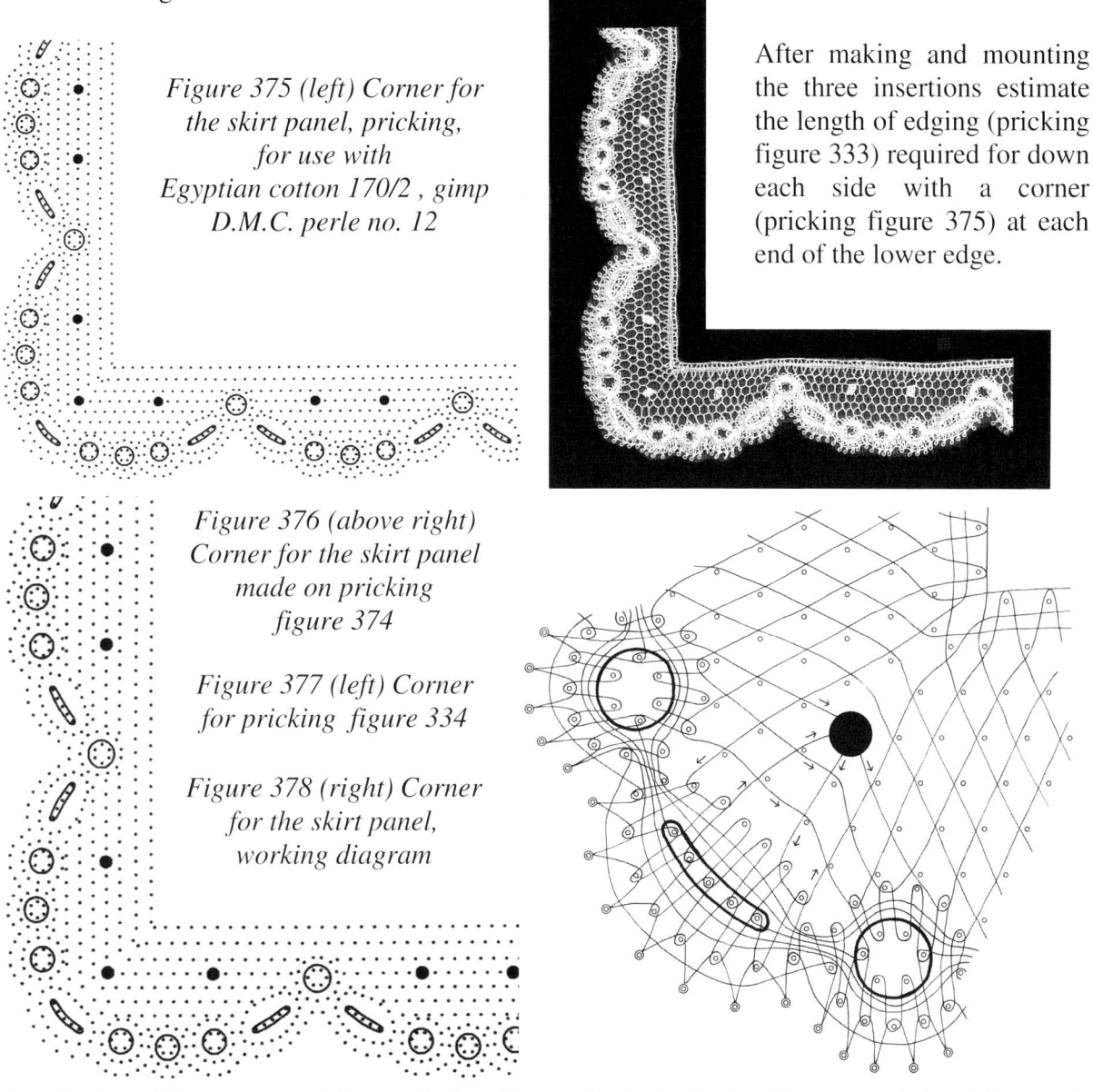

After making and mounting the three insertions estimate the length of edging (pricking figure 333) required for down each side with a corner (pricking figure 375) at each end of the lower edge.

Figure 376 (above right) Corner for the skirt panel made on pricking figure 374

Figure 377 (left) Corner for pricking figure 334

Figure 378 (right) Corner for the skirt panel, working diagram

Attach the edging to a machine-made heading and attach the heading around the skirt panel. Gather the top edge of the panel, place between the bodice and its lining and stitch together.

Belt

Emily's christening gown is finished with a belt (figure 379) with a lace insertion, the heading (figures 314 & 315). *Figure 379 (right) Belt*

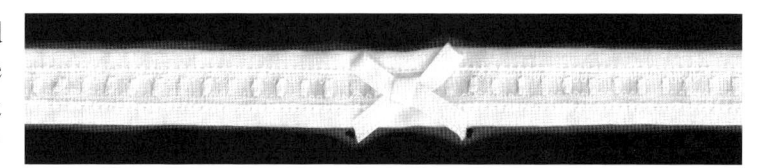

173

All about making—Floral Bucks Point Lace

END NOTES

1 Substituting threads
See Part 6.

2 Five-stitch filling
This is a popular filling in Regency Bucks, also found in Chantilly and other point ground laces, which is worked on a grid in which alternate vertical rows have been removed from the basic point ground grid (figures 380 & 381). For two adjacent pins, pins A & B (figure 380) make a cloth stitch with two pairs, pin, twist the pairs twice and cover with a cloth stitch. Cloth stitch one pair from pin A with one from pin B pairs at C and then cloth stitch each of these pairs with the remaining pair from the above pins, setting up pins D and E under these stitches. Twist all pairs twice and cover each pin with a cloth stitch. Repeat for pins F & G, H & J. Then cloth stitch one pair from pin E with one from pin H at K.

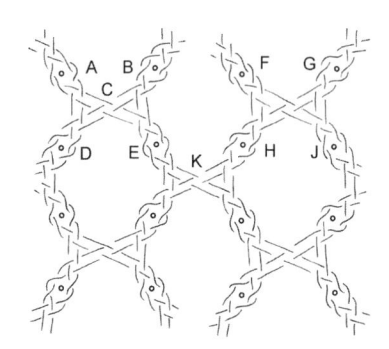

Figure 380 (left) Five-stitch filling

Figure 381 (right) Five-stitch filling

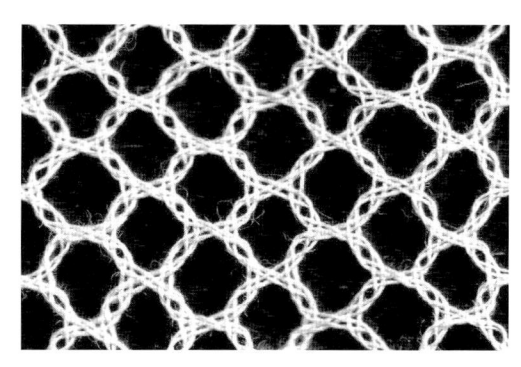

3 Closed Regency rings
When a Regency ring has a filled centre (figure 382), a gimp is introduced horizontally through selected passive pairs and the same number of rows of cloth stitch is worked across the ring, the gimps and the central passives, each gimp being paired with a fine partner within the ring. The gimps are doubled through the central passives and thrown out to complete the ring. At all times there should be a minimum of one passive pair outside the gimp, but there may be more. In this piece three passive pairs have been used for the centre, three rows worked across them and there is a minimum of one pair of passives outside the gimps.

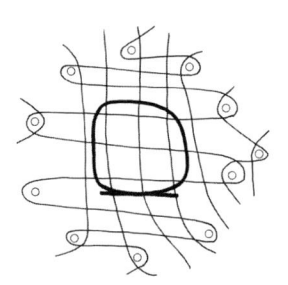

Figure 382 Closed Regency ring

4 Working the side branch
The point at which the side work starts to graft along the line is determined by the positions of the following rows. In figure 383 the workers from pin B need to travel to pin C. Therefore when the workers reach pin A it will be necessary to graft towards pin B. A similar situation occurs along the underside of the branch, where grafting is needed to enable the workers to continue at the required angle after the branch has been completed.

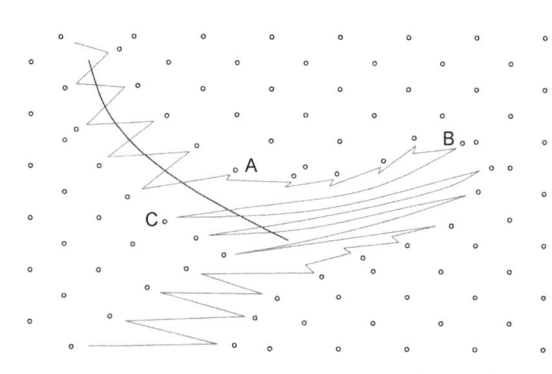

Figure 383 Working a side branch

All about making—Floral Bucks Point Lace

CHAPTER 19

PROJECTS 22 & 23: Bonnet crown and card decorations

Project 22: Bonnet with decorated crown
Project 23: Card with decoration

PROJECT 22: Bonnet with crown decoration

Materials Required for Projects 22
Egyptian cotton no. 170/2[1]
gimp single strand Anchor stranded embroidery
fabric for the bonnet according to the pattern
1m very narrow tape or thick thread for drawstrings

The bonnet (figures 384 & 385) has the sleeve frill edging (figures 304 & 305) around the crown and along the edge of the brim; the latter starting and finishing with a picot edge. A variation of the first skirt panel insertion (figures 350 & 351) is used for the insertion and a rabbit motif in the bonnet crown[2] (figures 386 & 387).

All measurements are the ones used to dress my doll and should be adjusted as required.

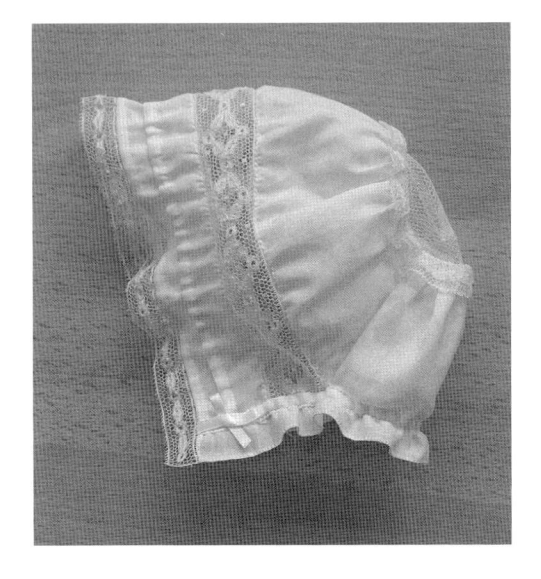

Figure 384 Bonnet side view 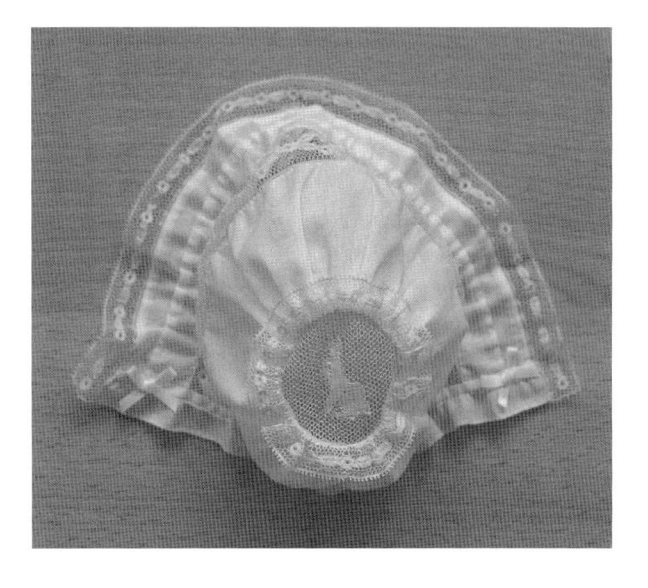   *Figure 385 Bonnet back view showing crown*

175

All about making—Floral Bucks Point Lace

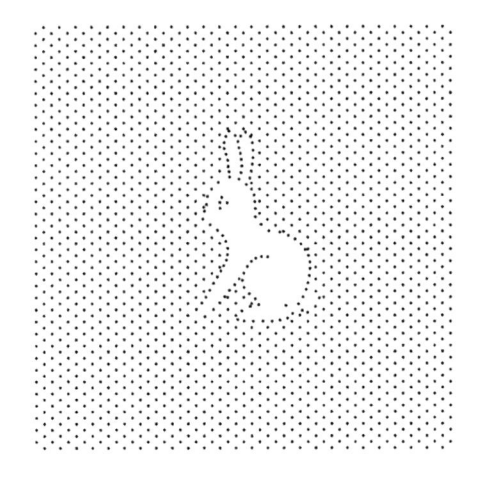

Figure 386 (above) Bonnet crown pricking for use with Egyptian cotton no. 170/2, gimp single strand Anchor stranded embroidery

Figure 387 (above right) Bonnet crown made on pricking figure 386 using Egyptian cotton no. 170/2, gimp single strand Anchor stranded embroidery

Figure 388 (right) Bonnet crown enlarged pricking for use with Egyptian cotton no. 100/2, gimp D.M.C. perle no. 12

The rabbit is worked in cloth stitch with a gimp surrounding the pins for his eye and a gimp around his tail.

The upper and lower pins for the eye are worked cloth stitch and twist, pin, cloth stitch and twist and the pin holes between them are winkie pins. The clothwork is divided at his hip where the workers make cloth stitch and twist, pin, cloth stitch when they meet. The shape of his haunch is indicated by twisting some of the passive pairs.

Figure 389 (right) Bonnet

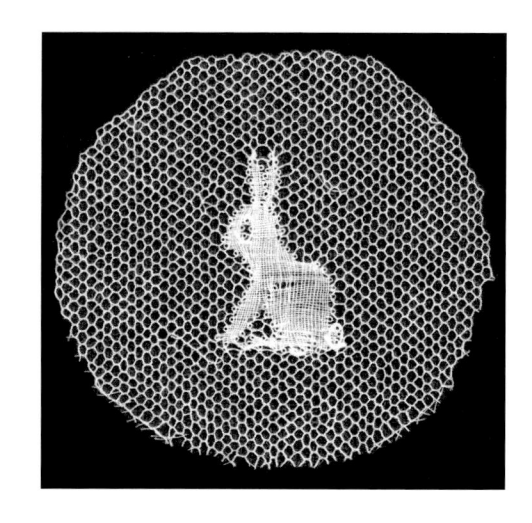

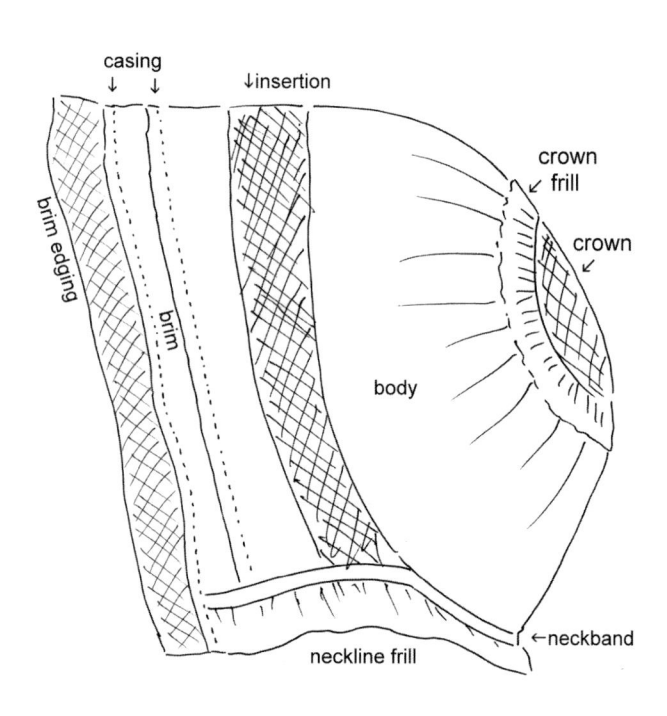

Making up the bonnet

The main body of the bonnet is a strip of fabric 42cm x 7cm, (16½in x 2¾in) including a 6mm (¼in) seam allowance and is joined end to end with a French seam. Make a rolled hem³ along both sides of the fabric. Start each hem with a knot at the end of a strong thread and slide the needle under the hem to pass out through the fabric at the outermost edge of the hem (figure 390) and with the stitches 2.5mm (1/10in) apart. Do not fasten off the thread.

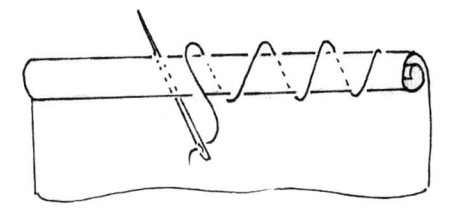

Figure 390 Rolled hem

Mounting the crown

Using the stitching thread, gather one rolled edge of the main body of the bonnet into a circle 4.5cm (1¾in) in diameter. Draw a circle 4.5cm (1¾in) in diameter on thick paper (traditionally brown paper was used) and tack the gathered edge right side down around this circle. Place the lace crown right side down on top of the gathered edge and tack in position. Make a line of small running stitches along the gathered edge to secure the lace in position and trim the excess to 3mm (⅛in). Oversew the lace securely to the gathered edge by taking a small stitch into each gather, collecting up the loose ends of the lace and oversewing them several times before discarding them. Finally trim the discarded threads.

Insertion

Gather the other edge of the main body of the bonnet to the required size and, working from the centre, oversew the insertion along the gathered edge. For mine the insertion was 25cm long (10in) leaving a gap of 10cm (4 in) along the back neckline.

Brim

The lace along the edge of the brim extends from the lower edge of the neck frill on one side to the lower edge on the other. It has two casings each 5mm (3/16in) wide and each containing a drawstring for adjusting the final size of the bonnet. Traditionally this was to allow the bonnet to be reused for different babies. Cut a strip 32cm x 5cm (12½in x 2in) and work a rolled hem along one edge as for the main body of the bonnet and along the other a plain hem 6mm (¼in) wide enclosing a drawstring leaving a central loop. Fold the strip lengthwise and make a row of running stitches 5mm (3/16in) from the fold for the casing. Because the casings are so narrow withdraw threads for the folds and stitching lines. Whilst stitching the casing, I enclosed the drawstring leaving a loop 15cm (6ins) long protruding between the stitches in the centre, or the drawstring may be inserted later. The loop provides the ends for gathering the brim to make the bonnet fit, and to tie a bow. Gather the rolled hem edge to fit the insertion and oversew together.

Neck band

The narrow neckband extends from the edge of the brim one side, across the end of the brim, the insertion, the back neckline, the other end of the insertion and the other end of the brim. The neckband also acts as a casing. Cut a strip 21.5cm (8½in) x 3.2mm (1¼in), fold in half lengthwise and turn in each long edge. (Withdrawing threads helps.) Starting from the centre back and with right sides together, stitch the neckband in position, taking care to stitch the cut ends of the lace securely. Trim the excess lace, fold over the neckband and stitch in place taking care across the lace. Insert a drawstring and hem in place leaving a long loop in the centre back. Secure both ends of the drawstring and neaten the ends.

Neckline frill

The neckline frill has a a finished size of 25.5cm (10in) x 12mm (½in), the latter being the length of the neckband plus an allowance for gathering. Cut a strip for the finished length, plus a turning at each end and sufficiently wide so that the long edge can be rolled and gathered. Then finish the other long edge and the ends with four-sided stitch. (Withdrawing threads may help to keep the stitching even.) Gather the rolled hem to fit the neckband and stitch in place.

Brim edging

With four-sided stitch, attach the lace edging along the edge of the brim from the lower edge of the neck frill on one side to its lower edge on the other.

Adjust the size of the bonnet using the drawstrings, securing each with a bow.

All about making—Floral Bucks Point Lace

PROJECT 23: Card with decoration

Figure 391 Christening card

Materials Required for Project 23
Egyptian cotton no. 170/2[1].
gimp single strand Anchor stranded embroidery
card with 6.5cm (2½in) aperture
acetate window to protect lace
self-adhesive silver letters
25cm (10 in) thick silver thread
fabric adhesive

Figure 392 Rabbit within a circular footside, pricking for use with Egyptian cotton no. 170/2, gimp single strand Anchor stranded embroidery

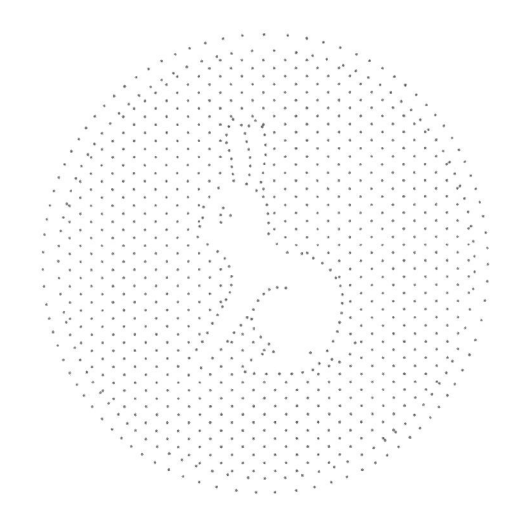

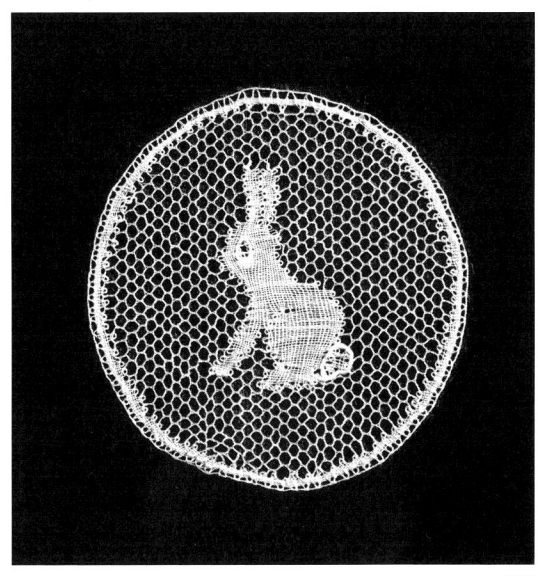

Figure 393 Rabbit within a circular footside, pricking for use with Egyptian cotton no. 100/2, gimp D.M.C. perle no. 12

Figure 394 (right) Rabbit within a circular footside made on pricking no. 392 using Egyptian cotton no. 170/2, gimp single strand Anchor stranded embroidery

179

All about making—Floral Bucks Point Lace

END NOTES

1 Substituting threads
See Part 6.

2 Bonnet crown
A horseshoe shaped or circular (also known as a roundel) insertion used in the back of a baby's bonnet. Particularly popular during the 1820s.

3 Rolled hem
Compare with rolled hem page 27.

All about making—Floral Bucks Point Lace

PART 4
VERY FINE BUCKS POINT

When I was relatively new to making Bucks Point I was puzzled as to how the very fine lace, those pieces with about 70 or more pins per 10 cm (4 in) along the footside, could have been made taking into consideration the fineness of the thread and the diameter of the pins being used; there appeared to be insufficient space for the pins. Later on I discovered that for the very fine Bucks Point (figure 395) many of the pins, although not all, are placed outside the gimp as in Lille and Beverse lace and, as in much of the Regency Bucks, a gimp can be worked as a passive thread, i.e. as part of a pair. Very fine Bucks Point, frequently abbreviated to very fine Bucks, has less clothwork and fillings than standard Floral Bucks, the design being the result of gimp work. The workers and passive pairs frequently follow the line of the design and do not necessarily keep to the horizontal and vertical directions to which we are accustomed.

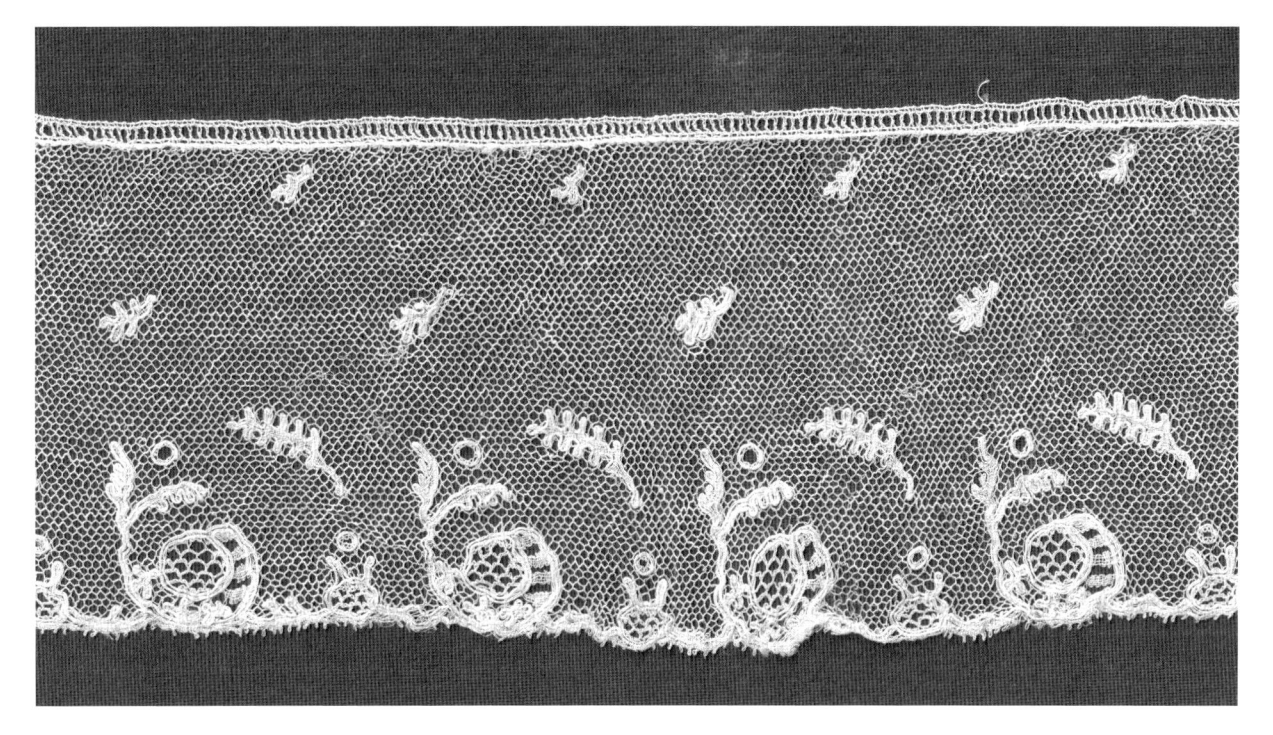

Figure 395 Very fine Bucks Point

The prickings for very fine Bucks usually have 70 or more pins per 10cm (4in) along the footside and the lace is worked using fine thread, e.g. Egyptian cotton 200/2 to 240/2. I have used 185/2 when I needed white thread as the finer thread is only available in unbleached and 170/2 for the fichu to match the thread of the net, although the lace would be improved by being made using a finer thread. Enlarged prickings for use with Egyptian cotton 100/2 are included, and the prickings may be further enlarged and even thicker thread used. However, when the lace is enlarged some of the techniques typical of this form of Bucks Point may show up as flaws which are not seen when the lace is made on the smaller scale.

All about making—Floral Bucks Point Lace

CHAPTERS 20-27

PROJECTS 24-29 Clothes trimmed with very fine Bucks Point for Lynette, a 45cm (18in) doll

Project 24: Drawers
Project 25a: Camisole edging
Project 26: Petticoat edging
Project 27a: Bodice insertion
Project 28: Skirt edging
Project 25b: Camisole galloon
Project 27b: Cuffs
Project 29: Fichu

The chapters are arranged according to the difficulty of the techniques included, thus Project 25b follows Project 28 and Project 27b follows Projects 28 and 25b.

As the heading implies, the thread used for these projects is very fine and varies from project to project. Care should be taken with the weight of the bobbins used for this lace[1]

Materials Required for Projects 20-24
commercial pattern for dress for 45cm (18 in) doll
a contrasting colour for her underwear will highlight the bodice insertions

Figure 396 Lynette wearing clothes trimmed with very fine Bucks Point lace

Lynette's fichu has nine repeats along each side with the ends modified to points. This edging cannot be worked satisfactorily in the reverse direction and therefore a reversing corner[2] would be unsuitable. Using a non-reversing corner allows the edging to continue in the same direction after the corner has been turned.

182

All about making—Floral Bucks Point Lace

CHAPTER 20

PROJECT 24: Drawers

Materials Required for Project 24
Egyptian cotton no. 240/2[1]
gimp one strand D.M.C. stranded embroidery thread
fabric for drawers according to pattern
small button

Figure 397 Drawers with lace trimming

The drawers were made up first so that the length of lace required for around the legs could be estimated. The lace was joined end to start.

Figure 398 Lace for Drawers, pricking for use with Egyptian cotton no. 240/2, gimp single strand D.M.C. stranded embroidery thread

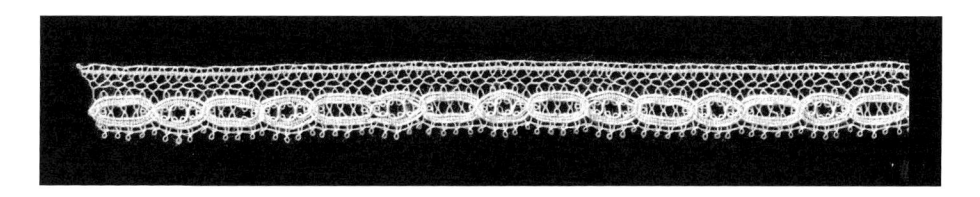

Figure 399 Lace for Drawers made on pricking figure 398 using Egyptian cotton no. 240/2, gimp single strand D.M.C. stranded embroidery thread

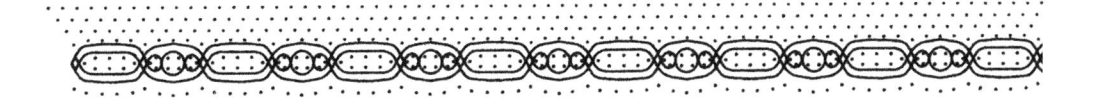

Figure 400 Lace for Drawers, pricking for use with Egyptian cotton no. 100/2, gimp D.M.C. perle no. 12

183

All about making—Floral Bucks Point Lace

Central passives
This pattern has trails each with two gimps and two passive pairs. The pairs cloth stitching across the trails can do so by making three cloth stitches, i.e. the two pairs of passives and two gimps add up to 6 threads, so when a pair works across them it can work three cloth stitches.

Trails crossing
When the trails meet, the inner gimps cross and then each weaves out across the other trail and makes a twist with the outer gimp. The passives from one side work through those from the other, first one pair crossing and then the other as when making a half spider. Finally the inner gimps weave through to the centre where they make a cross.

Headside
An alternative headside that has one pair of passives that may be twisted or untwisted was used for this piece and there may be one or two twists between the headside passives and the gimp.

The oval
The top pin of the oval (figure 401) is worked with a picot pair and a pair from the ground. The pairs are twisted once or twice and then worked cloth stitch, twist (usually twice), pin, cloth stitch and twist (once or twice). The pair on the headside works out through the gimps and central pairs and headside passives, makes a picot and returns to be twisted twice and pinned inside the oval. The other pair works through the other gimps and central pairs to make a catch-pin stitch and returns to be pinned and twisted within the oval. Now the pairs meeting within the oval make a kiss, i.e. work cloth stitch and twist twice to change sides. Then they work out through the opposite gimps and central pairs. The oval finishes when the two worker pairs enter through the gimps and central pairs, are twisted, work cloth stitch, twist, pin, cloth stitch, twist and pass out through the gimps and central pairs to the headside and ground. The gimps and central pairs are crossed as above before working the small ring.

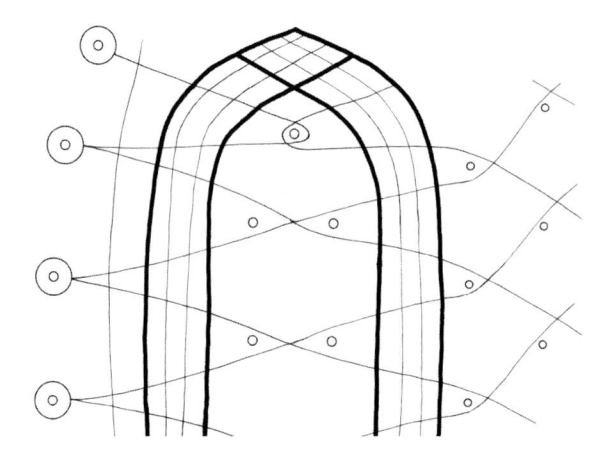

Figure 401 The oval

Crossing from the oval to the small ring

After crossing the trails the inner central passive pairs of each trail is brought into the ring across the gimp with no twists before the gimp (figure 402). The pairs are twisted and work cloth stitch, pin, cloth stitch and twist before passing out across the gimps to become central passives again. The headside and catch-pin pairs work across their gimps and central pairs to make winkie pins and return across their respective gimps and central pairs. Then the gimps are crossed.

The central ring is worked with two winkie pins each side and the gimps are crossed again.

The lower small ring has a winkie pin each side, then the inner passives pass into the ring, work the lower pin and pass out to resume their roles as inner passives and the trails are crossed.

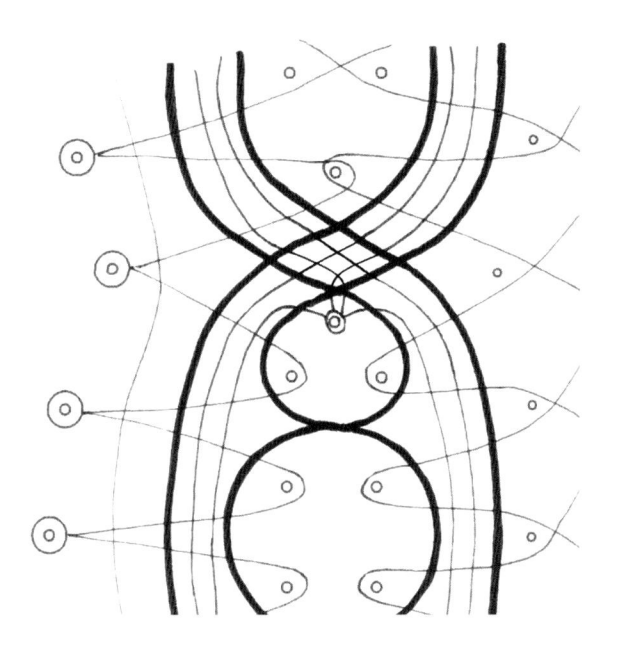

Figure 402 Crossing from the oval to the small ring

Attaching the lace
The lace was attached around the legs of the drawers using four-sided stitch[3].

END NOTES

1 Substituting threads
See Part 6.

2 Non-reversing corner
See pages 115 and 121.

3 Four-sided stitch
See 'All about making—Geometrical Bucks Point Lace' A. Stillwell, Salex Publishing pages 41-43.

All about making—Floral Bucks Point Lace

CHAPTER 21

PROJECT 25a: Camisole edging

Materials Required for Project 25a
Egyptian cotton no. 240/2[1]
gimp one strand D.M.C. stranded embroidery thread
fabric for camisole according to pattern
3 small buttons

Figure 403 Camisole with lace trimming

Figure 404 Camisole edging, pricking for use with Egyptian cotton no. 240/2, gimp single strand D.M.C. stranded embroidery thread

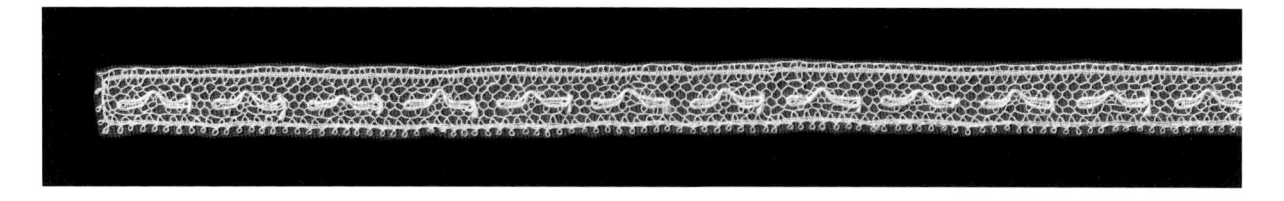

Figure 405 Camisole edging made on pricking figure 404 using Egyptian cotton no. 240/2, gimp single strand D.M.C. stranded embroidery thread

Figure 406 Camisole edging, pricking for use with Egyptian cotton no. 100/2, gimp D.M.C. perle no. 12

All about making—Floral Bucks Point Lace

The camisole was made up first so that the length of lace required for around the neckline and armholes could be estimated. The lace round the neckline was started and finished with a selvedge and the lace for the armholes was joined end to start.

Sycamore seed edging

The edging with a sycamore seed design has a separate gimp for each motif. Typically of very fine Bucks two pairs enter the top wing, work cloth stitch and twist, pin, cloth stitch and then one pair remains between the gimps while the other passes out to make a catch-pin stitch on one side.

Central passive pair between gimps

This pattern contains the typical method for working gimps with a central passive pair. Two pairs enter at pin A (figure 407), there are no twists between the gimps and the stitches, they then work cloth stitch, pin, cloth stitch. One pair exits across a gimp, the other remains as a central passive pair between the gimps. The following ground pairs cross the gimps and the central passive pair by making two 'cloth stitches', catch-pins are frequently used outside the gimps as shown here.

When the central passive pair is required for the ground at pin B a gimp passes through the pair (no twists), the two gimps now work as a single gimp and the former central passive pair is twisted prior to making a ground stitch. When a pair is no longer required for the ground it passes across a gimp to become a central passive pair at pin C.

When the gimps are to be cast off a pair enters across one gimp, works cloth stitch, pin, cloth stitch with the central passive pair at pin D and then the gimps are cast off through both pairs.

The edgings were attached to the camisole using four-sided stitch.

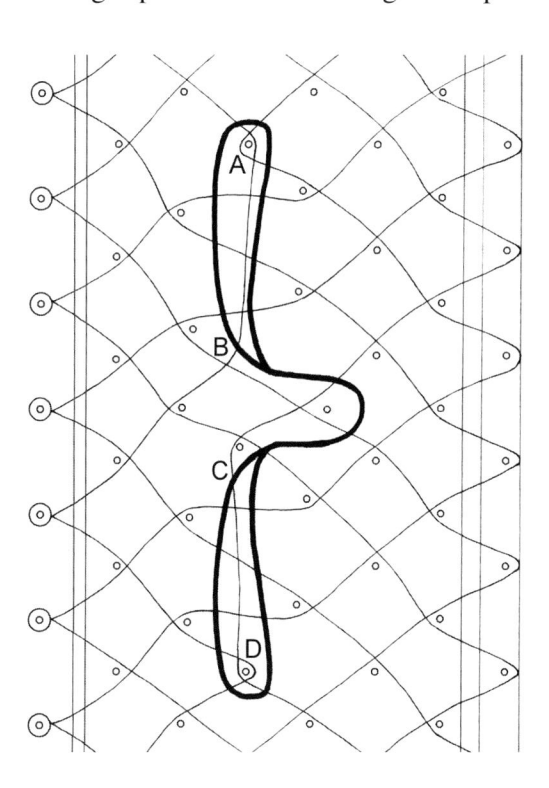

Figure 407 Central passives

END NOTES

1 Substituting threads
See Part 6.

CHAPTER 22

PROJECT 26: Petticoat edging

Materials Required for Project 26
Egyptian cotton no. 240/2[1]
gimp one strand D.M.C. stranded embroidery thread
fabric for petticoat according to pattern
small button

Figure 408 Petticoat with lace edging

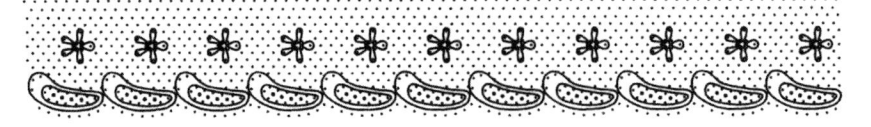

*Figure 409 Petticoat edging, pricking, for use with
Egyptian cotton no. 240/2, gimp single strand D.M.C. stranded embroidery thread*

*Figure 410 Petticoat edging made on pricking figure 409,
using Egyptian cotton no. 240/2, gimp single strand D.M.C. stranded embroidery thread*

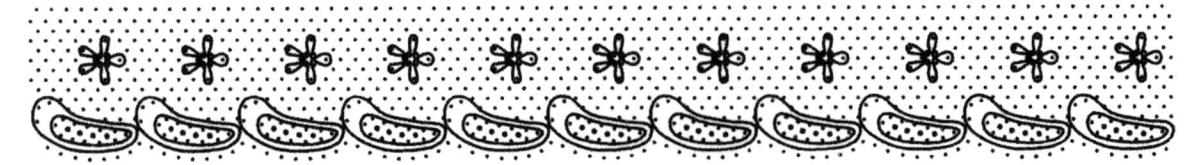

*Figure 411 Petticoat edging, pricking, for use with
Egyptian cotton no. 100/2, gimp D.M.C. perle no. 12*

All about making—Floral Bucks Point Lace

Starting the slipper-shaped motif
This motif has three pinholes in the wider top section (figure 412). Start at the one on the left, pin A, and work through four pairs towards the right to pin B. Return across the motif adding three pairs of passives, pass out across the gimp and one headside passive pair to make a picot, pin C, and return to work the next pin on the right, pin D. Return to make another picot at pin E. Take the workers back across the motif and gimp to become a ground pair. Leaving one passive pair inside the left gimp pass a new gimp towards the right through the next four passive pairs and start the honeycomb and tally centre at pin F. Pairs from the honeycomb stitches pass out through the gimps and passive pairs to make point ground stitches and return. From pin G a pair passes out from the honeycomb stitch to make a point ground stitch, pin H and the left pair from this stitch will be required to make the stitch at pin K. Therefore a pair from pin H cannot return across the clothwork to make the honeycomb stitch at pin J and a passive pair from the clothwork must be used. The right pair from the stitch at pin J passes out across the clothwork to make the point ground stitch at pin K. There must be many possible routes for finishing the clothwork, make sure you work at least one row after closing the gimps.

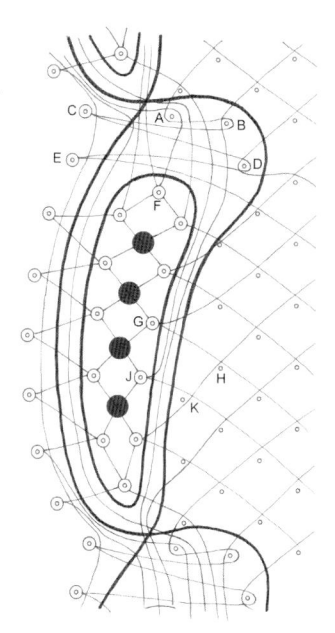

Figure 412 The slipper-shaped motif

Five-pointed star
This five-pointed star (figures 409, 410 & 413) has two points at the top. Start the left point, introduce the gimps and work cloth stitch, pin A, cloth stitch. In order to get the gimp into the correct position to work the pin in the right point make a nook pin at B then work the point at pin C. The left pair from pin C cloth stitches down through the pair from the nook pin to make a ground stitch outside the gimp at pin D and then works the left point at pin E. Make a ground stitch outside the gimp at pin F and work the right point, pin G. Cloth stitch the right pair from pin D with the left pair from pin F in the centre at H and then the gimps can be crossed. Make catch-pin stitches either side of the crossing at pins J and K and work the final point, pin L.

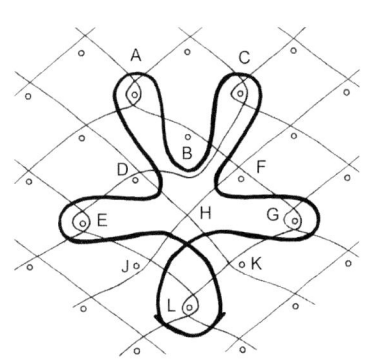

Due to the limitations of my computer and printer the pinholes in the centre of the star in the pricking are set wide. Counteract this by moving these pins closer together.

Attaching the lace
The lace was attached around the lower edge of the petticoat using four-sided stitch[2].

END NOTES

1 Substituting threads
See Part 6.

2 Four-sided stitch
See '*All about making—Geometrical Bucks Point Lace*' A. Stillwell, Salex Publishing, pages 41-43.

Figure 413 The five-pointed star

All about making—Floral Bucks Point Lace

CHAPTER 23

PROJECT 27a: Bodice Insertion

Materials Required for Project 27a
Egyptian cotton no. 185/2[1]
gimp single strand Anchor stranded
embroidery thread
fabric according to pattern
3 small buttons

Figure 414 Bodice

Figure 415 Right side bodice insertion, pricking for use with Egyptian cotton no. 185/2, gimp single strand Anchor stranded embroidery thread

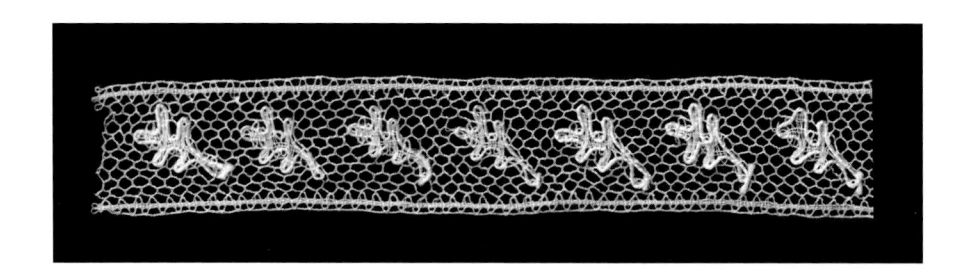

Figure 416 Right side bodice insertion, made on pricking figure 415 using Egyptian cotton no. 185/2, gimp single strand Anchor stranded embroidery thread

Figure 417 Left side bodice insertion, pricking for use with Egyptian cotton no. 185/2, gimp single strand Anchor stranded embroidery thread

190

All about making—Floral Bucks Point Lace

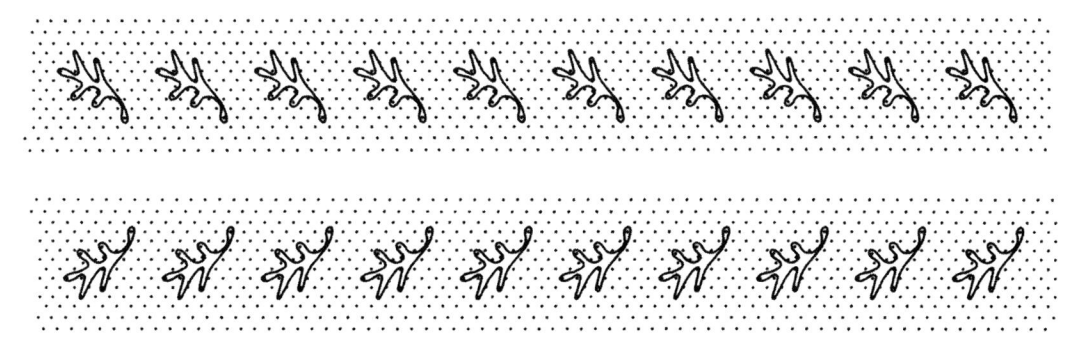

Figures 418 & 419 Bodice insertions, prickings for use with Egyptian cotton no. 100/2, gimp D.M.C. perle no. 12

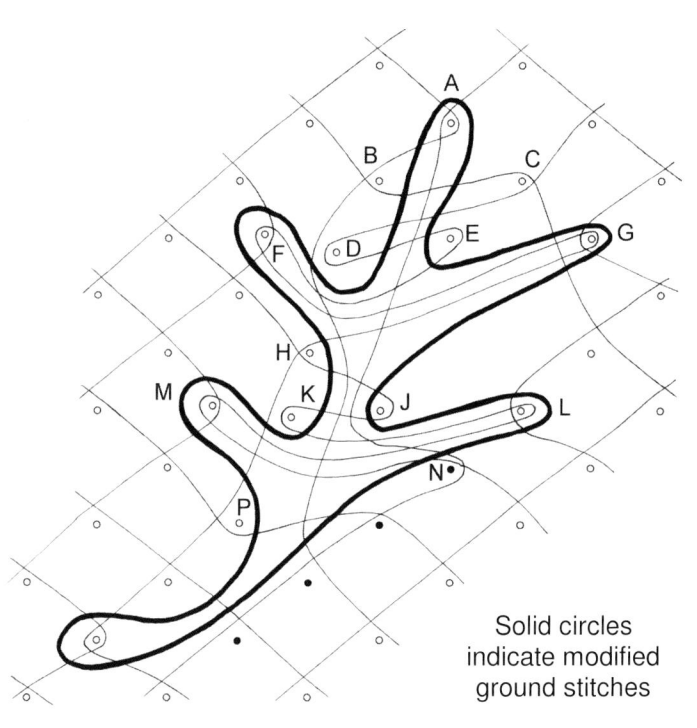

Figure 420 Bodice insertion

Solid circles indicate modified ground stitches

Standard methods

This leaf contains standard methods. A central pair is produced at the top pin inside the gimps. When there is a narrow stem the workers pass back and forth across the gimps and central pair (or pairs, there may be more than one) to make catch-pins on both sides. When the gimp angles up away from the central pair there is usually a nook pin.

The leaf

The leaf (figure 420) starts at A, the right pair becomes the central pair of passive pairs and the left pair passes across the gimp to the left to make a catch-pin stitch, pin B, then back across the gimps and central pair to make a catch-pin stitch, pin C, on the other side. The pair continues to pass across the gimps and passive pair but this time making nook pins at pins D & E.

The worker pair makes the next leaflet on the left by cloth stitching up through the available pairs to make cloth stitch and twist, pin, cloth stitch at the pin inside the points at pin F and back through all the available pairs to work the leaflet on the right at pin G. The workers return and make a catch-pin stitch on the left of the central stem, pin H, then a nook pin on the right of it and another on the left, pins J & K. Then the last two leaflets are made, pins L & M.

The right central pair and the workers pass across the right gimp and make a stitch catch-pin stitch at N; and the workers remain in the ground. A passive pair exits across the left gimp, makes a catch-pin stitch at pin P and passes back across the gimps and the central pair to make the point ground stitch below pin N. The central pair exits to make the next point ground stitch on the right.

All about making—Floral Bucks Point Lace

Modified point ground stitches
Sometimes honeycomb, catch-pin stitches and point ground worked adjacent to a gimp may look messy and traditionally the standard stitches may be replaced with modified stitches.

For honeycomb the following modified versions maybe used[2],
    (a) cloth stitch, twist twice, pin, cloth stitch, twist twice, or
    (b) cloth stitch, twist twice, pin, half stitch and twist.

For point ground and catch-pin stitches the stitch may be modified by working cloth stitch, twist three times (figure 421).

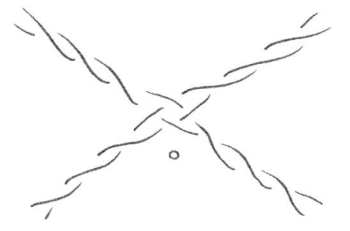

Figure 421 Modified point ground stitch

Point ground stitches occurring immediately below a sloping gimp are often improved by modifying them. In the bodice insertion (figures 415 & 416) the point ground stitches indicated by solid circles (figure 420) may be improved by being modified.

END NOTES

1 Substituting threads
See Part 6.

2 Modified honeycomb stitches
See *All about making*—Geometrical Bucks Point Lace, Alexandra Stillwell, Salex Publishing pages 75 & 80.

All about making—Floral Bucks Point Lace

CHAPTER 24

PROJECT 28: Skirt edging

Materials Required for Project 28
Egyptian cotton no. 185/2[1]
gimp single strand Anchor
stranded embroidery thread
pattern for skirt
fabric for camisole
lining for dress
1 small button

Figure 422 Skirt

*Figure 423 Skirt edging, pricking for use with
Egyptian cotton no. 185/2, gimp single strand D.M.C. stranded embroidery thread*

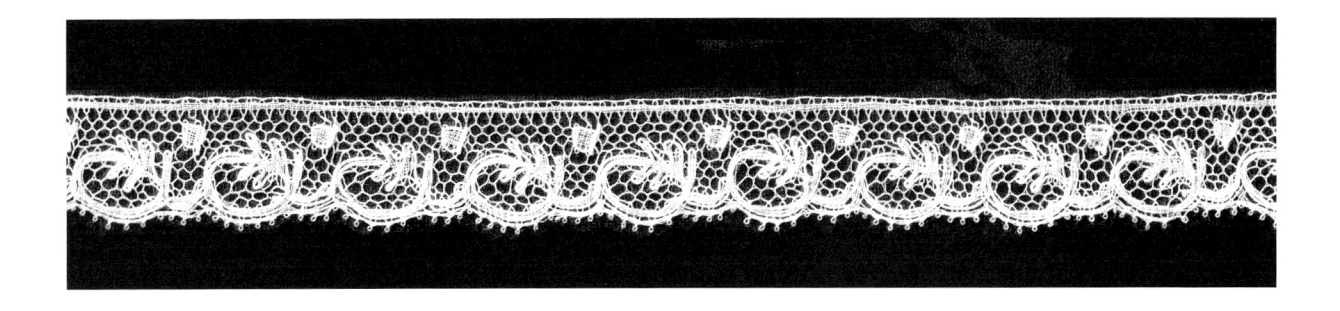

*Figure 424 Skirt edging, made on pricking figure 423
using Egyptian cotton no. 185/2, gimp single strand D.M.C. stranded embroidery*

193

All about making—Floral Bucks Point Lace

Figure 425 Skirt edging, pricking for use with Egyptian cotton no. 100/2, gimp D.M.C. perle no. 12

The majority of this pricking uses the techniques described previously. However, the gimped cloth stitch bud has no pins within the gimp (figure 426).

Gimped bud

Four pairs enter across the gimp (figure 426). Two from a point ground stitch above, pin A, and one from each side, pins B and C. One of the side pairs, in this case the one from pin B on the left, works across the other three pairs and passes out across the gimp to pin D. The workers twist two or three times and pass back across the gimp, the three passive pairs and the gimp on the other side to pin E. After three twists it passes back towards the right, this time to make a catch-pin stitch outside the gimp at pin F. A pair then returns across the clothwork to the left to make a catch-pin stitch at pin G and a pair returns across to exit the clothwork on the right side. Both gimps pass through the three remaining passive pairs and are thrown out. The two passive pairs on the left, those that entered the bud from the point ground stitch at pin A, make a modified point ground stitch (cloth stitch, three twists) at pin H and the right pair makes a point ground stitch with the remaining passive pair on its right at pin J.

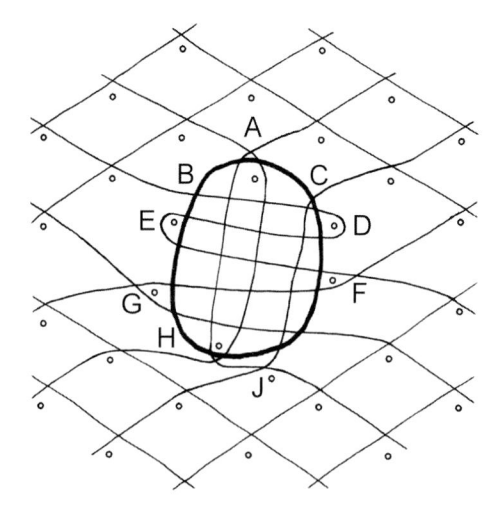

Figure 426 Gimped cloth stitch bud

All about making—Floral Bucks Point Lace

In this edging, the gimped bud is more tricky as it is situated close to the footside.

Compare the working of this leaf (figure 427) with the one in the previous pricking (figure 416). The general approach is the same. However, there is a pinhole in the second leaflet on the right that is used within the gimp as in Standard Bucks point. Before commencing the loop, use the pair left out at the end of the bridge to work two stitches without pins and at least a couple more point ground stitches.

As with all Floral Bucks, this figure is not the only way the lace may be made and there are many suitable variations, a pleasing alternative is to work honeycomb ground within the loop.

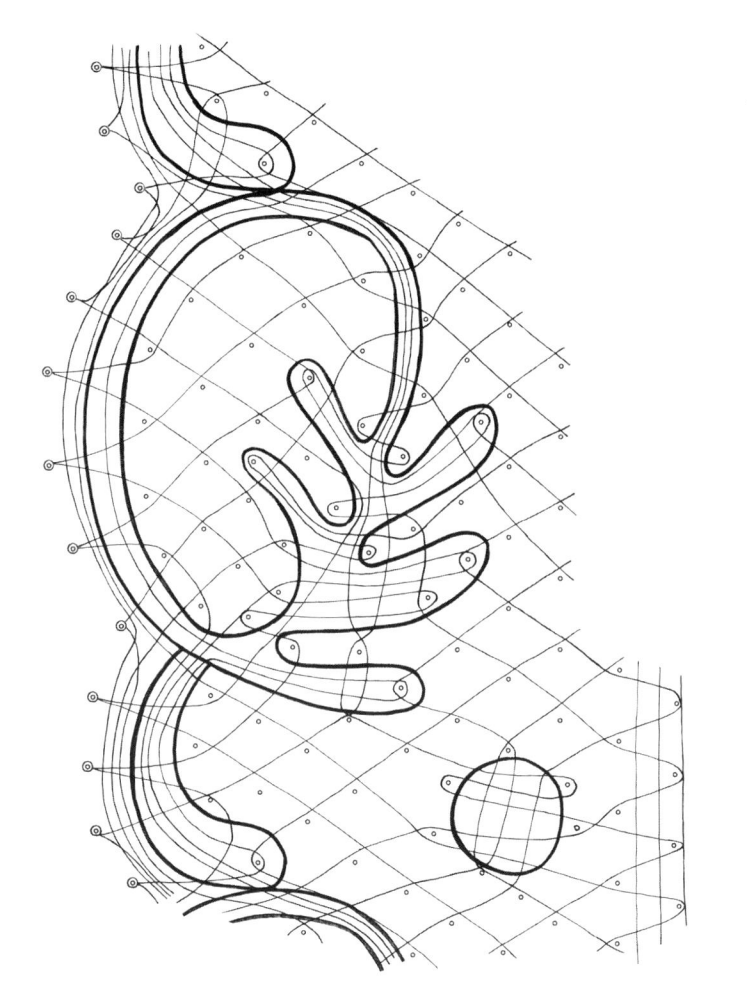

Note the variation for the valley at the lower end of the lower bridge linking the leaf motifs.

Figure 427 Working diagram for skirt edging.

The edging was attached to the skirt using four-sided stitch[2].

END NOTES

1 Substituting threads
See Part 6.

2 Four-sided stitch
See *All about making*—Geometrical Bucks Point Lace, Alexandra Stillwell, Salex Publishing pages 41-43.

195

CHAPTER 25

PROJECT 25b: Camisole galloon

As with the other forms of Floral Bucks, it is not necessary to follow this diagram exactly, there are many variations on how it may be worked. The flower (figures 428 & 429) contains many techniques that you can only use with very fine thread as they would look ugly if the pricking was coarser. The petals are worked as fingers with one or two pairs of passives travelling down them. The two petals in the centre are worked first then the gimp surrounding the honeycomb in the centre is introduced and the first stitch worked at the top of the honeycomb. The fingers of the right side are made before those of the left and when the pairs for the tally are left out from the right side they are incorporated into the left.

Materials Required for Project 25b
Egyptian cotton no. 240/2[1]
gimp one strand D.M.C. stranded embroidery thread

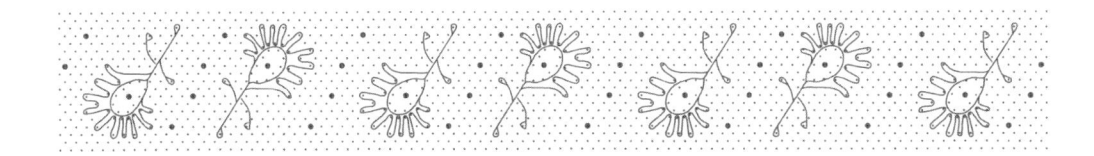

Figure 428 Galloon, pricking for use with
Egyptian cotton no. 240/2, gimp single strand D.M.C. stranded embroidery thread

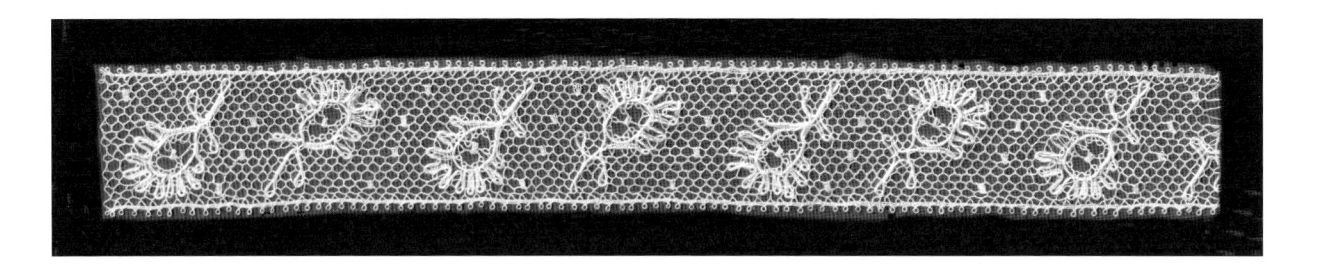

Figure 429 Camisole edging made on pricking figure 428 using
Egyptian cotton no. 240/2, gimp single strand D.M.C. stranded embroidery thread

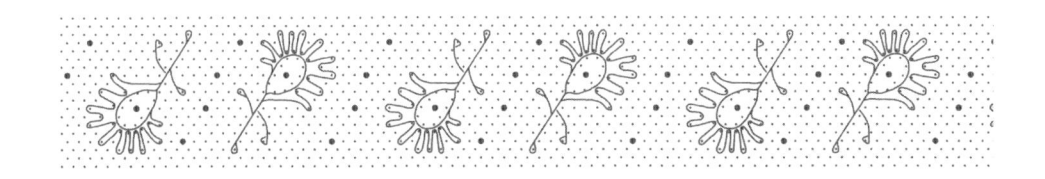

Figure 430 Camisole edging, pricking for use with
Egyptian cotton no. 100/2, gimp D.M.C. perle no. 12

All about making—Floral Bucks Point Lace

The two pairs meeting inside a gimp for the left finger at pin A work cloth and twist, pin cloth stitch (figure 431) The left pair passes out across the gimp to make a catch-pin stitch with the next ground pair at pin B, the other pair remaining within the gimps as a passive pair. The catch-pin pair adjacent to the gimp makes two cloth stitches across the gimps and passive pair, is twisted and makes a nook pin on the other side of the finger at C.

The right gimp passes through the next two pairs which then work cloth stitch and twist, pin, cloth stitch to start the next finger at pin D. The right pair passes out across the gimp to make a catch-pin stitch at pin E and the left pair from this stitch crosses the gimp, makes three cloth stitches to the left and passes out across the gimp to make a nook pin at pin F. It then works back across the same pairs to make another nook pin at pin G.

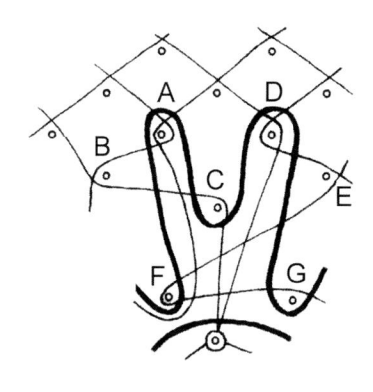

Figure 431 Starting the fingers.

A pair of gimps is introduced to surround the honeycomb centre which starts by making the first stitch using the nook pin pair, originally from pin C and the passive pair on its right, originally from pin D.

The next two fingers on the right are worked similarly. The pair making the nook pin at G passing through them to make a catch-pin stitch after working the second of these fingers (figure 432). A pair from the catch-pin at pin H enters a finger to become a passive pair and the other passive pair in this finger passes into the central ring to make a honeycomb stitch at pin J. A pair from this stitch works across and makes a nook pin at pin K and returns to make a honeycomb stitch at pin L with the other passive pair from the same finger. This side ends with a pair working across between catch-pin stitches in the ground and honeycomb stitches in the centre.

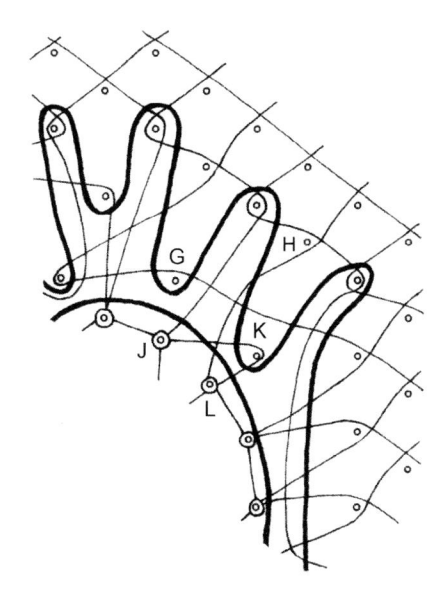

Figure 432 Working the next two fingers on the right.

197

All about making—Floral Bucks Point Lace

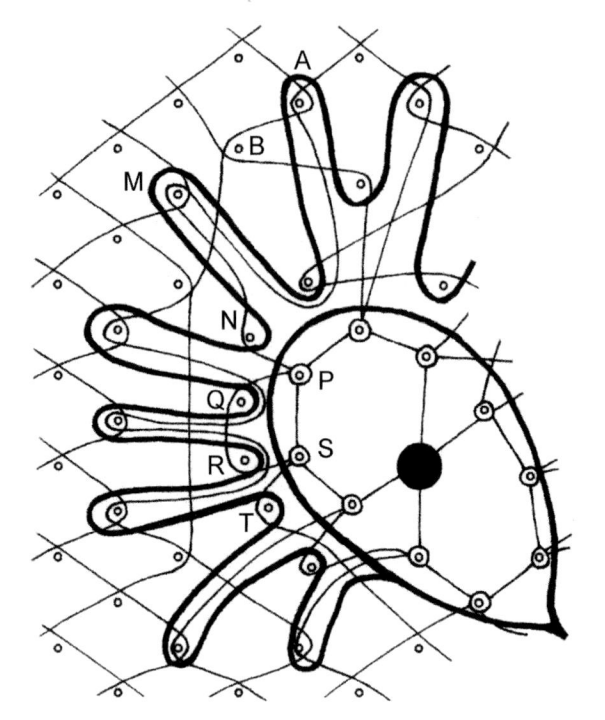

The passive pair from the left finger, the one that started at pin A, works up the next finger on the left crossing the pair from the catch-pin stitch at pin B and works cloth and twist, pin cloth stitch at pin M (figure 433). This passive pair then works back down the finger to make a nook pin at pin N. The pair that crossed the finger between pins M and N makes a catch-pin stitch and one pair drops down the cross the next three fingers. From pin N a pair makes a honeycomb stitch at pin P then makes nook pins at pins Q and R to return to the honeycomb at pin S and make a nook pin at T. After making the central tally the remaining two fingers and the honeycomb centre can be finished.

Figure 433 Working the fingers on the left.
The letters are for reference only, they are not the working order

The fingers use the same general techniques -
Gimps work cloth stitches with passives.

- The work is so fine that the doubling of threads does not show when you change from cloth stitches within the gimps, as at the top of a finger, to cloth stitches with gimps.
- Pairs may work uphill.
- Fingers may have a single pair of passives working from the tip to the base or may have a pair of passives working from the base to the tip then back to the base.
- Not all fingers have passives. (Not shown here.)
- Pairs may enter from the ground part way down the side of a finger to become passives or leave similarly.
- There is usually more than one way of working a pricking, certainly there are many different ways of working these fingers.
- When lace is this fine anomalies cannot be seen. The design is defined by the gimps and the workers and passives control them.

The galloon was attached by making a line of small running stitches down both sides through the edge passives and the lower edge neatened by hemstitching. The garment is fastened down the back with three very small buttons.

END NOTES

1 Substituting threads
See Part 6.

All about making—Floral Bucks Point Lace

CHAPTER 26

PROJECT 27b: Cuffs

Materials Required for Project 27b
Egyptian cotton no. 185/2[1]
gimp D.M.C coton á broder no. 25
embroidery thread
2 small buttons

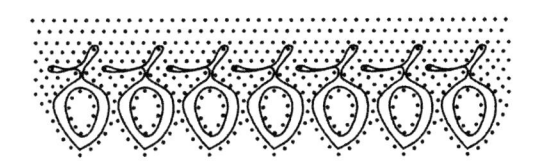

*Figure 434 Cuffs, pricking for use with
Egyptian cotton no. 185/2, gimp D.M.C. coton à broder no. 25*

*Figure 435 Cuffs made on pricking no. 434
using Egyptian cotton no. 185/2, gimp D.M.C. coton à broder no. 25*

*Figure 436 Cuffs, enlarged pricking for use with Egyptian cotton
no. 100/2, gimp D.M.C. perle no. 12*

199

The workers and passive pairs within the motif follow the design rather than horizontal and vertical directions (figure 437). A pair from the pin at the top of the fingers passes down through both the fingers to exit at the end of the lower one. Two pairs entering the clothwork at the top of the motif follow the gimp towards the left and continue under the central opening to exit into the ground on the right side. One pair entering at the top of the oval passes towards the right and continues around to exit when the oval is closed. It then passes into the next motif.

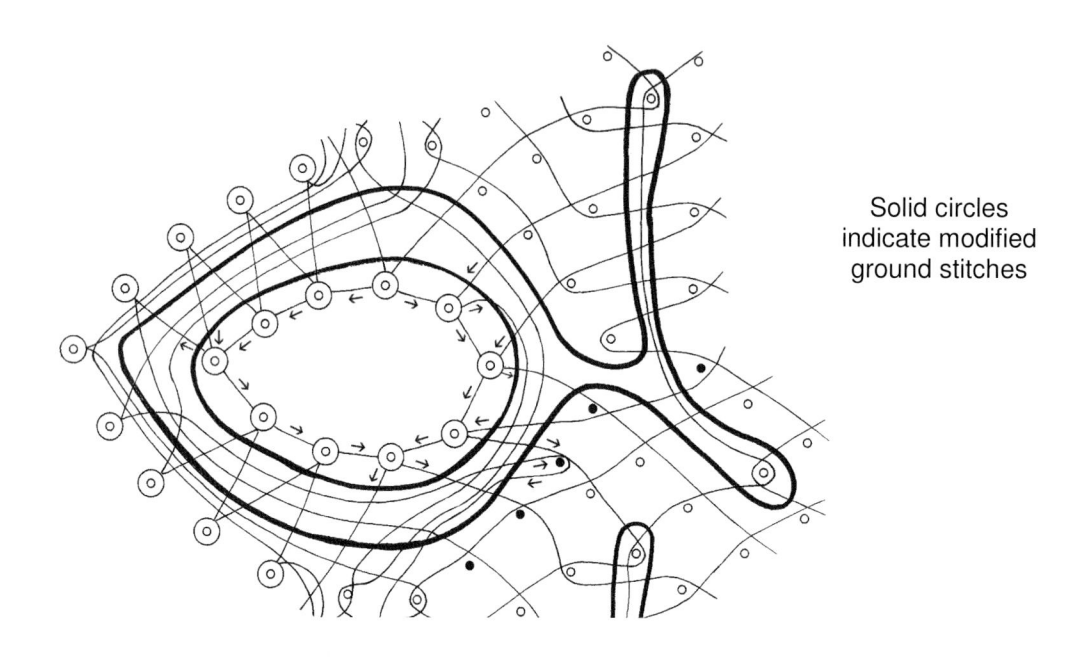

Solid circles indicate modified ground stitches

Figure 437 Working around ovals

The sleeves were finished by making a rolled hem either side of the sleeve opening and gathering the end with a rolled hem. The lace was attached to the edge of the rolled hem. A button was attached to one corner of the fabric and a chain loop buttonhole made.

END NOTES

1 Substituting threads
See Part 6.

All about making—Floral Bucks Point Lace

CHAPTER 27

PROJECT 29: Fichu

Figure 438 Fichu made using Egyptian cotton no. 170/2, gimp single strand Anchor stranded embroidery thread

Materials Required for Project 29
Egyptian cotton no. 170/2[1]
gimp single strand
Anchor stranded embroidery thread
30cm (12 in) x 30cm (12 in) cotton net

Figure 439 (left) Fichu edging, pricking for start and first side for use with Egyptian cotton no. 170/2, gimp single strand Anchor stranded embroidery thread

Figure 440 (right) Fichu edging, start and first side made on pricking figure no. 439 using Egyptian cotton no. 170/2, gimp single strand Anchor stranded embroidery thread

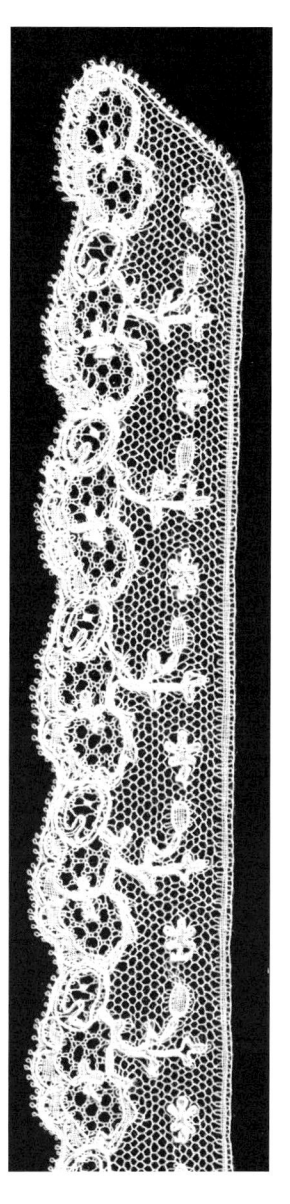

This is a complicated piece containing many of the more advanced techniques. As with all Floral Bucks do NOT attempt to follow the diagrams exactly; they only show one of many possible routes. Instead read the explanations, try to understand how to approach making the lace and experiment. This edging cannot be worked successfully 'upside down'[2], therefore a non-reversing corner has been designed and because a motif has been placed diagonally across the corner the filling within it is placed and worked on the diagonal.

201

All about making—Floral Bucks Point Lace

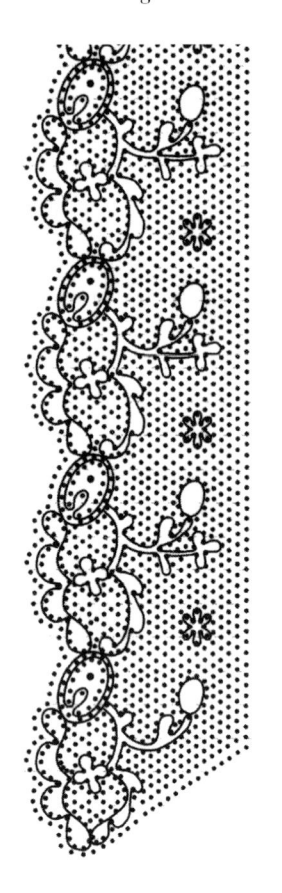

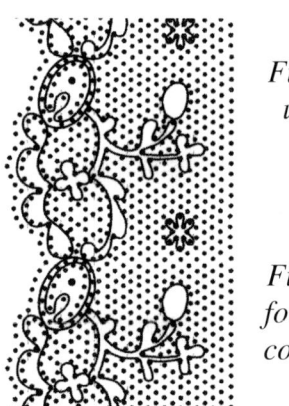

Figure 441 (left) Fichu corner, pricking for use with Egyptian cotton no. 170/2, gimp single strand Anchor stranded embroidery thread

Figure 442 (far left) Fichu edging, pricking for end of second side for use with Egyptian cotton no. 170/2, gimp single strand Anchor stranded embroidery thread

Figure 443 (below left) Fichu corner made on pricking figure 441 using Egyptian cotton no. 170/2, gimp single strand Anchor stranded embroidery thread

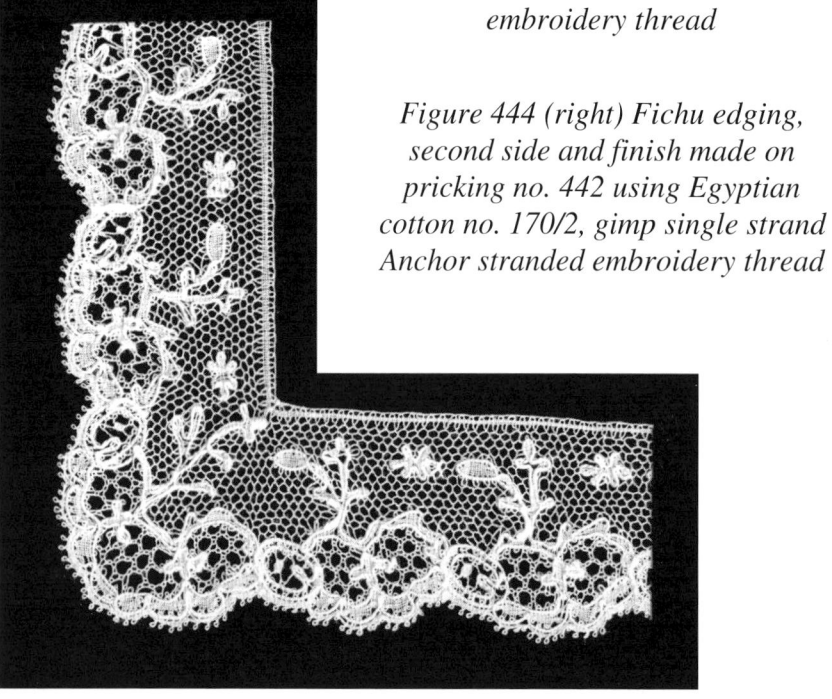

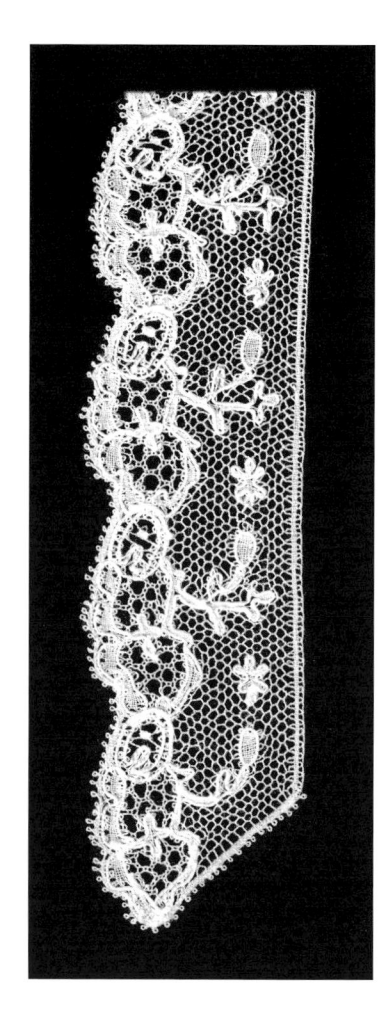

Figure 444 (right) Fichu edging, second side and finish made on pricking no. 442 using Egyptian cotton no. 170/2, gimp single strand Anchor stranded embroidery thread

All about making—Floral Bucks Point Lace

Figure 445 Fichu edging, pricking for start and first side for use with Egyptian cotton no. 100/2, gimp D.M.C. perle no. 12

Figure 446 (left) Fichu corner, pricking for use with Egyptian cotton no. 100/2, gimp single strand gimp D.M.C. perle no. 12

Figure 447 (far below) Fichu edging, pricking for end of second side for use with Egyptian cotton no. 100/2, gimp D.M.C. perle no. 12

All about making—Floral Bucks Point Lace

Setting in at the point (Read the End Notes before setting in)
The first repeat was modified to fit the diagonal start. The outer edge of the clothwork motif has pinholes along it, the inner edge does not. This means that pairs will exit across the gimp without twists on the clothwork side. The stems have no pins and pairs pass through them without twists. The lace was set in using previously explained techniques with three pairs of edge passives along the diagonal edge to match the three that will be required for casting off at the other end.

The workers leave the clothwork to make the stitch at A (figure 448) and return as workers.

Pin B is a support pin and there are twists between the edge passives and the gimp.

A pair enters the stem at C, works two stitches to right with pairs entering from picots and then leaves the stem at D to work a ground stitch at pin E. This is a technique whereby a pair enters to become a passive pair, works through other passive pairs and then leaves without any pins being set up, thus giving the opportunity for controlling the gimp. In this case the passive pair keeps the gimp lifted up and reduces any tendency for the outer gimp to sag against the inner gimp of the stem. The pair entering after the workers have returned from pin A exerts the same control.

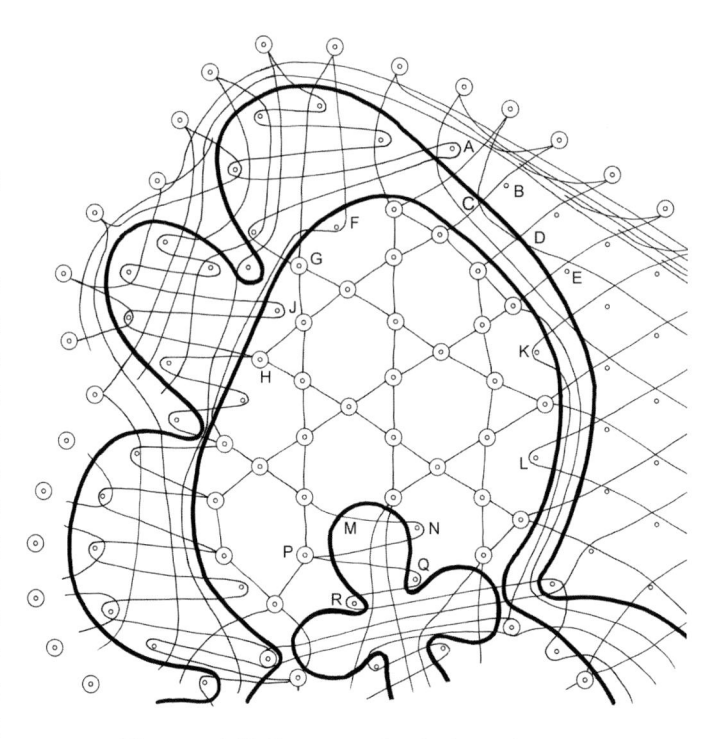

Figure 448 Starting the fichu edging

A passive pair exits the clothwork to make a winkie pin at pin F and returns as a passive pair.

Honeycomb stitches, modified if required, are worked around the rim when required, sometimes the worker remains in the honeycomb filling (pin G), sometimes it returns into the clothwork (pin H). Other pins are worked as winkie pins (J).

Pairs from the ground can cross the stem to make a winkie pin and return through the gimp to become passives (pin K) or pass back through the stem to continue making ground (L).

The cross
The central cross has a new pair of gimps. A pair enters from the left at M, passes through two pairs of passives and exits to the right to make a winkie pin at pin N; it returns across the clothwork and exits to the left to make a modified honeycomb stitch at pin P. To define the upper arm of the cross return across the clothwork to exit on the right to make a nook pin at Q and across the clothwork again to make a nook pin at R. There are no pins within the shape to support it, all the support comes from the tension on the workers.

Side arms of the cross
Pass the right gimp of the cross to the right through two pairs from pin S (figure 449) and work the pair from pin R to the right passing out of the cross and across the stem to make a catch-pin stitch at T, set up pin U between the passives in the stem. Pass the left gimp of the cross through the pair from the honeycomb stitch at pin V. Return the pair from pin T through all the passives of the cross and out across the gimps to work with the runners in the clothwork on the other side at pin W. The workers of the cross return through all the passive pairs of the cross and its right gimp to work with a passive pair that has passed out of the stem on the right at pin X.

Defining the lower arm of the cross
The cross workers return through the gimp and three pairs to work a nook pin at pin Y then back across the gimp, two pairs and the other gimp to make a nook pin at pin Z.

Lower arm of the cross
The workers pass to the left across the lower arm to make a honeycomb stitch in the ground, pin A, cross the arm to the right to make a honeycomb stitch on that side at pin B and back to make another on the left side at pin C. The gimps are cast off and the remaining pair makes a honeycomb stitch at pin D.

First clothwork lobe
The right gimp passes to the right through four ground pairs a, b, c and d. The passive pair that exited to work pin X returns across the gimp to resume its former role. Pair 'a' passes through the passive pairs to make a winkie pin at pin E and returns across the gimp to become a

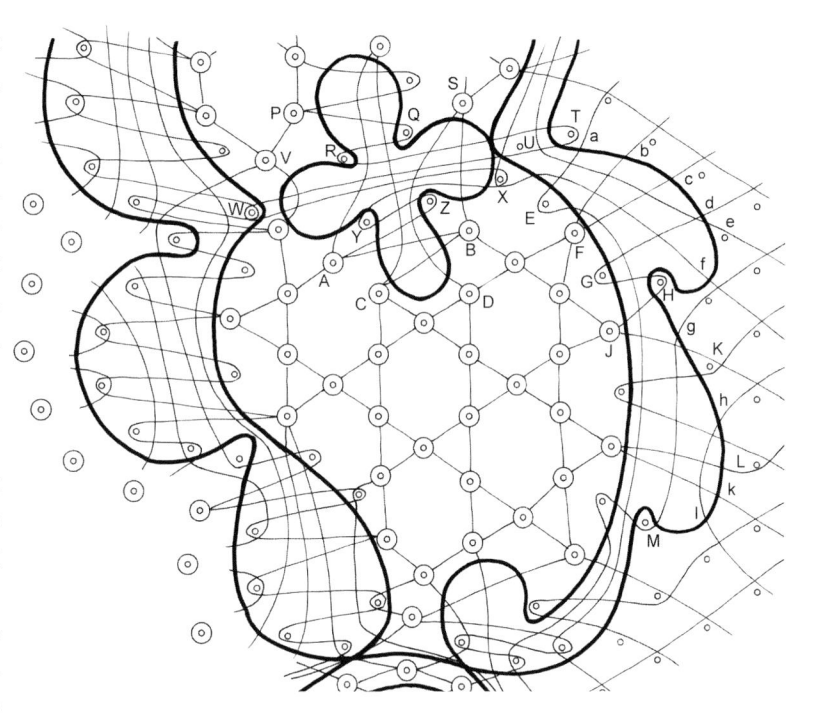

Figure 449 Cross and lobes

passive pair. Pairs b and c cross the passive pairs to exit across the gimp on the other side and work a honeycomb stitch at pin F. Pair d crosses the passive pairs and gimp to make a winkie pin at pin G. The right gimp passes through two passive pairs and then the workers pass back across to make a nook pin at pin H to define the lobe. The workers then cross back to the left to make a honeycomb stitch at pin J.

Second clothwork lobe
This time the workers make catch-pin stitches on the right, pins K and L but since the clothwork is widening towards the right a passive pair is brought in from the ground each time, pairs g and h. As the lobe finishes the worker, pair k, passes out into the ground followed by a passive pair, pair l. The next passive pair makes the nook pin, pin M that defines the end of the lobe.

All about making—Floral Bucks Point Lace

While working the clothwork adjacent to the headside the workers from winkie pin, pin X, (figure 450) travel across the clothwork to make a picot, pin Y, before continuing normally.

The scroll
From the nook pin, pin M (figure 450), the workers make a winkie pin at pin N and return across the gimp to become passives. A pair from the honeycomb stitch at pin P crosses the clothwork to make a catch-pin stitch on the other side, pin Q, returns across to make the nook pin, pin R, that defines the scroll and crosses back to work the ground at pin S.

The left gimp passes through a pair from pin P, one from pin T and one from pin U. The pair from pin P works towards the left, exits the clothwork and makes a honeycomb stitch at pin V. The clothwork then finishes normally using the last three pins.

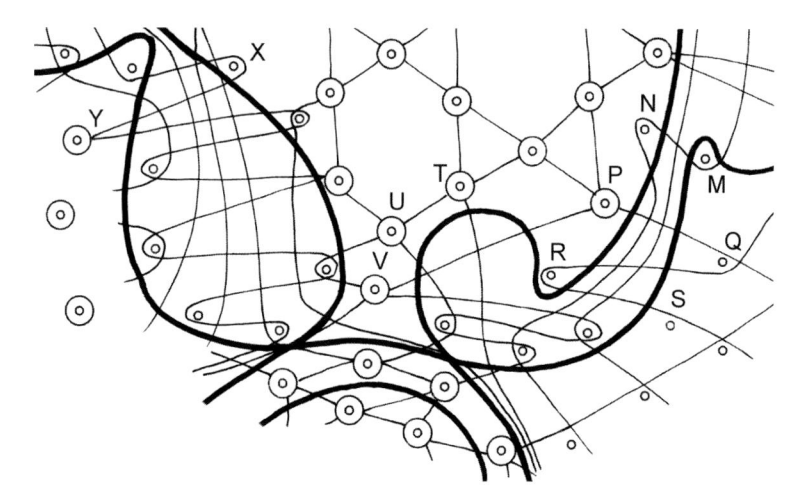

Figure 450 (right) Scroll

Six-pointed star
Various stars are used as motifs in very fine Floral Bucks Point. This one has six points which are regular with the ground, all stitches are cloth stitches and there are no twists between them and the gimp.

This star starts with two pairs and a new pair of gimps at pin A (figure 451). The workers pass out to make a nook pin at pin B, cross the star and make another at pin C. The workers work across to make the point at pin D and back to make the other top one at pin E. They then cross the centre to make catch-pins on either side, pins F and G, and then the lower two points, pins H and J, are worked. Nook pins K and L define the last point which finishes at pin M and the gimps are cast off.

Figure 451 Six-pointed star

All about making—Floral Bucks Point Lace

The oval
The oval is worked as a honeycomb stem containing honeycomb filling (figure 452). As the oval starts two pairs of passives will be needed on the outside gimp on the right (A) to be available when the side branch is reached.

Winkie pins (pins B) are worked along the rim when there is not a suitable honeycomb stitch available.

When the finger is reached and the inner left gimp and a pair rise up round pin C where two pairs entering across both work cloth stitch, twist, cloth stitch and these pairs exit the finger.

Now the side branch is started and worked until pin D has been worked providing a pair to make a honeycomb stitch at pin E in the stem. This in turn provides a pair to work with one of the pairs exiting from the finger to make a honeycomb stitch at pin F, the other pair from the finger making a nook pin at pin G.

From pin F a pair exits the stem to make a winkie pin at pin H and the same pair returns to make a honeycomb stitch in the stem at pin J with the other pair from pin F.

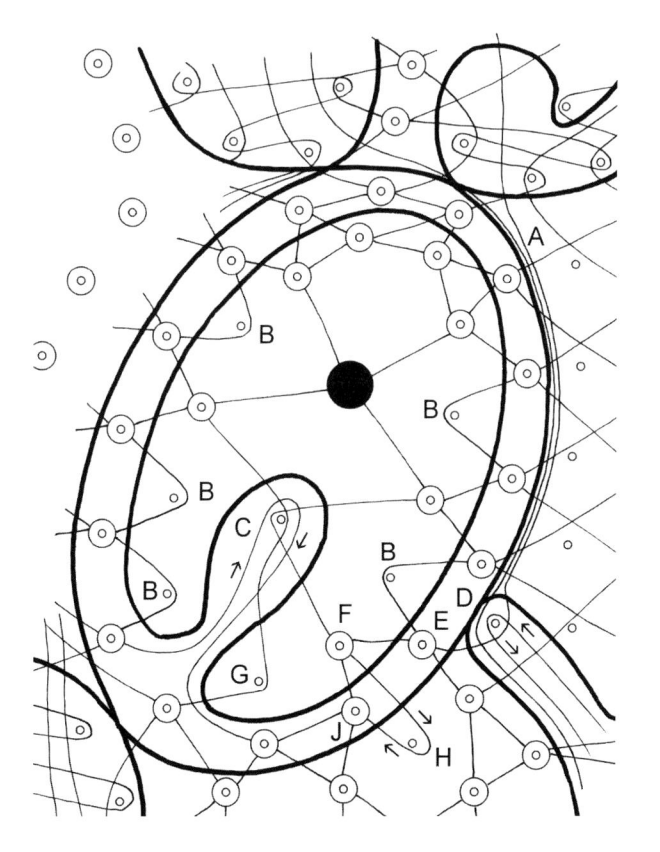

Figure 452 The oval

207

All about making—Floral Bucks Point Lace

Side branch
A new pair and two new pairs of gimps are introduced for the clothwork motif. The gimps will be cast off but usually the pair works its way through to the headside passives where it can be thrown out.

Top motif
A new pair, pair 'a', is slipped on the pair entering from the pinhole above the motif, pin A, so that it lies to the right of that pair. A new gimp is passed towards the left through this new pair, now the workers, passes through the next two pairs on the left (figure 453), the first being the pair it had been slipped onto and the second entering from the ground. The workers pass out across the gimp, are twisted and pinned at pin B. They then return across the gimp, the passives, a pair that has entered from the ground on the other side and exits to pass round a pin, pin C. The workers continue making rows across the motif exiting to be pinned outside the gimp and making catch-pin stitches or passing around pins before returning. When the last catch-pin, pin D, has been set up, a pair, pair b, is left out from the other side of the motif. The gimps are crossed and the workers bridge across the gimps (no stitches) to make a catch-pin stitch at pin E. The remaining two pairs of passives are left lying between the gimps. These two pairs work cloth stitch and twist, pin, cloth stitch at pin F and remain as passives. A pair from pin E works across the stem to make a catch-pin stitch at pin G and a pair works back across the stem to work a row of ground. The next pair from the ground on the left, pair c, works to the right making a ground stitch, stitch d, with the remaining pair from the catch-pin stitch at pin G, works across the stem and then makes two ground stitches, pins H and J. The left passive pair exits the stem, makes a nook pin, pin K, works across the stem and makes two ground stitches, pins L and M on the other side.

The bump on the left of the top motif
The passive pair inside the left gimp of the stem works with the remaining pair from stitch d to exit across the gimp to pass round pin N, return across the gimp and the pair from stitch d (figure 453). The gimp passes through the next ground pair on the left (pair e) and the pair from stitch D works across and exits the clothwork to pass round pin P and return across the gimp and two passive pairs to exit across the other gimp and make two ground stitches at pins Q and R.

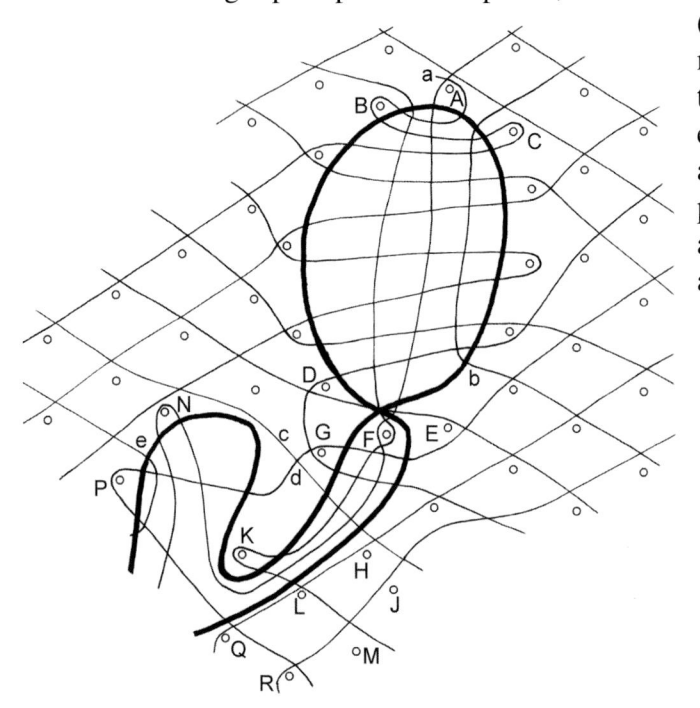

Figure 453 Starting the side branch and working the first bump on the left

All about making—Floral Bucks Point Lace

Starting left portion of the branch and the left bump
After working pin D of the oval (figure 454) work ground stitches at pins A and B. Take the left pair from pin B and pass it round a support pin, pin C, across the first of another new pair of gimps, across the other pair from pin B and exit across the other new gimp to make a catch-pin stitch at pin E. The right pair continues to make ground stitches at pins F and G and makes a catch-pin stitch, pin H, with a passive pair that has come from pin P in the clothwork on the right. The right pair from this stitch passes into the clothwork, works one stitch with the nearest passive and this pair exits across the gimp to be supported by pin J.

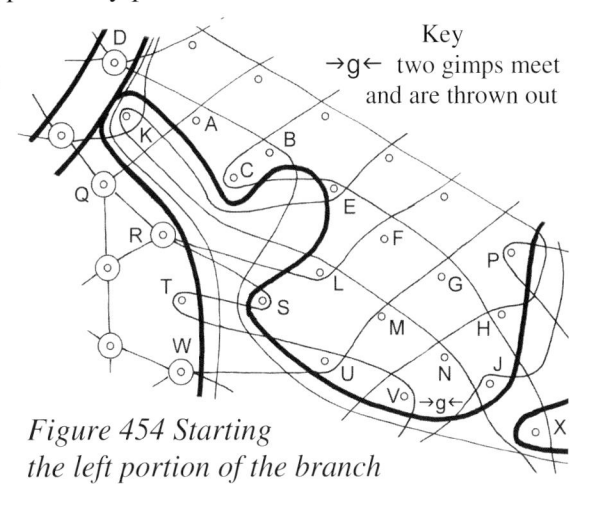

The other pair from pin E works to the left through the pairs from pins B and A and one of the extra pairs travelling along the gimp of the oval and a pin is set up under it at pin K. The same workers return across the previous pairs and the other gimp to make a catch-pin stitch, pin L. From here ground stitches are worked at pins M and N, a catch-pin stitch worked with the pair supported by pin J from which both pairs exit the ground.

A pair from the oval works a honeycomb stitch at pin Q with the pair crossing the stem from pin A and then one with the pair returning from catch-pin L at pin R. From here a pair crosses the stem to make a winkie pin at pin S, returns to one at pin T and works across again to make catch-pin stitch at pin U, then across once more to make a honeycomb stitch at W. The remaining pair at pin U makes a ground stitch at pin V and both these pairs enter the stem. Two gimps meet at →g← and are thrown out. The pair from pin H that entered across the gimp passes across the gimp on the other side of the clothwork and makes a nook pin at pin X. Using the passive pair that entered the clothwork from pin B as workers cloth stitch to the right through the pairs entering across the gimp from pins V, J and X.

Figure 454 Starting the left portion of the branch

Key
→g← two gimps meet and are thrown out

The trefoil
Place a pin at A above the pair from pin M to control the gimp and continue with the same workers through the pairs from pins R, M, A and J, take them across the gimp, round pin B and back into the stem of the trefoil to work across the pair from pin J (figure 455). The pair from pin J passes out to make a nook pin at pin C and re-enters the stem. The gimp passes through the next two pairs on the right, pairs a and b, to exit across the gimp where it is pinned at pin D. It then re-enters the stem to work across three pairs and the pair from pin C makes a nook pin at pin E. The ground must be made up as far as pin F. The leading ground pair enters the stem and works through two pairs. The second pair then exits the stem to be pinned at pin G and re-enters to pass up through the pairs from pins F and E and along the stem through the pairs from R. The gimp follows it through the same pairs. Pin H is placed under the pair that has crossed the finger from pin E. A row of ground starts at pin K with the two pairs that crossed the stem from pin R and then works towards the right.

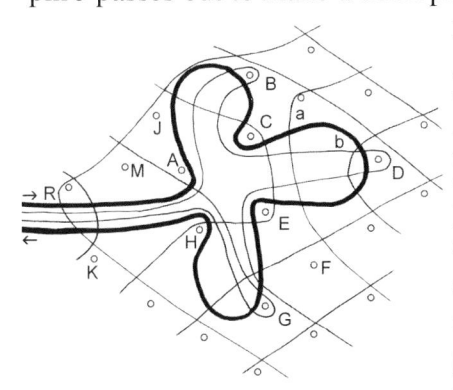

Figure 455 The trefoil

209

All about making—Floral Bucks Point Lace

Finishing the branch

After the workers have re-entered from the right through the passive pairs from pin R and the next passive pair pass the gimp through that pair and set up a nook pin at A (figure 456). Return the pair across the gimp and the next pair, the previous workers, the latter exiting the finger to work a row of ground towards the right starting with the stitch at pin B. Pass the gimp through a pair from B and one from the following stitch. The pair that crossed into the branch from nook pin X works down the branch and exits to make a ground stitch at pin C. The pair that entered the branch from pin J continues down the finger, exits to be pinned at pin D and returns to work up through all the pairs and parallels the original workers that entered the branch. The gimp follows it through the same pairs. A pin is set up at E under the pair crossing the branch from nook pin A. The pairs that crossed the branch from pins J and V work a ground stitch and another is worked with the pair supported by pin E. Then at n the lead pair is passed through the next pair it meets at the finger without any twists being made between it and the gimp. A pair from a honeycomb stitch in the motif passes out through the passive pair and the workers arriving from the branch, makes a nook pin at G and returns into the motif to make a winkie pin at pin H. A pair from here crosses stem of the motif to make a catch-pin stitch at K and four ground stitches towards the right. The next ground stitch, pin L, is made with the leading pair from the previous row.

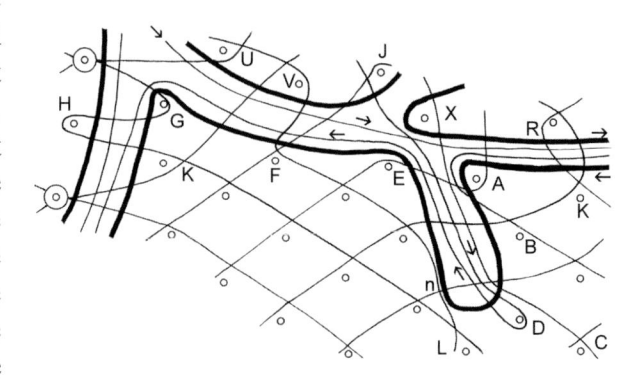

Figure 456 Finishing the branch

Making up the fichu

The cotton net chosen had the thickness of the thread making it and the size of the mesh as close as I could find to match that of the edging. The lace was mounted on the net as for the bonnet crown and the straight side of the triangle of net was hemmed.

END NOTES

1 Substituting threads
See Part 6.

2 Corners

Due to the techniques that are used in very fine Bucks many prickings cannot successfully be worked 'upside down' and for these non-reversing corners are more suitable. (Turn this book upside down and try following the thread diagrams.) It may be possible to discover different routes but there is another problem inherent in this pricking. In figure 449 pairs e and f and k, l and m drift out at the lower ends of areas of clothwork and the lace works successfully. If this is worked 'upside down' the pairs do not lie where they should as the stitches outside the clothwork area will be on the other sides of the pins. Also the weight of the bobbins, even if very light, will drag these passive threads out of place.

Some special characteristics of Very Fine Floral Bucks Point
Missing pinholes?
The distinguishing characteristic of very fine Bucks is that there are few pinholes, if any, within the clothwork. A trait that I suspect relates to the thickness of the pins; there being insufficient space for the pins if the lace was worked using the techniques for Standard Bucks. Many prickings for very fine Bucks with the headside gimp approximately parallel to the headside do not have pinholes along the edge of the clothwork by headside gimp, and the workers constantly pass from the filling to make a picot and return to continue as the workers. Also in this situation there is often only a single pair of headside passives which are twisted after every stitch. When such pieces have a valley it is usually worked using Standard Bucks methods. Once a second pair of passives has been stacked in the valley the twists disappear and the valley is worked in plain cloth stitch, the twists reappearing when the valley has been completed and there is only a single pair of headside passives remaining.

Line of the workers
Currently Standard Floral Bucks is made with the workers maintaining a horizontal line, in very fine Bucks Point they may work up hill and down following the line of a finger or stem (figures 420, 427 and 433). It all depends on the situation.

Controlling the positions of pairs in the clothwork
Since there are few pins within the clothwork the positions of the gimps and pairs in the clothwork are controlled by pairs passing through the clothwork to make stitches outside the gimp. This ability is severely compromised if the bobbins and spangles are too heavy and pull the pairs out of position.

Figure 448.
- A passive pair enters at C and exits at D. Tension on this pair will hold out the gimp on this side. The pair entering the cross at M and making a winkie pin at N controls the gimp at the top of the arm.
- The pair entering the cross at M and making a winkie pin at N controls the gimp at the top of the arm.

- Figure 449
- The pairs exiting the cross at the end of the lower arm hold the gimps out.
- The passive pair passing through at the constriction by pin T and passing out of the clothwork at 'e' holds the gimp up and prevents the clothwork collapsing.
- In the second lobe on the right the pair entering at 'h' and exiting at 'l' maintains the width of the clothwork.

- Figure 450
- The pair entering the scroll from pin P and exiting to make the honeycomb stitch at pin V controls the height of the scroll head.

Figure 453
- The workers from pin A to pin B control the top of the motif and the width by careful tensioning of the passives. This is best accomplished by firming up the stitch worked after the

gimp and heavy bobbins will pull them out of place.
- The top of the lobe is controlled by the workers from the catch-pin at pin G passing through and making a winkie pin at pin P.

Figure 454
- The workers from the nook pin, pin C, enter the clothwork and exit to make a catch-pin at pin E and control the top of the lobe.
- The passive pair entering before pin P and exiting after controls the width of the shape.

Figure 455
- The top of the upper lobe is controlled by the pair crossing from pin J to pin C.
- The gimp at the extreme right tip of the trefoil is controlled by the pair entering before the workers exit to work pin D and themselves exit after the workers have worked back though them.
- The length of the lower lobe is controlled by the pair passing through from pin F.

Figure 456
- The length of the lower lobe is controlled by the pair passing through from the ground stitch following the one at pin B.

Ground may be interrupted, disturbed or distorted to allow it to be made between stems, motifs and fingers.

Figure 453
- The ground pins, pins C and N, are also used to support workers that exits from and return into the clothwork.

Figure 454
- The leading ground pair working the row along pins A and B enters the clothwork and is replaced when a catch-pin is worked at pin E.

Figure 455
- The central pair exits to pass round a ground pin, pin B, before re-entering the finger. It may be easier to not pin the ground until this pair is pinned.
- Pin G is in line with the ground but the lead pair from the ground stitch at pin F crosses through the finger and pin G is used to control the central pair before it returns up the finger.

Figure 454
- The workers from the nook pin, pin C, enter the clothwork and exit to make a catch-pin at pin E and control the top of the lobe.
- The passive pair entering before pin P and exiting after controls the width of the shape.

Figure 455
- The top of the upper lobe is controlled by the pair crossing from pin J to pin C.
- The gimp at the extreme right tip of the trefoil is controlled by the pair entering before the workers exit to work pin D and themselves exit after the workers have worked back though

All about making—Floral Bucks Point Lace

them.
- The length of the lower lobe is controlled by the pair passing through from pin F.

Figure 456
- The length of the lower lobe is controlled by the pair passing through from the ground stitch following the one at pin B.

When clothwork abuts honeycomb ground various situations may arise.

Figure 448
- Along the rim of the ground there may be an incomplete honeycomb ring where a winkie pin may be necessary to provide anchorage for the clothwork workers to change direction at the end of a row, pins J and N.
- A clothwork passive pair may require anchoring under a shallow curve before it returns as a passive, pin F.
- A pair from the ground may pass through clothwork to make a winkie pin and return to the ground, pin L.
- A pair from the ground may pass through clothwork to make a winkie pin and return across the gimp to become a passive, pin K.
- Clothwork workers may pass into the honeycomb to make a stitch and return as workers, pin H.
- Two clothwork passive pairs may enter the honeycomb ground to make a stitch and remain there, pin G.
- A honeycomb pair may enter clothwork and pass through to exit on the other side, pins M and N.

Stems and fingers generally have central pairs of passives travelling through them.

Figure 448
- Two central passive pairs travel down the stem as in the lower half on the right of the honeycomb.
- A central passive pair may exit a stem and be replaced by another as seen in the upper half of the stem.

Figure 451
- Central passive pairs may swing across to make fingers on both sides of a central feature, pins D, E, H and J.

Figure 453
- There may be two pairs travelling in the same direction, pin F.
- Two central passive pairs may start at the same end of a stem, pin F.
- Passives may travel up through a stem or finger, pass out across the gimp and twist before returning down, pin N.
- The central passive pair may work with a pair entering the stem when a pin is set up and the central pair returns.

All about making—Floral Bucks Point Lace

Figure 454
- One pair may travel first in one direction and then return along the same path. In this figure a pair enters the stem from the catch-pin stitch at E, travels up the stem to pin K and returns to exit the stem, work a catch-pin stitch at pin K and return into the stem.

Figure 455
- A central worker pair travelling along the stem below pin R is controlled by a pin at A. The workers make the upper finger of the trefoil by rising up through a pair to be pinned at B and then returning down. The gimp is then controlled by a nook pin at pin C and the workers make the central finger by travelling out to be pinned at pin D and then returning. Nook pin E controls the gimp and the lower finger is made by the worker pair travelling down to be pinned at pin G and returning up the stem where pin H controls the gimp. The workers now start to return along its original path.

Figure 456
- After nook pin A has been worked the workers that were travelling towards the left pass out of the stem to work a ground stitch at pin B. Two pairs travel down the finger, one from pin J the other from pin X, and both pairs exit. The pair from pin J passes round pin D and returns up the finger to replace the workers lost at pin A.
- Central pairs may leave a stem and be replaced by others.

Ground may be interrupted, disturbed or distorted to allow it to be made between stems, motifs and fingers.

Figure 453
- The ground pins, pins C and N, are also used to support workers that exits from and return into the clothwork.

Figure 454
- The leading ground pair working the row along pins A and B enters the clothwork and is replaced when a catch-pin is worked at pin E.

Figure 455
- The central pair exits to pass round a ground pin, pin B, before re-entering the finger. It may be easier to not pin the ground until the central pair is pinned.
- Pin G is in line with the ground but the lead pair from the ground stitch at pin F crosses the finger, pin G is used to support the central pair before it returns up the finger.

Figure 456
- The lead pair from the row of ground starting at pin F cannot enter the finger as the gimp is travelling in the wrong direction. Instead, it parallels the gimp when the pair crossing it exits to make a stitch in the row below the one starting from pin F. The pair travelling down the gimp is used to make the next stitch of this row. It looks strange on paper but it works, especially if the bobbins are sufficiently light and the pin is placed close to the gimp.

All about making—Floral Bucks Point Lace

PART 3

BLACK HOLEY

This form of Bucks Point (figure 457) consists mainly of large irregularly shaped honeycomb rings and was traditionally made in black grenadine[1], a highly twisted silk thread, although other threads were used. The large rings usually have a stay, a pair across the corner that supports the corner of the ring and facilitates the movement of bobbins from one side of the ring to the other. When worked in black, 'clothwork', if present, was usually worked in half stitch. Point ground it not always present. Frequently the 'ground' is a complex filling often with large honeycomb rings and honeycomb bars. Many pieces and prickings do not have a footside. The pinholes are usually widely spaced, presumably so that the lace can be made quickly. However, this frequently results in untidy lace.

This lace is similar to some black blonde and the black lace of Pays-d'Enhaut, but there are differences in the techniques used for each lace. In particular, the stay used in black holey is absent from the others. I have found no information concerning the time when black holey was made, but as there are prickings for making the lace of Pays-d'Enhaut[2] dating 1823-1866, it is reasonably safe to assume that all three of these laces were fashionable and made at about the same time.

The 'rules' for making Black Holey are even less rigid than for Standard Floral Bucks and there is less attention to detail. Large honeycomb rings are frequently incomplete, gimps may not encircle motifs completely and stitches may work uphill.

Figure 457 Black holey

CHAPTER 28

Project 30a: Box lid edging with inward-facing corners

Figure 458 Box lid with rectangular insert and edging with inward-facing corners

Materials Required for Project 30a
Bart & Francis 150 denier silk[1]
gimp Shappe Super Best 30/2 silk
box with aperture 29.5cm (11½ in) x 25.5cm (10 in) approx.

The edging has inward-facing corners, i.e. the headside with picots is on the inside of the corner whereas a normal corner has the headside on the outside. A pricking with a normal corner is included and was made using 150 denier silk and 6 strands, loosely twisted, for the gimps.

All about making—Floral Bucks Point Lace

This edging has a series of trefoils, sets of three large honeycomb rings typical of black holey, each linked to the next by a curved honeycomb bar, a honeycomb stem with a row of honeycomb stitches on each side is also typical of black holey. There is a single pair of headside passives that is twisted twice after every stitch.

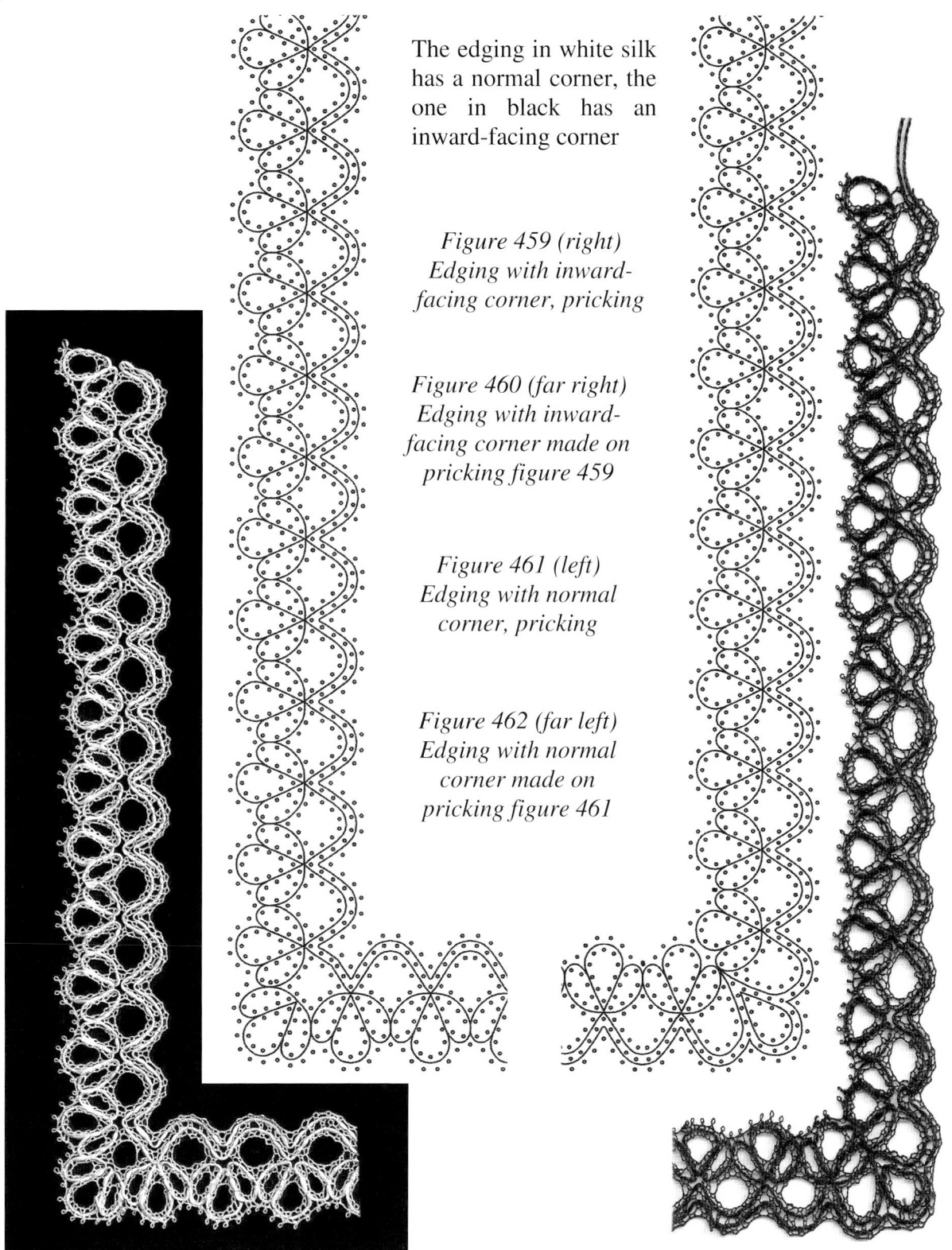

The edging in white silk has a normal corner, the one in black has an inward-facing corner

Figure 459 (right) Edging with inward-facing corner, pricking

Figure 460 (far right) Edging with inward-facing corner made on pricking figure 459

Figure 461 (left) Edging with normal corner, pricking

Figure 462 (far left) Edging with normal corner made on pricking figure 461

217

All about making—Floral Bucks Point Lace

Upper honeycomb ring and honeycomb bar
Set up with a false picot at the headside, 2a, three sets of two pairs at honeycomb stitches 2b, 2c and 2d and two single pairs added into honeycomb stitches 1a and 1b (figure 463). A pair of gimps is added for the petal and two single gimps for the honeycomb stem. There is a single headside passive pair starting at the false picot. Wherever pairs are twisted there are usually two twists. Apart from the picots all stitches are honeycomb stitches.

The upper ring of the trefoil starts part-way along the top of the petal at pin A with a pair from stitch 2b entering across the gimp and another added across the gimp. The left pair makes a stitch at pin B with a pair entering from the false picot, pin 2a, and the left pair passes out across the gimp to cloth and twist with the remaining pair from the false picot, make a picot at pin C, return across the headside passives with a cloth and twist and re-enter across the gimp. The returning pair makes a stitch with the remaining pair from pin B at pin D.

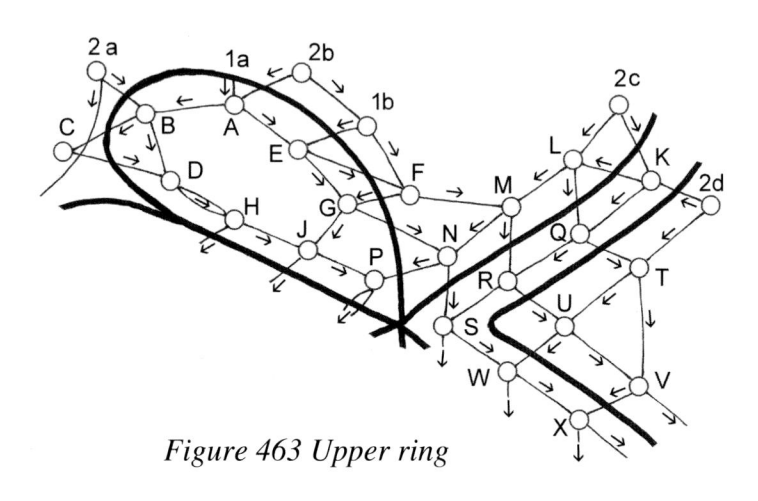

Figure 463 Upper ring

The remaining pair from pin 2b makes a stitch with a single pair at pin 1b and the left pair enters the petal to make a stitch at pin E with the remaining pair from pin A. The right pair exits the petal to make a stitch at pin F and re-enters to make a stitch at pin G with the remaining pair from pin E.

The two pairs from pin D make a pin-chain to pin H and the right pair makes a stitch at pin J with a pair from pin G. The pair from pin G to pin J forms the stay across the corner. This facilitates moving pairs from one side of the ring to the other and also strengthens the lace by supporting such a large ring across the corner.

The honeycomb bar is set up with honeycomb stitches at pin 2c and 2d and two single gimps. The stitch at pin K is made with pairs from pins 2c and 2d and the left pair makes a stitch with the remaining pair from pin 2c at pin L and then at pin M with the remaining pair from pin F forming the stay across the corner of the ring. Pairs from pins M and G make the stitch at pin N. The honeycomb bar continues with stitches at pins Q, R and S and the stem changes direction. A honeycomb stitch is made in the ring at pin T with a pairs from pins Q and 2d. and continues with a stitch at pin U in the corner and then one at pin V that is made using a pair from the corner and the pair left out from pin T, the pair from pin T to pin V forms the stay across the corner. Then stitches are worked in the bar at pins W and X.

In this piece the gimps for the trefoils are crossed after each petal, following a series of figure eights; the gimps of the bars do not cross each other, neither do they cross with the gimps of the trefoil.

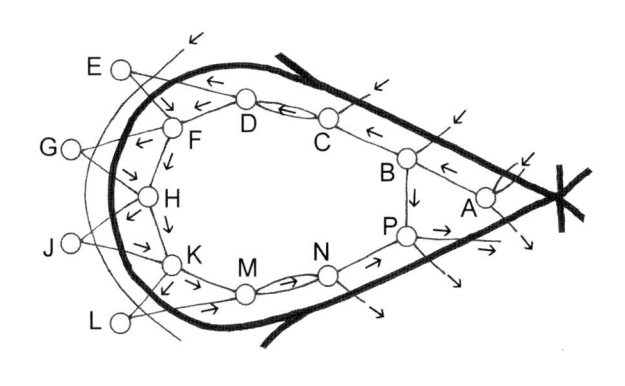

All about making—Floral Bucks Point Lace

Central honeycomb ring

This one starts in the corner at pin A (figure 464) with both pairs from the corner pin P of the upper ring (figure 463) and works uphill using the next pair to the left for the stitch at pin B and the next for the stitch at pin C. Both pairs from pin C then make the stitch at pin D. The left pair from pin D works out to make a picot at pin E and returns to make a stitch at pin F and this sequence is repeated for pins G-M. Both pairs from pin M make the stitch at pin N and the right pair from pin N makes a stitch at pin P with the pair remaining from pin B, the pair from pin B to pin P forming the stay.

Figure 464 The central ring

Lower honeycomb ring and honeycomb bar

The pinholes in the honeycomb bars at the top right relate to those in figure 463.

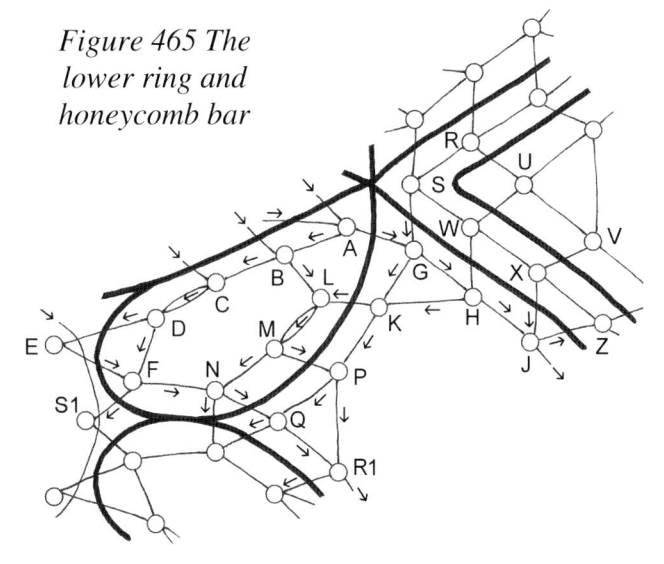

The lower ring starts in the corner at pin A with two pairs from the previous ring (figures 463 & 465) and the work travels around the ring with stitches made at pins B-F following a similar sequence to those used for the previous rings.

Figure 465 The lower ring and honeycomb bar

However, before working the remaining pins the pair from pin A exits the ring to work the stitch between the ring and the honeycomb bar at pin G. The right pair starts working along inside the bar to make stitches at pins H and J and the remaining pair from pin H makes a stitch with the remaining pair from pin G at pin K to form the stay. The left pair from pin K passes into the ring to make a stitch at pin L with the remaining pair from pin B, this forming the stay between pins B and L. Both pairs from pin L make a pin-chain to pin M and the ring is completed by working the stitch at pin N with pairs from pins F and M. Pairs exit the ring to make stitches with the remaining pair from pin K at pins P and Q and pairs from these pins make a stitch at pin R, the pair from pin P to pin R1 forming the stay.

The remaining pair from pin F makes a picot at pin S1 and continues into the next ring. The honeycomb bar continues with the stitch at pin Z. The edging is joined end to start.

219

All about making—Floral Bucks Point Lace

CHAPTER 29

Project 31: Fingerplate decoration also fits a bookmark sleeve

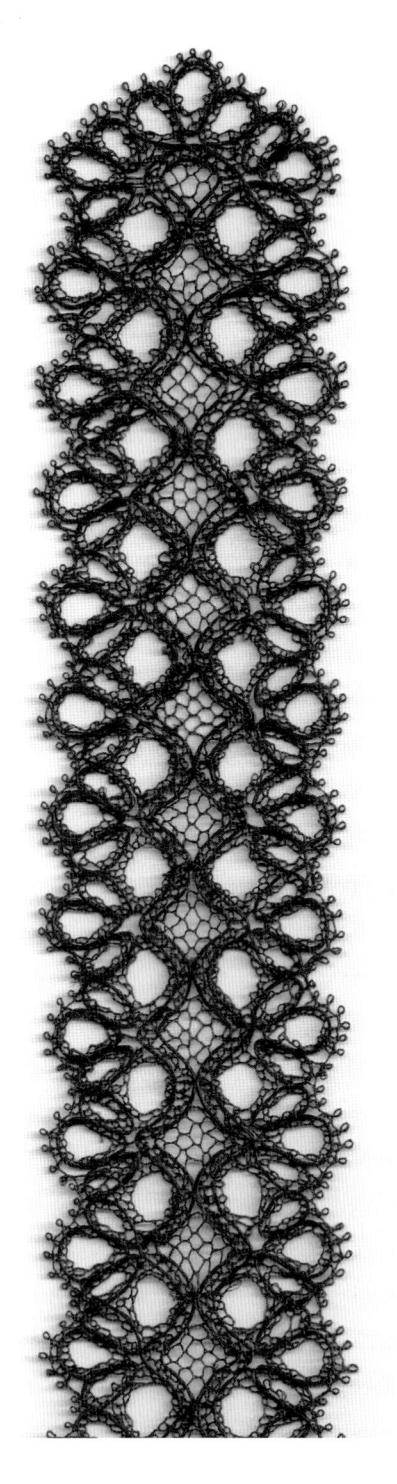

Materials Required for Project 31
grenadine no. 3/48 denier
gimp 6 x grenadine no. 3/48 denier threads (lightly twisted)
fingerplate
26cm ($10^1/_8$ in) x 6.5cm (2½ in)

Figure 466 (right) Fingerplate decoration (reduced)

Figure 467 (left) Lace made on pricking figure 468

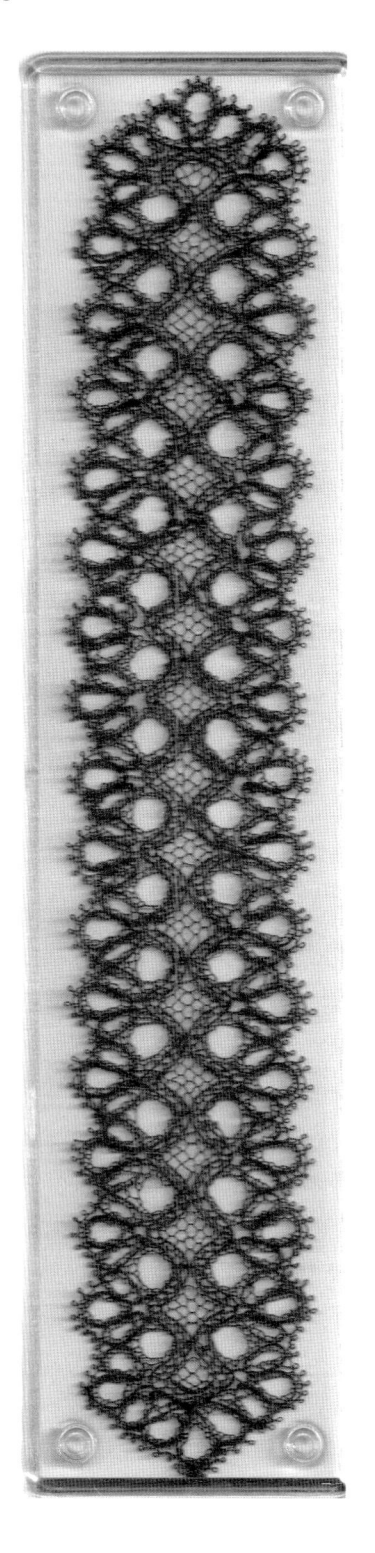

All about making—Floral Bucks Point Lace

Check the length of your fingerplate or bookmark and adjust the length of the pricking if necessary.

Do not expect to continue following the working diagrams exactly; they are designed to illustrate the techniques commonly used for making this type of lace, not to be used to 'make-lace-by-numbers'. A summary of the techniques is included at the end of the chapter.

This pricking has a similar arrangement of trefoils as the edging Project 30. However this time there is an area of point ground between honeycomb stems, not honeycomb bars and the number of pins is not the same in both prickings.

The arrangement of the pairs at the end of ring (12) (figure 477) does not match the arrangement at the end of ring (7) therefore the following rings cannot be made as rings (8) and (10).

Figure 468 (left) Bookmark, pricking

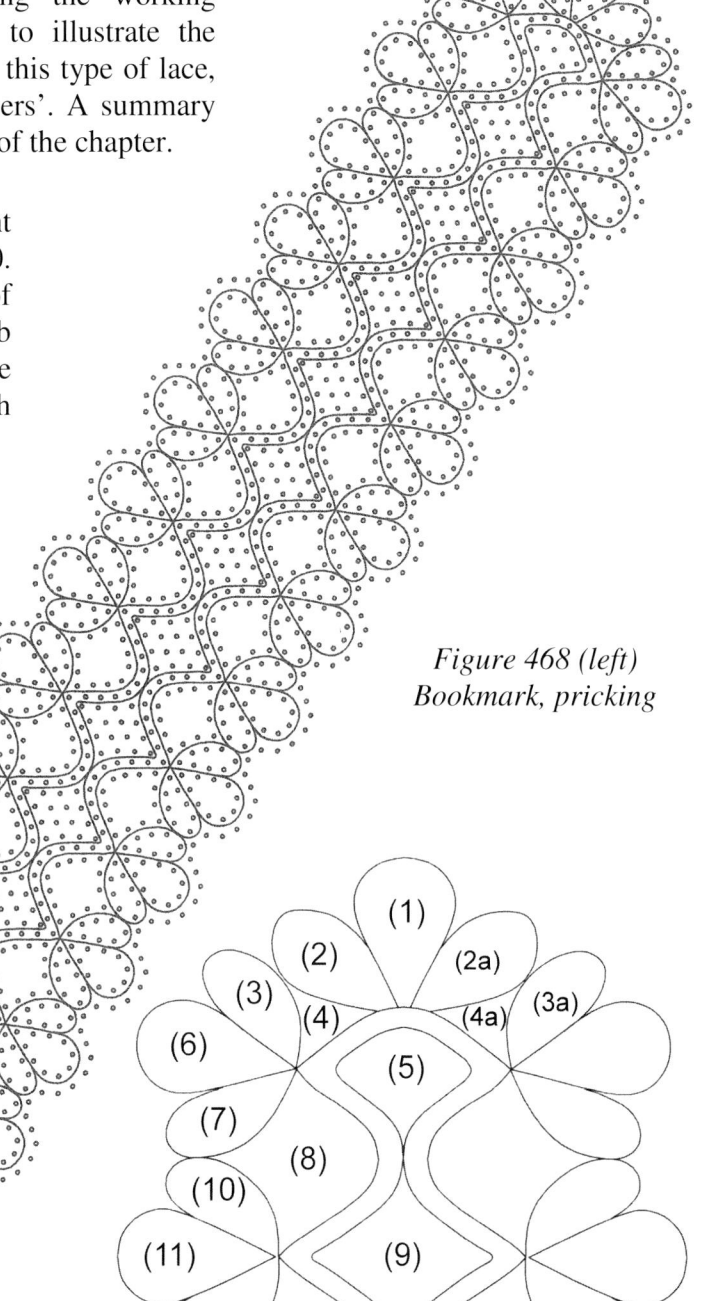

Figure 469 Plan of pricking figure 468, indicating the locations of the techniques described in the following figures. As you progress the right side is worked as a mirror image of the left, i.e. work (2a) after (2), (3a) after (3), (4a) after (4) etc.

221

All about making—Floral Bucks Point Lace

Setting in and headside passives
Set in across the top ring (1) with a picot edge using false picots and a single headside pair twisted once or twice. When working around the headside pairs pass across the gimp from a honeycomb stitch inside the ring, twist, cloth stitch and twist with the single headside passive pair, make a picot and return cloth and twist with the headside pair and back cross the gimp to make a picot at pin A (figure 470). When the ring is complete a new pair of gimps is introduced below the ring and the gimps crossed each side.

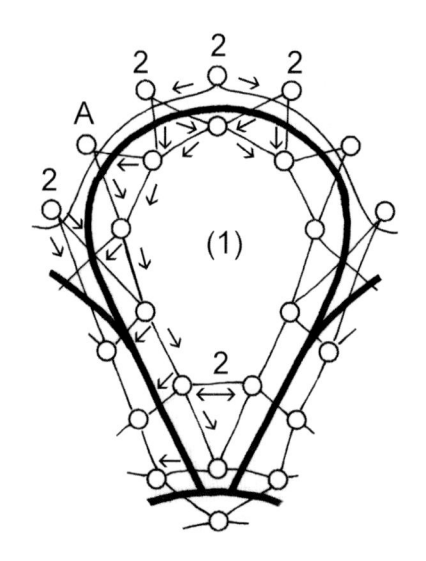

Figure 470 (right) Setting in

Honeycomb ring (2)
This starts part way along the top rim of honeycomb ring at pin B (figure 471) and the two resulting pairs split, one working towards the inner point, the other towards the outer edge. A pair, the stay, usually bridges across when two sides of a honeycomb rim meet at an angle as the pair C. After the stitch has been made at pin D both pairs make a pin chain to pin E. One pair continues to F to work with the pair approaching from the inner point, the other passes out across the gimp. The gimps are crossed. Work the mirror image ring (2) on the other side of ring (1).

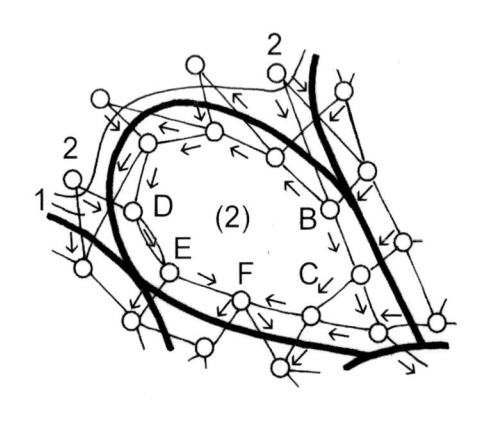

Figure 471 Ring (2)

Honeycomb ring (3) and into triangular ring (4)
Again this follows the typical route of starting part way along the top of the ring at pin G and then working both ways, making a pin chain when necessary (figure 472). After pin H has been worked a pair zig-zags across the gimp between ring (3) and ring (4) making stitches first one side of the gimp and then the other, pins J, K, L and M.

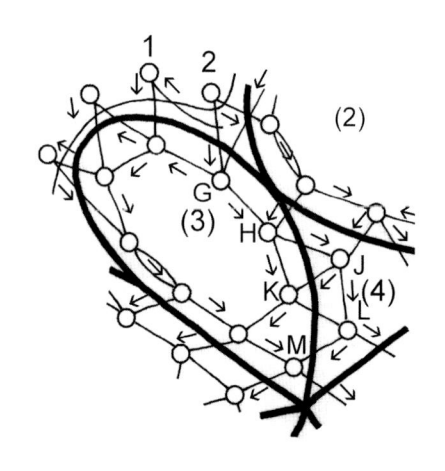

Figure 472 (right) Rings (3) & (4)

All about making—Floral Bucks Point Lace

Completing triangular honeycomb ring (4), honeycomb stem and point ground (5)

The right hand pin, pin N (figure 473) is made with two pairs from ring (2). A new pair of gimps is introduced below rings (1) and (2) and passes through the three pairs from ring (4) and one from ring (3). The honeycomb stem is started at pin P using pairs from ring (2) and its mirror image ring on the other side of ring (1). The stem continues towards the left using the two pairs from pin N, pins Q and R, and the next two pairs, the last pair from ring (4), pin S then one from ring (3) pin T. Repeat the stem travelling towards the right from pin P. Another new pair of gimps is introduced below the stem, passing through the pairs from the stem, i.e. from pins Q, R and S and the pairs from the stem on the other side.

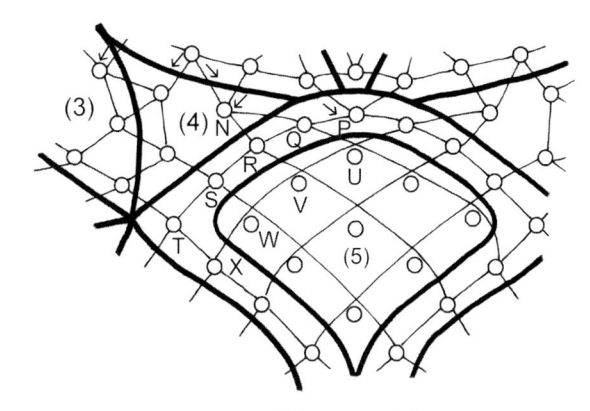

Figure 473 Ring (4), honeycomb stem and ground (5)

Point ground starts at U and travels across area (5) making stitches at pins V and W. When the ground is complete the gimps surrounding it pass towards each other through the pairs until they meet in the centre. The stem is continued, starting from pin X and the other gimp forming the stem passes through the stem pairs. I did not cross my stem gimps with those surrounding the honeycomb rings.

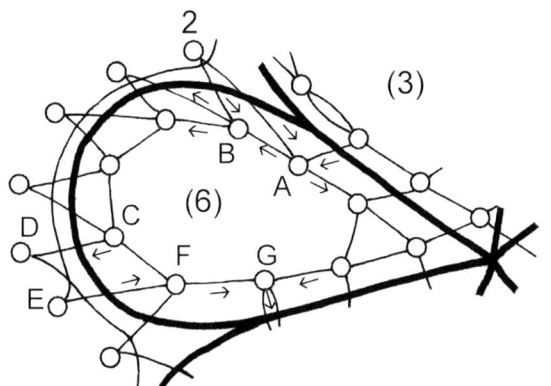

Honeycomb ring (6)

Two pairs are added at a false picot and the ring starts at pin A using one of these pairs (figure 474), the other being used at pin B and continuing to make the headside. From pin C a pair makes a picot, pin D and then exchanges with the headside passive pair which then makes the following picot at pin E. From here a pair returns into the ring to make a stitch at pin F and the ring is completed with the stitch at pin G.

Figure 474 (left) Ring (6)

Honeycomb ring (7)

This one starts with the stitch at pin H (figure 475) using both pairs from pin G, ring (6) (figure 474). The right pair travels uphill to the right to make stitches at pins J and K (figure 475) and downhill to the left to the stitch at pin L. Both pairs from the stitch at pin L make a pin chain to pin M. The left pair from pin H works round the headside making a stitch at pin N, leaving the ring to make a picot at pin P and returning into the ring to make a stitch at pin Q. The ring is completed at pin R with pairs from stitches at pins M and Q.

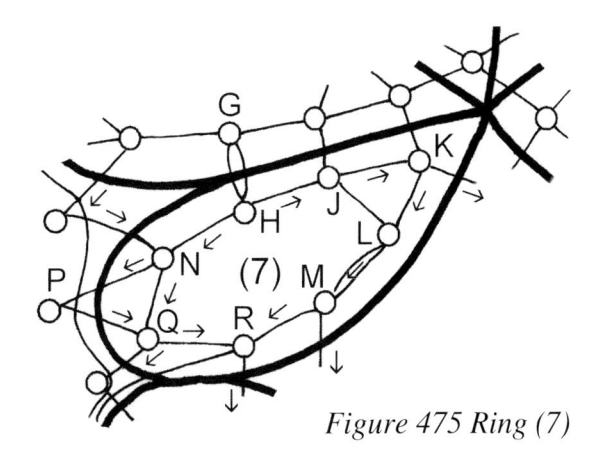

Figure 475 Ring (7)

223

All about making—Floral Bucks Point Lace

Honeycomb ring (8), honeycomb stem and point ground (9)
Ring (8) starts with a stitch at pin A with pairs from the honeycomb stem and ring (7) and progresses to the right using pairs from the stem at pins B and C (figure 476). One pair from pin C will go to pin E but since there is nowhere for the second pair from pin C to make a stitch lay it on the gimp.

Take both central gimps and the adjacent pair from the stitch at the end of one stem pin D, and pass through the pair from the pin D at the end of the other stem.

Work the other pair from pin D with the remaining pair from pin C to make the stitch at pin E. Make the stitch at pin F with a pair from E and the pair that passed across the central gimps from pin D in the opposite stem. Return a pair into ring (8) to make a stitch with the remaining pair from pin E at pin G then make a stitch at pin H with pairs from pins F and G. Take the pair off the gimp and use it with the left pair from pin G to make the stitch at pin J.

With pairs from A and B make a stitch at pin K, the stay from pin B bridging across the corner of the ring. Pin chain to pin L then make stitches at pins M and N and pairs from pins M and N cross the gimp to ring (10).

Ring (10) starts at pin P with pairs from rings (7) and (8). The right pair makes a stitch at pin Q with the pair from pin N and a pair returns across the gimp into ring (8) to make a stitch at pin R. The stay from pin R makes the stitch at pin S and the ring closes with a stitch at pin T.

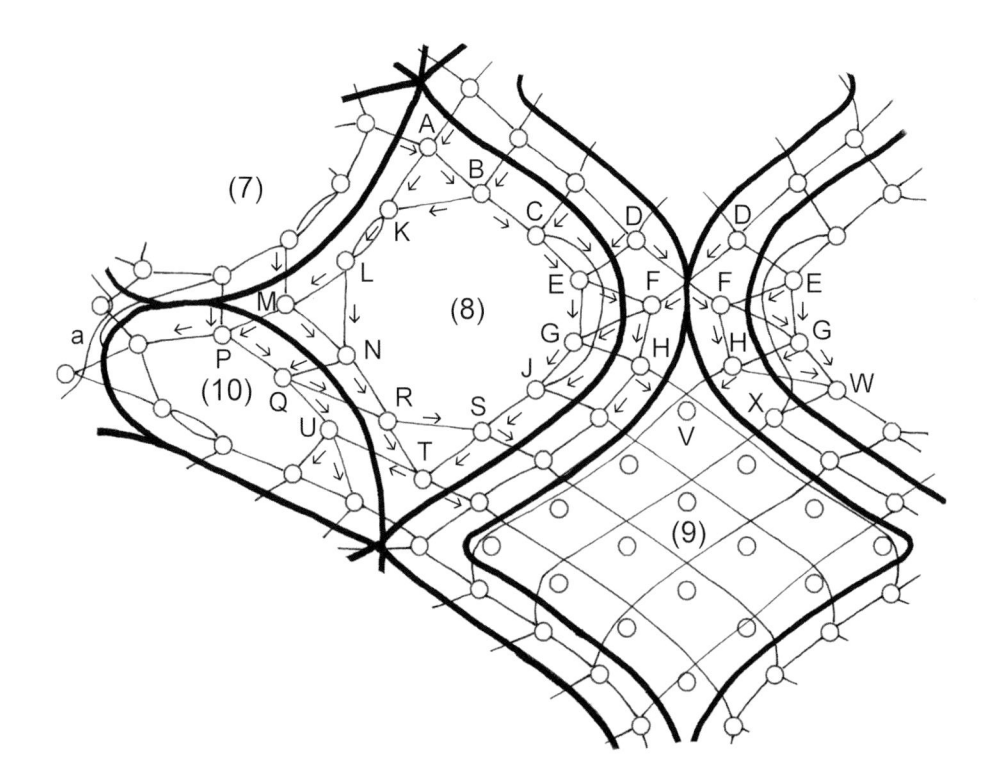

Figure 476 Honeycomb ring (8) and (10), honeycomb stems and point ground (9)

All about making—Floral Bucks Point Lace

The point ground (9) starts with pairs from pins H in the stem making a point ground stitch at pin V.

An alternate method for stitches following those at pins G and H is shown in the right hand ring (8) where the pairs from pins G and H make a stitch at pin W and one pair from pin W crosses the gimp to make a stitch with the pair carried along the gimp.

Complete the point ground (9), the honeycomb stem below it and honeycomb ring (10) (figure 476), laying the extra pair entering the headside on the gimp at 'a'.

Honeycomb rings (11)
Ring (11) starts at the inner point with a stitch at pin A with pairs from the previous ring (10) and the honeycomb stem and progresses uphill towards the headside pins B and C (figure 477). A pin chain is worked to pin D and the standard headside made until the picot pin F is reached. After working with the twisted edge the two pairs change roles and the former edge pair makes a picot at pin G and returns to make a stitch at pin H from where a pin chain is made to pin J and the work progresses to pin K and the gimps are crossed.

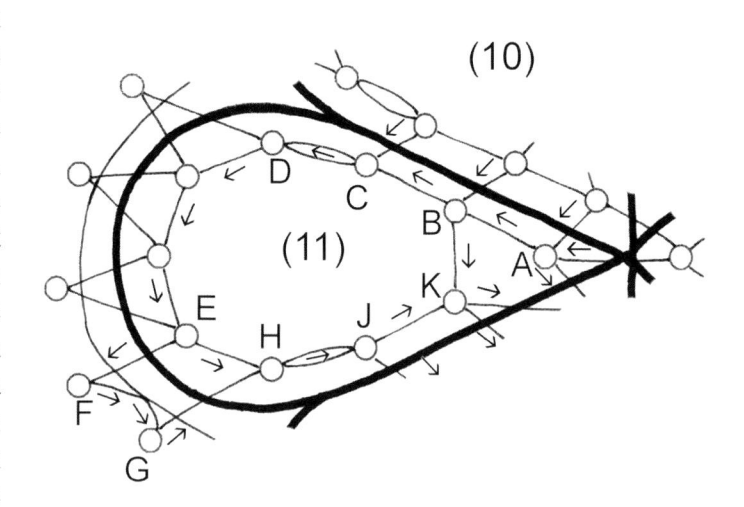

Figure 477 Honeycomb ring (11)

Honeycomb ring (12)
Ring (12) starts at the inner pin, pin L and progresses towards the headside, pins M, N and P (figure 478). The standard headside is made and a stitch made at pin Q. From pin L a pair exits across the gimp to start ring (13) at pin R with a pair from the honeycomb stem, then stitch at pin S with the next pair from the stem and one at pin T with the other pair from pin R. A pair then returns into ring (12) to work pin U then pin V.

The arrangement of the pairs at the end of ring (12) (figure 478) does not match the arrangement at the end of ring (7) therefore the following rings cannot be made as rings (8) and (10). You are now on your own, this is not 'making lace by numbers'.

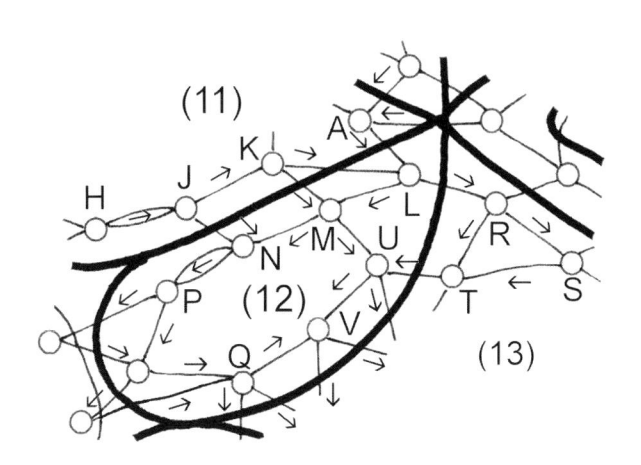

Figure 478 Honeycomb ring (12) and starting ring (13)

All about making—Floral Bucks Point Lace

Some special characteristics of Black Holey

The techniques for black holey are very flexible and the following may be mixed and matched, i.e. use any combination that seems appropriate according to the situation:

- This lace consists of honeycomb rings, mostly large ones, picots along the headside and sometimes, but not always, with small areas of point ground.

- The rim of honeycomb stitches within the rings can work uphill as well as downhill. Rings (2) (figure 471), (6) (figure 474), (7) (figure 475), (11) (477) and (12) (478).

- The rim of honeycomb stitches is not always complete, gaps frequently occurring in the corner next to a stay. Rings (3) (figure 472), (11) (figure 477) and (12) (figure 480).

- Rings with angled corners frequently have a stay, a pair connecting the two honeycomb stitches adjacent to the corner stitch. This stay braces the corner and assists stabilizing the shape and, when making the lace, it facilitates moving pairs. Note the direction they take in ring (8) (figure 476). At the top, pairs are leaving the point ground (5) so the stay is taken away from the ground to feed ring (10). As ring (8) closes the stay is taken the other way to feed the point ground following (9).

- The oval honeycomb rings may have four or more pins along the sides (excluding headside) and it is frequently necessary to work pin chain along these sides, but only one pin chain at a time. Rings (2) (figure 471), (3) (figure 472), (7) (figure 475), (8) (figure 476), (10) (figure 476), (11) (figure 477) and (12) (figure 478).

- Pairs may zig-zag across a gimp between two rings. Rings (3) (figure 472), (4) (figure 473), (8) and (10) (figure 476), and (12) and (13) (figure 478).

- In this fingerplate decoration (figure 467), the gimps were crossed after each ring along the headside was worked. The gimps on either side of the honeycomb stem remained along the sides of the stem and were not crossed with those surrounding the rings. In this piece the inner stem gimps were not crossed when they met.

- Pairs may be carried along the gimps as shown along the headside ring (10) and around the large honeycomb ring (8) (figure 476).

- Successive repeats need not be made following exactly the same routes.

END NOTES

1 Substituting threads
See Part 6.

CHAPTER 30

Project 30b: Rectangular lid insert worked in one direction

See Figure 458 Box with rectangular insert surrounded by edging with inward-facing corners

Materials Required for Project 31
Bart & Francis 150 denier silk[1], gimp Shappe Super Best 30/2 silk
box with lid aperture 29.5cm (11½ in) x 25.5cm (10 in) approx.

This insert is started with the upper edge of the pricking placed vertically on the pillow (figure 481 & 482). Pairs were added in two directions into the first motif and pairs left out for the central filling of bars and quatrefoils. More pairs were added in two directions into the second motif and pairs left out for the bars. More pairs were added in two directions as the corner was turned and completed.

Then the pillow was rotated so that the original top edge of the pricking was vertical and the motifs were on the right side. The remaining halves of the pairs added in two directions when the lace was started were then used to work the corner motif on the right. When the first half of this corner motif was complete the pricking was returned to its original position and the corner completed.

The other halves of the pairs that were added in two directions and the ones left out of the top motifs in the usual manner were then in the correct positions to work the edge motifs, the central filling of bars and quatrefoils and the point ground centre. The main part of the mat was worked in this direction, a few pairs were added when the point ground centre was reached and then thrown out as it was finished.

When the bar and quatrefoil centre was complete* and the first half of the lower left-hand corner motif worked, the pillow was rotated so that the lower edge of the original design was vertical then the motifs on the left and the corner motif were worked. Some threads and gimps then met 'head-to-head' along the gimp boundary between the motifs and the filling, i.e. threads that are about to enter from the ground meet others that are leaving from the motif. When this happened the threads that met were doubled along the gimp and thrown out. For security, threads that meet head-to-head were sometimes knotted before being throwing out.

*In principal the filling is completed before the lower edging is worked. In practice it is easier to work only sufficient ground and filling required for each motif as it is reached. Then turn the corner and rotate the pillow and again only work the amount of ground and filling necessary for each motif.

All about making—Floral Bucks Point Lace

Figure 479 Rectangular insert, pricking

All about making—Floral Bucks Point Lace

Figure 480 Rectangular insert

All about making—Floral Bucks Point Lace

Setting in a rectangle to be worked in one direction
Place the pricking on the pillow and rotate 90° to the left so that the motifs along the top edge of the rectangle are down the left side as you work. Starting at honeycomb ring A (figure 481) pin pairs above the ring so that the bobbins, including the gimps, will work in two directions. Work the ring and, adding pairs into the work as required, start working down both sides of petal B of the flower; the right side will need a total of 3 pairs, and start the single-gimp honeycomb bar C so that you can complete this side. The left side of petal B will need pairs added at two of the pins so they can cross the gimp into petal D. The centre of the flower is half stitch surrounded by a continuous honeycomb stem and pairs must be left out to accommodate it. As the base of the petal is reached, a nook pin is made and the gimp doubles back to the tip of petal D which is made by working up the first side, leaving a stay across the lower point and laying pairs along the gimp for use in the second side of the petal. Petals E and F are variations on this theme and another pair may need to be added. The techniques for black holey are very loose, as with the other forms of Floral Bucks Point, the general framework is important, not the detail.

Work the first half of the central petal G and start the double-gimp honeycomb bar J and work the four-pin honeycomb ring K in the centre of the flower. Then work the honeycomb stem, the half stitch centre of the flower and the remainder of the honeycomb stem. Pairs must be left out for the double-gimp honeycomb bar L.

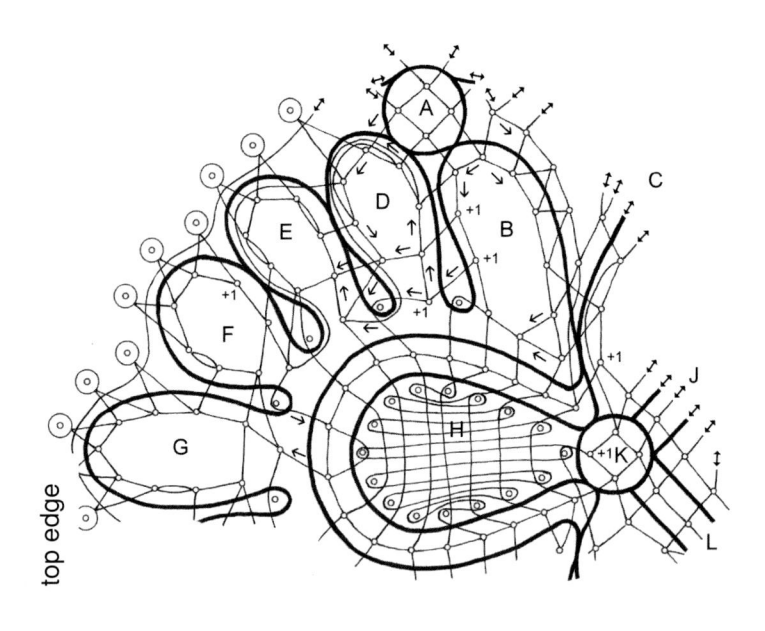

Figure 481 Setting in the rectangular insert

↔ pairs starting in two directions

All about making—Floral Bucks Point Lace

Continue setting in across the top of the pricking
Complete petal G and continue making petals M, N and P and lay surplus pairs along the gimps so they will be available for making the subsequent flowers (figure 482). Work both sides of the last petal Q, allow the single-gimp honeycomb bar R to break away.

Work the four-pin honeycomb ring S and continue down both sides of the first petal of the next flower, T. Pairs must be set up to travel in two directions to allow pairs for a single-gimp honeycomb bar U to enter the outer edge of petal T and again at V where the double-gimp bar meets the four-pin honeycomb ring and the pairs pass into the centre of the flower. These bars will exit as usual.

Pairs travelling in two directions will be needed when working the first half of the first flower at the corner and for the double-gimp bar that enters at the four-pin honeycomb ring between the two corner flowers.

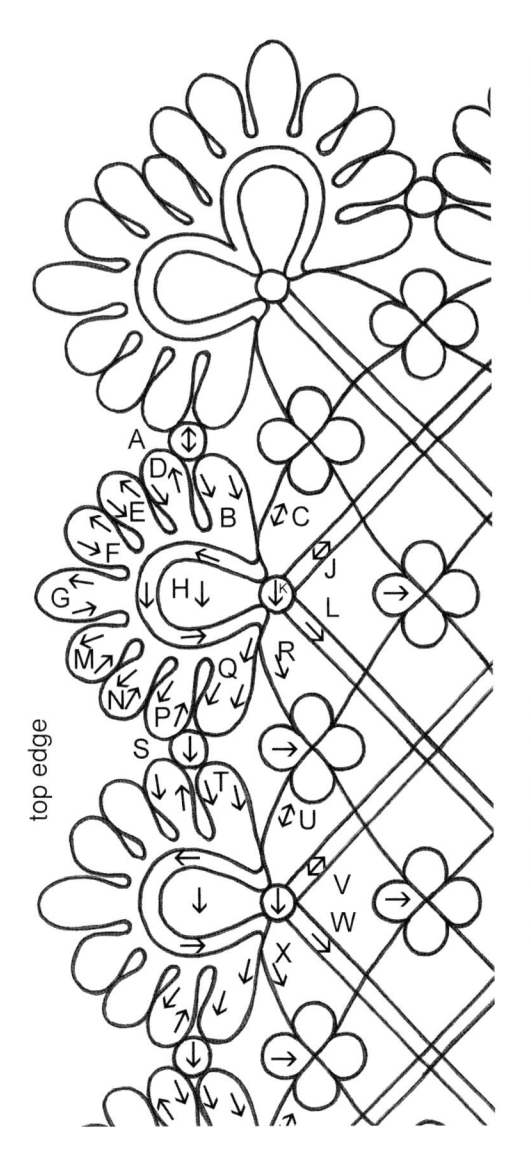

Now turn the pillow through 180° so that motifs along the top edge of the rectangle are down the right side. Make the corner motif, adding pairs in two directions as far as the double-gimp honeycomb bar entering the four-pin honeycomb ring between the two corner flowers. Work the second corner flower leaving out the single-gimp honeycomb bar.

Figure 482 Setting in the rectangular insert

↔ pairs working in two directions

Finally turn the pillow to the left through 90° so that the top edge of the pricking is at the top. The remaining pairs from those added to work in two directions are now available for making the flowers down the edges and the quatrefoil filling in the centre. Work down the pricking until you approach the flowers along the lower edge.

231

All about making—Floral Bucks Point Lace

Single-gimp honeycomb bars
Although the single-gimp bar can be made using only three pairs, when these bars are used as part of a filling the other elements may dictate that, as in this case, an extra pair is taken along the gimp from one of these motifs to the next.

A bar usually starts with a honeycomb stitch worked either side of the gimp, pins A and B and the surplus pair from pin A drops onto the gimp at 'a'. (figure 483).

The inner pair from pin B crosses the gimp to make a stitch at C and a pair returns across to make a stitch at pin D. The process of zigzagging a pair across the gimps is continued as required.

Double-gimp honeycomb bars
These require at least four pairs of bobbins.

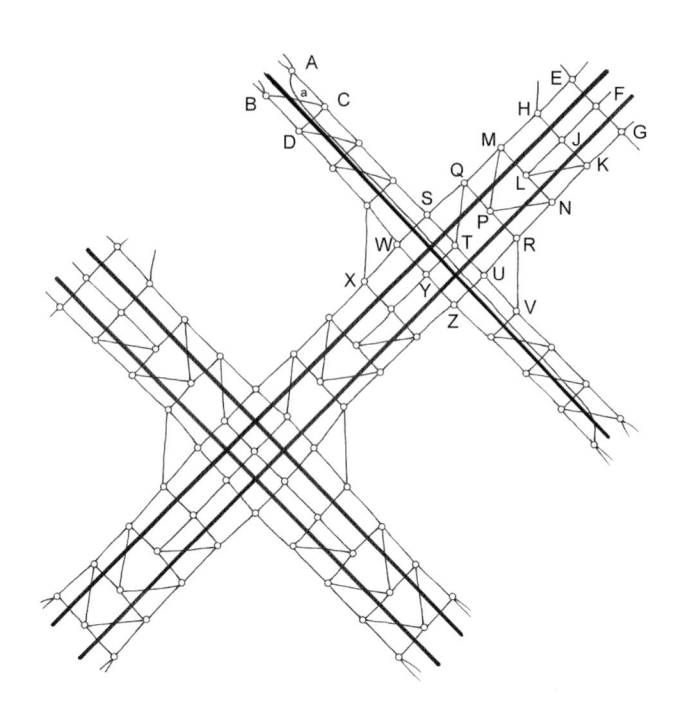

Figure 483 Single and double-gimp honeycomb bars and crossings

The bar illustrated starts with three honeycomb stitches E, F and G working towards the right. A pair for a stay had been left out from the stitch worked prior to starting the bar and now this pair works across the bar making honeycomb stitches with pairs from pins E, F and G, at pins H, J and K. The inner pair from pin K passes back to the centre to make a stitch with the central pair at pin L and then a stitch with the other outer pair at pin M. The remaining pair in the centre passes out to make a stitch with the outer pair at pin N. There is now no central pair, so the inner pairs from the outer stitches come together to make a stitch at pin P, and stitches at pins Q and R are made following the sequence for pins M and N. Continue the bar as required.

Crossing gimped honeycomb bars
When a single-gimp honeycomb bar crosses a double-gimp bar an edge pair from each bar is used to make the stitch where they meet, pin S. The left pair from pin S crosses the gimp (the spare pair remains with the gimp) and works across the double-gimp bar making stitches with the next three pairs, the first at pin T with the remaining pair from pin Q that has crossed the gimp, the next at pin U with the inner pin from the right side edge stitch, pin R, and then at pin V with the outer pair from the edge stitch at pin R, the latter pair forming a stay across the corner.

The remaining pair from pin S makes the corner stitch on the left of the junction with the next pair on the left, pin W, and making a stitch with the pair remaining on the left at pin X, the pair coming from the left forming a stay across the corner. With the remaining pair from pin W work towards the right making stitches at pins Y and Z. The two gimped honeycomb bars continue as usual.

Follow similar sequences when crossing two single-gimp and two double-gimp bars.

All about making—Floral Bucks Point Lace

Quatrefoil motif
The cloth stitches are usually followed by two twists, but this is optional. In some places where there are two pairs working parallel you may prefer to run one pair along the gimp. Pass the gimps through the pairs when they meet.

Finish the bars with a honeycomb stitch each side of the gimp at pins A, B, C and D.

Upper four-pin ring
Using the left pairs from pin B travel towards the left, cloth stitch through two pairs, make a picot, pin 1 and cover with a cloth stitch (figure 484). With the right pair from pin D work towards the right and cloth stitch through two pairs from pin C, make a picot at pin 2 and cover with a cloth stitch. With the right pair from this stitch make a picot at pin 3 and cloth stitch the picot pair through three pairs to the right. Take the other pair from covering the picot at pin 3 and work two cloth stitches towards the left. Pass the left gimp towards the right through five pairs and the right gimp towards the left through five pairs. Work the four-pin honeycomb ring, pins 4-7 and pass the gimps through until they cross.

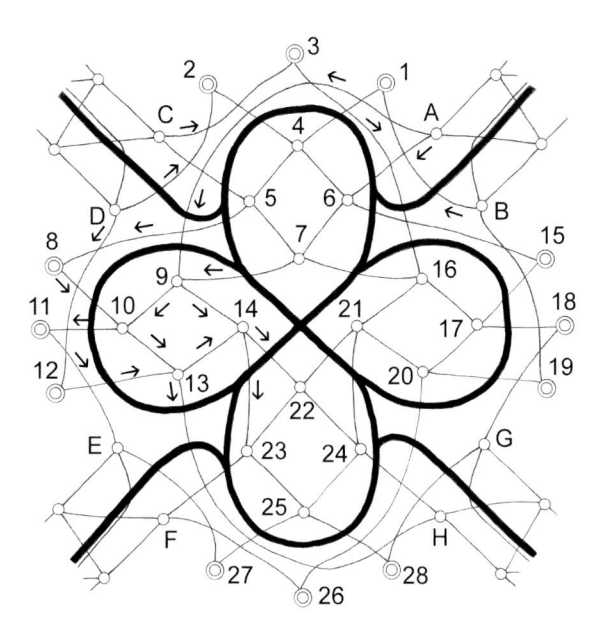

Figure 484 Quatrefoil, picots indicated by double circles, remaining pins are honeycomb stitches

Left hand side four-pin ring and picots
For the ring on the left side work the remaining pair from pin 5 of the upper ring to the left through two pairs, make a picot at pin 8, and cover the pin. Pass the left gimp, now in the centre, to the left through three pairs, i.e. up to and including the picot pair. Work the top stitch of the ring at pin 9 with a pair from pin 7 and the pair on its left. Work the left pair from pin 9 with the pair from the picot pin 8 at pin 10. From here take a pair out to make a picot at pin 11 and cover it with a cloth stitch, then make the next picot at pin 12. This picot pair returns to make the lower stitch of the ring at pin 13. The right stitch side stitch of this ring at pin 14 is made with right pair from pin 13 and the remaining pair from the upper stitch, pin 9. (I know, it goes uphill, and yes it is how it was made by the lace workers.)

Pass the left gimp towards the right, crossing the right gimp in the centre, and continue through the pairs for the right hand side four-pin ring. Make this four-pin ring and picots on the right similarly, pins 15-21.

Lower four-pin ring and picots
Cross the gimps and work the lower four-pin honeycomb ring, pins 22-25, using the two pairs from pin 14 and the two from pin 21. Cross the gimps and pass each out through two pairs of the ring and one more, the from the lower stitch of the side ring. These last pairs cloth stitch toward the centre until they meet where they make a cloth stitch and the pair now on the left makes a picot at pin 26. The picot pair cloth stitches with the pair on the left which then makes a picot at

233

All about making—Floral Bucks Point Lace

pin 27. The picot pair makes two cloth stitches to the left and then a honeycomb stitch when it meets the edge pair at pin E. One pair from this stitch becomes the edge pair of the bar, the other lays on the gimp. The next two pairs to the right make the other honeycomb stitch of the bar, pin F. The pair on the right of the central picot, pin 26 makes a cloth stitch with the pair to its right and that pair makes the remaining picot, pin 28, makes two cloth stitches to the right and a honeycomb stitch with the edge pair at pin G. One pair from this stitch becomes the edge pair of the bar, the other lays on the gimp. The remaining two pairs make a honeycomb stitch at pin H.

Finishing

After completing the point ground in the centre work the headside flower motifs down the left side and the quatrefoil motifs as far as motif A (figure 484). Work the first half of the corner motif, B and motif C. Turn the pillow and work the second half of the motif, D. As you work the honeycomb ring in the centre of the corner pairs will be entering from a double gimp bar that are surplus to requirements. Pairs surplus to future requirements, not necessarily those entering, may be knotted, doubled along a gimp through a few pairs and thrown out. As the corner progresses a single-gimp bar enters from motif C and is incorporated into the corner motif with surplus pairs being disposed of as before.

The pillow is returned to its previous position and the main part of the work is continued until motif E is completed. The pillow is turned and motif F worked. The bars entering as the first half is made enter normally but the pairs that normally exit while the second half is worked meet bars that are trying to enter. Knot the threads when they meet and dispose of them as before. Repeat for motifs G, H and the first half of L.

Return the pillow to its original position and complete the motifs down the right side to motif J and the quatrefoil motifs as far as K and M. Turn the pillow and complete motif L, disposing of surplus pairs. Turn the pillow and work the first half of motif N, disposing of surplus pairs. Turn the pillow and complete the corner disposing of surplus pairs and finish where the two flowers meet along the diagonal between the corner half stitch sections outlined with honeycomb stem P and N. Any pairs that cannot be laid on a gimp before being thrown out are knotted and left long, the remaining ends can be trimmed closely and the long ends sewn away after the pins have been removed.

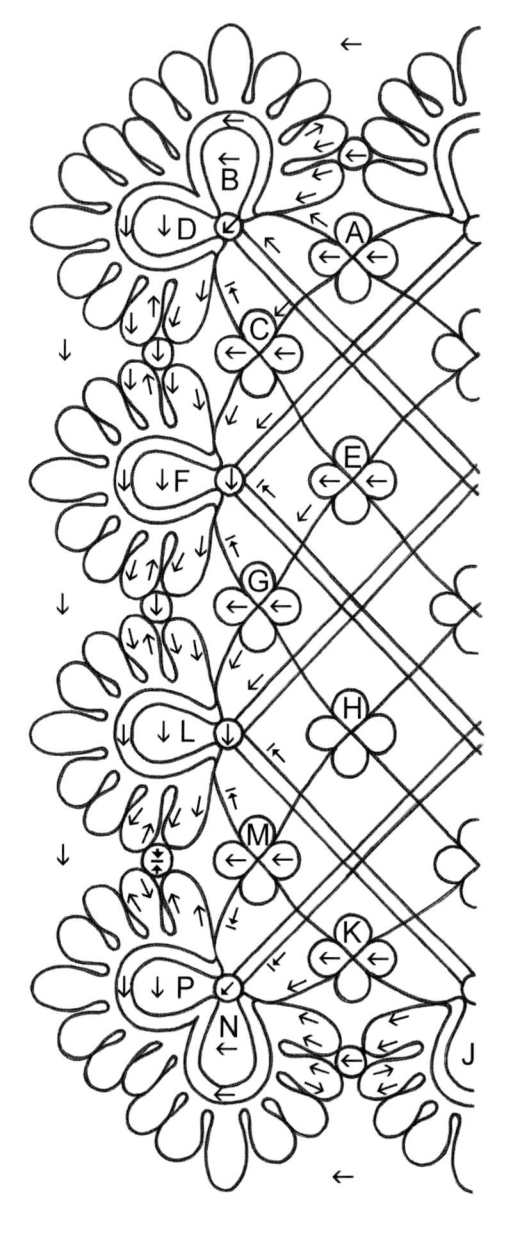

Figure 484 Finishing

⊥ - pairs meeting head-to-head

All about making—Floral Bucks Point Lace

CHAPTER 31

Project 32: Galloon used as a lid insert

Figure 486 Galloon used as a lid insert

Materials Required for Project 32
Bart & Francis 150 denier silk[1], gimp Shappe Super Best 30/2 silk
box with lid aperture 18cm (7 in) x 13 cm (5in) approx.

Although black grenadine or silk floss was used to make much of the antique black holey lace, some was made in white silk and some in cotton or linen thread.

This traditional pricking could be interpreted on other ways. All the large spaces could be honeycomb rings and the rims of the large spaces within the bars could also be honeycomb stitches. This one has the flowers worked in half stitch, but they could be cloth stitch and this one picots along all the bars.

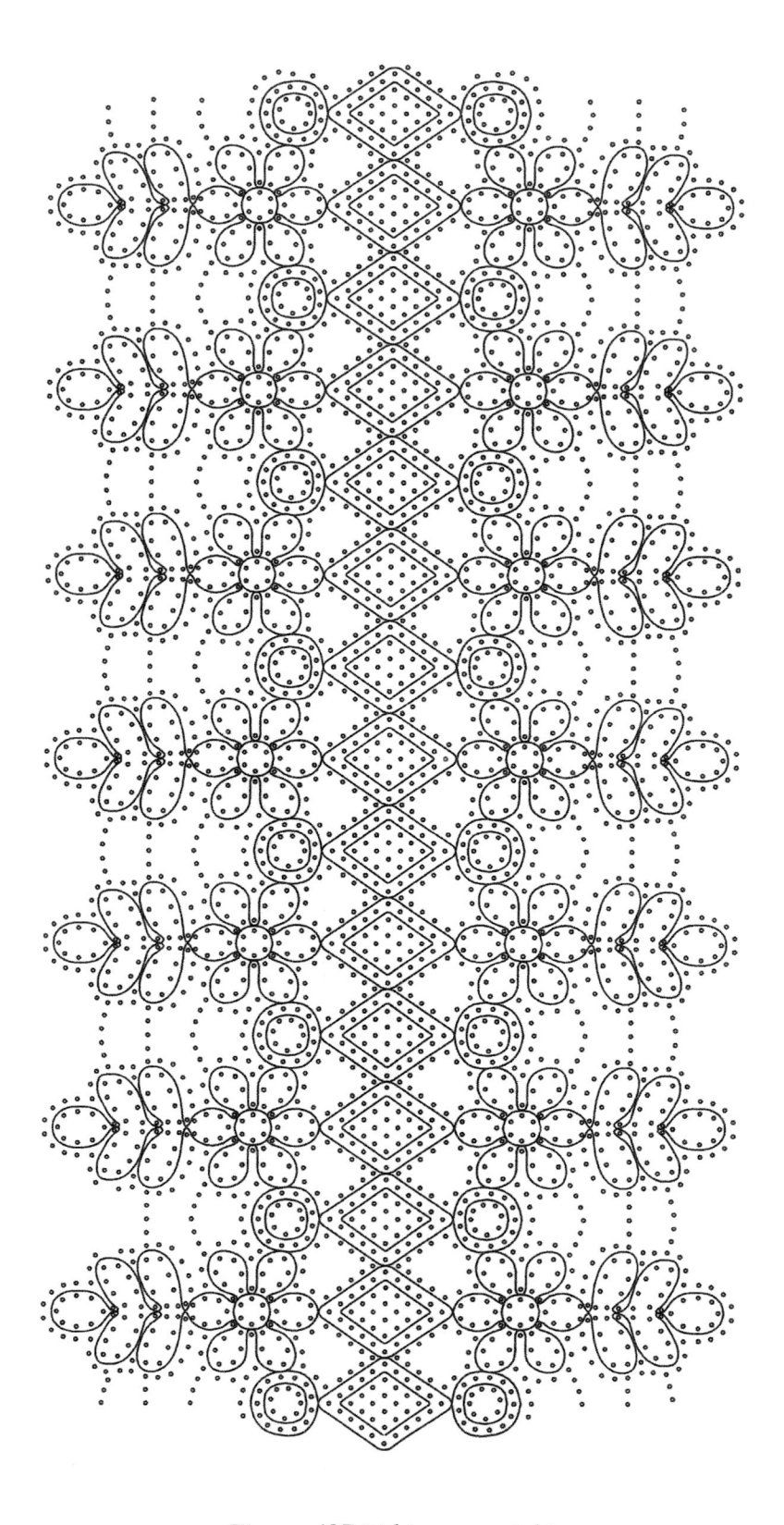

Figure 487 Lid insert, pricking

All about making—Floral Bucks Point Lace

Figure 488 Lid insert

All about making—Floral Bucks Point Lace

The techniques used to make this form of Bucks Point were developed for speed and the order of working each piece would again have been the quickest and time wasting adding and removing pairs would have been avoided. However, pairs have been added and removed while making this piece to give a better finish.

The gimps for the column of diamonds down the centre remain in that column and do not cross into the flowers (figure 489). The gimps in the centres of the diamonds and circular motifs are laid in and thrown out for each motif.

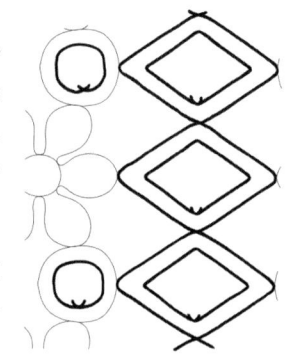

Figure 489 Gimps for the gimped picot bars and diamonds

Gimped picot bar

These have a minimum of a single gimp and two pairs (figure 490). However, these bars are a convenient means of carrying pairs from one section of the motif to another and there are usually several pairs being carried. The picot pair works cloth stitch twist twice with the passive pair. Then the gimp, with any pairs laid along it, is bound on by passing the gimp through the picot pair which twists twice and then the gimp passes back through the picot pair. The picot pair twists twice and works cloth stitch, twist twice with the passive pair before making the next picot.

Figure 490 Gimped picot bar

Working sequence (figure 491) and gimps sequences (figures 492-495)

Figure 491 and the numbers show the working sequence, figures 492-495 and their accompanying explanations do **NOT** describe the general working sequence, only the gimp sequences. Each gimp is explained separately and they occur concurrently.

Set in across the pricking with three gimped picot bars (figure 491, bars 1, 2 and 3). Then start the circular motif (4a) and diamond motif (4b). The gimp that is passed down the left side of the circular motif crosses the one from the right side beneath the motif and then works down the right side of the flower (figure 492). Later on it crosses below it to work the left side of the following circular motif.

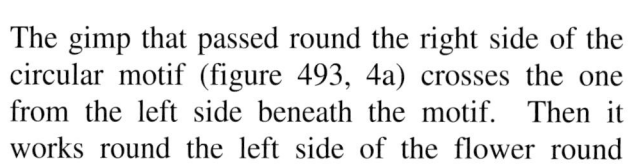

Figure 491 Working sequence

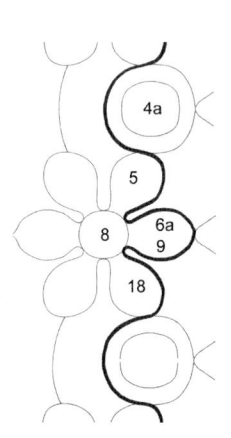

Figure 492 Gimp path

The gimp that passed round the right side of the circular motif (figure 493, 4a) crosses the one from the left side beneath the motif. Then it works round the left side of the flower round petals (5) and (7) and then it passes round the centre of the flower (8), where pin-chains may be required down both sides of the honeycomb ring and the right hand side petal may be completed. The gimp passes round the top of the left hand petal (10) and round petals (11) and (12). Later on it will return along a similar path round petals (14), (15), (16), (17) and (18).

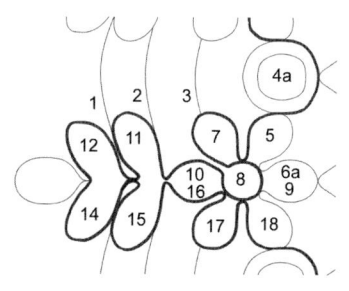

Figure 493 Gimp path

238

All about making—Floral Bucks Point Lace

The gimp from the picot bar (figure 494, 3) doubles the gimp passing down left side of petal (7) and then round the upper side of the side petal (10) (figure 495). It then continues on its own through the pairs from the upper two leaflets (11 and 12) and crossing the gimps from bars (2) and (1) on its way to the end leaflet (13). after working round the end leaflet it returns along a similar path to the tip of the lower left petal (17).

From bar (figure 495, 1) the gimp passes down the right side of leaflet (12) and waits for the gimp from the flower to pass through to work the end leaflet (13) and return. Later on it passes down the right side of the leaflet below (14). The gimp from bar (2) follows a similar path down leaflets (11) and (15).

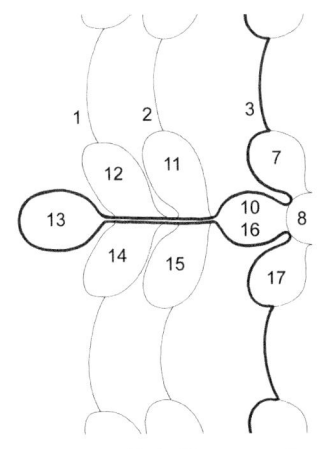

Figure 494 Gimp path

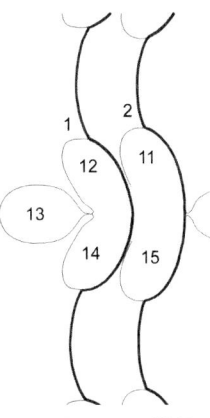

Figure 495 Gimp path

The progression from bars (1) and (2) to leaflets (11) and (12) is tricky (figure 496) and again there are many ways of tackling it. Leaflet (11) receives pairs from petal (7) via the honeycomb stitch at pin A, nook pin B and from the gimped picot bars (1) and (2) (figure 496). The pairs for the picots at pins D, E and F, from bar (2) must be made next and then the gimp from bar (2) can work down the right side of the leaflet and the gimp from the flower works from the base of the leaflet up the same side. Next the honeycomb stitches can be made down the right side of the leaflet at pins G, H, J and K. Now with the pairs from bar (1) work picots at pins L, M and N and the honeycomb stitch, pin P, between the leaflets. Complete leaflet (11) by working stitches at pins Q, R and S down its left side. Complete the leaflet at pin T and a pair from this stitch makes the nook pin at pin U.

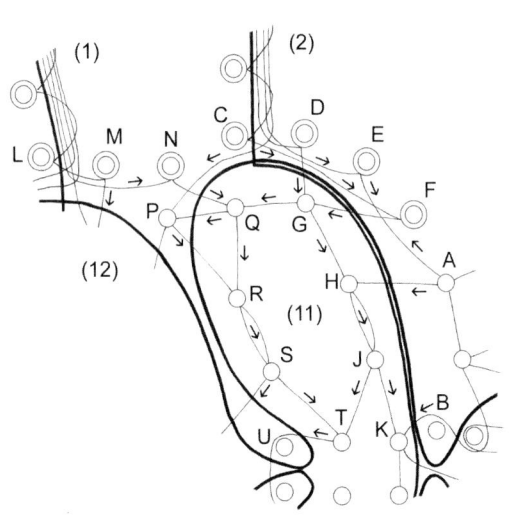

Figure 496 Progressing from bars (1) and (2) to leaflets (11) and (12)

Leaflet (12) also works downwards towards the leaf's central rib and leaflets (14) and (15) downwards way from the leaf's central rib.

As you are making this without following a route map at different times you will probably have different numbers of pairs carried along the bars.

All about making—Floral Bucks Point Lace

CHAPTER 32

Project 33: A Shaped Piece made on a Traditional Pricking

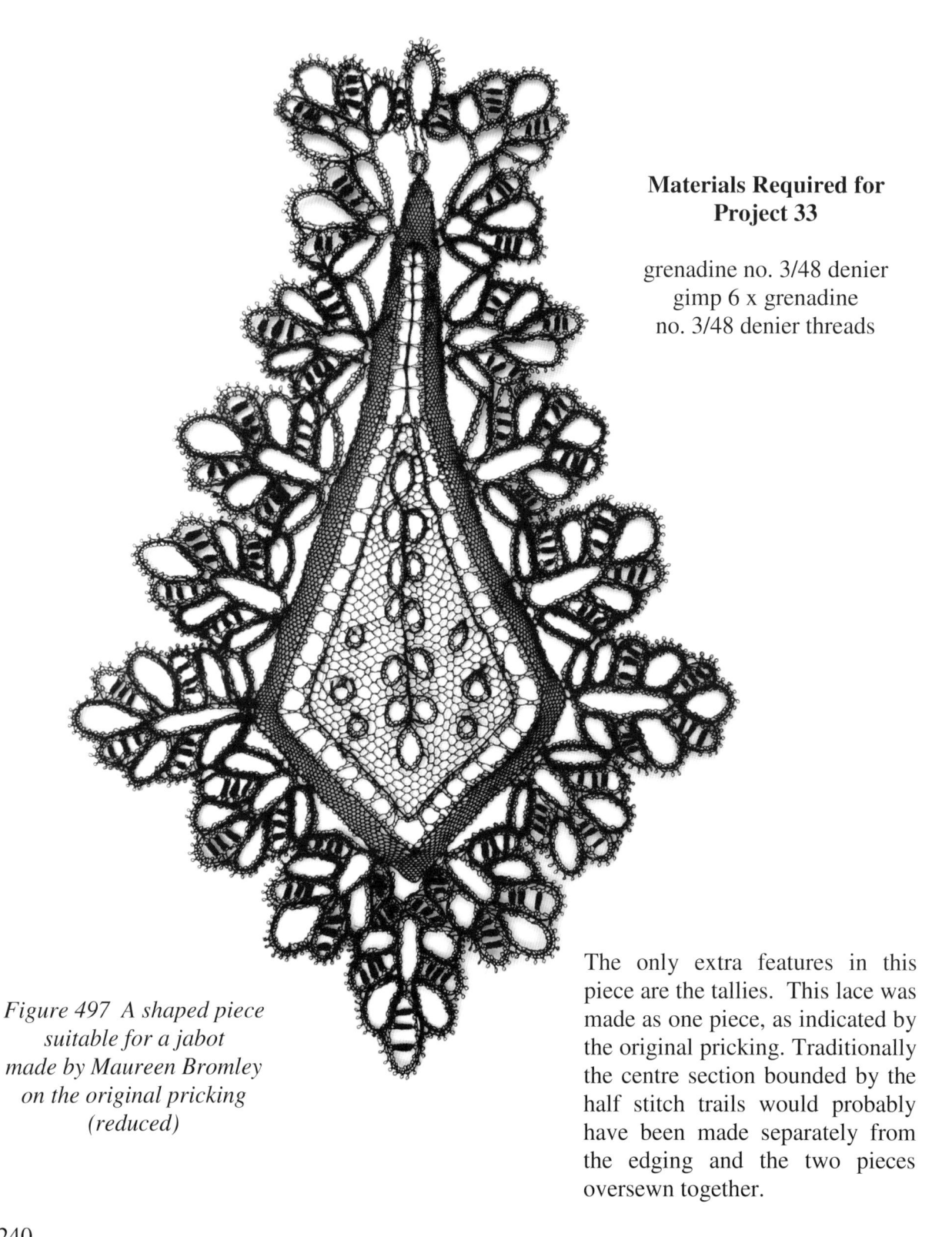

Materials Required for Project 33

grenadine no. 3/48 denier
gimp 6 x grenadine
no. 3/48 denier threads

Figure 497 A shaped piece suitable for a jabot made by Maureen Bromley on the original pricking (reduced)

The only extra features in this piece are the tallies. This lace was made as one piece, as indicated by the original pricking. Traditionally the centre section bounded by the half stitch trails would probably have been made separately from the edging and the two pieces oversewn together.

All about making—Floral Bucks Point Lace

Figure 498 Traditional pricking used to make lace figure 497

Reduced: the original measures 24 cm from tip to straight end.

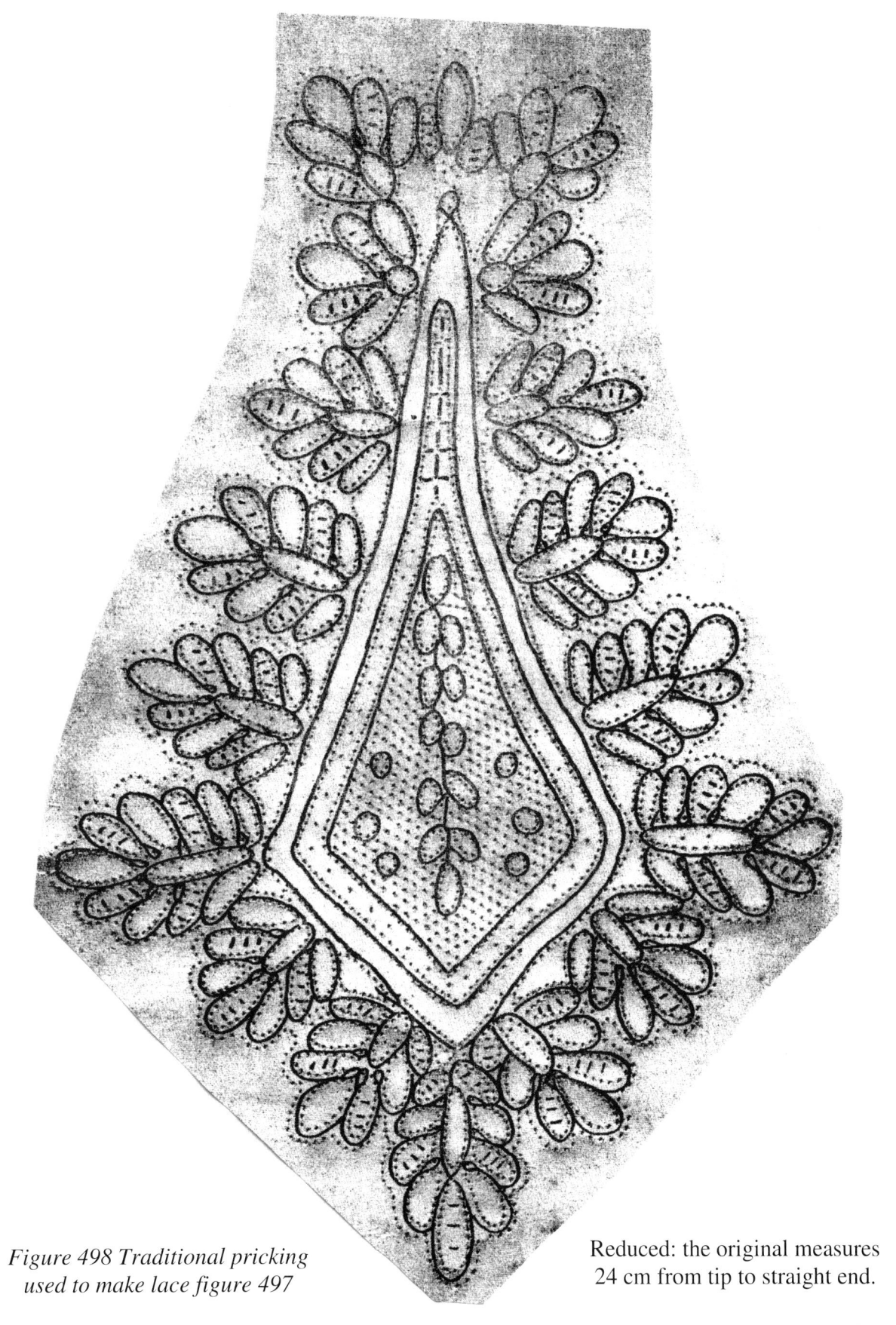

All about making—Floral Bucks Point Lace

Reduced: the original measures 24 cm from tip to straight end.

Figure 499 Pricking 498, trued up. To be made in two separate pieces joined together by oversewing

END NOTES

1 Substituting threads
See Part 6.

All about making—Floral Bucks Point Lace

PART 6

THREADS AND BOBBINS

Currently we use comparatively finer threads than the earlier lace workers would have used for the same pricking. Research shows that few standard Floral Bucks pieces had pairs added and thrown out. The laceworkers selected their thread so that clothwork would be of the required texture without resorting to the time consuming act of adding and throwing out pairs. The thread for the Jabot, Project 13, was selected using the same criteria and may feel rather coarse and the ground works up thicker than expected by today's standards. When making Bucks Point there is the freedom to change thread, and when a finer thread is used pairs may be added in/thrown out as necessary.

A laceworker would 'learn' her pricking, i.e. learn the routes taken by the pairs that would avoid adding and removing them. Pieces designed for a particular client would be made by the highly skilled workers. These pieces were made 'by eye', and it is in these that we are more likely to find extra pairs added in and thrown out. However, the form of Floral Bucks that frequently has pairs added and thrown out is the Regency. The fact that this form was only made for a comparatively short time may account for the lack of standardisation of the techniques. Antique samples made on very similar prickings vary widely in their interpretation and the techniques used to make them.

Today we do not have the constraint of having to earn a living from our lacemaking and we prefer the ground to be more transparent. We make lace for enjoyment and are more concerned with its final appearance than the time it takes to make it. It is now common practice to add and throw out pairs to improve the density of clothwork which should never be solid; the threads should be spaced evenly with the background showing through. When the thread is a little fine for the clothwork we compensate by adding pairs into it, and then removing them when there are too many. The skill of spreading passives to fill clothwork areas and managing the pairs so that they are in the places where they will be needed comes with experience.

Threads

The size of thread used for making lace is proportional to the spacing of the pins, which in turn is determined by the spacing of the grid on which it was drafted. Choosing a suitable thread for a particular pricking comes with experience, and experimenting using threads on grids with different spacing builds up this ability. It is useful to compile a collection of reference samples by using thread on bobbins leftover from an earlier project to work a few repeats on prickings with different spacings between the pins. Leave the ends long so they can be handled when comparing with other samples. Write the size and name of the thread, pin spacing etc. on a tag and attach to the sample (figure 500).

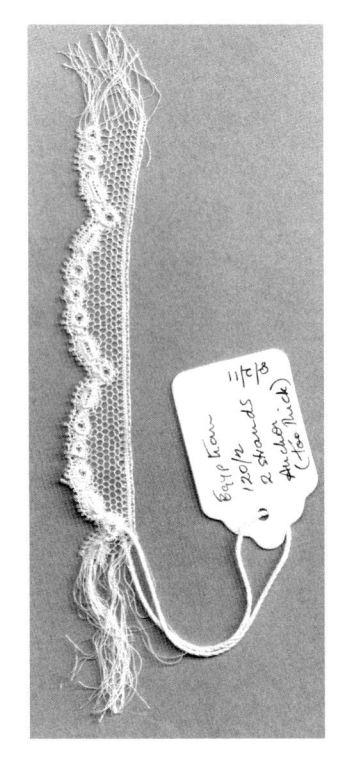

Figure 500 Sample

243

Thread quality
Lace to be worn and washed may require thicker thread than that to be protected by glass or other permanent transparent covering. Threads vary slightly in texture and those that work up stiffer are more suitable for jabots; those that work up softer are more suitable for handkerchiefs. These properties may be added to the tags on your samples.

Cotton is a natural fibre and varies according to the soil in which it is grown and the weather conditions when it grew. Hence different batches from the same manufacturer may vary slightly. Different brands have different properties due to their processing; some are softer, others whiter. Very fine cotton may not be available in white; the bleaching process weakens fibres resulting in too fragile a thread. Bleaching also reduces the bulk of the thread so the number of the thread is allocated after the spinning and before the bleaching which means that a fully bleached thread may feel a size smaller than an unbleached thread having the same number. The thickness of thread used for very fine prickings, e.g. the ones used in this book for Regency and the very fine Bucks is not as critical as that required for coarser patterns, thus in many cases several thicknesses above or below the one listed may well be suitable.

Working with black thread is more difficult, use a pale coloured pricking and cover cloths and draw guidelines in red. The former lace workers frequently worked using white thread and then dyed it black.

Authorities indicate that black grenadine, a tightly spun silk thread, was traditionally used for making Black Holey. During my research I have seen some Black Holey made using grenadine, some made using silk floss and some in cotton. Grenadine is a difficult thread to work with as it is stiff and springy. Silk floss gives good results but it is so loosely twisted the individual strands can get caught. I was not impressed with the way my cotton sample worked up.

Substituting threads
Floral Bucks can be very demanding regarding the size of thread when the lace is made exactly to a working diagram; substitute threads may not give satisfactory results. However, when not being made exactly to a working diagram this lace has facilities for adjusting and the tendency for the clothwork to look starved or choked may be easily compensated for by adding or throwing out pairs. This in turn leads to the freedom to use a large range of thread sizes. See *All about making* - Geometrical Bucks Point Lace, A. Stillwell, Salex Publishing 2006, pages 247-249.

Pins
Prickings requiring fine thread require the finest pins available. Apart from giving a little more space between the pins it also reduces the size of the hole remaining in the lace. Grenadine requires medium sized pins approximately 0.67mm diameter. Traditionally, picots are made using the same pins as the rest of the lace; using larger pins changes the overall appearance and character of Bucks Point. The needle in your pricker should match the diameter of the pins.

Pillows
Traditionally Bucks Point was made using spangled East Midlands bobbins on a plum pudding pillow (also known as a square pillow) or tapering bolster, both pillows being slightly domed across the top. These bobbins and pillows evolved together and are therefore well matched. The slight curvature of the pillow allows the weight of the bobbin and spangle to be active on the

All about making—Floral Bucks Point Lace

thread, creating the light tension necessary for point ground. Spangles also reduce the tendency for bobbins to roll. A modern cookie pillow is a suitable substitute as it has a similar curvature.

Bobbin/spangle weights
As I moved to using finer and finer threads, I realised how important it is to match the weight of the bobbin and spangle to the weight of the thread. If bobbins and spangles are too heavy the passives will be pulled straight rather than retain the gentle curve necessary for them to spread and fill an area of cloth stitch. Too strong a tension also causes the mesh of the ground to become harshly hexagonal rather than characteristically oval. Using a light bobbin/spangle combination is also very important when making very fine Bucks and when using a folded gimp in Regency lace, since the gimps in these laces are supported by the lace pairs of the clothwork, not by pins.

The bobbins I use with very fine threads are shorter than those usually available, making them lighter; the length of the bobbin should feel right for the weight (figure 501, natural size). The length of the bobbin and the weight of the bobbin and its spangle need to be in proportion, e.g. a 2gm bobbin works well with a 0.5cm spangle. The size and weight of bobbins and spangles is not an exact science and judging the size of the spangles from the illustration shown natural size (figure 501) is possibly as useful as weighing them. A light spangle on a long, heavy bobbin does not work as well as a more suitably proportioned one and vice versa.

Grenadine is a stiff, springy thread and needs a comparatively heavy bobbin so that the action of the bobbin on a curved pillow will keep the hitch in place.

The balance between thread size, bobbin length and weight and the spangle weight is individual and assessed by the appearance of the lace and the feel of the bobbins as the tension is created. Use the size and weight that works best for you but do not make do with thread, bobbins and spangles that are not suited to the pricking, they will spoil the lace.

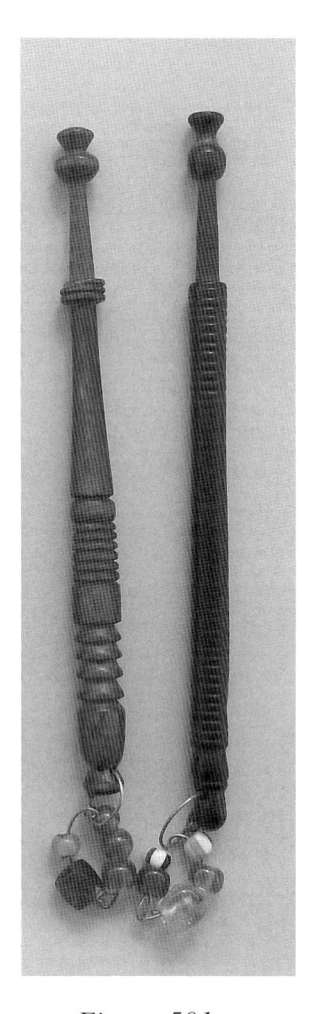

*Figure 501
(natural size)
East Midlands
bobbins, for use
with very fine thread*

Changing scale
Enlarging and reducing the scale of a pricking, together with the required change in thread thickness, affects the aesthetic appearance of lace that will be made on it. When the same pattern is made using different sized grids and matching thread, the design when viewed from the same distance appears to change. When very fine thread is used the clothwork appears a uniform colour, point ground appears as light shading and honeycomb as texture. As the scale is gradually increased first the individual stitches can be seen, then the twists on the pairs and later the texture of the thread. Thus the information we perceive changes as the lace increases in scale and we no longer enjoy it in the same way. Anomalies that cannot be seen when lace is very fine may be seen when the size is increased, thus changing scale can be tricky and something that should be approached with care.

All about making—Floral Bucks Point Lace

Mounting lace
Lace should be mounted on fabric with the same properties regarding washing, ironing and wear. Check that threads and fabric are the same colour. If the item is to be washed check that they colour match after washing; some ivory threads wash up whiter than their original colour

Grids, thread sizes and bobbin weight
NOTE: These are only suggestions, they are not the only threads that can be used with the listed grids, nor are they only to be used for the grids they are listed under; the finer the grid the more leeway you have with the size of the thread that can be successfully used. For more thread suggestions *see* 'Threads for Lace' by Brenda Paternoster, details in the bibliography.

The length and weight of the bobbins and spangles should be in sympathy with the chosen thread.

Group 1
Thread suggestions for use with grids having 40 pins per 10 cm (4 in) along the footside.

Thread	Gimp
Egyptian cotton no 60/2	no 8 perle
Madeira Tanne no 50	
Finca no 60	
DMC machine embroidery no 50	
Mettler 60/2	
Finca no 50	
Madeira Cotona no 50	
Egyptian cotton no 70/2	
Piper's 90 denier silk,	6-8 strands loosely twisted together

Group 2
Thread suggestions for use with grids having 50 pins per 10 cm (4 in) along the footside and 40 pins per 10 cm (4 in) along the footside for designs requiring a delicate effect.

Thread	Gimp
Madeira Tanne no 80	no 12 perle
Madeira cotona no 80	
Finca no 80/100?	
Egyptian cotton no 90/2	
Egyptian cotton no 100/2	
Brok 100/2	
Piper's 90 denier silk	4-6 strands loosely twisted together
Piper's 40 x 2 silk floss	Piper's 80 x 3

All about making—Floral Bucks Point Lace

As prickings become finer the size of thread is less critical and several sizes may be equally suitable.

Group 3
Thread suggestions for use with grids having 60 pins per 10 cm (4 in) along the footside and 50 pins per 10 cm (4 in) along the footside for designs requiring a delicate effect.

Thread	Gimp
Egyptian cotton no 100/2	stranded embroidery thread, one strand
Egyptian cotton no 120/2	stranded embroidery thread, one strand
Piper's 20 x 2 silk floss	4-6 strands loosely twisted together

Group 4
Thread suggestions for use with grids having 65-70 pins per 10 cm (4 in) along the footside.

Thread	Gimp
Egyptian cotton no. 100/2	D.M.C. perle no. 12
Egyptian cotton no. 120/2	
Egyptian cotton no. 140/2	
Egyptian cotton no. 160/2	
Egyptian cotton no. 185/2	stranded embroidery thread, one strand
Egyptian cotton no. 190/2	
Egyptian cotton no. 200/2	
Egyptian cotton no. 240/2	

Group 5
Threads suggestions for Black Holey. This lace usually looks better when made in black rather than white or ecru, and makes up better in silk than cotton.

Thread	Gimp
Grenadine 48 denier single and 3-ply	4-6x lace thickness
150 denier, Bart & Frances	Schappe Super Best 30/2 silk
Piper's silk floss	Piper's 30/3 silk gimp
80/2 Egyptian cotton	D.M.C. perle no. 12

Grenadine (also spelt grenedine) is highly spun silk thread. The single ply works ups a little fine and the 3-ply somewhat thick. A 2-ply would be more suitable.

BIBLIOGRAPHY

Instructions in the art of making the Buckingham Pillow Lace, Georgina M. Roberts, (unfinished manuscript) 1926, manuscript completed and revised by A Stillwell, Salex Publishing 2007

Practical Lace making Bucks Point Ground, C. C. Channer, Dryad, 1928

A Manual of Hand-made Bobbin Lacework, Margaret Maidment, Sir Isaac Pitman & Sons Ltd, 1931

A Guide to Lacemaking, M. E. W. Milroy, Brown, Son & Ferguson Ltd. 1934

Decorative Fillings for Bucks Point Lace, Geraldine Stott, Self-published

The Technique of Bucks Point Lace, Pamela Nottingham, Batsford, 1981

Lace, a History, Santina M. Levey, Victoria & Albert Museum, 1983

Designing and making Lace Fans, Christine Springett, British College of Lace, 1985

Dentelles du Pays-d'Enhaut, Ruth Doepfner-Wetterstein, Barbara Fay Verlag, 1994

Threads for Lace, Brenda Paternoster, Self-Published, 2001, regularly updated on her website http://paternoster.orpheusweb.co.uk/

All about making—Geometrical Bucks Point Lace, Alexandra Stillwell, Salex Publishing, 2006

The Grammar of Point Ground, Ulrike Voelcker, Schürmann & Klagges, 2008

Salex Illustrated Dictionary of Lacemaking, Alexandra Stillwell, Salex Publishing, 2009

Ilsoft Lace[8] www.ilsoft.co.uk

Lace[8] Explained, Ruth Budge, Self published 2012

INDEX

The original plan was to write one book '*All about making* - Bucks Point Lace'. However, as the book developed it soon became clear that there was too much material for a single book and it had to be divided into two parts, Part A Geometrical Bucks and Part B Floral Bucks. Providing you know your Geometrical Bucks techniques thoroughly there will be no need to refer to the former book. However, when I started writing this book my friends who were trying out my patterns asked for information about techniques that I had already explained in the Geometrical book. If I had included them all in this one, as they originally requested, this book would probably be 500 pages long. Therefore we decided that reference to them should be included in the End Notes at the end of each chapter.

adding pairs 4, 8, 21, 24, 31, 43, 48, 148, 156, 167, 171, *see also* slipping on pairs
adding pairs to be left out 4, 5, 11, 31
adding a pair across a gimp 24, 31
adjusting pinholes adjacent to gimp 13, 15
adjusting pins 33
angle to the footside 101
angling pins 33
attaching lace to a hem 27
back stitch 28, 33
back stitching the nook pin 50
beetle *see* Regency beetle
Beverse 181
binding on a gimp 5, 11, 46, 48
black holey 215
black lace/thread 1
blind spot 6, 11, 46
blonde 216
body 176-177
bonnet 175-177
bonnet crown *see* crown
bookmark, inserting into a sleeve 39
bow 47
bridge 46, 50, 78
brim 28, 176-178
bringing pair on a gimp back into work 7
by-passing 18, 31
carrying pairs along a gimp 5, 6, 7, 32 *also called* pairs laid along a gimp
casing 176-177
casting off 9, 12, 26, 33, 169
casting off along a diagonal picot edge 39
casting off along a horizontal or curved picot edge 23, 26, 144
casting off at a point 12, 39
catch-pin stitch 2, 10
central passives 184
changing working direction 131, 138-141, 143-144
church doll 23, 27-28, 32
circular piece 77, *see also* hexagonal piece
closed Regency ring 174
cloth and twist ground 128, 130
cloth and twist vein 152-153
cloth stitch with gimp 167, 189
clothwork 1, 4, 5, 36
clothwork divided by vertical gimps *see* vertical gimps through clothwork
continuing the weave 39
continuous row 103
corner, designing/drafting 60-63
corner, turning by reusing a pin 50
cover cloth, using them to 'keep your bearings' 68, 70
crown 175-177
crown frill 176
cucumber foot 154, 158
cutting out pairs 169
density *see* texture
designing a corner 50
designing, developing and interpreting 125, 128-129, 164-165, 173
designing a fan 144, 145
designing a hexagon 77-80
designing a non-reversing corner 121-124
designing a shaped piece 90-93

249

designing a side reverse 64-65
direction of working *see* working direction
dividing clothwork 32, 36 -39
double half hitch 136
doubling gimps 11, *see also* folded gimp
double gimp honeycomb bar 232, *see also* single gimp honeycomb bar
drafting a pricking 13-17, 51, 59-65, 77-80, 85-87, 90-93, 121-124, 125-129, 144-145, 164-165, 210
drafting corner *see* designing a corner
drafting a hexagon, *see* designing a hexagon
drawstring 177, 178
effective twists 36
engrêlure *see* heading
exchanging roles 10,
extra pair 5, *also called* spare pair, surplus pair
false picots 8, 12, 32
fan sticks 136
fillings 81, 84, 85, *see also* honeycomb and pin chain filling, old mayflower, whole stitch honeycomb filling, five-stitch filling
fine joining 94, 97-99
fingers 128, 194, 198
finishing *see* casting off
first row 4, 8, 11
five-pointed star 189
five-stitch filling 170, 174
flaws 96, 181
folded gimp 179-172
folding a fan 136
footside 13, 102, 147, *see also* kat stitch footside
forgetting to leave out pairs *see* tricks of the trade
four-pin honeycomb ring 5, 11
four-sided stitch 47, 50, 155, 195
French ground 101
French knot 28, 33
gap row 104
gaps by nook pin 50
geometrical Bucks 1
gimped beetle *see* Regency beetle
gimped bud 194
gimped division *see* gimped vein

gimped picot bar 238-239
gimped ring *see* Regency ring
gimped vein 69, 157,161, 164, 167-168
gimps 1, 5, 18-21, 32, 77, 147, 150, 154, 165-166, 167 *see also* doubling gimps, folded gimp. long loops
glue for sticking lace to fan sticks 137
grafting along a/the line 53, 73, 167, 174
grenadine 216
ground 4, *see also* point ground
ground with two twists 100
guard/guard stick
hair spray 128
half stitch 1, 129, 136
head (scroll) *see* scroll head
heading 154-156
headside 156, 159, 184
headside passives 4, 184
hemstitch 58, 65
hexagonal piece, edge motifs worked radially, centre from top to bottom 66-71, 79, 80
honeycomb 11, *see also* modified honeycomb stitch
honeycomb adjacent to the headside 6
honeycomb and pin chain filling 84-87, 96
honeycomb bar 217-218
honeycomb stem 2
honeycomb vein 157
Honiton no-pin filling, *see* no-pin filling
inner fan sticks 136
interpreting a design 59
interference 88
interpreting a design, *see* design, interpreting
inverting a design 57, 60
inward-facing corner 216
joining 53, *see also* fine joining
kat stitch 101, 128
kat stitch footside 101, 103-104, 106, 144
keeping your bearings 69 *also see* cover cloth
kiss 128, 129, 184
lacing 98
laying pairs across *see* adding in two directions, pairs laid across
laying pairs on a gimp, see carrying pairs on a gimp

All about making—Floral Bucks Point Lace

learning a pricking 243
leaving out pairs 5, 20
Lille 181
long loop 4, 11
loop edge 97, 100
loop pin 100
mayflower filling 128, *see also* old mayflower filling
mirror 50, 60
missing pinholes 211
mitred corner 58
mixing techniques 10
modified honeycomb stitch 20, 32, 44, 48 *see also* simulated honeycomb stitch
modified point ground stitch 191-192, 200
mounting 27, 110-111
mounting a fan leaf 136-137, 145
moving pairs between areas 5-6, 9, 10, 43
moving pins *see* adjusting pins
neckband 176-178
neckline frill 176-178
no-pin filling 128, 130
non-reversing corner 115, 121
nook pins 18, 19-21, 24, 25, 31-32, 44, 47, 50, *see also* back stitching the nook pin, nook pin used twice
nook pin used twice 50
off-set footside 1, 101, 147-148
old mayflower filling 82-83, 85-86
pairs laid across to travel in two directions 8, 12, *see also* setting in to work in two directions
pairs not left out *see* tricks of the trade
Pays-d'Enhaut iii
perforated sticks 136
photocopy 9, 12
pin-chain 86, 218
pin chain bar 118-119
pin chain filling *see* honeycomb and pin chain filling
pinned workers 37
pins 97
plantation doll *see* church doll
Point de Paris 101
point ground 1, 4, 11, 101, 128, 192 *see also* modified point ground stitch

prop *see* spacing pin
raccroc stitch 99, *see also* fine joining
Regency beetle 151, 152, 159
Regency Bucks 147
Regency headside 160
Regency ring 151-152, 157, 163, 167, *see also* closed Regency ring
Regency valley 160-161
reinforcement triangle/reinforcing triangle 111
removing pairs *see* throwing out pairs
reusing a pin 47, 50
reversing corner, *see* corner, drafting/designing
ring *see* Regency ring
rim 118, 235
rim pair 119
rolled edge/hem 27, 159, 177
roundel 180
scratches on prickings 69
scroll head 35, 75-76
scroll stem 35
setting in 4, 19, 24, 26, 53
setting in across a curved line of picots 8
setting in horizontally along a picot edge 8, 26, 143
setting in to work in two directions 8
sewings 48
shadow hole 4
shallow curves 53-54, 57
side reverse 57, *see also* designing a side reverse
simulated honeycomb stitch 44, 48, *see also* modified honeycomb stitch
single gimp honeycomb bar 232, see also double gimp honeycomb bar
six-pointed star 206
sleeve, inserting bookmark into, *see* inserting bookmark into a sleeve
slip stitch 27
slipping on pairs 5, 8, 19, 32
spacing pin 47, 50, 54 *also called* spacer
spare pair 5, 6, 21 *also called* extra pair, surplus pair, *see also* carrying pairs along a gimp, moving pairs between areas

251

spiders holding hands 128, 130
spiders in honeycomb stitch squares 127-130
stacking 39, 160-161
Standard Floral Bucks Point 1
starting line 53, 59
stay 215, 218-226
stem (scroll) *see* scroll stem
sticking lace to fan sticks 137
stiffening 128
stitch in the nook 31
stitches without pins 4, 152, 160
storing a fan 137
substituting fillings 85
substituting threads *see* Part 6
support pins 47
surplus pairs 5, *also called* extra pair, spare pair, *see also* carrying pairs along a gimp, moving pairs between areas
tally 9, 128, 164-165, 173 *see also* no-pin filling
tassel 39
tension 6, *see also* texture
texture 4, 6, 150, 156, 164
thread clamp 12

throwing out 4, 6, 9, 12, 21, 39, 156, 169
tricks of the trade 33, 45, 48, 59, 71, 76
twists 151, 156
twists around the pin 150
twists adjacent to gimps 32, 151, 156
two-twist ground 100
two-twist net 100
uncovered pin 76
uphill 198 *also see* tricks of the trade
unpinned workers 37
unwanted pair 5
up the creek without a paddle *see* tricks of the trade
valley *see also* Regency valley
vertical gimps through clothwork 36-38
very fine Bucks 181
vein *see* gimped vein
whole stitch honeycomb filling 166, 169
whole stitch round a pin 32
wire ground *see* kat stitch
working direction 4, 11, 201, 210, 216, 226, 230-231, 234 *see also* Projects 9, 10, 18, 19 and 30b